Design Thinking in Education

Christoph Meinel · Timm Krohn
Editors

Design Thinking in Education

Innovation Can Be Learned

 Springer

Editors
Christoph Meinel
Hasso Plattner Institute
Potsdam, Germany

Timm Krohn
Hasso Plattner Institute Academy
Potsdam, Germany

ISBN 978-3-030-89115-2   ISBN 978-3-030-89113-8   (eBook)
https://doi.org/10.1007/978-3-030-89113-8

This Springer imprint is published by the registered company Springer Nature Switzerland AG
The registered company address is: Gewerbestrasse 11, 6330 Cham, Switzerland

Foreword

The School of Design Thinking at the Hasso Plattner Institute in Potsdam was founded more than 13 years ago. Our goal was clear from the start: to convey a practical, user-centered Design Thinking approach using projects and real-world examples. The HPI D-School in Potsdam was a wonderful complement to the Hasso Plattner Institute of Design at Stanford University in California, which was founded back in 2003. Although the teaching modules differ to some extent in terms of content, there is a lively exchange of knowledge between the two institutions. Today, we are in the 13th program year of the *Hasso Plattner Design Thinking Research Program*, a research initiative conducted jointly by Stanford University in California and the Hasso Plattner Institute in Potsdam. Researchers in multidisciplinary teams funded under this joint program are conducting cutting-edge research in many fields, such as computer science, neuroscience, environmental studies, and education. In view of the diversity of disciplines of the researchers, this includes in particular the consideration of spatial, temporal, and cultural factors, as well as the question of how the Design Thinking innovation approach can be combined with traditional engineering and management approaches.

The focus of our work is always on establishing a common framework for international collaboration in the field of Design Thinking. This has led us to establish partnerships with four international universities over the past 20 years: University of Cape Town, Technion—Israel Institute of Technology, Nanjing University, and University of California, Irvine. The Hasso Plattner Institute awards scholarships to international doctoral students in South Africa, Israel, China, and the USA through these field offices. Expertise in different fields is developed, and various research topics are addressed at each site. The virtual classroom becomes a place of exchange for scientific debates and discussions. The Hasso Plattner Institute has had a branch office in South Africa since April 2009. The doctoral students at the "HPI Research School at University of Cape Town" focus primarily on information and communication technologies that are important for developing and emerging countries.

The human-centered Design Thinking approach is unique in that it is not limited to theories, but instead focuses on practical testing and development. As a result, Design Thinking is a powerful toolbox for promoting innovation in products, services, and operations that has been adopted by countless professionals. The timeless and powerful concept is finding its way into classrooms, the business sector, and society. It is thus all the more important to understand how the approach can be applied and what essential contribution it makes to a successful innovation culture.

This volume presents a comprehensive collection of articles intended to facilitate a greater appreciation of the potential of Design Thinking in education. Scientists associated with the Hasso Plattner Institute have collected research and observations and are contributing to a fundamental discussion of how people think, communicate, and implement Design Thinking in education.

Education needs innovative ways to prepare individuals and societies for the multitude of new challenges in the twenty-first century. In today's world, which is characterized by digitization, increasing speed, and complexity, Design Thinking has established itself as a powerful approach to human-centered innovation that can help address complex problems and guide change in all areas of life. Design Thinking formats create affective and cognitive outcomes in addition to teaching skills that benefit people as they expand their "toolbox." Besides that, Design Thinking formats also promote collaboration and a "We culture" across disciplines instead of competitiveness.

Design Thinking is an approach to understand everyday experiences and advancing transformation in different areas. The chapters in this volume invite readers to understand innovative educational approaches in a variety of fields and from different points of view, to open up new perspectives, and to recognize potential in their own fields of application.

Design Thinking is a long-established practice, but recent research and practical approaches are bringing new perspectives to the subject. The use of Design Thinking enables multidisciplinary collaboration and iterative improvement in real-world applications. Design Thinking offers well-suited methods and an innovative culture of collaboration for creating new forms of communication, interaction, and services in the educational sector.

Therefore, it is my pleasure to share the results of our latest research and findings with you. This book provides information about experiences and knowledge transfer that we were able to obtain with the help of Design Thinking in the educational sector. It also presents and analyzes different formats and methods. Specific examples of successes and failures associated with Design Thinking education projects are described. This volume presents a comprehensive collection of research studies, which were originally published in German on Design Thinking in the international educational sector. Discussions of the research results should not be limited to the scientific community. Instead, the discoveries should be available to all who strive for excellence in education. We invite you to experiment and think about how we can meet the challenges of today's world individually.

Potsdam, Germany/Palo Alto,   Hasso Plattner
California, USA

Acknowledgements

The editors of this book would like to thank all the contributors for their efforts and hard work.

The providers of useful input:

Jill Grinager, who coordinated the book as well as *Anne Greuling* who prepared all graphics and illustrations for this volume.

The translators at *HPI, Second Language* and *American Language Service in Bavaria*, who translated, copy edited and proofread particular chapters of this book as detailed here.

Copy Editing and Proofreading:

Dr. Sharon Therese Nemeth, HPI (Chapters "Beyond Brainstorming: *Introducing medgi, an Effective, Research-Based Method for Structured Concept Development*," "Integrating DT and Entrepreneurship: Case Study Universidad Mayor (Chile)"– "Towards a Culturally Responsive Design Thinking Education," "Strategic Design Thinking as a New Way of Leading Digital Transformation Processes," "Mastering the Fundamentals of Design Thinking by Teaching the Skills of Improvisation," "Design Thinking and the UN Sustainable Development Goals"–"IQ Grows in WeQ Mode")

Dr. Kelly Neudorfer, Second Language and *Monika Roehl*, American Language Service in Bavaria (Preface, Chapters "Introduction: Design Thinking in Education," "Combining Design Thinking and Entrepreneurship Education: The DTE Model"– "Walls, Furniture, People—Space in Design Thinking in Theory and Practice," "Human Centeredness in Professional Education – On the Benefits and Application of a Human-Centered Approach in Professional Education," "Certification Program for Design Thinking Coaches at the HPI Academy," "Design Thinking—Enabling Digital Engineering Students to be Creative and Innovate")

N. N. (Chapter "Design Thinking for Leaders—Leading Innovation and Agility")

Translation:

Dr. Sharon Therese Nemeth, HPI

Translated Chapter: "Strategic Design Thinking as a New Way of Leading Digital Transformation Processes"

Dr. Kelly Neudorfer, Second Language

Translated Chapters: "Design Thinking—Enabling Creativity and Innovation in Digital Engineering Students," "Human Centeredness in Professional Education – On the Benefits and Application of a Human-Centered Approach in Professional Education," "Certification Program for Design Thinking Coaches at the HPI Academy" and select short profiles

Monika Roehl, American Language Service in Bavaria

Translated Chapters: Preface, "Introduction: Design Thinking in Education," "Combining Design Thinking and Entrepreneurship Education: The DTE Model," "Walls, Furniture, People—Space in Design Thinking in Theory and Practice," "Design Thinking for Leaders—Leading Innovation and Agility"

Contents

Editors and Contributors

About the Editors

Prof. Dr. Christoph Meinel (Univ. Prof., Dr. sc. nat., Dr. rer. nat.) is Director and CEO of the Hasso Plattner Institute for Digital Engineering gGmbH (HPI) at the University of Potsdam.

Photo credit: Kay Herschelmann

He was born in 1954 and was founding Dean of the Digital Engineering Faculty at the University of Potsdam in April 2017. Currently he serves as Vice Dean. He holds the Chair of Internet Technologies and Systems and is also active in the fields of cyber-security and digital education, teaching in the bachelor's and master's programs in IT-Systems Engineering and at the School of Design Thinking. He developed the MOOC platform, openHPI.de, and also provided content on the site. His responsibilities include supervising numerous doctoral students, and he has authored or co-authored more than 25 books, anthologies, and various conference proceedings.

He has published more than 550 peer-reviewed articles in scientific journals and at international conferences and holds a number of international patents. He is a member of the National Academy of Science and Technology (acatech), director of the HPI-Stanford Design Thinking Research Program, honorary professor at the Technical University of Beijing, visiting professor at Shanghai University, professor at Nanjing University, and member of numerous scientific committees and supervisory boards.

Dr. Timm Krohn CEO of HPI Academy.

Photo credit: Kay Herschelmann

Timm Krohn studied law in Hamburg, Berkeley, Lausanne, Bonn (1st state exam) and Berlin (legal clerkship, 2nd state exam). This was followed by a doctorate in corporate law and work as a research assistant at the Chair of Business Law at the University of Bonn; he was a trainee/lecturer at Jura Intensiv in Cologne and Düsseldorf, a legal advisor at KPMG, a lawyer in various departments of L-Bank, Staatsbank Baden-Württemberg in Karlsruhe, and a lawyer in commercial and corporate law in downtown Hamburg. For more than 15 years, he was involved in growing HPI as COO, and in the meantime, he was also the founding managing director of the HPI Academy. Now, he is the managing director of the HPI Academy. Together with Christoph Meinel and Ulrich Weinberg, he has published books in the field of Design Thinking.

Contributors

Flavia Bleuel Hasso Plattner Institute Academy, Potsdam, Germany

Jonathan Antonio Edelman Hasso Plattner Institute for Digital Engineering, Potsdam, Germany

Ismael Espinoza Universidad Mayor, Santiago, Chile

Joann Halpern Hasso-Plattner-Institut, New York, New York, USA;
New York University, New York, USA

Mario Herane Universidad Mayor, Santiago, Chile

Katharina Hölzle Hasso Plattner Institute for Digital Engineering, Potsdam, Germany

Annie Kerguenne HPI, Hasso Plattner Institute Academy, Potsdam, Germany

Jan Koch Hasso Plattner Institute Academy, Potsdam, Germany

Timm Krohn Hasso Plattner Institute Academy, Potsdam, Germany

Lena Mayer HPI School of Design Thinking, Hasso Plattner Institute for Digital Engineering, Potsdam, Germany

Selina Mayer HPI School of Design Thinking, Hasso Plattner Institute for Digital Engineering, Potsdam, Germany

Christoph Meinel Hasso Plattner Institute for Digital Engineering, University of Potsdam, Potsdam, Germany

Steven Ney Hasso Plattner Institute Academy, Potsdam, Germany

Babajide Owoyele Hasso Plattner Institute for Digital Engineering, Potsdam, Germany

Richard Perez The Hasso Plattner School of Design Thinking at University of Cape Town (d-School), Cape Town, South Africa

Shama Rahman Hasso Plattner Institute for Digital Engineering, Potsdam, Germany

Joaquin Santuber Hasso Plattner Institute for Digital Engineering, Potsdam, Germany

Martin Schwemmle HPI School of Design Thinking, Hasso Plattner Institute for Digital Engineering, Potsdam, Germany

Christina Stansell Hasso Plattner Institute Academy, Potsdam, Germany

Caroline Szymanski Hasso Plattner Institute for Digital Engineering, Potsdam, Germany

Mana Taheri Hasso Plattner Institute for Digital Engineering, Potsdam, Germany

Annie V. Talbot Potsdam, Germany

Christine Thong Design Factory Melbourne at Swinburne University of Technology, Melbourne, Australia

Hanadi Traifeh HPI School of Design Thinking, Hasso Plattner Institute for Digital Engineering, Potsdam, Germany

Falk Uebernickel Hasso Plattner Institute at the University of Potsdam, Potsdam, Germany

Karen von Schmieden HPI School of Design Thinking, Hasso Plattner Institute for Digital Engineering, Potsdam, Germany

Julia von Thienen Hasso Plattner Institute for Digital Engineering, University of Potsdam, Potsdam, Germany

Cornelia C. Walther POZE Space, New York, NY, USA

Ulrich Weinberg HPI School of Design Thinking, Hasso Plattner Institute for Digital Engineering, Potsdam, Germany

Theresa Weinstein Hasso Plattner Institute for Digital Engineering, Potsdam, Germany

Introduction: Design Thinking in the Field of Education

Timm Krohn and Christoph Meinel

Abstract Design Thinking has become an established approach in science and the commercial sector so that companies and institutions worldwide are benefiting from this new problem-solving and innovation mindset. At HPI, we have learned over the past 15+ years that design thinkers, whether students or professionals, develop a more thorough awareness of problems, take a user-focused approach to thinking and solving as a team, and achieve amazing results when working in groups. The expertise of individuals is bundled to form a group's overall knowledge. If the process is moderated and focused, the team's problem-solving power exceeds the sum of the available specialized knowledge. Thus, Design Thinking turns students into creative problem solvers and socially competent team workers. These skills are in demand and are increasingly required in managerial positions in the networked economy. HPI and its Design Thinking facilities continue to research this approach while educating and teaching students. In this book, researchers and practitioners from the HPI cosmos present their research approaches and results. We would like to share our experience of about 15 years of working in Design Thinking education.

Design Thinking has become an established approach in science and the commercial sector so that companies and institutions worldwide are benefiting from this new problem-solving and innovation mindset. In the course of a solution finding process using the Design Thinking approach, the specialized knowledge of individuals is merged in such a way that the combined creative power of a team flows into the overall process of finding a solution: from the preparation and analysis of an issue (what is *really* the problem?) to the generation of ideas for solving a problem, all the way to the construction and testing of the prototypical manifestation. Or to put it more simply: multidisciplinary teams work in a flexible environment, applying an iterative process to develop "user-centered" products, services, or business models.

T. Krohn (✉)
Hasso Plattner Institute Academy, August-Bebel-Str. 88, 14482 Potsdam, Germany

C. Meinel
Hasso Plattner Institute for Digital Engineering, Campus Griebnitzsee, Prof.-Dr.-Helmert-Str. 2-3, 14482 Potsdam, Germany

1

Yet Design Thinking is still a comparatively young approach: in 2007, Hasso Plattner founded the School of Design Thinking at the Hasso Plattner Institute (HPI) in Potsdam, laying the foundation for the first Design Thinking hub in Europe, which has since spread across borders and supported the establishment of new Design Thinking educational institutions worldwide. Four years earlier, he had already founded the Hasso Plattner Institute of Design—the d.school—at Stanford University. The two institutions have been working closely together since 2008 as part of the joint *Design Thinking Research Program* (HPDTRP). One year later, the HPI Academy was founded as a continuing education provider of the HPI. Since then, it has been able to educate more than 20,000 professionals in Design Thinking.

The Design Thinking approach has advanced significantly over the past two decades. It was originally used in classical design disciplines to develop innovative products or services. However, it then rapidly stood out as an effective method in other areas as well. Thus, Design Thinking can help address pressing social problems just as well as it can help develop and introduce technical innovations. The team-oriented approach supports an agile learning and working culture, which is particularly important in times of digital change. Researchers and practitioners have also become interested in Design Thinking as a means of building creative trust and creative abilities. More and more universities are therefore opening up to the Design Thinking approach to support students in acquiring creative problem-solving and collaboration skills.

As an IT school with engineering-based computer science courses, the Hasso Plattner Institute itself benefits significantly from Design Thinking in all its facets. The students at HPI are particularly interested and strong in the field of algorithm and number-oriented mathematics and computer science. When they start their studies after school, they come from a system in which individual learning success counts and is graded. The team-oriented, interdisciplinary approach challenges them, opens up new views and broader perspectives on problems and approaches to solutions, and makes their knowledge more "connectable" and applicable in a more targeted way. Instead of focusing primarily on technical aspects during software development, the needs of future users, for example, already play a major role when the software is being designed. In this way, Design Thinking helps to develop IT solutions in the context of their usefulness, comprehensibility, and user-friendliness rather than merely from the perspective of technical feasibility.

At HPI, we have learned over the past 15+ years that design thinkers, whether students or professionals, develop a more thorough awareness of problems, take a user-focused approach to thinking and solving as a team, and achieve amazing results when working in groups. The expertise of individuals is bundled to form a group's overall knowledge. If the process is moderated and focused, the team's problem-solving power exceeds the sum of the available specialized knowledge. Thus, Design Thinking turns students into creative problem solvers and socially competent team workers. These skills are in demand and are increasingly required in managerial positions in the networked economy.

HPI and its Design Thinking facilities continue to research this approach while educating and teaching students. In this book, researchers and practitioners from the

HPI cosmos present their research approaches and results. We would like to share our experience of about 15 years of working in Design Thinking education.

1   HPI School of Design Thinking

The Hasso Plattner Institute's School of Design Thinking, or "D-School" for short, started in 2007 with 40 students from 30 different disciplines. Due to rapidly increasing numbers of applicants from all over the world, since 2015, the D-School has been educating 120 students per semester who currently come from 20 different nations and have educational backgrounds in about 70 different disciplines. There are now more than 2000 graduates in total. Students devote two days a week to their Design Thinking education, either for a semester or for a full year. On the remaining three days of the week, they continue their regular university education. In the Design Thinking courses, which are always aligned to a Design Thinking process, students develop a passion for their work that is rarely seen in other degree programs. This may be because Design Thinking courses especially foster a work culture of joy, collaboration, action, wild experimentation, and rapid learning. After all, Design Thinking is not so much about building explicit knowledge as it is about the student's mindset. Turning students into creative problem solvers and socially competent team workers through Design Thinking, as we have learned, does not require soft skills training, but rather hard skills training. We have also observed students regularly reporting profound impacts on their entire lives. They tell us about major changes in their self-image, private habits, work style, and career preferences. All alumni credit their time at D-School with gaining a high degree of confidence in their creative abilities.

Works related to teaching at the HPI D-School:

> Prof. Dr. Christoph Meinel/Dr. Julia von Thienen: Design Thinking - Enabling Creativity and Innovation in Digital Engineering Students

> Prof. Dr. Katharina Hölzle: Combining Design Thinking and Entrepreneurship Education: The DTE Model

> Prof. Dr. Christoph Meinel/Karen von Schmieden/Lena Mayer/Hanadi Traifeh: Massive Open Online Design: Learning from Scaling Design Thinking Education

> Annie Talbot: Mastering the Fundamentals of Design Thinking by Teaching the Skills of Improvisation.

2   Hasso Plattner Design Thinking Research Program

The Hasso Plattner Design Thinking Research Program (HPDTRP) aims to foster and coordinate innovative Design Thinking research at Stanford and HPI so that new scientific findings can be disseminated immediately to the academic and business communities. Since the beginning of the program, the research results have been published annually in the program's own book series, "Design Thinking Research" by Springer-Verlag.

The HPDTRP includes a variety of research foci that primarily concentrate on the three pillars of Design Thinking, namely *Process, Place, and People*: for example, the unique *look and feel* of Design Thinking, which is so different from traditional education, is explored, as is the impact of spaces and their furnishings on the process. The ideal composition of teams is another subject of research: whenever possible, Design Thinkers work in multidisciplinary and multicultural teams. Achieving diversity is particularly relevant in the composition of teams and is a criterion when the D-School applicants are selected. That is because every academic discipline produces students with a unique vocabulary, a unique methodology, and a unique worldview from which a mixed team can benefit.

Examining the neurocognitive effects of the educational program is another focus of the research. Research conducted as part of the HPDTRP shows that Design Thinking education improves focused attention and information processing. The results of the neurocognitive studies also seem to support a general philosophy of Design Thinking: To guide students towards a mindset that is more action and implementation oriented.

Works about the Hasso Plattner DT Research Program:

Jonathan Edelman, PhD: Beyond Brainstorming: introducing medgi, an effective, research-based method for structured concept development

Dr. Julia von Thienen/Dr. Caroline Szymanski/Theresa Weinstein/Dr. Shama Rahman: Design Thinking, Neurodesign and Facilitating Worthwhile Change: Towards a Curriculum for Innovation Engineering

Dr. Martin Schwemmle: Walls, Furniture, People – Space in Design Thinking in Theory and Practice

Mana Taheri: Towards a Culturally Responsive Design Thinking Education.

3   D-Schools International

More and more international educational institutions have joined the Design Thinking initiative in recent years. In 2012, HPI and the HPI Academy jointly helped establish a D-School Malaysia in Kuala Lumpur and, in 2015, another D-School in Cape Town, South Africa. Both institutions have been supporting the establishment of a D-School in Santiago de Chile since 2018 and the establishment of an HPI D-School Middle East in the United Arab Emirates since the beginning of 2020. Two works from the respective Design Thinking schools provide insight into the culture-specific characteristics of Design Thinking in the corresponding countries and regions:

Mario Herane/Ismael Espinoza: Integrating DT and Entrepreneurship: Case Study Universidad Mayor (Chile)

Richard Perez: Where Context Matters - Design Thinking in South Africa.

4   Design Thinking International

New teaching formats and programs emerge regularly in this "Design Thinking cosmos." Some examples are: the Global Design Thinking Weeks, conference and event formats such as the D-Confestival, global networks such as the Global Design Thinking Alliance, which supports high standards in DT teaching and research internationally, and the SUGAR Network, which brings together universities and companies worldwide.

Related works:

Prof. Dr. Falk Uebernickel: Contextualizing Design Thinking with Multiple Intelligences – The Global SUGAR Program as a Case

Joann Halpern, PhD/Cornelia Walther, PhD: DT and the UN Sustainable Development Goals, Design Thinking and Youth Empowerment, *Case Study ForUsGirls (US) and Start-up Africa (Kenya)*

Prof. Ulrich Weinberg: IQ grows in WeQ mode.

5   HPI Academy—DT in the Field of Continuing Education and Corporate Training (Professional Education)

Since 1999, the HPI Academy has been offering customized courses and workshops for professionals, specialists, and managers at the Potsdam-Babelsberg campus and on-site in companies. With its range of training and continuing education courses, the HPI Academy provides "professionals" with the necessary knowledge, the appropriate mindset, and array of tools in various formats and workshops. With this, participants can efficiently initiate innovation in a manner that is oriented to actual practice, and at the same time, they can control and manage change processes in their companies, successfully master digital transformation, and develop new business models. The HPI Academy program managers have many years of experience in international strategy and innovation projects and are part of a network of well over 200 experienced Design Thinking coaches. All offers are tailored specifically to the needs of each participant.

Works from the field of adult education:

Flavia Bleuel/Selina Mayer/Christina Stansell: Design Thinking for Leaders – Leading Innovation and Agility

Annie Kerguenne: Strategic Design Thinking as a New Way of Leading Digital Transformation Processes

Jan Koch: Human-Centeredness in Professional Education – On the Benefits and Application of a Human-Centered Approach in Professional Education

Dr. Steven Ney: Certification Program for Design Thinking Coaches at the HPI Academy.

Dr. Timm Krohn Timm Krohn studied law in Hamburg, Berkeley, Lausanne, Bonn (1st state exam) and Berlin (legal clerkship, 2nd state exam). This was followed by a doctorate in corporate law and work as a research assistant at the Chair of Business Law at the University of Bonn; he was a trainee/lecturer at Jura Intensiv in Cologne and Düsseldorf, a legal advisor at KPMG, a lawyer in various departments of L-Bank, Staatsbank Baden-Württemberg in Karlsruhe, and a lawyer in commercial and corporate law in downtown Hamburg. For more than 15 years, he was involved in growing HPI as COO, and in the meantime, was also the founding managing director of the HPI Academy. Now he is managing director of the HPI Academy. Together with Christoph Meinel and Ulrich Weinberg, he has published books in the field of Design Thinking.

Prof. Dr. Christoph Meinel was born in 1954 and was founding Dean of the Digital Engineering Faculty at the University of Potsdam in April 2017. Currently he serves as Vice Dean. He holds the Chair of Internet Technologies and Systems and is also active in the fields of cybersecurity and digital education, teaching in the bachelor's and master's programs in IT-Systems Engineering and at the School of Design Thinking. Christoph Meinel developed the MOOC platform, openHPI.de, and also provides content on the site. His responsibilities include supervising numerous doctoral students, and he has authored or co-authored more than 25 books, anthologies, and various conference proceedings.

He has published more than 550 peer-reviewed articles in scientific journals and at international conferences and holds a number of international patents. He is a member of the National Academy of Science and Technology (acatech), director of the HPI-Stanford Design Thinking Research Program, honorary professor at the Technical University of Beijing, visiting professor at Shanghai University, professor at Nanjing University, and member of numerous scientific committees and supervisory boards.

Design Thinking in Higher Education Setting

Design Thinking—Enabling Digital Engineering Students to be Creative and Innovate

Christoph Meinel and Julia V. Thienen

Abstract Digital transformation is changing every aspect of our world. Some of these changes are for the better, others less so. Software, for instance, can make the everyday life of the user exhausting if new products have to be used at work that are difficult to understand and handle. On the other hand, very welcome avenues of action can be opened up that would be inconceivable without digital technology. Digitization thereby provides a chance to change many things in the world for the better, but this is not a foregone conclusion. In order for digitization to make a positive difference, developers of software systems need to be more than proven experts in technical subjects, they also need to be capable innovators. The Hasso Plattner Institute (HPI) offers digital engineering degree programs to train the internationally competitive next generation of managers who will help shape and advance the digital world. Meeting this demand depends on developing technical expertise and creative innovation skills in equal measures. At the HPI and Stanford University, Design Thinking is an important part of education and work culture, where students learn to make good use of their specialist knowledge when shaping the digital future. This way, technical education is being modernized and opened up, ensuring that it goes far beyond the usual analytical and deductive engineering education, thus preparing students for their work as innovators. Technical degree programs in the past primarily sought to enable students to incrementally improve existing solutions and optimize systems. Especially in the field of digitization, however, software developers and architects are always working in areas where immediate changes are necessary and highly desirable. Design Thinking helps students learn to explore what is desirable and then realize these desirable solutions by applying cross-disciplinary expertise.

C. Meinel · J. V. Thienen (✉)
Hasso Plattner Institute for Digital Engineering, University of Potsdam, Campus Griebnitzsee, Prof.-Dr.-Helmert-Str. 2-3, 14482 Potsdam, Germany
e-mail: Julia.vonThienen@hpi.de

C. Meinel
e-mail: office-meinel@hpi.de

1   Why Design Thinking is an Integral Part of Digital Engineering Education at the HPI

The Hasso Plattner Institute (HPI) was founded in 1998, privately funded and endowed by Hasso Plattner. In decades of personal experience, he had combined business and science, and therefore, he was well-familiar with challenges of merging the two fields. Hasso Plattner was one of the co-founders of the software company SAP, which today employs around 100,000 people worldwide. In the corporate context, he noticed that classic computer science courses at universities did not adequately prepare students for what they would later be expected to do in their jobs. While the application of computer science knowledge in business or research was focused on developing forward-looking technologies and innovations, many graduates evidently found it difficult to mentally separate themselves from the status quo of existing technical solutions they had studied before. It also seemed that many computer scientists had difficulties working in interdisciplinary teams, as they were not accustomed to doing so by means of their academic training. However, interdisciplinary teamwork is necessary in business contexts and beyond to develop good solutions to problems from a variety of perspectives. It also helps ensure the quality of new solutions by involving diverse expertise at all levels. Hasso Plattner saw another critical shortcoming, especially when comparing computer science education in Germany to that in the USA. In Germany, students were generally not trained to develop their own forward-looking ideas in order to actively introduce these into the market, for example as entrepreneurs. The Hasso Plattner Institute at the University of Potsdam was thus intended to test and enable a form of education that was urgently needed in Germany, but also worldwide. The aim was—and continues to be—to combine top-class technical knowledge transfer with practical experiences and intensive innovation education.

The Institute's rapid development shows how productive this new model of technical training can be. While the HPI educated 77 students in 1999, ten years later there were around 460 bachelor's and 190 master's graduates in addition to many doctoral candidates, and even one postdoctoral lecturing qualification. The Institute then experienced another growth spurt when the *Digital Engineering Faculty* was founded at the University of Potsdam in 2017. Since then, it has offered a selection of degree programs that include IT Systems Engineering, Digital Health, Data Engineering, and Cybersecurity. The HPI currently has 21 departments led by internationally renowned professors, and the number continues to grow, as does the number of students.

How can technical education prepare students for their role as innovators in society? This was a central question for Hasso Plattner from the very beginning in his search for new educational formats. Learning about Design Thinking at Stanford University was a crucial experience for him. There, a group of professors in the engineering faculty's mechanical engineering department taught Design Thinking with the goal of training students to be creative thinkers and innovators who also enjoyed collaborating with representatives of other disciplines. Students from all the departments were able to participate in the courses. Course attendees learned how to use their interdisciplinary diversity of perspectives in teamwork as an important resource in the development process.

In one Design Thinking project, for example, a team of eight students tried to invent a reading lamp that would enable people in developing countries to read after sunset. Leading electronics companies had estimated that such a lamp would cost at least US$120 to produce. The students made it their mission to provide it for less than US$20 so that many more people could afford it. The fact that the students actually succeeded had a lot to do with excellent interdisciplinary teamwork.

> The medical student advised the electrical engineering student on which lamps [...] were best for the eyes with minimal energy consumption. The electrical engineering student sourced the right rechargeable batteries and purchased the solar panel inexpensively over the Internet. The software student described the charging process so that the energy was stored in the battery in the right form [...]. The business student went to New York and negotiated with the World Bank to get funding for a large-scale trial. The mechanical engineering student negotiated via the Internet with India, where the outer shape of the lamp could be molded from plastic. And the sociology student flew to Mexico and South Africa to set up the field trial.
>
> The project was carried out successfully [...]. Today, these lamps are available for purchase.
>
> (Plattner, 2009, p. 15f., our translation)

Impressed by projects like this, Hasso Plattner asked me (author Christoph Meinel) to set up this kind of innovation education at the HPI in Potsdam as well. He helped fund a comprehensive expansion of Design Thinking education to that end, which was initially begun at Stanford. The *Hasso Plattner Institute of Design*, or *d.school* for short, was founded at Stanford University in 2004 and began teaching in 2005.

In 2007, we were able to establish a sister institute to the Stanford *d.school* in Potsdam, the *HPI School of Design Thinking*, or *D-School* for short. Education in Potsdam is based on the successful Stanford model, but has also taken the approach in novel directions. For example, innovation education at the HPI is designed to be even more open. Not only can students from different disciplines at the University of Potsdam participate, but even students from different institutions around the globe. The course structure is also adapted to the German system, in which there are semesters (and not quarters, as at Stanford); moreover, courses are graded for credit. It also makes a difference whether Design Thinking shapes the day-to-day working culture in the field of computer science, i.e., in digital engineering as at the HPI, or in mechanical engineering as at Stanford.

Innovation education in Germany at the HPI School of Design Thinking quickly turned out to be extremely promising. Just like the HPI as a whole, the D-School grew rapidly within a short period of time. In 2007, it started with 40 students from 30 different disciplines. Not least due to the quickly growing number of interested students from all over the world, the Institute now educates 400 students per year. They currently come from 20 different nations, 65 universities, and 70 disciplines.

Design Thinking, as it has been taught at the Stanford d.school since 2005 and at the Potsdam D-School since 2007, offers a highly hands-on education. This practical relevance contributes significantly to the ability of course participants to apply their experience to their specialist knowledge and new work projects. This enables them to develop the intuition and inclination necessary to pursue not only technically obvious developments, making incremental improvements, but also to look with an open mind for entirely new solutions that can truly make a difference in people's lives.

The HPI School Cloud is a good example of digital engineering projects in the spirit of Design Thinking. This project aims to rethink educational access and collaboration among all stakeholders in the school environment based on the possibilities of digital technology. Traditionally, the teaching materials for students are conveyed via books. Once printed, the content in the book cannot be changed, although teachers and students are sure to find things that are hard to understand, outdated, or just plain wrong. The books that are paged through often and carried around in backpacks soon become unsightly and look even older than they actually are. In analog instruction, there are also social dynamics that are not always desirable. For example, many class discussions demand courage and self-confidence from the students. Shy students might not answer at all and will be heard less.

In a direct attempt to transfer the analog teaching model to the digital space, book texts could simply be digitized and displayed on screens. When discussing texts, everything would go on as before: Everyone reads their text. Those who dare to say something speak up. It would also be possible to set up expensive computer rooms in which the software and hardware are installed locally and must then be maintained, often by teachers who are not trained for this task. Again, once installed, they quickly become obsolete, and each school must reinvest money to upgrade the teaching material and equipment. All in all, such an approach re-deploys principles familiar from analog teaching and transfers them unquestioningly to the digital world.

That is where Design Thinking invites you to first take a big step back and consider the situation without predetermined solutions. What is classroom instruction about? What are the needs of students, teachers, and other stakeholders in the school context? How can we use the possibilities of digitization to support everyone in the best possible way? What might be completely new approaches to solving given problems?

In the fall of 2016, the pilot project "HPI School Cloud" was started at the HPI. An interdisciplinary team was assembled that included digital engineering experts as well as educators, media technicians, sociologists, and others. The project entered a pilot phase in 2017. Unlike many other areas of product development, the School Cloud was not dreamed up behind closed doors. The idea was not to create another system that would first be developed in a resource-intensive way and then presented to customers as a ready-made package solution. After all, customers can do no more than accept or reject such package solutions. If they have suggestions for changes, however, these might be almost impossible to implement due to the expense of development. Instead, the HPI School Cloud team worked closely with users from the very beginning. Users came from 27 schools of the national Excellence School Network MINT-EC and actively participated in developing the product. Initial School Cloud prototypes were tested at these schools by an increasing number of teachers and students. They met regularly with the HPI development team to exchange experiences and ideas. This resulted in solutions that were not thought up only by computer specialists in their development laboratories, but solutions emerged also from the experiences of teachers and students.

Today, the HPI School Cloud offers a digital teaching platform with a wide range of teaching materials. The platform is centrally maintained and continually updated. It is easy for teachers and students to access. All they need is a computer with an Internet connection—even a cell phone can suffice. Usability is simple and clear, so that the site can be used intuitively without special training. Data access complies with the strict guidelines of the German Data Protection Act, and users have the possibility to modify and improve teaching material. For example, teachers can easily adapt existing worksheets so they fit into the context of their teaching units. A wide variety of resources can be combined: texts, videos, audio files, etc. Teachers can choose from an immense amount of reviewed teaching materials, all of which have been approved for classroom use. This is different from searches on the global Internet, where teachers can find a lot of potential materials for their classes, but many of them are copyrighted—sometimes in a way that is difficult to see—and can only be used after a fee has been paid. There are also differences in social interactions. For example, students can simultaneously post their thoughts on the subject matter by using small digital notes and making them visible to the class. As a result, students are much more willing to contribute to group discourse. Whereas usually only the more confident students respond to questions, many more students join in discussions with the new approach. And if you have already shared a few key words, it is not that difficult to explain things verbally when asked. Thus, discussions amongst students gain momentum (Fig. 1).

Fig. 1 The HPI School Cloud does not just transfer familiar, analog forms of teaching into the digital realm. It also enables fundamentally new forms of interaction, such as sharing and sending thoughts about the subject matter on digital notes. This means that shy students who do not speak up in class can participate in class discussions more easily

While 27 schools were initially involved in the HPI School Cloud project in 2017, the number had already increased to around 300 in 2018, that is, all the schools from the national Excellence School Network MINT-EC. In 2020, the HPI School Cloud was then opened to all interested schools across Germany in response to the challenges of the Corona pandemic, so that it is now used by thousands of schools. The project development as well as the state-wide offer to all interested schools was and is supported by the German Federal Ministry of Education and Research.

If you would like to read more about digital engineering projects in the spirit of Design Thinking, Meinel and von Thienen (2016) describe several developments such as SAP HANA, the digital documentation system Tele-Board MED to support doctor–patient cooperation, or *open.hpi.de,* with its offer of Massive Open Online Courses (MOOCs). Those who are particularly interested in the topic of "digitization and education" can find further discussion in Meinel (2020a, 2020b, 2020c). Moreover, the site *www.thisisdesignthinking.net* provides numerous examples of how IT companies are successfully using Design Thinking in their projects, including IBM's and German companies' involvement in the Internet of Things (IoT). Other examples from the field of neurodesign (von Thienen et al., 2021a, 2022) specifically focus on projects that use Design Thinking in the context of digital engineering.

Overall, it is clear that digital engineering experts are capable of developing forward-looking solutions, especially if they are more than just technical experts. It is important to consider the basic needs of people in everyday life and at work with an open mind. How can new solutions really make a positive difference in people's lives? This involves changing the starting point for development. Those trained in Design Thinking no longer start by looking at familiar products to refine details or by optimizing existing systems. Instead, the focus shifts to people's living environment, searching for completely new solutions if this brings about a lasting change for the better. This is best achieved through collaborative, careful experimentation, a constant exchange of experiences and ideas from a wide variety of perspectives—especially across disciplinary boundaries. At the HPI, it is primarily Design Thinking that enables students to work in this way.

2 Design Thinking Balances Different Creative Approaches

Creativity research has long described two different approaches or work modes that people use to develop creative products (Arnold, 1959/2016; Maslow, 1959/2016; McKim, 1959/2016; von Thienen & Meinel, 2019; von Thienen et al., 2021b). Over time, different authors have used varying terms to describe these two approaches, but they have always been very much in agreement on the content.

In the first approach, creative developments are tackled within a specialized domain using in-depth expertise as a basis. Rational planning is characteristic of this way of working. Ideas are developed based on subject expertise, by reflecting on, and analyzing, relevant content areas. People generate new approaches to solutions by working with the concepts they are familiar with from the relevant discipline.

Overall, the process is characterized by a high degree of meta-cognitive control. The methodology is usually structured as a step-by-step approach. Often, creative developments of this kind are easy to plan in light of domain knowledge. It is roughly foreseeable how much time the process will take, what its outcome will be, and what difficulties, if any, will have to be overcome at various points. The effectiveness of the work is highly dependent on the developers' subject matter expertise. The better they know the concepts and methods of their field, the better they can plan ahead. The greater the subject matter expertise, the faster and more error-free the targeted solution can be produced.

The second type of creative developments is based on a broad range of life experiences. In the early stages of projects, the developers do not even know themselves what creative product will emerge in the end. Other largely unpredictable factors include the difficulties that might arise in the creative process and what kind of breakthrough might be achieved. The process is characterized in large part by unforeseen, unplanned experiences and "flashes of inspiration." So while developers by the nature of their work cannot anticipate and plan ahead for the exact stages of their design journey, they do move through characteristic processes to increase the chances of obtaining interesting, unexpected insights and experiences. Their way of working also reflects an openness to experiences beyond specialized concepts, an openness that is crucial for successful developments in novel terrain. The methodology is for the most part unstructured; it involves spontaneous trial-and-error approaches, or open conversations with others not limited by specific outcome expectations. Developers follow their intuitions, impulses, and sense of curiosity. They explore new perspectives, are spontaneous, playful, often humorous, and do what feels right in the moment. There is also a strong physical involvement in many cases: The developers do not just sit at their workstations, but are on the move, changing positions, tinkering with objects, and working with different senses. In this second form of creative work, empathy and compassion can be important vehicles of the creative process: Developers immerse themselves in the users' lives and take their needs as sources of inspiration and motivation to find completely new solutions for problems at hand—far removed from the pre-paved solution avenues of a particular academic discipline. Another often observed source of motivation and inspiration can be the dream of a visionary innovator. Overall, this approach is characterized by an openness to, and enjoyment of, experiences that lie beyond the conceptual pigeonholes of established subject domains.

Creative developments at the highest level, though, can only be achieved when both approaches are merged. Providing meta-cognitive control and subject matter expertise is critical to perfecting existing solution ideas and establishing functioning systems. At the same time, open-mindedness toward experiences beyond technical debates is essential in order to become aware of problems that are important, and therefore truly need to be solved. People's fundamental problems often lie outside of academic disciplines and cannot be solved by only applying the knowledge of isolated domains. The sense-approach, which transcends the boundaries of specialist disciplines, is therefore important for finding worthwhile objectives in creative work, for productively bringing together different perspectives, and for discovering entirely new points of view with resultant new solutions.

All in all, there are typical patterns in creative processes: Developments driven by the knowledge and methods of a single discipline almost always produce incremental innovation. By contrast, leaps in performance and disruptive innovations usually originate from real-life experiences and unstructured, curiosity-driven explorations beyond the boundaries imposed by single domains of expertise. Disruptive ideas alone are not enough, though. It takes a considerable amount of specialist expertise, often from different disciplines, to develop ideas and implement them in a technically adept and highly professional manner.

Figure 2 illustrates the interplay of the two different approaches, which only produce high-caliber, fundamental innovation if they are merged and carefully balanced.

The technical education of engineers is traditionally characterized by an analytical, structured approach, by systematic considerations of content areas with the help of subject-specific concepts, by deductive thinking, and by planning project progress in advance. All of this enables students to produce state-of-the-art engineering solutions and to incrementally improve existing solutions. However, when this way of thinking, planning, and working is used on its own, it limits the developer to what is

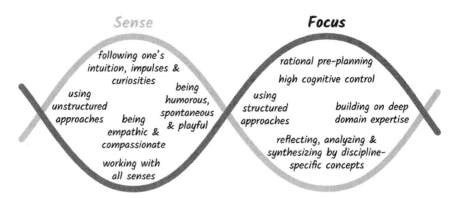

Fig. 2 "DNA" of a creative process: High-profile creative developments and innovations require the effective combination of two approaches, here referred to as *sense* and *focus*. On the one hand, it is important to discover new, worthwhile perspectives and goals for creative projects (sense). This is how disruptive innovations are made possible. In the process, "meaning" and "finding meaning" play an important role. The way of working is often "sensory"; that is, different sensory channels are used. On the other hand, it is also important to benefit from the already existing knowledge of the community in creative processes and to apply it in a targeted manner (focus). Qualified work with methods and concepts of a professional community helps to develop technically skilled solutions that do not fall short of the level of performance already achieved. However, simply reusing existing specialist concepts results in solutions that are only level with the state of the art or go a little beyond it, i.e., incremental innovations, not radical leaps. High-quality creative developments combine the sense and focus ways of working. In this way, it is possible to create highly novel, desirable, and in-demand solutions that are also technically mature. Figure adapted from von Thienen et al. (2018)

feasible in the subject area. As emphasized above, finding fundamentally new solutions additionally requires an open approach that differs in many ways from what is taught as a process in classical engineering projects.

The more engineering education focuses on teaching work processes that are structured analytically, the more this approach becomes entrenched as a "comfort zone" among students. It then becomes increasingly difficult to "break out" into open explorations beyond what is plannable based on existing, technical concepts. This was recognized early on in Design Thinking projects and has therefore strongly influenced the development of curricula. Based on such experiences, already many decades ago Stanford developed an innovation curriculum for engineers that "values incoming students' analytical skills while introducing new ones" (Faste, 1994, p. 2).

Against this backdrop, Design Thinking courses to this day specifically train such creativity skills and impart processes that are usually neglected, or sometimes even trained away in engineering studies: empathy as a basis for work, long phases of exploring problems before thinking about solutions, story-telling instead of quantitative analysis, thinking up wild approaches to solutions (temporarily) without questioning their feasibility, many kinesthetic experiences in the creative process, such as walking around frequently during working hours and physically tinkering with prototypes instead of physically quiet thinking while seated, and much more.

At first glance, you might think Design Thinking is just a wild, unconventional way of working, in contrast to classic engineering approaches, but that would actually be a misunderstanding. The developers of Design Thinking have always been aware that both approaches and both types of competencies must be joined in order for valuable fundamental innovations to emerge. The Design Thinking approach to teaching at engineering institutes like Stanford and Potsdam focuses primarily on conveying the "wild" side, on "sense" more than "focus," because students at both institutes already bring with them, or learn elsewhere, the analytical and domain-specific skills that are just as essential.

3 Effects of Design Thinking Education on Digital Engineering Students

So how does Design Thinking education affect students? Is it possible to measure the desired impact and effect of such an education? Yes, in fact, there are now quite a number of studies on the influence and impact of Design Thinking education that demonstrate the favorable effect of this approach.

Royalty et al. (2012) surveyed alumni of the Stanford d.school. They found significant outcomes of Design Thinking education which persisted in the long term. In particular, alumni reported influences of Design Thinking on their career choices and preferred ways of working, on their creative confidence, on how they dealt with uncertainty and failure, and on how they designed creative work environments for themselves. The majority of respondents said that they still used what they had learned at the d.school on a weekly basis—and they reported this even years after graduating. It is certainly rare for courses to have such a lasting impact on students. For most courses, it is more likely that students will later have little recollection of course content and practices when asked about them years later. The fact that individual courses have a lasting impact on people's lives, including their later professional careers, is truly exceptional.

A different research approach was taken by Bott et al. (2014) and Saggar et al. (2015), who used neuroscientific methods. They found changes in brain activation after Design Thinking training. By participating in a design thinking training course as part of a controlled, randomized experiment, not only the creative performance of the participants increased, but it was also possible to measure how brain dynamics had changed through training. For example, graduates of the Design Thinking training showed a stronger involvement of the cerebellum during creative thinking. Other research has found that the cerebellum is important for fluid body movements and movements in space. It seems, what is supported by real movement in normal life— exploring views from different perspectives—can occur mentally as well. Similar brain structures are involved, whether they support fluid body movements and perspective changes in real life or fluid mental shifts in the creative thinking process.

For a review of various studies on Design Thinking education and its effects, see von Thienen et al. (2017). Across the board, significant positive effects of Design Thinking have been found in the areas of "training creative processes," "fostering creative mindsets and interdisciplinary collaboration," as well as "designing creative work environments." Overall, Design Thinking has a positive effect on the social skills and interactions of course participants. Trainees are empowered to develop more novel ideas and are significantly better able to solve problems creatively by using the Design Thinking approach. Other frequently observable effects of Design Thinking education include a high degree of enjoyment of creative work, independence in innovation development, good social networking skills, and interaction that is beneficial—also in the long term—for all those involved.

The majority of studies on Design Thinking education examine all the course participants without paying specific attention to individual disciplines. Traifeh et al. (2020) specifically studied the effects of Design Thinking education on digital engineering students. In their study, HPI students were surveyed about their participation in the *Global Design Thinking Week*. This workshop has been developed by the HPI D-School to introduce Design Thinking practically in a highly condensed time frame. The course lasts for one week during which students jointly develop innovative solutions to real-world problems with an international project partner. In the process, they are assisted by experienced Design Thinking coaches and go through the entire Design Thinking process. Traifeh et al. administered a questionnaire to course participants before and after they attended the *Global Design Thinking Week*, in order to assess the development of important facets of a creative mindset. After the training, there was a change in almost all recorded dimensions, although the training only lasted one week. Consistently, Design Thinking education strengthened creative attitudes (Figs. 3 and 4).

How confident IT-students feel that they can …

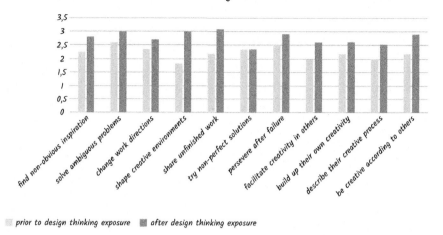

prior to design thinking exposure   after design thinking exposure

Fig. 3 Creative self-efficacy is critical to overcoming multiple challenges that typically arise in innovation projects. The Competency-Based Creative Agency Scale (Royalty et al., 2014) captures such self-efficacy in eleven key competency domains. Traifeh et al. (2020) thus recorded the mindset development of IT students, comparing the situation before and after the *Global Design Thinking Week*. Almost across the board, there was a clear increase in creative confidence over the course of the Design Thinking training. Values can vary from 1 (respondent felt "a little confident" in handling the challenge) to 4 (respondent felt "completely confident"). Before-and-after comparisons of eleven students were included in the analysis for each topic area. We would like to thank Traifeh and her colleagues for sharing their raw data, which we reproduce here in aggregated form

First, Traifeh et al. explored a phenomenon known as "creative confidence" (cf. Royalty et al., 2014). It questions how comfortable and confident people feel when working on creative projects. When students have a high level of self-efficacy in innovation work, they have the confidence to deal with unforeseen difficulties. This means they even remain capable of action and continue working (often with good strategies for action) when unexpected setbacks occur in the process. Unlike incremental innovation projects based on expertise (focus), in disruptive innovation projects (sense), the course of the project is genuinely unpredictable, and serious difficulties almost always arise at one point or another. Self-efficacy is therefore essential so that difficulties can be overcome with courage and the ability to act. Otherwise, the creative process would not come to a good end. In almost all areas included in the study, a significant increase in creative self-efficacy was observed among respondents after just one week of Design Thinking education (Fig. 3).

Another area that Traifeh et al. (2020) examined concerns empathy and cultural sensitivity. As discussed above, disruptive innovation almost never develops within the confines of one discipline alone where existing ideas from a single specialist community are merely recombined and then applied. Disruptive innovation occurs when people experience new perspectives which they usually learn about in their own lives and through their interactions with others. In order to benefit from other

How comfortable IT-students feel when working with people from ...

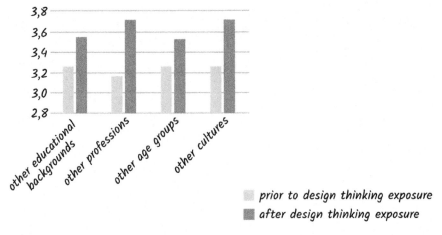

prior to design thinking exposure
after design thinking exposure

Fig. 4 Empathy and cultural sensitivity are important prerequisites for the success of innovation projects. They help developers embrace new, unfamiliar ways of looking at things, which in turn fosters the emergence of disruptive innovation. Traifeh et al. (2020) observed that a one-week Design Thinking training course already had very favorable effects in helping digital engineering students collaborate with individuals from other social groups. Values can vary between 1 (the respondent does not feel at all comfortable in the heterogeneous team) and 4 (the respondent feels very comfortable). We would like to thank Traifeh and her colleagues for sharing their raw data, which we reproduce here in aggregated form

perspectives in innovation projects, one must first and foremost recognize them, engage with them, and follow up on them. In the work process, this very often means being able to deal with other people and their view points. They may introduce unfamiliar perspectives due to the fact that they have a different educational background/a different profession, or that they come from a different age cohort or cultural background. Thus, Traifeh et al. also asked how comfortable IT students felt when working with people from other social groups. Here, too, the *Global Design Thinking Week* had a positive influence. After the week-long course, participants consistently felt more comfortable working in heterogeneous teams (Fig. 4). This is another important prerequisite for the success of innovation projects.

In summary, we can report how Design Thinking at the HPI is proving to be an integral part of engineering education. At a time when our living environment is changing rapidly and radically as a result of digital transformation, we at educational institutes bear a great responsibility. It is no longer enough to teach students how to incrementally improve existing solutions, how to optimize systems, and how to transfer solutions from the analog into the digital world (often, unfortunately, without questioning these solutions). The digital engineers we train create new environments that shape the daily experiences of many people. It is therefore critical to also prepare students for their role as innovators. They need a creative mindset with a pronounced awareness of their own innovator role, methodological tools for the creative process, experience with and enjoyment of interdisciplinary collaboration, and a sharpened eye for the needs of people who should benefit from new, digital solutions. The digital transformation is bringing about major changes for all of us. Whether these are positive changes that truly make a difference in people's lives depends to a large extent on the education we are able to offer digital engineering students. Design Thinking is instrumental in educating engineering students to become thoughtful innovators who first explore thoroughly what people really need, and then use cross-disciplinary expertise to implement desirable solutions.

References

Arnold, J. E. (2016). Creative engineering. In W. J. Clancey (Ed.), *Creative engineering: Promoting innovation by thinking differently* (pp. 59–150). Retrieved from http://purl.stanford.edu/jb100v s5745

Bott, N., Quintin, E.-M., Saggar, M., Kienitz, E., Royalty, A., Hong, D.W.-C., Liu, N., Chien, Y.-H., Hawthorne, G., & Reiss, A. (2014). Creativity training enhances goal-directed attention and information processing. *Thinking Skills and Creativity, 13*, 120–128. https://doi.org/10.1016/j.tsc.2014.03.005

Faste, R. (1994). Ambidextrous thinking. In *Innovations in mechanical engineering curricula for the 1990s.* American Society of Mechanical Engineers. Retrieved from http://www.fastefoundat ion.org/publications/ambidextrous_thinking.pdf

Maslow, A. H. (2016). Emotional blocks to creativity. In W. J. Clancey (Ed.), *Creative engineering: Promoting innovation by thinking differently* (pp. 188–197). Retrieved from http://purl.stanford.edu/jb100vs5745

McKim, R. H. (2016). Designing for the whole man. In W. J. Clancey (Ed.), *Creative engineering: Promoting innovation by thinking differently* (pp. 198–217). Retrieved from http://purl.stanford.edu/jb100vs5745

Meinel, C. (2020a). Digitale Kompetenzen und Schulbildung. In M. Friedrichsen & W. Wersig (Eds.), *Digitale Kompetenz* (pp. 29–35). Springer Gabler.

Meinel, C. (2020b). Die HPI Schul-Cloud: Eine zukunftssichere IT-Infrastruktur für das deutsche Bildungswesen. In A. Ternès von Hattburg & M. Schäfer (Eds.), *Digitalpakt—was nun?* (pp. 81–87). Springer VS.

Meinel, C. (2020c). Die Bildungscloud—smarte Bildung für ein smartes Deutschland. In C. Etezadzadeh (Ed.), *Smart city-made in Germany* (pp. 175–182). Springer Vieweg.

Meinel, C., & von Thienen, J. P. A. (2016). Design thinking. Aktuelles Schlagwort. *Informatik-Spektrum, 39*(4), 310–315. https://doi.org/10.1007/s00287-016-0977-2

Plattner, H. (2009). Entstehungsgeschichte der HPI School of Design Thinking. In H. Plattner, C. Meinel, & U. Weinberg (Eds.), *Design thinking. Innovation lernen. Ideenwelten öffnen* (pp. 11–25). mi-Wirtschaftsbuch.

Royalty, A., Oishi, L. N., & Roth, B. (2012). "I use it every day": Pathways to adaptive innovation after graduate study in design thinking. In H. Plattner, C. Meinel, & L. Leifer (Eds.), *Design thinking research. Measuring performance in context* (pp. 95–105). Springer. https://doi.org/10.1007/978-3-642-31991-4_6

Royalty, A., Oishi, L. N., & Roth, B. (2014). Acting with creative confidence: Developing a creative agency assessment tool. In C. Meinel & L. Leifer (Eds.), *Design thinking research. Building innovation eco-systems* (pp. 85–101). Springer.

Saggar, M., Quintin, E.-M., Kienitz, E., Bott, N. T., Sun, Z., Hong, W.-C., Chien, Y. H., Liu, N., Dougherty, R. F., Royalty, A., Hawthorne, G., & Reiss, A. L. (2015). Pictionary-based fMRI paradigm to study the neural correlates of spontaneous improvisation and figural creativity. *Scientific Reports, 5*, 10894. https://doi.org/10.1038/srep10894 PMID:26018874.

Traifeh, H., Nicolai, C., Refaie, R., & Meinel, C. (2020). Engaging digital engineering students in design thinking. In *DS 101: Proceedings of NordDesign 2020* (pp. 1–14), Lyngby, Denmark, 12th–14th August 2020.

von Thienen, J. P. A., Traifeh, H., & Meinel, C. (2018). Design thinking powered learning experiences. Invited talk at the *Stanford-Potsdam Hasso Plattner design thinking research community building workshop*, Stanford, USA, March 14.

von Thienen, J. P. A., & Meinel, C. (2019). Balancing child-like and adult approaches in creative pursuits: The sense-focus model of creative mastery. Presentation at the *European Collaborative Creativity Conference EC3*, June 20–22, Bologna, Italy. Retrieved from https://mic.fgm.it/wp-content/uploads/2013/07/ec3-mic-conference-2019_book-of-abstracts_online2.pdf

von Thienen, J. P. A., Royalty, A., & Meinel, C. (2017). Design thinking in higher education: How students become dedicated creative problem solvers. In C. Zhou (Ed.), *Handbook of research on creative problem-solving skill development in higher education* (pp. 306–328). IGI Global.

von Thienen, J. P. A., Szymanski, C., Santuber, J., Plank, I. S., Rahman, S., Weinstein, T., Owoyele, B., Bauer, M. & Meinel, C. (2021a). Neurodesign live. In H. Plattner, C. Meinel, & L. Leifer (Eds.), *Design thinking research. Interrogating the doing* (pp. 357–425). Springer.

von Thienen, J. P. A., Clancey, W. J. & Meinel, C. (2021b). Theoretical foundations of design thinking. Part III: Robert H. McKim's visual thinking theories. In H. Plattner, C. Meinel, & L. Leifer (Eds.), *Design thinking research. Interrogating the doing* (pp. 9–72). Springer.

von Thienen, J. P. A., Kolodny, O., & Meinel, C. (2022). Neurodesign: The biology, psychology and engineering of creative thinking and innovation. In N. Rezaei (Ed.), *Thinking: Bioengineering of science and art*. Springer Nature.

Prof. Dr. Christoph Meinel (Univ. Prof., Dr. sc. nat., Dr. rer. nat.) is Director and CEO of the Hasso Plattner Institute for Digital Engineering gGmbH (HPI) at the University of Potsdam.
Photo credit: Kay Herschelmann.

Christoph Meinel was born in 1954 and was founding Dean of the Digital Engineering Faculty at the University of Potsdam in April 2017. Currently he serves as Vice Dean. He holds the Chair of Internet Technologies and Systems and is also active in the fields of cybersecurity and digital education, teaching in the bachelor's and master's programs in IT-Systems Engineering and at the School of Design Thinking. Christoph Meinel developed the MOOC platform, openHPI.de, and also provides content on the site. His responsibilities include supervising numerous doctoral students, and he has authored or co-authored more than 25 books, anthologies, and various conference proceedings.

He has published more than 550 peer-reviewed articles in scientific journals and at international conferences and holds a number of international patents. He is a member of the National Academy of Science and Technology (acatech), director of the HPI-Stanford Design Thinking Research Program, honorary professor at the Technical University of Beijing, visiting professor at Shanghai University, professor at Nanjing University, and member of numerous scientific committees and supervisory boards.

Dr. Julia V. Thienen Initiator of HPI Neurodesign and Senior Researcher at the Hasso Plattner Institute for Digital Engineering.

Photo credit: Kay Herschelmann.

Dr. Julia von Thienen studied psychology, neuroscience, computer science and philosophy at the Free University of Berlin. She has taught research methodology at the Free University of Berlin, the University of Chicago and the University of Potsdam. In 2008, Dr. Julia von Thienen joined the Hasso Plattner Institute for Digital Engineering, specifically the Stanford-Potsdam Design Thinking Research Program. Her studies are concerned with design thinking as an approach to creativity and innovation. She specifically seeks to encourage creativity in engineering—all in the service of worthwhile innovation—, and to integrate more body-related perspectives in the process. In design thinking education, one challenge Dr. Julia von Thienen finds important concerns the breadth of approaches taken, so as to orchestrate classes from highly practice oriented approaches to deep treatments of theory and research, from classes on creativity in engineering to innovation projects in all areas of life. Here, design thinking values of diversity, flexibility and collaboration are key. They help to advance rich design thinking programmes, where educators, students and project partners meet in a spirit of curiosity, appreciation and mutual support, so that collaborations emerge naturally.

Mastering the Fundamentals of Design Thinking by Teaching the Skills of Improvisation

Annie Talbot

Abstract This chapter makes the connection between design thinking and improvisation and the skills required by each discipline. Further, we make the argument that the skills needed for successful design thinking and effective team interaction can be taught and that improvisation is the perfect medium for teaching them. We offer simple, practicable exercises that teach fundamental design skills like flexibility, risk taking, careful observation, and building on the ideas of others.

1 Introduction

Design thinking and team-based design rely heavily on flexibility, creativity, and risk taking. These skills are buzzwords in business, education, and in almost every other industry. Creative problem solving is deemed one of the most important skills necessary for success in the workplace and in life. Design thinking and team-based design are *built* on flexibility, creativity, and risk taking, which raises the very important question: How do we teach these skills?

This chapter explores the connections between improvisation and team-based design and suggests improvisation exercises that teach specific design-related skills, giving design practitioners and educators a foundation for teaching and practicing fundamental design skills.

Design thinking has been defined as an iterative, user-centered approach to solving complex problems. Improvisation, or improv, can be defined as the ability to improvise or act without a script, or, to make things up spontaneously, using the people and things available to you. We can use the principles of improv to teach the skills needed in design thinking, making them accessible and easy to practice.

In design thinking, teachers and coaches encourage teams to "be creative", "take risks" and "build on the ideas of others" but they rarely tell them *how* to perform these behaviors. Telling a designer to "be creative" without providing the mechanisms for doing so, is like a sports coach telling an athlete to "run faster." Athletes practice drills

A. Talbot (✉)
Potsdam, Germany

© The Author(s), under exclusive license to Springer Nature Switzerland AG 2022
C. Meinel and T. Krohn (eds.), *Design Thinking in Education*,
https://doi.org/10.1007/978-3-030-89113-8_3

25

for successful performance just as musicians practice scales. The same holds true for designers: in order to excel at user-centered design, we must first teach designers the skills and drills needed for successful performance. Improvisation relies on many of the same skills as design thinking and has proven to be an extraordinary vehicle for teaching these skills. Repeating the exercises and practicing the skills of improv gives the designer a "road map" to follow—a practical guide to navigating the unknown (Talbot, 2022).

The benefits of improvisation have been widely recognized by businesses, industry, and academic institutions. Companies like Google, Siemens, and IBM use improvisation for promoting innovation and improving team dynamics, and graduate schools like Harvard Business School, MIT, and Stanford, have made improvisation a part of their curriculum.

2   Training Improv Skills for Team-Based Design

One of the fundamental concepts in design thinking is the notion of "building on the ideas of others." In order to build on someone else's ideas, we must first listen to their ideas. Active listening is a skill. It involves more than just perceiving sound. It requires our full attention and letting go of one's own agenda. It involves trust. Improv helps us develop this ability to listen attentively, to observe, and to promote empathy. Teaching us to say "yes," to our teammates' suggestions, asks us to be accepting and non-judgmental, thus promoting open-mindedness and collaboration. Improv encourages us to take risks, thereby helping us to become more flexible and less afraid to fail. It teaches us to make useful "offers" or suggestions that our teammates can build on. It teaches us to let go of our preconceived outcomes, opening us to discovery and innovation. These are valuable life skills, business skills, and problem-solving skills. They are the fundamental skills of team-based design.

When combined with design thinking as a way of solving problems, improv can be the key to successful innovation and creative solutions because it gives students actual practice learning the skills they need to succeed. It takes the mystery out of successful design and design thinking by giving us methods for learning these skills and an opportunity to practice them.

3   Improvisation and Cognition

In good design, we are never just designing an object by itself. We are always creating something in relation to the objects or people around it. We are creating both the *experience* of using or engaging with the object as well as *the story* that goes along with the object. When we design a new pen, we are designing the experience of holding and writing with that pen. We are creating the story of a user using that pen in a variety of situations. If done well, we are *envisioning* and *enacting* the story of our object being used. We make the story come alive in our bodies, not just in our heads, in our imaginations. This kind of "thinking with the body" is what researchers call "extended cognition" and it is a hallmark of high-performance teams.

We tend to think of cognition, or thinking, as happening mostly in the brain. However, research has shown that we think with our bodies and with things as well. Thinking with our bodies and interacting with the objects around us actually *helps* us think. When we think with "things," holding them in our hands, using them, and when we think with our bodies, acting something out, pointing, gesturing, pantomiming, we think better, faster, and more creatively (Kirsh, 2011; Tversky, 2019). In short, the combination of mind, body, and objects actually enables cognition.

If thinking is enhanced by engaging on these three levels: mind, body, and with objects, how can we practice this kind of engagement and thus train ourselves to think more creatively? Improvisation involves the body but also happens in the mind and in relation to other people and things around us. Improv operates on all three of these levels, often at the same time. It allows us to switch easily between body, mind, and object and to explore the interplay between them. Improvisation gives us a way of practicing different kinds of thinking, and "extending" our cognition, and it gives us a practical way of teaching students to do the same.

Another area of cognitive research that is relevant to the design process is *distributed* cognition, or problem solving distributed within or across the group (Hutchins, 1995). The nature of improvisation is spontaneous and unscripted. No one knows the outcome of an exercise or a scene at the start. We only know our individual parts. The same is true in design. When we are working on a design challenge, no one knows what the final outcome or solution will be. It emerges as a result of individual efforts. Becoming comfortable with only knowing our individual contribution and relying on team members to complement our contribution is a lesson in trust. Each team member brings his or her unique skills and point of view to the process, such that the whole is "an intersection," not just the sum, of the individual parts. When done well, distributed cognition can take a team from "coordinating" to "collaborating," that is, from merely working well together into the realm of discovery and innovation (Leifer, 2005).

4 Designing the Story

In improvisation, we are continually building on what has come just moments before. We create the story moment by moment, allowing it to unfold, piece by piece. Recognizing and learning to "build" on individual pieces and weaving them into a compelling narrative is also the job of the designer and design thinker.

There are many improv exercises that teach the skill of story building. In the exercise "Questions Only," two people build a scene or a story by alternating one line at a time. But unlike "One-Word Story," where we build a story by adding one word at a time, or "One-Sentence Story", where we alternate adding one sentence at a time, in this exercise, we are only allowed to ask questions.

When playing "Questions Only", we would give two "players" or volunteers a made-up relationship and a situation, for example; "siblings at their sister's wedding." Player One might start the exercise by saying, "Can you believe our sister is getting married?" Player Two might respond, "Do you think she'll really go through with it?" To which Player One might say, "Why? Do you think she knows about the affair?"....

This exercise can be incredibly challenging. We often disguise statements as questions, thinking we are asking something when we are really providing information, usually to further our own idea of where the story should go. We want to answer the question. Designers have the same tendency. We want to solve the problem. We often resist staying in the "question space" and are eager to jump to the "solution space". However, there are many benefits of staying longer in the "question space" including opening up to a greater understanding of the problem.

The Quaker religion has something called a "clearness committee," which helps anyone in the community find clarity when faced with a big decision. Rather than try to solve the problem or offer advice, the committee has one rule: "ask questions only." The idea is that by asking only questions, the committee seeks to listen and to help the person seeking clarity, to listen. Contrary to our culture of wanting to fix things and offer solutions, the "clearness" process assumes that we provide more help by listening than by "fixing" (Levoy, 1997). It suggests that asking questions and listening attentively leads to solutions.

Asking the *right* questions helps us formulate a good story. Researcher Ozgur Eris describes two types of questions necessary for informed design, DRQs or Deep Reasoning Questions, and GDQs, Generative Design Questions. DRQs ask about specifics: how big something will be, where the buttons will go, what material it will be made of. Deep Reasoning Questions are concerned with specifications, comparison, and verification. Generative Design Questions, on the other hand, help us to generate, asking questions like, "What if we made it out of this? What if we changed the shape or material?" Because these two types of questions do very different things, we would therefore want to use them at different stages in the design process. The most effective teams know when to ask which type of question and how to move easily between the two types (Edelman, 2011; Eris, 2003). Improv exercises like "Questions Only" can help designers recognize the different types of questions and become adept at utilizing them appropriately.

5   Re-thinking the "How Might We" Question

In design thinking, we often use the technique of asking "How might we...?" questions (HMW) as a way of generating possibilities during ideation. However, "How might we" questions are actually *not* generative questions. "How might we" questions are really deep reasoning questions disguised as generative questions. By their very nature, they seek a specific answer. "How might we do such and such...? We do it like this..." The moment these questions are asked they move us immediately from exploring the problem to finding possible solutions. What if we reframe the

HMW question as a "What happens if..." question? "What happens if" is a generative question. It seeks to open the space, it asks for possibilities. It asks for more. It takes a risk. "What happens if" questions get us comfortable with staying in the "question space." When proposed by a teammate, "What happens if" is a suggestion, an "offer." We can practice building on our teammate's ideas by building or adding to their scenario. We build on their ideas by asking generative questions and lingering in the question space. Ask "What happens if..." questions, then play out the scenarios—enacting them in the body, the mind, and with objects.

6 Teaching the Core Skills

This section focuses on several skill sets necessary for good team-based design: careful observation, deep listening, and empathy, as well as building on the ideas of others, flexibility, collaboration, and trust, and finally synthesizing information, telling a good story, and taking risks. Specific improv exercises aimed at developing these skills are described in detail, as well as notes for reflecting on the exercises.

7 The Basic Rule

There is one basic rule in improvisation, "Yes, and." Whatever your partner or another player says or does, you say "yes" to it. You accept all "offers," (that's the "yes") and then build on that offer (the "and"). Every suggestion, idea, or outrageous statement is met with an enthusiastic, "Yes!" even if they ask you to let go of what you had planned. Letting go of pre-conceptions is another essential skill for designers. Staying open to possibilities, resisting stereotypes, seeing things from a new and varied perspective are all ways to build the trust, cooperation, and collaboration necessary for teams, students, and businesses to succeed.

Saying "yes" and accepting your partner's offers shows you are listening, you are validating their suggestions. This makes your partner feel and look good. Then when you make an offer they say "yes" to your idea, making you look and feel good. This leads to another rule of improv, "Make your partner look good". Del Close, one of the early founders of modern improvisational theater, said, "If you want your partner to be a poet and a genius, then be a poet and a genius." (Salinsky & Frances-White, 2008) It is much easier to come up with good ideas when all of your ideas are received enthusiastically. Focusing on your partner also keeps you present at the moment, gets you "out of your head," and takes your attention off of yourself and what you will say or do next.

In improv, we are taught to accept every offer or suggestion, but not every offer is a "good" offer. A good offer, in improv and in design, is one that propels the story forward, offering something in addition to, or "more than" what came before. Through practice, we can learn to turn a "weak" offer into an offer our teammates can use and build on, an offer that contributes something, risks something. It's how we begin to develop the skill of risk taking.

8   A Few Notes on Improv

Improvisation is fun, so learning these skills is also fun. Improv requires no previous knowledge and very little preparation. It is flexible and can be done almost anytime, anywhere.

Improv involves the whole body. It can help us practice embodied cognition, enabling us to think "better, faster and more creatively" (Tversky, 2019). Additional research on what makes a successful team and on ways to increase team efficacy shows that embodiment and gesture correlate with successful team interaction (Edelman et al., 2019). Improv is one way to become more comfortable with embodied movement and gesture.

9   Making Mistakes

Improv, like design thinking, is about doing. In design thinking, we "do to know," prototyping quickly so we can test our idea and see if we're on the right track. By making "mistakes" we learn from our "failures." In improv, because there is no script, we also have to act quickly. We learn to act on instinct regardless of the outcome. Improv exercises are designed to get us "out of our head." They're fast-paced and unpredictable.

Learning to "jump in" without thinking trains us to take risks and face our fears. We become willing to fail, and we get comfortable making mistakes. In improvisation, there are no mistakes. Everything is useable. In improv, mistakes are often celebrated with applause. With practice, we can become skilled at seeing "mistakes" as a challenge, an opportunity.

10   Teaching the Skills

Throughout this chapter, I use the term students, participants, or players to refer to those who are learning the improv exercises. These could be adults, children, or professionals. When teaching adults, I have found that most prefer the security of knowing what they will be doing before they do it. They often want to discuss and analyze the exercises before trying them. Instead, have them try the exercises first. Defer questions and observations to the end.

Conduct a brief reflection after each exercise. Ask the students what they noticed or learned, and see if they can name some of the skills used in the exercise and their relevance to team-based design and to life. The reflection period is like synthesis; it's where we make sense of what we just observed or experienced. It's often where the real insights occur.

11 The Exercises

"Mirroring"

One of the simplest exercises for developing observation skills is the "Mirroring" exercise. The goal is to develop deep observation skills by teaching students to look carefully and pay close attention. It's like "deep listening" with the body.

Playing the Game

Have students form two lines facing each other, pairing up with the person opposite them. (If there's an odd number you can step in). Have them decide who will lead first. One player leads and the other "mirrors" them simultaneously. Switch leaders after a minute or so. You can make suggestions about varying the speed or using all parts of the body, including the face.

Reflection

Almost always, one group will say that there came a point where they were so "in synch" with each other that neither person was leading or following, they were acting in unison. Although this is not the goal of the exercise, it shows how carefully they were observing each other so as to seem to be moving together seamlessly. As the facilitator, you can ask what other skills this exercise develops. Some of these skills are empathy, focus, being present, slowing down, paying careful attention, working together, cooperation, and getting "out of your head."

How It Relates to Team-Based Design

The skills taught in the Mirroring exercise can be helpful in several phases of a design challenge. These phases are "understanding" the problem, because of empathy and teamwork, "observing" by looking carefully and noticing and especially in "synthesis," where being "in sync" with our user and seeing things from the user's point of view (empathy) is key to successfully making sense of our findings.

Additional exercise: "**Change Three Things**"

"Change Three Things" is another improv exercise that helps develop observation skills. It can be done using the same set-up as mirroring (two lines, partners facing each other) and is often a good warm-up to start a session. Partners take a minute or so to "study" each other, paying careful attention to details. Then they turn back to back to each other and change three things about their physical appearance (rolling up their sleeves, taking off glasses, etc.) When both partners are ready, they turn back to face each other and take turns trying to guess the three changes. It's good to do a second round as the players get more confident and the changes become more subtle and harder to detect.

11.1 "Yes, And!"

Listening well requires putting all of your attention on the other person and letting go of any thought about what you're going to say next. This requires a great deal of trust. Trust in your partner and trust in yourself that when it comes times for you to speak, you will know what to say. It requires you to let go of any preconceived notion of where the story or the idea should go. Saying yes to your partner or teammates says, "I hear you. I'm listening" and "What a great idea!" The "And!" says, "I like your idea and I'm going to build on it." Accepting someone else's ideas gives them permission to take risks by releasing them from the fear of saying something wrong, or failing. It builds cooperation and trust, freeing other members of the team to take chances and to trust their instincts. "Yes, And!" is used frequently in business for brainstorming and team-building, and in design thinking in the "iteration" phase.

11.2 Playing the Game

This exercise is usually played in three rounds. However, if time is an issue, you can skip to the third round, "Yes, And!" Give the instructions for each round just before the round, so there is no planning ahead or trying to "figure out" the exercise. Have the group split into pairs or 3's. Suggest an activity that they will plan together (a surprise party, vacation, company picnic, etc.).

As the facilitator, you can pick someone from each group to go first (or come up with a fun way of deciding who will start, for example, "whoever is taller" or "whoever is not wearing black"). In the first round, instruct the players to say "no" to every suggestion. The first player starts with what they are going to do and the other player, or players, respond with "no" and make another suggestion. Let the players know they have permission to really discount the idea. They take turns coming up with and rejecting suggestions. For example, if we decide the activity is to plan a retirement party for our boss, the first round might sound something like this:

Let's have a surprise party for our boss and invite the whole company!

No. That would be way too expensive. How about we take her to dinner with the team?

No, she doesn't even like us. We should get her something, like a watch.

No. Watches are stupid. No one even wears watches anymore.

In the second round, players say "yes, but…" It might sound something like this:

For the party, everyone could prepare a little rhyme about our boss.

Yes! But you never know what people might write. What if we do a skit?

Yeah, that'd be so cool, but it would take a lot of planning. We could hire a band?

Yes, music would be great, but a band is so expensive!

In the last round, players say "yes, and!" to every suggestion. They respond enthusiastically to the idea and then build on or add to it. Remind the players to "accept" whatever their partner suggests.

The third round might go something like this:

Hey, why don't we have the party on a boat, like a dinner cruise?

Yes! And we could hire one of those giant cruise ships with basketball courts and swimming pools on the decks!

Yes! And we could stay overnight on the cruise ship, with every employee getting their own Presidential suite!

Pitfalls: Besides trying to be clever or funny (which usually means not really listening to your partner), there can be a tendency with the "Yes, And!" round for players to just list a bunch of ideas. This kind of associative list is usually related to the topic but doesn't build on the previous idea. One reason brainstorming often fails is that it generates a "laundry list" of suggestions that lack depth. Remind the players instead to really engage with their partner's suggestion, expanding on and adding to it. This is how we can turn a weak offer into a more useful offer and how we can "stack the deck" for distributed cognition, with each individual contribution building upon the one that came before.

11.3 Reflection

After all three rounds are finished, ask the players what they noticed about each round. Usually, players either love the "no" round, because it gives them a chance to speak in a way they never would, or they hate it because it doesn't go anywhere and no one is really listening to each other. If players don't come up with this insight for the "yes, but" round, you can make the point that "*yes, but*" is really a "*no*." Even though you have said "yes," in effect, the "but" renders it a "no." In the third round players usually get very excited, the volume in the room goes up and there is often a lot of animation and gesturing, a good sign that players may be moving into a new level of awareness, that is, embodied or extended cognition (Edelman, 2019).

11.4 How It Relates to Team-Based Design

"Yes, And!" is often used for "iteration" or idea generating. Saying "yes," supporting your teammates, and building on their ideas is helpful throughout the entire design process.

11.5 "What Cha Doin'?" (Aka: What Are You Doing?)

This is a great exercise to warm up a group, especially if they are nervous about improv. The point of the exercise is to "mis-name" or "get it wrong" so no one has to worry about "getting it right." It is also physically active so good for getting people moving and it is always a lot of fun.

11.6 Playing the Game

I like to do this exercise in a circle with the whole group because I think there is much to be learned by watching other players. It can also be done in pairs or smaller groups. Players form a circle. Decide who will go first and in which direction the game will go. The person who starts begins by pantomiming an activity, like brushing their teeth. After watching for a few seconds, the person next to them asks, "What cha doin'?" They can join in the pantomime while they are observing if they want. The first person responds by naming an activity completely different from what they're acting out, like "I'm doing yoga." The second person begins pantomiming the answer, in this case, they do some yoga poses, as best they can. Then the player next to them asks, "What cha doin'?" Rather than say, "I'm doing yoga" they respond with something unrelated, like, "I'm changing a tire." And so on around the circle.

11.7 Reflection

This exercise operates on all three levels of extended cognition: thinking with mind, body, and objects around us. In addition to thinking with the body by physically enacting an activity, there is an "implied" object or objects with which we are interacting, and we are also thinking with our mind and communicating with language. It is here that this exercise operates on another, much deeper level. By acting out one thing but calling it something else, we are challenging our usual thinking process. We disrupt the connection between things and what we call them, essentially giving us a new way of looking at something, a fresh perspective. This disruption lays the groundwork for the subsequent "re-naming" of these objects. The re-naming of objects, interactions, and experiences, is an advanced design skill linked to highly effective teams (Mabogunje, 1997). Seeing beyond our limited notion of what something is, seeing a chair as "not just a chair" or "more than what we think of as a chair" is an invaluable skill for designers and educators alike. It allows us to imagine what could be, what is not yet in existence—a necessary skill for radical innovation.

11.8   How It Relates to Team-Based Design

This exercise can help us with "synthesis"; the ability to recognize patterns, put things together, and make something new. It is also good for developing "observation", "understanding" and "ideation."

Additional exercise: **"Mis-Naming Objects"**

Another exercise for practicing the advanced design skill of renaming, is called "Mis-Naming Objects". In this exercise everyone walks around the room, points at random objects, and "mis-names" them out loud, all at the same time. It is much harder than it sounds to separate what we call something from what it actually is. However, breaking this association is crucial for the designer if we want to redesign anything.

12   We Are All Improvisers

We are all improvisers. None of us knows what will happen next and life does not follow a script. We have all had to deal with failure or the unexpected. Improvising is a part of life. Improvising "*well*" is a skill that can be taught. Practicing the skills of improvisation lays the foundation for mastering the skills of team-based design, helping us to become better designers and greater agents of change.

Annie V. Talbot

Hasso Plattner Institute

November 2, 2020

May 28, 2021.

References

Edelman, J. (2011). *Understanding radical breaks: Media and behavior in small teams engaged in redesign scenarios.* Doctoral Dissertation, Stanford University http://purl.stanford.edu/ps394d y6131

Edelman, J. A., Owoyele, B., Santuber, J., Talbot, A. V., Unger, K., & Von Lewinski, K. (2019). Accessing highly effective performative patterns. In Design thinking research. Springer Berlin Heidelberg New York

Eris, O. (2003). *Asking generative design questions: A fundamental cognitive mechanism in design thinking.* Springer.

Hutchins, E. (1995). *Cognition in the wild.* MIT Press.

Kirsh, D. (2011). How marking in dance constitutes thinking with the body. In *The external mind* (pp. 183–214).

Levoy, G. (1997). Callings finding and following an authentic. In *Life,* (41), Random House, Inc.

Mabogunje, A. (1997). Noun phrases as surrogates for measuring early phases of the mechanical design process. In *The Proceedings of the 9th International Conference on Design Theory and Methodology*.

Salinsky, T.., & Frances-White, D. (2008). *The improv handbook: The ultimate guide to improvising in comedy, theatre, and beyond,*. Bloomsbury Academic.

Talbot, A. V. (2022). Improvisation as the foundation for teaching the fundamental skills of design thinking in education. In *Design thinking in education management—successfully developing and implementing innovation in educational contexts*. Springer.

Tversky, B. (2019). *Mind in motion: How action shapes thought*. Basic Books.

Annie Talbot Design Thinking and Presentation Coach, HPI Academy.

Annie Talbot is a Design Thinking and Presentation Coach who combines her background in theater and education with her love of team-based design, bringing her own unique perspective to teaching the skills of design thinking. She grew up in the U.S. and was a professional actress in New York and Los Angeles and worked in early childhood education in Northern California. Before moving to Germany, Annie Talbot taught "Improvisation for Artists" at the Royal College of Art London, a curriculum she developed after watching artists and designers struggle with how to practice the basic skills of creativity. She works with the HPI Academy as a design thinking coach and is an integral part of their Certification Program for DT Coaches.

The greatest challenge to using DT in education is our failure to provide a way to learn and to practice the fundamental skills of team-based design. The simplest step to remedying this is to teach Improvisation. Once the connection between the skills of Improv and the skills of DT, becomes obvious, we've given students a "road map" to follow to team-based success.

Combining DT and Entrepreneurship Education: The DTE-Model

Katharina Hölzle

Abstract Entrepreneurship consists of recognizing opportunities and taking advantage of them; i.e., entrepreneurial thinking and action is the act of taking responsibility for oneself and others. This is the philosophy of Entrepreneurship Education at the Hasso Plattner Institute and the University of Potsdam. Entrepreneurial thinking means to perceive and seize entrepreneurial opportunities. This requires a combination of analysis and synthesis; mindset, process and tools, and a new way of learning. The Design Thinking Entrepreneurship model (DTE model) responds to the current demands of Entrepreneurship Education, prioritizing the recognition of entrepreneurial opportunities with a user-centered approach and combining it with active doing, experimenting, and reflecting.

1 Motivation

When looking at current challenges, it is clear that we need a new approach to how we educate students: The aftermath of the COVID-19 pandemic, climate change, demographic change, and digital transformation is impacting virtually every aspect of our lives and working environments. Students will shape a future that will look radically different from our world today. A transformation of this magnitude, where social, environmental, and economic challenges will be front and center, calls for mindsets that borrow from all fields, from the natural sciences to economics to the humanities (Hillgren et al., 2011). It will be about identifying and solving *wicked problems*.[1] This is difficult to achieve with linear thinking or isolated tools and mindsets from just one discipline (Glen et al., 2014). If we look at the innovations currently found in the market, it becomes clear that many services offered do not

---

[1] *Wicked problems* are multidimensional complex problems that cannot be defined or solved unambiguously (Rittel & Webber, 1973, p. 161).

K. Hölzle (✉)
Hasso Plattner Institute for Digital Engineering, Campus Griebnitzsee, Campus III, Haus G-1, Raum G-1.E.08, Rudolf-Breitscheid-Straße 185-189, 14482 Potsdam, Germany
e-mail: Katharina.Hoelzle@hpi.de

© The Author(s), under exclusive license to Springer Nature Switzerland AG 2022
C. Meinel and T. Krohn (eds.), *Design Thinking in Education*,
https://doi.org/10.1007/978-3-030-89113-8_4

meet the expectations of users or society. Innovation is often incremental rather than radical, and the call for a new startup spirit goes unheard. The demand for new ways of thinking and acting goes beyond the conventional agenda of value creation and profit-oriented thinking found in traditional research and teaching.

Design Thinking is one possible approach for dealing with wicked problems. It complements the conventional analytical perspectives and methods of the natural sciences and economics, offering a mindset (Carlgren et al., 2016), a process (Lockwood, 2010), and tools (Seidel & Fixson, 2013) that are characterized by different approaches, the combination of various disciplines, and a human-centered approach. It can thus help to better identify entrepreneurial opportunities and find more innovative solutions to problems than other methods of teaching. Combining Design Thinking and Entrepreneurship Education is not without its problems, however, as the two sides have different emphases. This can lead to problems and misunderstandings during implementation (Sarooghi et al., 2019).

Building on a brief historical review of Entrepreneurship Education, this paper aims to introduce the DTE model with a focus on perceiving entrepreneurial opportunities and the commonalities of Design Thinking and Entrepreneurship Education. The goal of this model is to train people who, through a combination of Design Thinking and entrepreneurship, learn and apply ways of thinking and acting with which they can identify problems creatively, responsibly, and in a visionary way as well as find and implement solutions: in other words, become entrepreneurial.

2 Entrepreneurship Education and Entrepreneurial Opportunities

Entrepreneurship Education has changed significantly since the first entrepreneurship course was offered at Harvard University in 1947 (Daniel, 2016). For many decades, it was primarily characterized by the planning school, which follows the *recognition theory* in assuming that entrepreneurial opportunities are identified using systematic searches or prediction and are implemented by developing a business plan (Fiet, 2000). This is still evident in the textbook by Grichnik et al., (2010, p. 29) where entrepreneurship is described as an economic process of identifying, evaluating, and exploiting entrepreneurial opportunities. Scholars and practitioners say that without opportunities, there is no entrepreneurship (Brülhart, 2013, p. 2). How this is used to trigger the entrepreneurial process, though, depends on various influencing factors (perception of the opportunity, the opportunity itself, and the contextual factors).

The entrepreneurial opportunity arises from detecting decision errors made by other market actors and in this sense tends to be reactive, equilibrium-building, and not very innovative (Grichnik et al., 2010, p. 35). It is often referred to as a Kirznerian opportunity. According to the *discovery theory*, the entrepreneurial opportunity exists independently of the individual and is waiting to be discovered or exploited (Fueglistaller et al., 2012, p. 61). By consciously shaping the

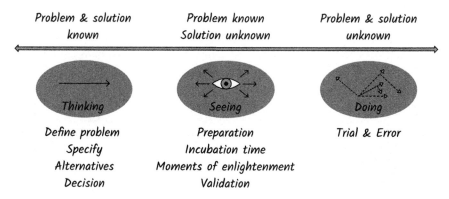

Fig. 1 Different perspectives on perceiving opportunities (Author's own figure)

process through the creation of either supply or demand, the entrepreneur becomes a change agent. In this role, and in the spirit of Schumpeter's *creative destruction*, an entrepreneur conceives something new and takes advantage of existing opportunities, but also creates new opportunities. The Schumpeterian opportunity stimulates change processes and imbalances through creative destruction. It is radically innovative, proactive, and rather rare. Such an opportunity can arise from a new combination of resources, impacting entire industries and triggering economic developments through fundamental innovations (Grichnik et al., 2010, p. 35f.). According to the *creation theory*, opportunities are not simply there waiting to be found, but only emerge when entrepreneurs engage in an iterative process to create them (Fueglistaller et al., 2012, p. 61).

There are three courses of action with regard to the process of perceiving opportunities (see Fig. 1).

Here, *thinking* is considered to represent the planning and systematic approaches. The approach is rational and analytical, using facts and figures as a basis (cf. Mintzberg & Westley, 2001, p. 91). Problems and solutions are largely known. The problem is defined and specified, then alternatives are generated and presented so a decision can be made. *Seeing* as a basis for decision-making can be viewed as the artistic approach. The focus is on visual aspects and the ideas, visions, and fantasies associated with them (Mintzberg & Westley, 2001, p. 91). In this case, the problem is known, but it is too complex to capture and analyze all the possible strategic alternatives. Intuition, imagination, and interpretive skills are required to visualize a picture of the future. *Doing* can be characterized as a craft (Mintzberg, 1996, p. 459). It is distinguished by a culture of learning and experimentation (Mintzberg & Westley, 2001, p. 91). In a new, complex, and ambiguous situation, the principle of *trial and error* is applied until appropriate behaviors can be selected. This approach is also referred to as enlightened experimentation (Schindehutte et al., 2009, p. 207f.).

These three courses of action are also found in the two main logics of the entrepreneurial process: causation logic and effectuation logic (Nielsen & Stovang, 2015). Causation logic *(thinking)* is based on prediction, control, planning, and rational analysis to achieve predefined outcomes (Sarasvathy, 2001). In contrast, according to effectuation logic *(seeing & doing)*, the entrepreneur uses the available means to shape opportunities (Sarasvathy, 2001). Effectuation is connected to the idea of bricolage (Baker & Nelson, 2005; Baker et al., 2003) and is based on many features found in design research (Nielsen & Stovang, 2015). It is closely related to the work of Herbert Simon (1969). In their recent study on Entrepreneurship Education, Garbuio et al. (2018) emphasize the importance of design cognition, including the cognitive acts of *framing*, analogical reasoning, abductive reasoning, and mental simulation. They find that teaching ways of thinking is far more effective than teaching processes and showing tools that are often not easily transferable to other areas.

3 Integration of Design Thinking into Entrepreneurship Education

The longstanding debate over whether opportunities are more likely to be discovered or created (Alvarez & Barney, 2007) has been resolved in practice in that aspiring entrepreneurs show a clear preference for opportunity creation (Garbuio et al., 2018). This has implications for Entrepreneurship Education. The conventional tools of strategy, such as SWOT analysis, are primarily taught in causation logic regarding opportunity discovery (Porter, 1980). However, opportunity creation requires fundamentally different skills, such as a willingness to experiment and the ability to learn from those experiments (Alvarez & Barney, 2007). This learning needs creativity, mental flexibility, the ability to be open to conflicting feedback, and a willingness to fail and learn from experience.

Opportunities are seized when appropriate cognitive skills are present (Baron & Shane, 2007; McGrath & MacMillan, 2000), and these can be trained and developed (DeTienne & Chandler, 2004; Muñoz et al., 2011). Design provides a well-researched and teachable set of cognitive skills, such as convergent and divergent thinking, framing, analogical reasoning, pattern recognition, counterfactual thinking, mental simulation, and abductive reasoning (Baron, 2004; Cornelissen & Clarke, 2010; Gaglio, 2004; Grégoire et al., 2015; Mitchell et al., 2002). Yet many educators do not know how these processes help create opportunities or how to effectively introduce students to these actions.

Design Thinking teaches how to deal with uncertain situations and uncover unexpected problems early on (Fixson & Rao, 2014; Fixson & Read, 2012). Accordingly, there are increasing calls from entrepreneurship scholars and practitioners for Design Thinking concepts and design methods to be used in Entrepreneurship Education (see, e.g., Glen et al., 2014; Van Burg & Romme, 2014; Nielsen & Stovang, 2015). Sarooghi et al., (2019) call for successful entrepreneurship programs to develop a common understanding of Design Thinking and a consistent set of tools/methods for implementing Design Thinking concepts in developing a successful entrepreneurship curriculum. Teaching mindset rather than processes has emerged as an important pedagogical perspective (Eastman, 1999; Oxman, 2004), where cognitive actions rather than the process of design constitute the teaching content.

The lean startup and business model canvas approaches refer to important elements of Design Thinking in their basic assumptions. However, they are primarily concerned with the application of the tools rather than teaching the underlying cognitive skills. Due to the increasing speed and dynamics of the business environment in which entrepreneurs pitch their ideas, a detailed business plan is often not very effective or feasible. Following the philosophy of lean startup approaches (Blank, 2013; Ries, 2011), it is more promising to present ideas at a very early stage and then test and iterate them until a commercially viable concept emerges. These approaches and the Business Model Canvas approach (Osterwalder & Pigneur, 2010) are much more useful in hands-on training than the tools of strategy.

Despite some changes in recent years, the teaching in many entrepreneurship courses at universities and other institutes of higher learning still relies heavily on causation logic and focuses on finding the ONE AND ONLY business idea and writing the ONE AND ONLY business plan (Solomon, 2007). Courses are often more "about" entrepreneurship than "for" or "through" entrepreneurship (Pittaway & Edwards, 2012).[2] In addition to business planning, they focus primarily on methods of starting a business and predicting a successful business model (Daniel, 2016). Students are often required to develop a business idea very quickly at the beginning of the semester and then conduct planning and forecasting activities with the goal of demonstrating the commercial viability of the idea at the end of the semester (Daniel, 2016). Accordingly, grading is frequently based only on the outcome of the course, namely the business plan, rather than evaluating the process of learning entrepreneurial skills and thinking. This has a negative impact on students' aspirations to start a business and on their image of entrepreneurship (von Graevenitz et al., 2010). A learning journal, also called a reflective journal, for example, would be a much more effective way to record the learning process (Robinson et al., 2016). In order to learn entrepreneurial thinking and action, a student must learn by doing and reflecting on the entrepreneurial process (Kassean et al., 2015). Entrepreneurship Education should therefore focus primarily on students learning to navigate uncertain environments in uncertain times (Neck & Greene, 2011). Courses that focus on developing entrepreneurship skills and competencies are more likely to lead to business start-ups (Nabi et al., 2017).

---

[2] Most of the entrepreneurship education approaches prevalent today can be categorized as the "about" approach, which corresponds to a more traditional pedagogy that does not involve students in activities and projects, or does so only peripherally (Nielsen & Stovang, 2015; Pittaway & Edwards 2012).

4   The Design Thinking and Entrepreneurship Model (DTE Model)

We supplement the Design Thinking approach taught at the HPI School of Design Thinking with the cognition approach of Design Thinking (Johansson-Sköldberg et al., 2013) and merge the two approaches with an effectuation/opportunity approach to entrepreneurship. Students of the natural sciences/engineering (systems software engineering) and economics are our primary target group. We are thus following the thinking of Herbert Simon, who advocated this integration as early as 1967. While the pure natural scientist uses analytical techniques in the search for the unambiguous laws of phenomena, the practitioner is concerned with developing actions, processes, or physical objects that effectively serve a specific purpose. The scientist analyzes by breaking phenomena down into their component parts, whereas the practitioner synthesizes by assembling these parts into larger systems and ideas (Simon, 1969). The cognitive skills of analysis and synthesis are combined with engineering, natural sciences, economics, and design by merging these two approaches. Students learn to analyze problems carefully and go through a problem-solving process in a structured manner. This is done against the backdrop of a user-centered, empathic, and iterative Design Thinking mindset.

The DTE model starts by recognizing a problem or a need (see Fig. 2). Using the tools and mindset of the Design Thinking process such as empathy, point of view, and ideation, students analyze the problem and the users' needs to then map out initial

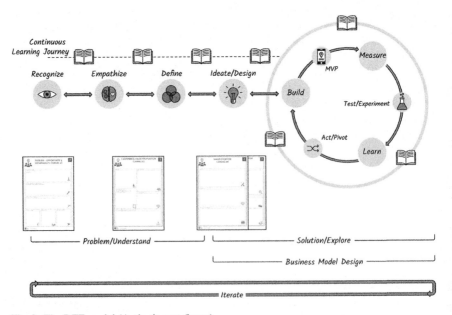

Fig. 2 The DTE model (Author's own figure)

ideas for solving the problem. This leads to the creation of an entrepreneurial opportunity corresponding to an artifact in the form of a problem-solution pair (Ardichvili et al., 2003). The result is also referred to as the mean-ends relationship (Shane & Venkataraman, 2000) or product-market fit (Grégoire & Shepherd, 2012). It signifies a first milestone towards the (preliminary) completion of the problem-solving process. Students present their artifacts and receive feedback on the quality and potential of the analyzed user needs as well as on their ideas and artifacts.

In the next step, an artifact is implemented by designing a mechanism of commercialization. To this end, we use the business model concept, which is inherent to the entrepreneurial process in the shape of the evolving artifact. We consider the business model to be the third constitutive component of an opportunity alongside the problem and solution. The choice of components is consistent with the concepts of problem-solution fit and business model fit in the philosophy of the lean startup (Blank & Dorf, 2020; Osterwalder & Pigneur, 2010). In the second part, we apply the concept of lean methodology, focusing on experimentation and on creating a *minimum viable product* (MVP), i.e., a product with minimal features for the customer. Based on customer feedback, the product can be quickly adapted (*"pivoted"*) or modified. Thus, the lean approach encourages speed and iteration but simultaneously focuses more on a prototype that works and is commercially viable (see Fig. 2). This distinguishes the approach from Design Thinking, which is more focused on problem definition and idea generation. The lean startup approach further involves formulating hypotheses about the product and testing the product and its features by users in the market. The lean startup method is widely used, including in incubators, accelerators, and government initiatives such as the U.S. National Science Foundation and its Innovation Corps program (Garbuio et al., 2018).

The DTE model includes continuous reflection along the process in addition to the combination of Entrepreneurship Education with Design Thinking. We have chosen a way to focus on opportunity creation and practice entrepreneurial thinking in the spirit of education with a "through" approach. Learning/reflective journals are an essential tool when learning through entrepreneurship (Robinson et al., 2016). These reflections help students link practical knowledge with their understanding of the theoretical perspectives of entrepreneurship. When students look back at the end of the process, they often find that their understanding of the challenge has changed and that the most obvious solution is not always the best one.

5 Discussion

Using the DTE model, students learn to proactively identify problems, create opportunities, and develop solutions to a problem or a challenge. They create artifacts, present their solutions, learn to work iteratively, and experiment. Our model with a combination of Design Thinking and entrepreneurship follows the results of recent investigations that underline the usefulness of Design Thinking in fostering entrepreneurial skills (Johann et al., 2020). Iteration is an important aspect of our approach (Neck &

Greene, 2011). Ideas are developed more broadly and comprehensively compared to entrepreneurship courses that do not follow the DTE model. The pieces of the ideas fit together better and do not need to be forced to fit together at the end. Students are more confident and more likely to iterate and show what they have learned, rather than develop ideas of a more "make-believe" character. The use of Design Thinking for Entrepreneurship Education also shifts the center of attention away from the instructor and more towards student-centered learning (Daniel, 2016; Robinson et al., 2016). The workshop formats and reflective journals help students engage with their own learning in a way that is very different from the traditional learning style at universities.

Based on theory-driven considerations of why and how Design Thinking and entrepreneurship fit together, we build on the findings of Garbuio et al., (2018), Sarooghi et al., (2019), and Johann et al., (2020) and design a concrete example of such a combination with the DTE model. We thus contribute to conceptually linking previous research calling for a methodological approach (Neck & Greene, 2011) and Entrepreneurship Education with an end-to-end and reflective perspective (Pittaway & Edwards, 2012). The DTE model has been used several times in bachelor's, master's, and executive courses in recent years, tried out in semester, workshop, and virtual formats, and adapted several times based on participant feedback. We have created a reflective, iterative, and active model to train people who are creative, responsible, and visionary in identifying problems, finding solutions, and implementing them. In other words, they think and act entrepreneurially.

The author would like to thank Dr. Katja Puteanus-Birkenbach and Dr. Claudia Nicolai for jointly developing, testing, and implementing the Potsdam Entrepreneurship Experience Lab (PEEL). Many considerations and aspects of the DTE model presented in this paper have been tested and implemented in this format.

References

Alvarez, S. A., & Barney, J. B. (2007). Discovery and creation: Alternative theories of entrepreneurial action. *Strategic Entrepreneurship Journal, 1*(1–2), 11–26.

Ardichvili, A., Cardozo, R., & Ray, S. (2003). A theory of entrepreneurial opportunity identification and development. *Journal of Business Venturing, 18*(1), 105–123.

Baker, T., Miner, A. S., & Eesley, D. T. (2003). Improvising firms: Bricolage, account giving and improvisational competencies in the founding process. *Research Policy, 32*(2), 255–276.

Baker, T., & Nelson, R. E. (2005). Creating something from nothing: Resource construction through entrepreneurial bricolage. *Administrative Science Quarterly, 50*(3), 329–366.

Baron, R. A., & Shane, S. A. (2007). *Entrepreneurship: A process perspective.* Cengage Learning.

Baron, R. A. (2004). The cognitive perspective: A valuable tool for answering entrepreneurship's basic "why" questions. *Journal of Business Venturing, 19*(2), 221–239.

Blank, S., & Dorf, B. (2020). *The startup owne's manual: The step-by-step guide for building a great company.* Wiley.

Blank, S. (2013). Why the lean start-up changes everything. *Harvard Business Review, 91*(5), 63–72.

Brülhart, A. (2013). *Opportunity recognition and entrepreneurship education* (Vol. 72). BoD–Books on Demand.

Carlgren, L., Rauth, I., & Elmquist, M. (2016). Framing design thinking: The concept in idea and enactment. *Creativity and Innovation Management, 25*(1), 38–57.

Cornelissen, J. P., & Clarke, J. S. (2010). Imagining and rationalizing opportunities: Inductive reasoning and the creation and justification of new ventures. *Academy of Management Review, 35*(4), 539–557.

Daniel, A. D. (2016). Fostering an entrepreneurial mindset by using a design thinking approach in entrepreneurship education. *Industry and Higher Education, 30*(3), 215–223.

DeTienne, D. R., & Chandler, G. N. (2004). Opportunity identification and its role in the entrepreneurial classroom: A pedagogical approach and empirical test. *Academy of Management Learning and Education, 3*(3), 242–257.

Eastman, C. M. (1999). Special issue on design education. *Design Studies, 20*(2), 99–103.

Fiet, J. O. (2000). The theoretical side of teaching entrepreneurship. *Journal of Business Venturing, 16*, 1–24.

Fixson, S. K., & Rao, J. (2014). Learning emergent strategies through design thinking. *Design Management Review, 25*(1), 46–53.

Fixson, S. K., & Read, J. M. (2012). Creating innovation leaders: Why we need to blend business and design education. *Design Management Review, 23*(4), 4–12.

Fueglistaller, U., Müller, C., Mueller, S., & Volery, T. (2012). *Entrepreneurship modelle—Umsetzung—Perspektiven.* Gabler Verlag.

Gaglio, C. M. (2004). The role of mental simulations and counterfactual thinking in the opportunity identification process. *Entrepreneurship Theory and Practice, 28*(6), 533–552.

Garbuio, M., Dong, A., Lin, N., Tschang, T., & Lovallo, D. (2018). Demystifying the genius of entrepreneurship: How design dognition can help create the next generation of entrepreneurs. *Academy of Management Learning and Education, 17*, 41–61.

Glen, R., Suciu, C., & Baughn, C. (2014). The need for design thinking in business schools. *Academy of Management Learning and Education, 13*(4), 653–667.

Grégoire, D. A., Cornelissen, J., Dimov, D., & Burg, E. (2015). The mind in the middle: Taking stock of affect and cognition research in entrepreneurship. *International Journal of Management Reviews, 17*(2), 125–142.

Grégoire, D. A., & Shepherd, D. A. (2012). Technology-market combinations and the identification of entrepreneurial opportunities: An investigation of the opportunity-individual nexus. *Academy of Management Journal, 55*(4), 753–785.

Grichnik, D., Brettel, M., Koropp, C., & Mauer, R. (2010). *Entrepreneurship: Unternehmerisches Denken, Entscheiden und Handeln in innovativen und technologieorientierten Unternehmungen.* Schäffer-Poeschel.

Hillgren, P. A., Seravalli, A., & Emilson, A. (2011). Prototyping and infrastructuring in design for social innovation. *CoDesign, 7*(3–4), 169–183.

Johann, D. A., Nunes, A. D. F. P., dos Santos, G. B., da Silva, D. J. C., Bresciani, S. A. T., & Lopes, L. F. D. (2020). Mapping of scientific production on design thinking as a tool for entrepreneurship education: A bibliometric study of a decade. *World Journal of Entrepreneurship, Management and Sustainable Development. Preprint online.*

Johansson-Sköldberg, U., Woodilla, J., & Çetinkaya, M. (2013). Design thinking: Past, present and possible futures. *Creativity and Innovation Management, 22*(2), 121–146.

Kassean, H., Vanevenhoven, J., Liguori, E., & Winkel, D. E. (2015). Entrepreneurship education: A need for reflection, real-world experience and action. *International Journal of Entrepreneurial Behavior and Research, 21*(5), 690–708.

Lockwood, T. (2010). *Design thinking: Integrating innovation, customer experience and brand value.* Allworth Press.

McGrath, R. G., & MacMillan, I. C. (2000). *The entrepreneurial mindset: Strategies for continuously creating opportunity in an age of uncertainty.* Harvard Business Press.

Mintzberg, H. (1996). Strategy as a craft. In C. Montgomery & K. Omae (Eds.), *Strategy. Die brillanten Beiträge der weltbesten Strategie-Experten* (pp. 459–476). Ueberreuter.

Mintzberg, H., & Westley, F. (2001). Decision making: It's not what you think. *Sloan Management Review,* 89–93

Mitchell, R. K., Busenitz, L., Lant, T., McDougall, P. P., Morse, E. A., & Smith, J. B. (2002). Toward a theory of entrepreneurial cognition: Rethinking the people side of entrepreneurship research. *Entrepreneurship Theory and Practice, 27*(2), 93–104.

Muñoz C, C. A., Mosey, S., & Binks, M. (2011). Developing opportunity-identification capabilities in the classroom: Visual evidence for changing mental frames. *Academy of Management Learning & Education 10*(2), 277–295.

Nabi, G., Liñán, F., Fayolle, A., Krueger, N., & Walmsley, A. (2017). The impact of entrepreneurship education in higher education: A systematic review and research agenda. *Academy of Management Learning and Education, 16*(2), 277–299.

Neck, H. M., & Greene, P. G. (2011). Entrepreneurship education: Known worlds and new frontiers. *Journal of Small Business Management, 49*(1), 55–70.

Nielsen, S. L., & Stovang, P. (2015). DesUni: University entrepreneurship education through design thinking. *Education + Training, 57*(8/9), 977–991.

Osterwalder, A., & Pigneur, Y. (2010). *Business model generation: A handbook for visionaries, game changers, and challengers.* OSF.

Oxman, R. (2004). Think-maps: Teaching design thinking in design education. *Design Studies, 25,* 63–91.

Pittaway, L., & Edwards, C. (2012). Assessment: Examining practice in entrepreneurship education. *Education + Training, 54*(8/9), 778–800.

Porter, M. E. (1980). *Competitive strategy.* The Free Press.

Ries, E. (2011). *The lean startup: How today's entrepreneurs use continuous innovation to create radically successful businesses.* Random House LLC.

Rittel, H. W. J., & Webber, M. M. (1973). Dilemmas in a general theory of planning. *Policy Sciences, 4*(2), 155–169.

Robinson, S., Neergaard, H., Tanggaard, L., & Krueger, N. F. (2016). New horizons in entrepreneurship education: From teacher-led to student-centered learning. *Education + Training, 58*(7/8), 661–683.

Sarasvathy, S. (2001). Causation and effectuation: Toward a theoretical shift from economic inevitability to entrepreneurial contingency. *The Academy of Management Review, 26*(2), 243–263.

Sarooghi, H., Sunny, S., Hornsby, J., & Fernhaber, S. (2019). Design thinking and entrepreneurship education: Where are we, and what are the possibilities? *Journal of Small Business Management, 57,* 78–93.

Schindehutte, M., Morris, M., & Pitt, L. (2009). *Rethinking marketing: The entrepreneurial imperative.* Pearson Prentice Hall.

Seidel, V. P., & Fixson, S. K. (2013). Adopting design thinking in novice multidisciplinary teams: The application and limits of design methods and reflexive practices. *Journal of Product Innovation Management, 30*(1), 19–33.

Shane, S., & Venkataraman, S. (2000). The promise of entrepreneurship as a field of research. *Academy of Management Review, 25*(1), 217–226.

Simon, H. (1969). *The science of the artificial.* MIT Press.

Solomon, G. (2007). An examination of entrepreneurship education in the United States. *Journal of Small Business and Enterprise Development, 14*(2), 168–182.

Van Burg, E., & Romme, A. G. L. (2014). Creating the future together: Toward a framework for research synthesis in entrepreneurship. *Entrepreneurship Theory and Practice, 38*(2), 369–397.

von Graevenitz, G., Harhoff, D., & Weber, R. (2010). The effects of entrepreneurship education. *Journal of Economic Behavior and Organization, 76*(1), 90–112.

Prof. Dr. Katharina Hölzle Experience with DT: Katharina Hölzle has been researching and teaching Design Thinking for over ten years. Her research focuses on the introduction of Design Thinking at companies and organizations and the resulting change, as well as the combination of Design Thinking and entrepreneurship. Since 2009, she has been a coach at the HPI School of Design Thinking, bringing together Design Thinking and entrepreneurship in teaching at the university and in executive education.

What does Katharina Hölzle view as the biggest challenge to applying DT in education and the easiest step in doing it? Only when viewing Design Thinking as a mindset that can be learned and then applied, can the true potential of Design Thinking be leveraged. Merging Design Thinking with other methods and tools from the fields of entrepreneurship, innovation, and management can aid this goal. Many aspects of Design Thinking are familiar to learners, but combining them in a consistent curriculum that addresses the needs of learners can bring about a flash of insight into how it all fits together (Design Thinkers often refer to this as the "aha" effect). Empathy and observation are two of the most important skills of Design Thinking, as putting people and their needs at the center of attention is the key to successful innovation and change.

Massive Open Online Design: Learning from Scaling Design Thinking Education

Karen Schmieden, Lena Mayer, Hanadi Traifeh, and Christoph Meinel

Abstract This chapter focuses on the opportunities and limitations of teaching design thinking in Massive Open Online Courses (MOOCs). MOOCs, often free and easily accessible, are becoming increasingly popular in academic and organizational contexts. Creating a MOOC comes with a range of design issues, though, and conveying design thinking skills via an online course causes a number of additional challenges. We describe these challenges and our strategies to solve them by explaining how we designed three online courses on design thinking skills for several thousand participants. We also examine learning interventions in the different course designs.

1 Introduction

Massive Open Online Courses (MOOCs) are becoming increasingly popular. The courses, often free and easily accessible, have gained widespread interest beyond academic structures. With the aim of conveying creative skills to learners all over the globe, several renowned universities and institutions have conceptualized MOOCs on design thinking (Taheri, 2016a).

Our research focuses on the opportunities and limitations of teaching design thinking in MOOCs. MOOC creators face a range of design issues, and there are a number of additional challenges in conveying design thinking skills via an online

K. Schmieden (✉) · L. Mayer · H. Traifeh · C. Meinel
HPI School of Design Thinking, Hasso Plattner Institute for Digital Engineering, Campus Griebnitzsee, Prof.-Dr.-Helmert-Str. 2-3, 14482 Potsdam, Germany
e-mail: Karen.Schmieden@hpi.de

L. Mayer
e-mail: Lena.Mayer@hpi.de

H. Traifeh
e-mail: hanadi.traifeh@hpi.de

C. Meinel
e-mail: meinel@hpi.de

course. In this chapter, we describe these challenges and our own learning design attempts to solve them. We explain how we designed three online courses on design thinking skills for several thousand participants. Further, we examine the learning interventions and items we added for each new course design.

2   Challenges of Design Thinking MOOC Design

2.1   MOOC Design Challenges

MOOC instructors perceive a range of difficulties for conceptualizing courses. Zhu et al. identified ten design challenges from interview data with 12 MOOC instructors, including "unknown audience, limited assessment methods, engaging learners, time limitation of designing MOOCs, a lack of instructor and learner interaction, building community, recording short videos, time zone differences, conservative opinions from colleagues, and copyright issues." They described the key challenges as "assessment, engaging learners, time limitations in designing MOOCs, and getting to know the audience" (2018, p. 219).

Throughout our MOOC conceptualization, we additionally perceived the challenge of audiences being large, international, and heterogeneous; the difficulty of offering qualitative feedback to learners in assessments; and the complexity of encouraging learners to transfer their newly acquired knowledge and skills to their professional and private contexts.

2.2   Challenges for Design Thinking MOOCs

We have described how teaching and learning in an online course come with a range of issues. Teaching and learning *design thinking* in an online course adds another set of challenges to the pile. Traditionally, design disciplines are associated with a physical studio setting, where learners are exposed to the work and thinking processes of their peers (Brown, 2005; Lynas et al., 2013). Similarly, design thinking is usually taught in studio-based learning environments that encourage hands-on teamwork in an open environment (Plattner et al., 2011).

In our role as course designers, we perceived a range of challenges. Firstly, documenting physical design actions and design objects that learners produced as independent homework tasks in the digital space. Secondly, the challenge of enabling learners to give valuable feedback on the design thinking work of others. Finally, the process of breaking down design thinking teamwork processes into separate skills that can be learned individually. We, therefore, focused on the Taheri et al.

model for design thinking learning outcomes (2016a), which differentiates skill-based outcomes, cognitive outcomes, and effective outcomes. Focusing on skill-based outcomes, we defined learning outcomes that allow learners to explore skills on an individual level and to consequently apply them independently in later (group) projects.

The first distance learning designers have taken on these challenges since the seventies. The Open University in the UK offered its first remote design course in 1975. Lloyd (2013) named several developments that had a major impact in enabling design education over distance. Two of these developments are "creative social networks" and "technological development in design education". Creative social networks established the digital custom of exposing design work to and receiving feedback from a broader audience. Technological development in design education has shifted even traditional university courses from a purely studio-based learning model toward a hybrid environment in which students also work and communicate online.

There are also several advantages to teaching design thinking in Massive Open Online Courses. First, it allows for a diverse pool of learners. This heterogeneous group offers more perspectives and experiences than many homogeneous groups in localized university or business settings. Second, design knowledge transfer in design schools is often a mix of one-to-one and many-to-many transfer, whereas the focus in an online environment is many-to-many knowledge transmission (Lloyd, 2013). Thirdly, MOOCs allow for scaled dissemination of design thinking educa-tion. With an ever-growing need—and demand—for design thinking skills in diverse professional settings, online courses manage to enable learners in busy professional contexts, remote areas, or disadvantaged societal positions to acquire design thinking skills (Taheri et al., 2016b).

3 Major Learnings from ProtoMOOC to MOOC #1

3.1 Introducing an Iteration Approach

To start our MOOC design process, we conceptualized a MOOC prototype (proto-MOOC) in a closed setting. Around 100 learners participated in the hidden course. We consequently iterated the course and ran it publicly, with over 4000 enrolled learners at course start. Our goal was to learn from the protoMOOC group, which contained a considerable number of learners but was still small in comparison to a public international MOOC sample. We aimed to understand how to scale learning, design exercises and assignments in such a way that they resonate with a broad audience. To do so, we conducted a threefold iteration approach: (1) gathering data through learning satisfaction and self-efficacy surveys as well as qualitative inter-views, (2) sorting data in feedback grids to extract a list of topics, and (3) transforming structured feedback into actionable iteration tasks (von Schmieden et al., 2019).

In total, we defined 82 tasks and chose 57 of these actions for implementation in the first course iteration.

3.2 MOOC #1: "Inspirations for Design: A Course on Human-Centered Research"

The first public MOOC from the series is "Inspirations for Design: A Course on Human-Centered Research." The course focused on skills related to design thinking research, including careful observation and qualitative interviewing. It ran from August to September 2017 on the openHPI.de platform. The enrollment number totaled 5491, of which 3040 (58%) were active learners who visited the course at least once. Much of learner-learner and learner-instructor interaction took place in the discussion forum: 1145 learners used the forum. We observed lively discussions in the forum: Course participants started 191 discussion threads and wrote 1912 posts.

Learners from 87 countries enrolled in the course. The majority of learners were from Germany (64%), followed by the United States (4.6%), India (3.54%), and Switzerland (2.76%).

3.3 Learning Interventions and New Items: MOOC #1

- **Course structure and timeline**: As the biggest change between protoMOOC and MOOC #1, we stretched the module on qualitative interviewing over two weeks. We focused one week on preparing for qualitative interviewing and conducting an interview, and the second week on inferring meaning (=interpreting interview notes). We witnessed some confusion about deadlines and course requirements and thus introduced a course timeline illustration on the MOOC landing page. This visual aid contained all relevant content releases and assignment deadline dates. With most MOOCs created in the global West, a regular flaw is setting assignment deadlines on weekend days (e.g., Sunday). This conflicts with the weekly rhythm of other cultures, (e.g., with Middle Eastern countries) where Friday is the day of rest. Based on protoMOOC participants' feedback we changed the release and deadline days to Thursdays, allowing for a full weekend before a deadline.
- **Additional reading material**: We created a list of additional reading materials and resources for learners who wanted to explore specific topics in greater depth. We opened this list up for participation and asked learners to add their own resources. In this way, we hoped to encourage learner engagement and to provide a further path of learning.
- **Subtitles**: Non-native learners commented on difficulties encountered in following the videos. We consequently added subtitles to all videos. Additionally,

we offered the possibility to download the video scripts. This can be a helpful way for learners with bandwidth limitations to have full access to MOOC video content.

- **Template Redesign**: In the assignment, learners had to upload a picture of a "design workaround". ProtoMOOC feedback showed that interpretations of this workaround were sometimes quite localized, and that additional space to reason and discuss the workaround context was missing. We iterated all templates with the aim of creating more understanding among learners in the peer-reviewed assignment process.
- **Wrap-Up video**: Learners respond positively to instructor engagement. While we pre-recorded protoMOOC content and created interaction or reaction to learner activities solely in the discussion forum, we decided to increase interaction for MOIC #1. We shot a wrap-up video for the last MOOC week displaying and praising several learner assignments. We chose assignment submissions from a range of countries to exemplify the diversity in our course.
- **Summary**: To offer learners a *tangible* takeaway, we created a two-pager with a course summary including all topics and terminology.

4   Interventions for MOOC #2

4.1   MOOC #2: "Human-Centered Design: From Synthesis to Creative Ideas"

"Human-Centered Design: From Synthesis to Creative Ideas" ran from September to October 2018. In total, 3641 learners enrolled during the course, of which 1945 (53%) were active learners who visited the course at least once. 1202 learners used the discussion forum and 526 learners posted in the forum.

According to platform data, most enrolled learners participated from Germany (24.01%), followed by the United States (1.48%) and Switzerland (1.02%). Overall, learners from 69 countries took part in the MOOC. With 53% of survey participants identifying as "male", slightly less female participants attended the course. 77.57% of pre course survey participants ranked their prior experience with design thinking as "none" or "beginner" (163 and 570 respectively out of $n = 945$). 72% of survey participants had previous experiences with MOOCs, and 24% had even participated in more than five MOOCs. Only 262 out of $n = 946$ were first time MOOC participants.

4.2   Learning Interventions and New Items: MOOC #2

For the second MOOC, we aimed to create a more flexible structure for learners to engage with the content and work through modules at their own pace. To achieve

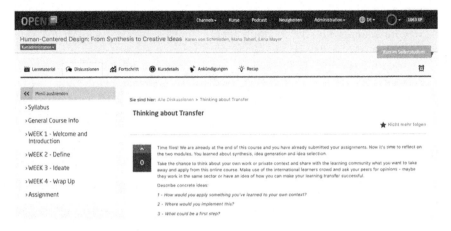

Fig. 1 "Thinking about Transfer" Post (author's own figure)

this, we opened all modules at the same time—in contrast to the common structure of modules opening sequentially each week. Instead of two assignments, we
consolidated both skill assessments in one assignment at the end of the course. We
found that learners preferred this learner mode more. We added some further learning
interventions in the course:

- **Podcasts**: Our podcasts allowed advanced learners to explore the theoretical
  contexts of skills in more depth and provided an audio format as a new medium.
- **Thinking about Transfer Posts**: We created transfer posts in the discussion forum
  after each learning module (see Fig. 1). These encouraged learners to share their
  plans to bring their new skills back to their professional context. The research goal
  was to find out "to what degree are learners thinking about skill transfer during
  online learning" (Mayer et al., 2018).
- **Question Flowchart**: In MOOC #1, many helpdesk mails and technical problem
  inquiries in the forum were identical. We created a question flowchart for MOOC
  #2 to channel learners' questions into the right area in the MOOC (see Fig. 2).
  Mails to the helpdesk accounts decreased and forum threads became more
  clustered.
- **Course Ethics Video**: We produced a short video called "Learning goals and
  course ethics" in MOOC#2. Our aim was to create a safe environment to foster
  mutual respect among learners (Ginsberg, 2005). The ethics video asked participants to be mindful of the diverse learner group in the course and encouraged
  a focus on written and valuable peer feedback in the assignment, rather than on
  grades. Learner behavior in the assignment process of MOOC#1 showed that
  participants benefited more from written feedback than from the allocated points
  for their submission. Hence, we wanted to nurture constructive feedback, also in
  the light of different cultures dealing with feedback in various ways (Bailey et al.,
  1997). Western cultures emphasize the importance of providing direct. feedback

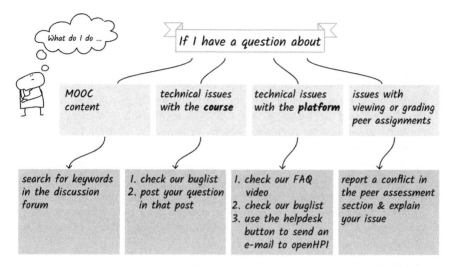

Fig. 2 Question flowchart (author's own figure)

in teaching, in other cultures this might be perceived as impolite (Taheri et al., 2019).

5 Interventions for MOOC#3

5.1 MOOC #3: "Human-Centered Design: From Synthesis to Creative Ideas"

The last MOOC from the series is "Human-centered Design: Building and Testing Prototypes". This course focused on different prototyping techniques, user tests, and working with user feedback. The MOOC ran from August to October 2019. There were 3,356 learners enrolled at the midpoint of the course, 1583 (47%) of them were active learners who showed up at least once in the course. The number of learners to use the discussion forum was 1188 while 379 learners posted in the forum. This course also attracted international learners, with the majority coming from Germany, followed by the USA and India.

Finally, the overall satisfaction with the course seemed high according to the survey results from 284 learners who ranked their satisfaction. Of these, 255 rated 7 or higher.

5.2 *Learning Interventions and New Items: MOOC #2*

For the third MOOC, we introduced:

- **Assignment How To video**: After they receive the written instructions for their assignments, learners are usually left on their own to pursue the assignment task. We realized that many learners still had difficulty following the instructions correctly and reporting back their results in templates sufficiently. To support learners, we produced an "Assignment How To" video in which we described the different steps of the assignment once more and demonstrated how to fill in the template in a way that allowed for feedback.
- **Personalized Learning Objectives** (PLOs). For the third course, we used the PLO function established by Rohloff et al. (2020). PLOs allow learners to set their own goals for an online course upfront, with visual cues pointing them to the course items that are relevant for them.

During previous MOOCs, we perceived that a number of participants only explored specific modules of the course or searched for educational material to download. Based on these observations of user behavior, we offered six learning objective paths:

1. *Complete Course Experience.* This objective comprised all course material including the graded exercises and the peer assessment. Taking this path allowed learners to gain a Record of Achievement.
2. *Explore.* This objective comprised all introductory material about design thinking, prototyping, and testing. Following this objective was sufficient if the goal was to receive a Confirmation of Participation.
3. *Deep Dive Prototyping.* This objective focused on content about prototyping only.
4. *Deep Dive Testing.* This objective focused on content about testing only.
5. *Material Collector.* This objective highlighted the material items for users who were mainly interested in collecting resources and templates.
6. *Inspirational Trip.* This objective offered an option to look at different aspects of the course, specifically more inspiring content such as podcasts.

As results by Rohloff et al. (2020) showed, most learners who opted to set learning objective paths for themselves chose the "Complete Course Experience" (71.88%). This reflects that most learners are eager to receive a certificate for participating in a course. Nonetheless, we see a distinct number of learners choosing an "Explore" path (14.73%) and an "Inspirational Trip" (4.91%) (see Table 1). As course instructors, PLOs offered us insights into our learners' motivations and the considerable numbers of participants who are curious to explore a course first before committing themselves to a full course experience.

Table 1 Personalized learning objectives

Objective	Selected	Quota (%)	Objective achieved (%)
Complete course experience	322	71.88	28.75
Explore	66	14.73	46.97
Deep dive prototyping	31	6.92	19.35
Deep dive testing	4	0.89	0.00
Material collector	3	0.67	0.00
Inspirational trip	22	4.91	18.18

Adapted from Rohloff et al. (2020)

6 Summary

In this chapter, we described why we set out to develop MOOCs on design thinking: online courses allow us to convey design thinking skills to audiences in contexts beyond traditional university or business education. They also allow us to reach a more heterogeneous group, which can greatly benefit the discussion on design thinking.

Challenges for teaching and learning with MOOCs are manifold and focus on learner engagement, offering qualitative feedback and skill transfer.

Challenges for creating design thinking MOOCs focus on documenting and presenting physical design work in digital spaces and enabling learners to give helpful feedback to each other.

The changes and improvements we did over the course of the three design thinking MOOCs tackle a number of these challenges. They include interventions to amplify learner engagement (through participatory forum items and reaction videos shot during the course), encouraging planned skill transfer (Transfer Forum Posts), and documenting design work through iteratively designed templates and rubrics.

To conclude, we have seen that basic design thinking skills can be conveyed through Massive Open Online Courses. It is also evident that many learners can benefit from this scaled approach of dissemination. We need to encourage learners to apply—and practice—these skills in their real life contexts, to further advance their design thinking skill development as the move towards a design thinking mindset.

References

Bailey, J. R., Chen, C. C., & Dou, S. G. (1997). Conceptions of self and performance-related feedback in the US, Japan and China. *Journal of International Business Studies, 28*(3), 605–625.

Brown, H. R. (2005). *Physical relativity: Space-time structure from a dynamical perspective.* Oxford University Press on Demand.

Ginsberg, M. B. (2005). Cultural diversity, motivation, and differentiation. *Theory into Practice, 44*(3), 218–225.

Lloyd, P. (2013). Embedded creativity: Teaching design thinking via distance education. *International Journal of Technology and Design Education, 23*(3), 749–765.

Lynas, E., Budge, K., & Beale, C. (2013). Hands on: The importance of studio learning in design education. *Visual Inquiry, 2*(2), 127–138.

Mayer, L., Hölzle, K., & Meinel, C. (2018). Investigating training transfer of design thinking skills in online education. In *ISPIM Innovation Symposium* (pp. 1–4). The International Society for Professional Innovation Management (ISPIM), Boston, USA.

Plattner, H., Meinel, C., & Leifer, L. (2011). *Design thinking: Understand—Improve—Apply.* Springer.

Rohloff, T., Sauer, D., & Meinel, C. (2020). Students' achievement of personalized learning objectives in MOOCs. In *Proceedings of the Seventh ACM Conference on Learning @ Scale,* 147–156.

Taheri, M., Hölzle, K., & Meinel, C. (2019). Towards culturally inclusive MOOCs: A design-based approach. In *Proceedings from the 11th International Conference on Computer Supported Education* (CSEDU 2019).

Taheri, M., Unterholzer, T., & Meinel C. (2016a). Design thinking at scale: A report on best practices of online courses. In H. Plattner, C. Meinel, L. Leifer (Eds.), *Design thinking research. Understanding innovation.* Springer.

Taheri, M., Unterholzer, T., Hölzle, K., & Meinel, C. (2016b). An educational perspective on design thinking learning outcomes. In *ISPIM Innovation Symposium* (p. 1). The International Society for Professional Innovation Management (ISPIM).

von Schmieden, K., Mayer, L., Taheri, M., & Meinel, C. (2019). Iterative course design in MOOCs: Evaluating a protoMOOC. In *International Conference on Engineering Design*, Delft, Netherlands.

Zhu, M., Bonk, C. J., & Sari, A. R. (2018). Instructor experiences designing MOOCs in higher education: Pedagogical, resource, and logistical considerations and challenges. *Online Learning, 22*(4), 203–241.

Karen Schmieden is a researcher in the HPI-Stanford Design Thinking Research Program, where she designs, enhances, and delivers Massive Open Online Courses (MOOCs). Her research focuses on learner-centered course development and learner behavior in MOOCs. She also designs and oversees digital and analog Design Thinking learning experiences for students and companies. Spending enough time on the problem is a major challenge, both online and offline: How can we help learners have enough courage (and patience) to not think immediately in terms of solutions? Inspiration helps: That is why Karen von Schmieden curates "ThisIsDesignThinking.net," the largest online resource for Design Thinking case studies in organizations. In this work, she noted that learners find individual and unique ways to adapt Design Thinking for their own use—and then sometimes contribute their own case studies shortly afterward.

Lena Mayer is an organizational psychologist and works in the HPI-Stanford Design Thinking Research Program, investigating innovation behavior, e-learning, and training transfer in organizations. She is working on her doctorate, focusing on a case study at BASF. In addition, she leads workshops and seminars in industrial and academic contexts as an alumna of the HPI School of Design Thinking. Lena Mayer's biggest challenges in terms of Design Thinking Facilitation were to design Massive Open Online Courses with her research team at the HPI, to prepare her Design Thinking Navigator card set for use by organizations, and to explain important Design Thinking elements in just a few words. She believes the art of conveying Design Thinking lies in not necessarily using the label of Design Thinking, but in cleverly integrating elements and attitudes of the Design Thinking approach or culture into workshops or teamwork, thus giving the participants something to take away with them.

Hanadi Traifeh Over the past 20 years, Hanadi Traifeh held positions in different design and consulting firms in the UK and Canada, and worked as an advisor for several organizations in Europe, the Middle East, and North America. She led and contributed to the design and implementation of several educational and capacity building programs around the world for organizations that include the University of Cambridge, BBC World Trust, the International Development Research Centre of Canada, and the World Affairs Council of North California. Since introduced to design thinking about a decade ago, design thinking became the passion that guides all her endeavors. In addition to developing practical skills in the field, Hanadi Traifeh decided to contribute to the development of the theory behind design thinking and joined the Hasso Plattner-Stanford Design Thinking Research Program in 2017. A significant challenge in higher education is getting educators to adopt a human-centered approach in which they can develop empathy for their students to better understand their needs and design new innovative learning experiences. As a first step, educators may view students as co-creators of the learning experience by observing their behavior and feelings, ask them purposeful questions about their current experience, and listen to their ideas on how to make it better. Once a collaborative relationship is built between students and educators, transforming the whole educational system may become a little bit easier.

Prof. Dr. Christoph Meinel (Univ. Prof., Dr. sc. nat., Dr. rer. nat.) was born in 1954 and was founding Dean of the Digital Engineering Faculty at the University of Potsdam in April 2017. Currently he serves as Vice Dean. He holds the Chair of Internet Technologies and Systems and is also active in the fields of cybersecurity and digital education, teaching in the bachelor's and master's programs in IT-Systems Engineering and at the School of Design Thinking. Christoph Meinel developed the MOOC platform, openHPI.de, and also provides content on the site. His responsibilities include supervising numerous doctoral students, and he has authored or co-authored more than 25 books, anthologies, and various conference proceedings. He has published more than 550 peer-reviewed articles in scientific journals and at international conferences and holds a number of international patents. He is a member of the National Academy of Science and Technology (acatech), director of the HPI-Stanford Design Thinking Research Program, honorary professor at the Technical University of Beijing, visiting professor at Shanghai University, professor at Nanjing University, and member of numerous scientific committees and supervisory boards.

Design Thinking, Neurodesign and Facilitating Worthwhile Change: Towards a Curriculum for Innovation Engineering

Julia V. Thienen, Caroline Szymanski, Theresa Weinstein, Shama Rahman, and Christoph Meinel

Abstract Innovation is in great demand today, just like curricula for innovation training. At the Hasso Plattner Institute for Digital Engineering (HPI), design thinking has been used successfully over many years to train students and help them become capable innovators. Notably, this curriculum does not stand still but undergoes its own innovation processes. Innovation is change and good innovation education is itself open to planned as well as serendipitous developments. Neurodesign courses have been created at the HPI as an amendment to the design thinking curriculum. The approach encourages creative engineering in a promising field of innovation: at the intersection of digital engineering, neuroscience and design thinking. While such serendipitous discoveries of fruitful work areas are important for the development of innovation curricula, equally important is a good overview of competence domains that students need to practice to mature as innovators. In this chapter, we discuss a number of innovation competencies, which are now taught in complementary courses at the HPI. The classes distinguish themselves for instance by the role that subject-specific knowledge plays in the teaching, as from the area of digital engineering. In addition, inspiration for creative work is drawn from varying sources, such as empathy with user needs in some classes, while other classes focus more on the innovator's own visions and passions. Overall, a collaborative spirit has proven itself invaluable for a positive teaching and learning experience. This collaboration is evident in both the individual courses, as well as in the fruitful development of the

J. V. Thienen (✉) · C. Szymanski · T. Weinstein · S. Rahman · C. Meinel
Hasso Plattner Institute for Digital Engineering, Campus Griebnitzsee, Prof.-Dr.-Helmert-Str. 2-3, 14482 Potsdam, Germany
e-mail: Julia.vonThienen@hpi.de

C. Szymanski
e-mail: Caroline.Szymanski@hpi.de

T. Weinstein
e-mail: Theresa.Weinstein@hpi.de

S. Rahman
e-mail: Shama.Rahman@hpi.de

C. Meinel
e-mail: meinel@hpi.de

innovation curriculum as a whole. Through a generous interplay, marked by curiosity and mutual support across various disciplines, institutions and social roles, the best conditions emerge for innovation and innovation education.

1   Introduction

Neurodesign is a new academic area at the Hasso Plattner Institute (HPI), which creates synergies at the intersection of three areas: (i) engineering, (ii) neuroscience and (iii) design thinking: creativity, collaboration and innovation. Neurodesign aims to expand and combine the basic knowledge and methods in these three areas, ultimately in order to promote innovation that is both urgently needed in the world and which sustainably improves people's quality of life. This work area of neurodesign has evolved from design thinking training at the Hasso Plattner Institute, in collaboration with Stanford University. The emergence of this new academic area is an example of how curricula for innovation education themselves demonstrate what the students are taught in class: openness to desirable, yet often initially unplanned change. In Sect. 2 of this chapter, we describe the history of neurodesign education as an example of the development of innovation curricula—highlighting principles that can be reused in the design of innovation curricula at other institutes and with other work foci. The basis is openness to desirable change. Subsequently, we provide an overview of innovation education at the HPI, covering the field of innovation engineering. Section 3 describes various existing courses and the areas of competence they convey. Section 4 discusses the creative processes of students in class. Here, we particularly address the question of how specialist knowledge shapes creative processes (Sect. 6.1). It is also discussed how empathy with user needs in comparison to personal passions and visions, each influence creative processes (Sect. 6.2). The chapter closes in Sect. 5 with an overview of our team-teaching approach in the field of neurodesign and the development of collaboration networks, which are particularly important for a favourable development of innovation potentials in individuals and the community as a whole.

2   Developing Curricula for Innovation Education by Facilitating Worthwhile Change

Innovation is change. Incremental innovation means progress that takes place step-by- step. This type of change can be planned and incrementally new solutions are usually foreseeable. Radical innovation differs from this. It often arises unexpectedly. Radically new perspectives and approaches to solutions are new to the world. Nobody has ever tried these approaches before, nobody knows what exactly will or will not work. Therefore, radical innovation can be courted and promoted. But the process of radical innovation is not a process of planning ahead and meeting milestone plans. It's a process of exploring and learning from what you discover and try, what works and what doesn't.

Innovation education teaches how to deal with change. The training creates a framework to enable change (cf. Leifer & Steinert, 2011) and at the same time helps to handle difficulties of the process. The more a curriculum aims to promote radical innovation, the more it has to be open to unexpected and unplanned future scenarios. At the same time, it needs to provide the resources and mindsets for people to discover initially unexpected opportunities, to explore and establish novel realities.

In the realm of design thinking, we don't want change for the sake of change. Innovation is not an end in itself. The key question is how to better satisfy basic needs of people, in ethically sound, healthy, socially and environmentally responsible ways. The design thinking curricula that we develop at the Hasso Plattner Institute (HPI) are all bound to this perspective of exploring areas of opportunity, where things can change for the better because there are chances of addressing basic needs in more comprehensive and balanced ways by means of novel solutions. Often, however, a markedly positive change succeeds primarily through radical innovations that go beyond incremental refinements of existing approaches. Accordingly, our curricula place great emphasis on conveying skills for ethically reflected, radical innovation. At the same time, plannable, incremental progress is also an indispensable part of human innovation and appropriate training needs to be part of any systematic innovation education. Consequently, our curricula support unexpected change, while also facilitating plannable progress—they train incremental and radical innovation capacities.

Today the new area "neurodesign" already offers a wide range of courses for students at the institute. A few years ago, however, it was not even foreseeable that such an area would come into existence. In the development of design thinking education, the concept of neurodesign is one such serendipitous advancement, which was initially unexpected and unplanned. Based on a highly change-facilitating, supportive and collaborative community spirit, this novel area of research and teaching was discovered, probed and realized at ever-increasing scales at a rapid pace.

In the past, the corporal basis of creativity and innovation has been discussed in various strands of discussion for a long time. Historically, design thinking pioneers were closely involved in such considerations. As one example, many decades ago this interest in how the body influences the mind already inspired the use of warm-up exercises with movement elements in design thinking innovation training (Roth, 2015). Moreover, already in the 1950s and continuously ever since, such considerations have influenced the way in which design thinking work environments were designed. The rooms are specifically equipped and laid out in such ways that they stimulate various forms of movement during working hours (Arnold, 1959/2016; von Thienen, 2018a, 2020b), such as getting up, walking around and changing one's perspective, or manual work with prototypes.

When the Hasso Plattner Design Thinking Research Program (HPDRP) started to operate in 2008, soon research projects began to elucidate the corporal basis of creativity and collaboration in scientifically ever more rigorous ways. For instance, at Stanford, Allan Reiss, Manish Saggar and their teams pioneered neuroscientific studies (e.g. Saggar et al., 2016; Xie et al., 2019), where they focused in particular on state-of-the-art measurements of brain activity, while test subjects worked on creative tasks alone or in teams.

In parallel, studies into the history of design thinking showed how detailed theories, numerous hypotheses and insights about (neuro-)psychological processes have informed the development of design thinking ever since its early beginnings in the 1950s at Stanford University (Clancey, 2016, 2019; von Thienen et al., 2016, 2017, 2019, 2021b). These studies add to our theoretical understanding of why and how design thinking works. They also reveal hypotheses of what could be achieved through specific design thinking interventions and approaches, how they would impact human bodily processes and thereby change the scope of people's creative potential. Building on this, empirical research can confirm, correct and amend our understanding of how to facilitate creative thinking and collaboration through people's bodily engagement in the world. After all, people's creative work can harness a small subset of possible bodily engagements, or people may be flexible and harness a grand spectrum of possibilities: hearing, seeing, reading, sniffing, touching things and changing them, formulating words, calculating, demonstrating and gesturing, walking—approaching things or leaving them behind and so on. The range of related research questions is manifold: Does someone who spends her workday reading and writing have the same creative prospects as someone who spends her time touching and manipulating objects? How exactly do different kinds of bodily involvement impact creative projects? For instance, is visual thinking important and helpful to foster radical innovation, as some design thinking educators have suggested? What kinds of bodily involvement can be recommended depending on the desired kind of creative outcome? E.g. might reading and writing be specifically favourable to foster incremental innovation in mathematics (or in some other selected field of interest)? How about manipulating objects, listening or smelling and their impact on innovation developments? How might tools be developed, such as novel digital environments, to facilitate beneficial bodily engagements with the world, including other humans and/or objects?

The new neurodesign area was "born" at a symposium on the neuroscientific foundations of design thinking, taking place at the HPI in autumn 2018 (von Thienen, 2018a, 2018b). Colleagues from various institutions contributed to this event, all of whom were researching the bodily basis of creativity and collaboration from various angles. The community was thrilled to observe increasingly comprehensive and coherent understandings of why and how design thinking works. Moreover, novel and promising research questions arose in short order, pushing the boundaries of understanding innovation. At this event, Larry Leifer, founding director of the Center for Design Research at Stanford and head of the Design Thinking Research Program at his institute, coined the term "neurodesign" as a headline for promising new avenues in the development of design thinking. Soon afterwards, Jan Auernhammer became Executive Director of the newly inaugurated Leifer Neurodesign Research Program at Stanford. Together, Larry and Jan hosted the first neurodesign symposium in March 2019, where the HPDTRP research community was joined by other experts from within the NeuroDesignScience field.

At the HPI Potsdam, a number of scholars with initially diverse affiliations discovered their joint passion for this research domain and began to build up neurodesign education at the institute. Julia von Thienen had been a design thinking creativity and innovation researcher, long affiliated with Christoph Meinel's design thinking research groups. Caroline Szymanski had been a design thinking coach at the HPI D-School. Theresa Weinstein had worked in design thinking research on the impact of places, together with Martin Schwemmle, Claudia Nicolai and Uli Weinberg. Shama Rahman was initially located in London, where she worked as an innovation entrepreneur. Despite these differences of affiliation, they all had received training in neuroscience in their academic education and they were all passionate about the topics of creativity, collaboration, innovation and design thinking generally.

Beginning in 2019, the emerging team offered neurodesign classes at the HPI, starting with a neurodesign lecture and a seminar. The topic portfolio increased rapidly, driven by further interested and collaborative colleagues, like Joaquin Santuber from Jonathan Edelman's design thinking research team and Irene Sophia Plank from the Berlin School of Mind and Brain at Humboldt-Universität zu Berlin.

At the beginning of 2021, there were already 35 teachers at the HPI in the neurodesign field. Seven professors, 15 postdoctoral researchers and four practice experts acted as lecturers, while nine Master and Ph.D. students additionally accompanied the courses and student projects in class. The neurodesign teachers come from thirteen different leading institutions in the field of creative engineering and neuroscience. 15 teachers are now permanent members of the HPI—not least because they came to the HPI through neurodesign, like Shama Rahman, who moved from London to Berlin-Potsdam, to help set up neurodesign at the institute. Other lecturers come from Stanford University, the Berlin School of Mind and Brain at Humboldt Universität zu Berlin, the Max Planck Institute, the Marconi Institute for Creativity from Italy, Oxford University and others.

Overall we introduced neurodesign at the HPI as a field that seeks synergies at the intersection of (i) engineering, (ii) neuroscience and (iii) design thinking: creativity, collaboration and innovation (cf. Fig. 1).

The novel neurodesign classes were very well received by the students, who helped to shape this novel work area by means of their own creative projects conducted in class and by means of their suggestions for activities outside of class. While the content of neurodesign classes and projects is reviewed elsewhere in detail (von Thienen et al., 2021c), here one example shall suffice.

In a typical neurodesign class project, one student team re-analyzed neuroscientific data of people's brain activity during team collaboration. With standard tools used in neuroscience, 74% of the variance in team-collaboration performance could be explained, based on the synchrony of people's brain activity, measured via electroencephalography (EEG). By means of machine learning, the students achieved an increased prediction accuracy of about 99%. With this improved data processing, completely new possibilities are opened up to facilitate team collaboration live by analyzing brain activities in real time. For example, the brain activities of team

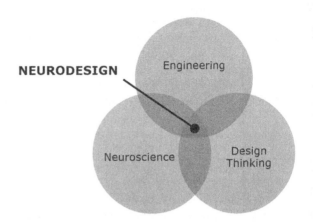

Fig. 1 Neurodesign is a novel academic work domain at the HPI, which combines knowledge from the fields of (i) engineering, (ii) neuroscience and (iii) design thinking, to foster worthwhile innovation

members can be measured via EEG headbands available for consumers and evaluated via neural networks. Thus, teams could obtain immediate feedback about how well they are synchronized, which is highly predictive of their team performance. In addition, they could obtain suggestions for interventions upon demand, such as joint motion warm-ups known to increase team synchrony and performance.

Beyond in-class projects, a number of notable activities emerged outside of class, which helped to explore fruitful work areas for neurodesign beyond the topics that had originally been planned in the curriculum. For instance, neurodesign students became curious and wanted to conduct fMRI studies themselves. This was rendered possible by Irene Plank at Humboldt Universität zu Berlin, who invited interested course participants to the MRI facilities of the Berlin Center for Advanced Neuroimaging (BCAN), where they could prototype their own little study on the brain activity of digital engineers when reading and thinking about computer code (cf. von Thienen et al., 2021c).

Another example is the initiative of one neurodesign guest lecturer, Chris Chafe, director of the Center for Computer Research in Music and Acoustics (CCRMA) at Stanford University. Based on the great interest of the audience during his guest talk at the HPI, Chris spontaneously offered to organize a workshop on his lecture topic. He soon delivered this, choosing the Technical University of Berlin as the venue, where he himself was spending a semester abroad. Although for many HPI members attending the workshop involved the effort of changing location, numerous HPI students accepted the invitation, as did a number of other (guest) lecturers from the HPI neurodesign course, next to further interested colleagues. Chris worked on data sonification, making data audible as an alternative or supplement to the more common approach of data visualization. In neurodesign, this topic was initially picked up with a specific interest in the sonification of brain data. After all, the human sense of hearing is particularly good at recognizing patterns such as rhythms, and brain activity is highly rhythmical. This is why humans might be better at understanding brain activity when listening to it, rather than looking at the data in the form of graphs. In one pioneering project by Chris and colleagues, such an approach had already been demonstrated to be highly effective. Based on well-designed sonification algorithms for EEG data, medical novices can detect critical conditions of epilepsy in silent-seizure-patients with a higher degree of accuracy than trained medical personnel visually inspecting the same EEG data in the form of graphs (Parvizi et al., 2018). This area of work proved so fruitful that HPI students and staff, together with students from two other universities in the area, came to work extensively on the subject in a highly collaborative spirit, giving rise to a number of conference presentations in just one year (Danz, 2020; D'Aleman Arango, 2020; D'Aleman et al., 2020a, 2020b; Hartmann et al., 2020; Strauch et al., 2020). In addition, this work also brought together teaching staff, such as Henrik von Coler as a specialist in music informatics and Marisol Jimenez as a sound artist, who helped to create a new course "Data Sonification and Opportunities of Sound" at the HPI in 2020. In 2021, training and work in this area were intensified even further, so that two additional courses emerged, a lecture and a seminar on "Sonic Thinking: Methods of Working with Sound".

Examples like this show the value of serendipity, which comes to fruition when people are free to explore their curiosities and passions beyond pre-planned schedules. Chris Chafe's class-external workshop could only inspire subsequent developments, because many persons followed their curiosities and passions, instead of opting for the least amount of work or attending obligatory class sessions only. Moreover, the development was based on the collaborative spirit of persons with varying academic and institutional backgrounds. Finally, at the HPI the rapid curriculum development was rendered possible by comparatively little bureaucracy and maybe even more importantly: highly supportive colleagues in administrative roles, who worked to facilitate favourable developments as best they could in the realm of given institutional regulations. All these contributions from people in varying roles were necessary to facilitate fruitful curricula developments at a rapid pace.

Overall, from design thinking over neurodesign to data sonification, the HPI curriculum for innovation education has grown considerably in a relatively short time. Classes offered in 2021 were not foreseen and they were not foreseeable in 2018. However, persons and institutions were open to change. Driven by passion and a collaborative spirit, highly novel and fruitful work areas can be discovered, implemented and elaborated. This is a design thinking innovation process in the realm of education and curriculum design.

3   Course Content and Imparted Skills in Innovation Engineering

To date, numerous courses for innovation education have already been established at the HPI and the Digital Engineering Faculty, which was founded together with the University of Potsdam in 2017. Since we primarily train engineers in the field of digital engineering, the various innovation courses can also be summarized under the headline of "Innovation Engineering". Design thinking lies at the centre of innovation education at the HPI. A respective course program has been offered at the institute from 2007 onwards. The curriculum has been developed in close collaboration with partners from Stanford University, where the related Hasso Plattner Institute of Design had started operation in 2005. While the official institutions are relatively young, design thinking has had a long legacy at Stanford (von Thienen et al., 2016, 2017, 2019, 2021b). A continuous stream of content has been created since the 1950s, to offer innovation education for mechanical engineering students. Prior to courses headlining *Design Thinking*, other headlines had been used. In particular, classes evolved to teach *Creative Thinking, Visual Thinking* and *Ambidextrous Thinking* (Fig. 2). All content developed under these headlines is highly pertinent in helping students develop worthwhile innovation. Therefore, all this content remains central for our newly emerging curricula on innovation engineering at the HPI.

Neurodesign emerged as a teaching concept decades after design thinking. However, newer teaching concepts are not "better" than earlier ones. Rather, each teaching concept is concerned with particular competency domains that matter for high-level creative performance. Thus, for comprehensive skill building, all these domains need to be covered in education. In terms of curriculum design, this means dedicated training is required for each conceptual field. At the HPI, we offer at least one dedicated class per concept and often more.

The teaching concept of **Creative Thinking** is specifically concerned with theories of creativity and innovation. This includes conceptual clarifications, such as

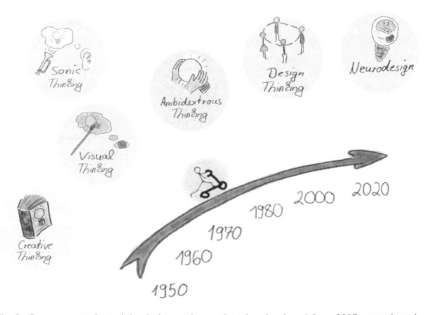

Fig. 2 Core concepts for training in innovation engineering developed from 2007 onwards at the HPI and previously at Stanford University

defining characteristics of creative products, a systematic overview of attributes that characterize a creative mindset and models of the creative process. Early course scripts on this teaching concept were collocated by John Arnold (1959/2016; see von Thienen et al., 2017, for a summary). Today, similar kinds of content, amended by more recent theories and research, are rendered available to students at the HPI in the course *Design Thinking for Digital Engineering*. It was taught in 2018 for the first time.

The teaching concept of *Visual Thinking* pursues increasing differentiations in creative skill building. Stanford educators recognized that creative projects would be much affected by the way in which students chose to represent and process project information. The educators began to distinguish respective thinking modes, such as visual, acoustic (sonic), olfactory, kinaesthetic, language-based, number-based and emotional information processing. The basic idea is that each information-processing channel can be more or less suited for specific tasks that come up in problem solving. So, it would be important to be well-versed in the different processing approaches, to tackle all kinds of upcoming problems flexibly and effectively. For instance, it was assumed that visual information processing is particularly useful for driving radical innovations, i.e. to achieve leaps in knowledge and to think up fundamentally new solutions (McKim, 1972). In order to be able to benefit optimally from this type of information processing, the students should first train visual thinking methods in order to develop appropriate skills. Teaching content on different thinking modes was elaborated especially by McKim (1972) and Adams (1974); see von Thienen et al. (2021b) for a summary. An early historic class in this teaching tradition was *Rapid Visualization* offered by Robert McKim in 1962 (Stanford University, 1962). Later on, the course *ME 101: Visual Thinking* was established and is taught up to this day (Stanford University, 2021). On behalf of language-based information processing, John Arnold had offered dedicated courses, such as the senior collo- quium *SC49: How to Ask a Question* (Clancey, 2016). At the HPI, we have offered *Visual Thinking* beginning in 2019. To broaden out the skill-building spectrum, in 2020 we added a class on *Sonic Thinking,* named *Data Sonification and Opportu- nities of Sound*. Due to important yet underexplored creative opportunities in this realm, two further classes, a seminar and a lecture on *Sonic Thinking: Methods of Working with Sound* were added in 2021. Classes on other modes of information processing, including language- and number-based approaches (which are especially important for programmers at the HPI), are likely to follow in subsequent semesters. All along the way, it is an important aim in neurodesign education to include ever more scientific studies on how modes of information processing impact creative thinking and innovation development, in terms of empirical data.

Ambidextrous Thinking is specifically concerned with the role of the whole body in creative projects, including the impact of body motion and of tactile experiences in the interaction with tangible prototypes. Overall, this teaching concept promotes the development of balanced skill sets in creators, including focused-analytic work modes next to more intuitive, holistic, emotional approaches. Thus, as much as *Visual Thinking* has been concerned with differentiation of thinking modes—like visual versus sonic versus numeric information processing—*Ambidextrous Thinking* is concerned with the re-integration and balanced use of all kinds of thinking modes, methods and abilities. A respective university class, *ME 313: Ambidextrous Thinking*, was created in 1988 for Stanford Mechanical Engineering students (Faste, 1994). This conceptual content is continued in the HPI seminar **Ambidextrous Thinking**, taught in 2020 for the first time.

Design Thinking introduces three specific objectives compared to earlier teaching concepts. One is to facilitate teamwork, in particular, collaboration in interdisciplinary teams (Carleton & Leifer, 2009; Plattner et al., 2009; Weinberg, 2015). A second course characteristic is to build creative confidence rapidly (e.g. Jobst et al., 2012; Kelley & Kelley, 2013; Rauth et al., 2010; Roth, 2015; Royalty et al., 2012, 2014; Traifeh et al., 2020). A third characteristic is the massive use of empathy techniques and user research at the outset of creative processes (cf. Plank et al., 2021, for a review). Human needs had been a central concept in the innovation curricula at Stanford Engineering ever since John Arnold's elaboration of *Creative Thinking*. Additionally, empathic user research was introduced by Robert McKim in the context of *Visual Thinking* as a source of creative inspiration. However, design thinking courses dedicate unique amounts of time and methodological concern to empathic user research, and "user needs" are invoked as a primary source of inspiration for creative processes. At the HPI, there are numerous excellent design thinking classes available to students, such as the *Global Design Thinking Weeks*, the *Basic Track*, the *Advanced Track* as well as Massive Open Online Courses (MOOCs) offered at openHPI, such as *Inspiration for Design: A Course on Human-Centred Research* by Taheri, Schmieden and Mayer, *Human-Centred Design: From Synthesis to Creative Ideas* and *Human-Centred Design: Building and Testing Prototypes*. In view of such a large number of excellent courses on design thinking at the institute, the neurodesign work group has not yet set up any further courses that specifically aim to convey experiences in interdisciplinary student teamwork, rapid creative confidence building or empathic user research.

Neurodesign introduces two unique teaching concerns. One is to illuminate the biological basis of creativity, collaboration and innovation (von Thienen et al., 2021c, 2022). Such biological insights are invoked to better facilitate creative work and also to promote worthwhile innovation that is respectful of broad ranges of basic human needs (Borchart, 2020; von Thienen, 2020a). A second priority is to explore specialist knowledge and personal passions or visions as drivers of creative processes. This complements classic design thinking courses, which rather emphasize the role of creative self-confidence and empathy (see Sects. 6.1 and 6.2). At the HPI, we currently offer two kinds of courses for these particular teaching objectives. One is the **Neurodesign Seminar**. Here students learn the basics of research methodology, both in terms of physiological studies and social science research. As a major part of the course, students become familiar with neuroscientific data and tools for data acquisition. In addition, there is the **Neurodesign Lecture**, which pursues changing research foci from year to year. In 2019 the course focused on the neuroscience of collaboration, curated by Julia von Thienen and Caroline Szymanski. In 2020 the lecture addressed artificial intelligence and creativity, curated by Shama Rahman based on her area of innovation entrepreneurship and networks encompassing neuroscience, art/science and business.

In parallel to these developments, the HPI curriculum on innovation engineering is also growing in further directions. After all, many innovation initiatives emerge in the realm of companies or entrepreneurship. What to be mindful of to foster worthwhile innovation in *business contexts* is taught by colleagues at the HPI, who are building respective portfolios of classes, such as Katharina Hölzle, who took on the chair of IT-Entrepreneurship in 2019 and Falk Uebernickel, who took on the chair of Design Thinking and Innovation Research in the same year. Under Falk Uebernickel's direction, the latter addresses, in particular, the question of how human-centred design (HCD) leads to sustainable business innovations in a corporate context. The connection between neurodesign and business is a promising area of work and teaching at the HPI as well—not least because neurodesign experts Shama Rahman and Caroline Szymanski have a professional background in entrepreneurship and business counselling, respectively. Neuroscientific knowledge about optimal conditions versus blockages in the creative process and in teamwork are valuable resources for organizations. Based on research findings, dedicated tools, interventions and measurement approaches can be developed to promote creativity and collaboration in corporate settings. For the winter semester 2021, the neurodesign work group has announced the class *Neurodesign Lecture: Designing for Empathy in Business Contexts*, which is currently being prepared by Irene Plank. As a new development, Christoph Lattemann (founder of the design thinking lab D-Forge at Jacobs University Bremen, professor of business administration and information management) together with team members Pia Gebbing, Xingyue Yang and Raoul Pilcicki will be involved as external experts.

In addition, design thinking has a strong focus on the role of **environments**, as they promote, block or channel innovation developments in selective directions. The study of how places impact people's feelings and behaviours have a long tradition in design thinking, both in theory and design practice. Here places can be understood in a broad sense, ranging from concrete environments such as a room or desktop background, over organizations in terms of buildings and organizational culture, up to larger-scale places as when considering Europe or America in different time epochs, or even the Earth compared to other planets. From a design thinking point of view, a key question is how exactly environments influence the development of innovations and what the main determinants are (Clancey & Arnold, 2018; Doorley & Witthoft, 2012; Katz, 1990; Klooker et al, 2019; Leifer & Steinert, 2011; McKim, 1972; von Thienen et al., 2012b). In the field of neurodesign, particular attention is paid to how environments affect the body. How does a certain environment influence people's movements, their gestures, postures, sitting positions, the interactions between different participants or modes of information processing (McKee, 2021; von Thienen, 2018a, 2020b; von Thienen et al., 2021c)? In addition to specific spatial designs, political regulations are being researched as another important environmental factor that has a very high predictive power for innovation developments (Bartsch & von Thienen, 2020; Mitchell & Bartsch, 2020). After all, law forbids or allows novel developments

in different areas of technology. In addition, political regulations and their implementation determine bureaucratic processes and the associated effort for all parties
involved. The amount of bureaucracy that individuals or organizations have to deal
with in order to obtain project approval from the state is a quantitative measure of
how the creative flow of the population is disturbed. Due to costs in terms of money
and lifetime, bureaucracy determines how high the entry barriers are for creative
projects in society. In addition, (un-)certainties about future political regulations have
a major impact on the willingness of investors to finance innovative developments
in respective technology domains (Hartmann, 2020). As an example, Europe facing
uncertainties of how New Genomic Techniques will be regulated in the near future
faces little financial investment in this area. Overall, the spatial environment—from
the immediate workplace to large political or geographical regions—has a significant
influence on innovation developments. A comprehensive curriculum on innovation
engineering will need to cover the role of environments in shaping innovation by
means of at least one dedicated course.

4   The Creative Process in Class

Neurodesign education—like design thinking education—helps students become
innovators who make worthwhile inventions. In all courses, students are able to work
on creative projects and gain experience in managing their own creative processes.

In creativity research, the topic of work processes has been investigated intensely
over at least one century. Notable commonalities have been found across the creative
processes of various work domains and historical times (Agnoli & Corazza, 2015;
Arnold, 1959/2016; von Thienen et al., 2012a; Wallas, 1926). Figure 3 shows a design
thinking model of the creative process. Similar descriptions of creative workflows
are available from many different creativity research communities.

To illustrate the reconstruction of creative processes in terms of the *Domain-
General Design Thinking Process Model*, we can return to the neurodesign student
project described above, where the team re-analyzed EEG data on team synchrony.

The **understanding** of a project domain is largely dependent on people's knowledge. In the case of the neurodesign student project, the whole creative endeavour
was strongly informed by the students' knowledge of machine learning, which they
had acquired in previous classes.

In terms of **experiences**, the student team listened to numerous guest talks in the
neurodesign lecture, which covered various neurodesign topics—often content areas
that were very novel and unfamiliar to the students. Emotionally, some topics would
be experienced as more exciting and meaningful than others. Caroline Szymanski's
discussion of her Ph.D. research stood out to the students because it included the kind
of data that could easily be used for machine learning, although Caroline had pursued
a completely different analysis approach (which did not convince the students).

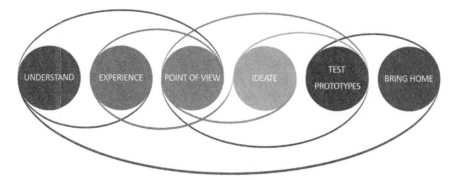

Fig. 3 The *domain-general design thinking process model*. This model of the creative process has been developed for scientific study purposes. It is used to describe, explain, predict and support creative processes in any application domain, including classic design thinking work areas such as the redesign of user experiences as much as new developments in science, art, philosophy, technology, sports or any other area of creative work. The model covers incremental and radical developments; it is used to pinpoint differences in the work process that predict the emergence of incremental vs. radical innovation (figure adapted from von Thienen et al., 2018)

In the **point of view** phase, the students decided that they wanted to see how far they could get with Caroline's data, using machine learning. They reached out and Caroline was ready to share her data sets.

Ideating, the students came up with several machine learning approaches they wanted to examine. In this endeavour, numerous crucial decisions had to be taken (e.g. how many layers to use in the models and which filters to apply for a pre-processing of the data).

The team pioneered four major **prototypes**—in this case machine learning models. These were trained on half of the data, while model performance was then tested with the other half. Moreover, the team presented their project twice in class, prior to final submissions, thus getting feedback on the overall project idea and the concrete steps taken.

To **bring home** what the students had achieved in their creative project, they did not only submit a poster and abstract. Rather, the students also created a public repository[1] so that neuroscientists can reuse the machine learning models they had developed. This allows neuroscientists to easily test whether such models are useful for other types of research questions and physiological data. This neurodesign project—like others—was also discussed in scientific publications (von Thienen et al., 2021c). This means that the working methods and project results are comparatively well documented and easily accessible so that subsequent neurodesign projects can build on what has been achieved (e.g. McKee, 2021).

Did this neurodesign student project pursue incremental or radical innovation? Insofar as previous knowledge on machine learning was used and the creative process was well-planned, incremental innovation emerged. However, ideas from

---

[1] https://pypi.org/project/deepeeg/0.1/.

one domain—digital engineering or machine learning—were transposed to a very different context: social neuroscience, team-collaboration research. Here novel analysis approaches like this can be revolutionary, opening up novel avenues of prediction and tooling that would have been unimaginable before.

Overall, innovation in real life can be built on any degree of novelty, from incremental developments to radically new approaches. It is therefore important that our process models for comprehensive innovation education are able to explain and support the entire spectrum of possible developments. In addition, the models ideally allow precise predictions and regulations in the direction of incremental versus radical novelty, depending on what is currently desired in a particular project.

In all courses that we offer, a self-chosen creative project is the main work for students during the semester. The nature of the creative process is very similar in classic design thinking classes and neurodesign courses. In all cases, it is a highly iterative learning journey. Participants are encouraged to delay decisions about a particular solution approach in order to first gather inspiration and gain a better understanding of potential problem spaces to work in. All courses have a strong focus on teaching creative mindsets. The participants learn to bias toward action, experiment, collaborate, share and test unfinished solutions in the process, work with multiple rough prototypes at first, include wild ideas, learn from feedback as well as successful or failed tests and so on.

Beyond these overarching commonalities, there are two subtle differences in the creative processes of classic design thinking classes versus neurodesign courses (cf. Sects. 6.1 and 6.2). These are pinpointed in the *Sense-Focus Model of Creative Mastery* (Fig. 4).

A comprehensive skill-set for innovation includes versatility in two work approaches, here named SENSE and FOCUS. On the one hand, it is important to discover new and worthwhile perspectives and goals for creative projects ("sense"). This working mode promotes disruptive innovation, i.e. the development of radical novelty. In the process, "sense/meaning" and "sense-making/finding meaning" play an important role. The way of working is often perceptual, i.e. different channels of sensory perception are involved. On the other hand, it is also important to benefit from

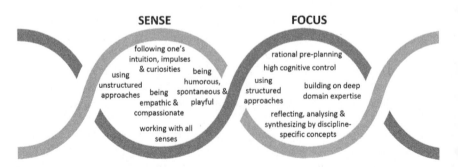

Fig. 4 The "DNA" of a creative process: sense and focus activities are closely interwoven (graphic adapted from von Thienen et al., 2018)

existing specialist knowledge in creative projects ("focus"). Sophisticated concepts and methods of a professional community help to develop technically adept solutions that do not fall short of the already achievable level of performance. The mere reuse of existing specialist concepts, however, promotes solutions that are only state-of-the-art or go a little further, i.e. incremental innovation. Radical leaps in performance are not to be expected. Top class creative developments typically combine the approaches of sense and focus. In this way, it is possible to create highly new, desired and sought-after solutions that are also technically mature. (The *Sense-Focus Model* and related research is discussed in more detail in the chapter "Design thinking—enabling creativity and innovation in digital engineering students" in this volume, by Meinel & von Thienen, 2021).

The work in classic design thinking courses is carried out primarily in a sense mode, while less emphasis is placed on the acquisition and application of discipline-specific concepts. The reason is that design thinking classes are meant to complement discipline-specific training.

By contrast, some of the neurodesign courses pay a lot of attention to the intertwining of sense-mode approaches with subject-matter knowledge used in focus-mode activity (Sect. 6.1). Ultimately, neuroscientific expertise and digital engineering competencies are discipline-specific, and students learn to use this knowledge in creative ways for purposes of ethically sound innovation.

Moreover, in the realm of sense-mode activity, neurodesign classes are more concerned with inventors "following their own intuitions, impulses and curiosities", while classic design thinking classes dedicate more time to inventors "being empathic & compassionate" (Sect. 6.2).

4.1 The Role of Domain Expertise in Creative Developments

Research has shown very clearly that specialist knowledge (domain expertise) is an important predictor for the sophistication and effectiveness of new solutions. A major reason for this is the path dependency of inventions (Altman & Mesoudi, 2019; Corazza & von Thienen, 2021; Kolodny et al., 2016; von Thienen et al., 2022). Later inventions build on earlier inventions. That is, they use the expertise that was previously developed. For example, the Internet could not be invented without prior inventions in the fields of electricity, computer technology, telecommunications, etc. Internet solutions become more and more effective, the more sophisticated the reused, earlier inventions are. In this sense, a stable power supply is a prerequisite for stable internet connections. Knowing the most effective solutions that are available in different areas, which can be reused and recombined for new purposes, is essential to developing state-of-the-art solutions even in novel terrain.

However, acquiring knowledge is time-consuming for people. It takes a long time to build deep domain expertise. Research on creative people has shown that it takes about ten years of training in a domain before people publish internationally recognized creative works in the field (Bloom, 1985; Ericsson et al., 1993; Hayes,

1989). Many more years of training are necessary before people reach their peak creative performance in life. This means that only after considerably more than ten years of practice in a specialist domain do people succeed in playing creatively with ideas from their specialist domain in the most ingenious way (Kaufman & Kaufman, 2007; Simonton, 1997, 2000). It is true that "knowledge" may appear to be easily and quickly accessible via books or the Internet. But years of practice in a knowledge domain are required before people can use culturally available knowledge in profound, creative ways.

Design thinking acknowledges this importance of training and domain expertise by encouraging students to begin design thinking education when they have already undergone extensive domain-specific training. As design thinking educators emphasize: "Being advanced in one's university studies or even having completed one's degree is the best precondition to not only learning about design thinking, but also making effective use of it" (Plattner et al., 2009, p. 67, our translation).

At the same time, in recent decades there has been a very strong concern for building creative confidence in students straightforwardly (Jobst et al., 2012; Kelley & Kelley, 2013; Rauth et al., 2010; Roth, 2015; Royalty et al., 2012, 2014). Creative confidence means that students experience themselves as effective in creative work, feel apt to handle potential difficulties along the way and trust in their ability to manage their own creative processes well.

To quickly endow students with creative confidence, some tweaks have been made in design thinking classes, compared to previous curricula in the innovation education for engineers at Stanford. In particular, four measures came into play, all of which shift the focus of the training away from the role of domain expertise in creative processes. After all, building up domain expertise takes multiple years and thus building up creative confidence based on domain expertise is also time-consuming. The following changes in course designs were made:

(1)   All creative projects pursued in class became projects to redesign someone's (user) experiences. After all, user experiences can be understood and designed without much specific domain expertise (e.g. one needs no time-intensive training in mathematics, medicine, philosophy or any other academic discipline). Compared to the previous innovation education at Stanford, however, this new teaching approach means a radical reduction in creative projects that are treated in class. Originally, John Arnold's discussion of creative processes also included classic engineering projects, mathematical problem solving, chemical inventions and other domain-specific developments that were essentially based on specialist knowledge (whereas user experiences were hardly discussed in the project analyzes of that time).

(2)   Students were granted the freedom to decide themselves what particular project goal and solution approach they wanted to pursue. Thus, no particular knowledge domain is prescribed anymore where students need to demonstrate their creative ingenuity and come up with novel, worthwhile solutions. This means, intentionally or unintentionally, students can move towards those knowledge fields where they feel comfortable and develop creative projects in this realm.

(3) Lectures, discussions of theories and research, as well as reference lists in publications were eliminated or kept to an absolute minimum. There should not be any implicit message regarding time-intensive studies that would be required before people could act as master innovators. In the new courses, experienced moderators impart the necessary process knowledge to enable the course participants to start successful creative projects straight away. This takes place in very precisely pre-planned courses with clear instructions and work templates. Even the mood of people is not left to chance, but interventions like playing selective pieces of music are used to convey moods considered favourable for creative work.

(4) Design thinking courses invite radical collaboration within multidisciplinary teams and beyond. With this team-collaboration strategy, each group benefits from a certain amount of domain expertise from different areas of knowledge that the various team members bring to the table. In addition, the radical collaboration approach helps team members to actively use social networks and, if necessary, to quickly organize additional knowledge for the projects.

The authors of this chapter believe that such adaptations in the innovation education for engineers are ingenuous moves to instil creative confidence rapidly in students. The effectiveness of such training has been evidenced widely in research. Indeed, already after some days of design thinking training students report significant increases in creative confidence (cf. Traifeh et al., 2020).

At the same time, neurodesign education seeks to complement classic design thinking courses by promoting knowledge-intensive creative competencies as well. Respective course adaptations have been made in two major directions.

First, more emphasis is placed on theory. This means that more time is made available for theoretical input. There are longer frontal lectures and even content tests. The teaching materials contain numerous references. Even relevant original sources, which are not always easy to read, may be discussed in detail.

Second, constraints are placed on the knowledge domain, in which students shall demonstrate their creativity. The HPI educates students in the field of digital engineering. Therefore, our course participants should develop and demonstrate their own creative skills in this area. Moreover, there are further requirements in the neurodesign lecture and the associated seminar. Here, the students should not only develop creative projects in the field of digital engineering, but they should also work with physiological data.

One reason why we find it important to include some courses in the overall curriculum where project topics are confined to digital engineering is due to student feedback and the re-analysis of experimental data. A number of course attendees, who had enrolled in extensive design thinking education at the institute before, reported that they had never conducted design thinking projects where they could apply their own digital engineering expertise. All their design thinking projects had evolved towards non-technical solutions.

Based on this feedback, we re-analyzed experimental data from von Thienen et al. (2011). Here the same creative challenge was posed to 40 study participants, who came to work in newly assembled teams of three to four persons. Their task was to design a solution that would help people suffering from psychological trauma. Twenty participants came to work in single-discipline digital engineering teams, while the other 20 participants came to work in multidisciplinary teams with no or only one digital engineer. In the end, all single-discipline digital engineering teams presented a technical solution to address the creative challenge; almost all of these teams provided a functioning prototype by the end of the project week. Among the multidisciplinary teams, only one team presented a technical solution and it was only described by means of storytelling without a functioning prototype. Notably, in both study conditions (single- vs. multidisciplinary teams) half of the teams comprised experienced design thinkers, while the other half consisted of design thinking novices. However, in this experiment, the level of design thinking experience was not a predictor of what type of solution the teams would produce. Only the team members' educational backgrounds predicted whether the teams would develop technical or non-technical solutions. These data clearly show the influence of domain expertise on the course of creative projects. The teams moved towards solution areas in which they had specialist knowledge; so single-discipline digital engineering teams developed technical solutions. Conversely, the study participants moved away from solution areas in which they had little specialist knowledge. In this sense, multidisciplinary teams with no or only one technically trained team member developed non-technical solutions. This shying away from technical solutions observed in multidisciplinary teams was also not explicable in terms of a search for "better solutions," because feedback indicated that on average technical solutions received better ratings for addressing user needs compared to non-technical solutions.

Against such a background, some of the novel classes added to our curriculum seek to ensure that students get to deploy creative skills in their own academic discipline. In all courses offered by the neurodesign work group at the institute, students work on creative engineering projects of their own choice, while the classes offer process and community support.

4.2 Empathy, Personal Passion and Vision as Drivers of Ground-Breaking Innovation

In recent decades, design thinking educators have placed a strong focus on empathy with user needs as a means to inspire worthwhile creative projects. This is reflected in process models depicting empathy as the first design phase (Fig. 5). Students learn to interview and observe users as a key methodological qualification in order to develop desirable, new solutions.

Notably, empathy with other people's needs is not the sole candidate for valuable sources of inspiration at the beginning of the creative process. Indeed, debates are ongoing about the empirical relationship of empathy and innovation. A number of scholars believe that empathy with user needs usually leads to incremental innovation.

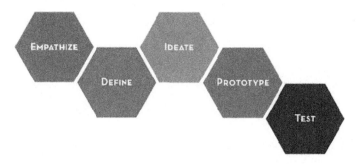

Fig. 5 According to a well-known process model from Stanford University, innovation projects begin with empathy (http://web.stanford.edu/group/cilab/cgi-bin/redesigningtheater/the-design-thinking-process); see the design thinking bootcamp bootleg (d.school, 2012) for methods in the empathy phase

Instead, radical, ground-breaking innovation would typically result from personal visions and passions. To say the least, there appear to be additional routes to ground-breaking innovation, next to empathy with user needs.

Thoughts in this direction were already expressed by John Arnold, one of the founding fathers of design thinking in the engineering department at Stanford University. He used the term "Design Thinking" as early as the 1950s. In his understanding, personal visions and passions are one of the most important paths to ground-breaking innovation. Methodologically, he spoke of the *big dream* approach.

> The big dream approach [...] is carried out by asking yourself the biggest question you possibly can, by dreaming the biggest dream that you possibly can, by sort of soaring off into space with a grand idea and then expending every possible effort to answer this big question, to make this big dream come true, to get some tangible tie between your flight into space and solid reality.
>
> (Arnold, 1959/2016, p. 76)

To gauge the impact of different creative approaches, Arnold analyzed the work processes of several outstanding innovators. He found big dreams, personal passions and visions as recurring precursors for the emergence of ground-breaking innovation. One example was the inventor Edwin Land who worked for Polaroid.

> His biggest dream was a camera that would give a full colour picture in a matter of a few seconds after exposure. In trying to make this big dream come true, he ran into a number of seemingly insurmountable difficulties. So, he stepped down a dream [...] and finally settled for the original sepia-toned print that first came on the market. [...] At this point he turned the models over to his research staff and they, using the controlled, empirical approach, have made steady improvements of the original invention. [...] A large, creative step was made using the big dream approach. This was a functional [i.e. radical] innovation and looking back through the history of invention, it seems that a large share of the functional changes were brought about in this fashion. Less creative acts, improvements to the big dream, are usually made in a step-by-step fashion, following one or more of the organized approaches.
>
> (Arnold, 1959/2016, p. 76)

In addition to Edwin Land's invention of Polaroid pictures, King Camp Gillette's invention of the disposable razor is also discussed by John Arnold, who then sums up:

> In both cases, reason and analysis (the experts) said that it couldn't be done. […] In both cases, a certain amount of confidence, or intuition or faith provided the emotional energy or drive to carry the project through and make the big dream come true.
>
> (Arnold, 1959/2016, p. 104)

Empathic user research, on the other hand, is not mentioned as a path to ground-breaking innovations. Arnold formulates an innovation theory based on human needs. Methodologically, however, this does not imply any systematic user research at the beginning of creative projects. Rather, Arnold describes the inventor as having emotional reactions to human needs that are not well met in society, which motivates a search for better solutions and thus initiates the innovation process. For example, an inventor develops the vague feeling that something is wrong with cars and traffic, because too many people die in traffic accidents, traffic jams are frustrating and it can be difficult to find a parking space. Such rather general experiences inspire questions and big dreams about how mobility needs in society can be satisfied differently and better in the future.

In contemporary works, Norman and Verganti (2014) discuss the effects of empathic user research on innovation projects. Donald Norman himself is considered to be one of the founding fathers of Human-Centred Design (HCD), which "starts with extensive design research to determine user needs" (p. 89). However, the authors come to the conclusion that the HCD process "unwittingly restricts the potential solutions to incremental innovations" (ibid.). Similar to John Arnold, Donald Norman conducted extensive case studies. Contrary to his own expectations as a human-centred designer, Norman found that projects starting with empathy ended up producing incremental innovation. In contrast, radical innovations were the result of visionary approaches, as Arnold had previously described.

> Norman was bothered by his analysis and tried to find examples that refuted this conclusion; he failed. Every radical innovation he investigated was done without design research, without careful analysis of a person's or even a society's needs. The list of such innovations starts out long before design research existed, with such technologies as indoor plumbing, electric lighting in homes, the automobile and airplane, radio and television. But even today, radical innovations, such as Facebook's and Twitter's development of social networks, have come about simply because their inventors thought there were interesting things to try. Norman was unable to find any example of radical innovation that resulted from the HCD process.
>
> (Norman & Verganti, 2014, p. 79)

Researchers from the MIT Media Lab come to similar conclusions. According to their analysis, a "focus on user needs" has a limiting effect on innovation projects. Ground-breaking innovations are much more likely to arise from the visions and passions of the developer.

> Looking back through the history of HCI [Human Computer Interaction], we see that quantum leaps have rarely resulted from studies on users' needs […]; they have come from the passion and dreams of visionaries such as Douglas Engelbart [inventor of the computer

mouse]. We believe that vision-driven design is critical in fostering quantum leaps and it complements needs-driven and technology-driven design by looking beyond current-day limits.

(Ishii et al., 2012, p. 49f.)

In the history of design thinking, empathy methods to identify user needs were introduced in the engineering department of Stanford University by Robert McKim, a direct successor to John Arnold. McKim asked the students to explore user needs empathically, not least because some of the course participants found it difficult to develop big dreams by themselves; they seemed to lack inspiration. In terms of curriculum design, there can be different interventions to address such a challenge. Introducing empathy work is one way to inspire students. Another avenue may be to help students explore their own passions and experiences in order to dream big.

In neurodesign education, we believe that empathy can be a fruitful avenue towards breakthrough innovation—when the methodology is worked out for that purpose. Not every kind of empathy promotes ground-breaking developments. Design Thinking conveys a portfolio of empathy methods that can very well promote radical innovation if one works specifically in this direction. Here it is crucial to address basic human needs, which are enduring, instead of dealing with temporary user needs that only exist in specific time-bound, cultural contexts.

We also believe that the "focus on human needs" in the creative process is important for a completely different reason, not to promote radical innovation. Taking human needs into account helps create products that are ethical, desirable and healthy—products that make a positive impact in the world rather than causing frustration or even direct harm. Thus, a focus on human needs is important whether the emerging product is radically novel or just slightly new. Especially in late design phases, a comprehensive focus on human needs is indispensable to ensure good design. In some cases, good design requires extensive user research right from the start of a project, for instance when a product is to be tailor-made for certain user groups that the designer hardly knows. In this sense, empathy primarily serves good design, rather than the promotion of radical innovation.

As sources of inspiration to advance ground-breaking innovation, we believe it is reasonable to explore and teach multiple pathways. Existing design thinking courses already offer comprehensive training in empathy techniques and draw the course participants' attention to the needs of users as sources of inspiration for creative developments. To complement this already existing, sophisticated training, our newly added classes teach students to explore their own experiences and passions, to dream big, follow their intuitions and try out what they find interesting as avenues to promising creative endeavours.

Notably, however, in addition to curricula developments, the neurodesign work group also looks systematically into human needs and empathy. Szymanski et al. (2017), Szymanski (2019a, 2019b) and Plank et al. (2021) explore from a neuroscientific perspective how it is even possible for people to understand each other, what works well and when failures of mutual understanding or team coordination arise. In addition, there is research on technologies, methods and training programs to support empathic understandings, teambuilding and mindfulness of needs. For instance, in order to support innovators in developing desirable solutions, the neurodesign work group has introduced reflection templates for creators to assess product risks and benefits based on human needs in comprehensive ways (Borchart, 2020; von Thienen, 2020a). Moreover, tools and interventions are developed to help people synchronize during teamwork, to enhance team performance and feelings of togetherness—even in remote interaction (von Thienen et al., 2021a).

5   Team Teaching and Collaboration Networks

Creativity and innovation research shows that many experts are needed to cover a wide range of knowledge fields in depth (see Sect. 6.1). In turn, deep knowledge is required to create highly sophisticated solutions. However, in-depth knowledge alone is usually not enough to initiate ground-breaking innovation. When experts tackle problems by means of discipline-specific concepts only, this leads to a fixation on already known, common solutions approach (cf. Luchins, 1942; Wallisch, 2017). In this case, problems are always approached with the same concepts and thus the same types of solutions are developed over and over again. Sometimes a problem-solving approach is very effective for certain purposes and many sophisticated solutions emerge. But the same work approach is then reused in cases when it is not ideal. Advantageous alternative solutions are easily overlooked if they require a different perspective and a different conceptual toolbox in order to be discovered.

Bringing together experts from different knowledge domains creates an optimal environment for ground-breaking innovation. The experts contribute deep knowledge in multiple areas. By means of their different training backgrounds, they introduce varying perspectives, conceptual toolboxes, interests and points of view. This encourages attempts of trying out diverse approaches, radically re-combining ideas and exploring powerful conceptual toolboxes in completely new application domains. Moreover, as design thinking research has noted (Salehi & Bernstein, 2018), an exchange of ideas does not happen as reliably when there is only exposure to other people's ideas by means of written words or images. The exchange of ideas across domains is most effective when people meet in person. Ideas travel best with people, within personally meaningful interaction. This is one reason why innovation education benefits a lot from teaching with diverse lecturer teams. Such an approach has been pioneered for a long time in Stanford's design thinking education. Bernard Roth explains how this team teaching is conducted and how it helps students to learn about academic perspectives, while not becoming fixated on any one of them:

> In my teaching and administrative roles as the academic director of the d.school, most of my day is filled with different group experiences. In the d.school, all classes must be team-taught. The way we do team teaching is different from many other team-taught courses at Stanford: we expect that the entire teaching team be present at every class [...].
>
> My colleague Jim Adams loves this kind of teaching. He tells me, "I like to team-teach, so we teachers can trash-talk each other, thereby giving the students a better insight into

professors as people and the nature of their world." [...] [It] does benefit everyone to have different view-points in the same room.

(Roth, 2015, p. 149f.)

A related approach of team teaching with lecturers from different disciplines is also pursued in our new courses. For instance, the neurodesign lecture focuses on a specific topic each year. In 2019 the overarching topic was collaboration. In 2020 it was creativity and artificial intelligence. To best shed light on the bigger topic, we set up a team of lecturers and researchers, who all work on different subtopics in the field, to look at the chosen overall subject from a 360-degrees perspective. In addition, the lecturers come from a wide variety of fields, such as neuroscience, psychology, engineering and more. By bringing together such a diverse community of experts, we want to inspire our students to select projects on different aspects of the overall topic and to look at their project topics from different perspectives.

Just as we change the main topics of the lecture from year to year, we also work with varying research and teaching teams from one semester to the next. But the teams are not simply replaced by a completely new group of experts. Rather, we seek organic developments and team re-formations by bringing lecturers together in different groups over time and occasionally inviting new colleagues. Thus, we ensure continuity of carrying on lessons learned from one semester to the next while maintaining a high degree of innovativeness through continuous input from new and different directions. Occasionally, the diverse inputs also help to question previous views in the teaching team and they always help to push the curriculum boundaries.

Another aspect of team teaching is extensive co-creation. We co-create the curriculum and study material and also collectively decide what new perspectives, subtopics and experts to bring into the program. For example, the team that sets up the neurodesign lecture series is not the same as the one that sets up the seminar, but both teams extensively co-create the curricula to ensure our students receive an educational experience that is both theoretically sound, but still open to new topics and most importantly open to experimentation. By having individual experts with different backgrounds (e.g. research and academia vs. start-up environment) that reach out in their networks to set up a new team to teach and experiment around a specific sub-topic, our program can benefit from the input of different teams with not only different expertise but also with different approaches to teaching itself. This enables our program to experiment and even create different educational approaches, such as *Data Sonification* in 2020, which combined engineering skills with music informatics and art education. We are confident that our approach of team teaching will help to continuously shape the innovation engineering program towards directions yet unknown and unexpected—directions that ultimately prove powerful and beneficial for everyone involved.

And how about the students? Based on our intention to provide comprehensive education for innovation engineering we invite, but do not prescribe, teamwork among students. After all, in real life, innovation projects can be conducted alone as well as in teams. Moreover, historically, many ground-breaking innovations have been brought about by visionary individuals, who pursued their own creative passions and visions often without much social support, sometimes even surrounded by doubts or criticism in their immediate social environment (cf. Corazza & von Thienen, 2021). Thus, we let all students decide for themselves whether they want to pursue their creative projects alone or in teams. When they opt for teamwork, they can choose team members freely, in a self-organizing fashion. Sometimes students develop project ideas they are eager to pursue and they start off doing so alone. Then other students become convinced of the idea in the course of the semester and they jump on the bandwagon to then form a team. It also happens regularly that a person who pursues a project alone in one semester works in a team in the next semester and sometimes vice versa.

All along the way, innovation benefits from the breadth and depth of available knowledge and perspectives. Thus, every student—whether working alone or in a team—is embedded in a highly collaborative and supportive social network. The diverse neurodesign community includes, of course, organizers, classmates, invited guest lecturers and sometimes project partners and external experts. Every time a project is presented in class, all other students are explicitly viewed as *extended team members*, whose task it is to contribute as much as possible with knowledge, resources and ideas. In addition, there is a lot of spontaneous communication and collaboration between class participants and also with neurodesign lecturers. No sharp distinction is made between lecturers responsible for one class, lecturers responsible for another class and those who taught a former class. Rather, everyone is available based on expertise and interests. Thus, it is not pre-planned who is working with whom or who supervises whom, but the students commence with creative ideas they are passionate about and then depending on the subjects they chose, the network evolves organically, so as to best facilitate developments in this particular subject domain.

Meanwhile, we are well aware that there is still untapped potential in the field of neurodesign courses to promote innovative developments, particularly in neuroscience, through multidisciplinary mixed student teams. Students from digital engineering and neuroscience could learn much by working with each other. For example, digital engineers can bring in their expertise with IT systems, data handling and elegant code writing (skills much needed in neuroscience research), while neuroscience students could help with grounding projects in neuroscientific theory and fundamental research, with the proper handling of measurement equipment and the meaningful interpretation of body-related data. Thus, organizationally, even more, interdisciplinary collaboration on a student level is currently being prepared, which will complement the already well-established interdisciplinary collaboration among students and lecturers.

In summary, innovation is change. We seek to advance a comprehensive curriculum for innovation engineering at the HPI, which is an exercise in facilitating worthwhile change. Each course does so in the form of creative projects that students pursue in class. Here students learn to identify "sweet spots" for innovative developments, where something novel and desirable can be created. Beyond this, the curriculum is not set or pre-planned for the long term, but rather open to serendipitous developments. Building on the skill sets and classes that have shaped innovation education for engineers at Stanford University over multiple decades, we have built up a comprehensive course portfolio for digital engineering students at the HPI. As an important addition, we have introduced neurodesign courses that familiarize students with the biological foundations of creativity and collaboration. Moreover, beyond a focus on selective user needs, students learn to be mindful of basic human needs in comprehensive ways, which helps to ensure healthy, gratifying and ethically sound solutions in digital engineering and beyond.

To enable comprehensive skill building, we offer a variety of courses that focus on different areas of expertise. Some courses invoke a traditional design thinking approach, where empathy with user needs serves as a primary source of inspiration for creative projects. Other courses start with the students' personal passions and visions in order to initiate creative developments. Moreover, in some classes, the aim is to build up creative confidence rapidly. These classes de-emphasize the role of domain expertise for the emergence of ground-breaking innovation. Other classes are specifically designed to help students become creative in their primary expertise domain, i.e. digital engineering at the HPI. Yet other classes exemplify for the students how they can build up expert knowledge in a novel field (such as neuroscience) and combine this with already acquired expertise (digital engineering), so as to gain creative inspiration and develop worthwhile innovation. In all cases, a working spirit of mutual support and collaboration has been found to be ideal for innovation education. Innovation curricula thrive in organically evolving networks of collaboration, where everyone—students, teachers, project partners or alumni alike—can contribute outside the rut of bureaucratically established roles, and instead are driven by curiosity and a desire to take on novel avenues of work that feel personally meaningful and prove to be worthwhile.

References

Adams, J. L. (1974). *Conceptual blockbusting*. Stanford Alumni Association.

Agnoli, S., & Corazza, G. E. (2015). TRIZ as seen through the DIMAI creative thinking model. *Procedia Engineering, 131*, 807–815.

Altman, A., & Mesoudi, A. (2019). Understanding agriculture within the frameworks of cumulative cultural evolution, gene-culture co-evolution, and cultural niche construction. *Human Ecology, 47*(4), 483–497.

Arnold, J. E. (2016). Creative engineering. In W. J. Clancey (Ed.), *Creative engineering: Promoting innovation by thinking differently* (pp. 59–150). Stanford digital repository. Retrieved from http://purl.stanford.edu/jb100vs5745 (Original manuscript 1959).

Bartsch, D., & von Thienen, J. P. A. (2020). *Modellierung von Innovationsräumen und -prozessen zur Europäischen Biotechnologie*. Tagung „Was heißt Innovation in der Bioökonomie?", Dialogreihe „Innovation und Verantwortung". Evangelische Akademie Tutzing, in Kooperation mit der Deutschen Akademie der Technikwissenschaften (acatech) und dem Institut Technik-Theologie-Naturwissenschaften (TTN) der LMU München, 4.-5. Oktober 2020, Tutzing, Deutschland.

Borchart, K.-P. (2020). Exploring ethical perspectives on digital engineering developments—using design thinking templates for risk-benefit assessments. Presentation at the research meeting *Design Thinking—Innovation, law and politics*, December 3–4, Hasso-Plattner-Institute at the University of Potsdam, Potsdam, Germany.

Bloom, B. S. (Ed.). (1985). *Developing talent in young people*. Ballantine Books.

Carleton, T., & Leifer, L. (2009). Stanford's ME310 course as an evolution of engineering design. In *Proceedings of the 19th CIRP design conference–Competitive design*. Cranfield University Press.

Clancey, W. J. (Ed.). (2016). *Creative engineering: promoting innovation by thinking differently— by John E. Arnold*. Retrieved from http://purl.stanford.edu/jb100vs5745 (Original manuscript 1959).

Clancey, W. J. (2019). *Cognition and design: A developmental perspective*. Talk at the Stanford Neurodesign symposium. March 6, Stanford, U.S.A.

Clancey, W. J., & Arnold Jr, J. E. (2018). Training creative engineers: The Arcturus IV case study and its relation to MDRS. Retrieved from http://www.marspapers.org/paper/Clancey_2018.pdf

Corazza, G. E., & von Thienen, J. P. A. (2021). Invention. In V. P. Glăveanu (Ed.), *The Palgrave encyclopedia of the possible*. Palgrave Macmillan.

D'Aleman Arango, N. (2020). Brainwave sonification: Virtual instrument. Presentation and demo in J. von Thienen, & T. Weinstein (chairs), *innovation modelling based on human needs*. Session at the Stanford-Potsdam design thinking research meeting, May 18–20, organized by Stanford University.

D'Aleman Arango, N., Chafe, C., & von Thienen, J. (2020a). *Brainwave etudes: Composition and improvisation with brain data*. Presentation at the MIC Conference of Creativity, September 14–16, Bologna, Italy.

D'Aleman Arango, N., von Thienen, J., & von Coler, H. (2020b). The brainwave virtual instrument: Musical improvisation and brainwave sonification via Faust programming. *Proceedings of the 2nd international Faust conference (IFC-20)*, Maison des Sciences de l'Homme Paris Nord, France, December 1–2.

Danz, N. (2020). *Real-time EEG sonification with the BITalino platform*. Presentation at the MIC conference of creativity, September 14–16, Bologna, Italy.

Doorley, S., & Witthoft, S. (2012). *Make space*. Wiley & Sons.

Ericsson, K. A., Krampe, R. T., & Tesch-Roemer, C. (1993). The role of deliberate practice in the acquisition of expert performance. *Psychological Review, 100*, 363–406.

Faste, R. (1994). *Ambidextrous thinking. In Innovations in mechanical engineering curricula for the 1990s*. New York: American Society of Mechanical Engineers. Retrieved from http://www.fastefoundation.org/publications/ambidextrous_thinking.pdf

Hartmann, C. (2020). *"Sandkastenregulierung" als Mittel zur Ermöglichung von Innovationen. Beitrag im Harnackhauskreis der Berliner Wissenschaftlichen Gesellschaft zum Thema Modellierung von Innovationsräumen und -prozessen zur Europäischen Biotechnologie*, December 3, Potsdam, Germany.

Hartmann, L, Hilbrich, L., Steigerwald, P., & Strauch, T. (2020). Audible spatialization of EEG data. Presentation and demo in J. von Thienen, & T. Weinstein (chairs), *Innovation modelling based on human needs*. Session at the Stanford-Potsdam design Thinking Research Meeting, May 18–20, organized by Stanford University.

Hayes, J. R. (1989). *The complete problem solver*. Erlbaum.

Ishii, H., Lakatos, D., Bonanni, L., & Labrune, J.-B. (2012). Radical atoms. *Interactions, 19*(1), 38–51.

Jobst, B., Köppen, E., Lindberg, T., Moritz, J., Rhinow, H., & Meinel, C. (2012). The faith-factor in design thinking: Creative confidence through education at the design thinking schools Potsdam and Stanford? In H. Plattner, C. Meinel, & L. Leifer (Eds.), *Design Thinking Research. Measuring Performance in Context* (pp. 35–46). Springer.

Katz, B. M. (1990). *Technology and culture: A historical romance*. Alumni Press.

Kaufman, S. B., & Kaufman, J. C. (2007). Ten years to expertise, many more to greatness: An investigation of modern writers. *The Journal of Creative Behavior, 41*(2), 114–124.

Kelley, T., & Kelley, D. (2013). *Creative confidence*. Harper Collins.

Klooker, M., Schwemmle, M., Nicolai, C., & Weinberg, U. (2019). Making use of innovation spaces: Towards a framework of strategizing spatial interventions. *Design thinking research* (pp. 75–96). Springer.

Kolodny, O., Creanza, N., & Feldman, M. W. (2016). Game-changing innovations. How culture can change the parameters of its own evolution and induce abrupt cultural shifts. *PLoS Computational Biology, 12*(12), e1005302.

Leifer, L. J., & Steinert, M. (2011). Dancing with ambiguity: Causality behavior, design thinking, and triple-loop-learning. *Information Knowledge Systems Management, 10*(1–4), 151–173.

Luchins, A. S. (1942). Mechanization in problem solving: The effect of Einstellung. *Psychological Monographs, 54*(6), i–95.

McKee, H. (2021). *Remote collaboration, motion and creativity.* Presentation in the Neurodesign Lecture, Feb 8, Hasso-Plattner-Institute at the University of Potsdam, Potsdam, Germany. Retrieved from https://www.tele-task.de/lecture/video/8545/

McKim, R. H. (1972). *Experiences in visual thinking.* Wadsworth Publishing.

Meinel, C., & von Thienen, J. P. A. (2021). Design Thinking—Enabling creativity and innovation in digital engineering students. In C. Meinel, & T. Krohn (Eds.). *Design thinking education. Innovation can be learned.* Springer.

Mitchell, H. J., & Bartsch, D. (2020). Regulation of GM organisms for invasive species control. *Frontiers in Bioengineering and Biotechnology, 7*, 1–11.

Norman, D. A., & Verganti, R. (2014). Incremental and radical innovation: Design research vs. technology and meaning change. *Design issues, 30*(1), 78–96.

Parvizi, J., Gururangan, K., Razavi, B., & Chafe, C. (2018). Detecting silent seizures by their sound. *Epilepsia, 59*, 877–884.

Plank, I. S., von Thienen, J. P. A., & Meinel, C. (2021). The neuroscience of empathy: Research-overview and implications for human-centred design. In H. Plattner, C. Meinel, L. Leifer (Eds.), *Design thinking research.* Springer.

Plattner, H., Meinel, C., & Weinberg, U. (2009). *Design thinking. Innovation lernen. Ideenwelten öffnen.* Mi-Wirtschaftsbuch.

Rauth, I., Köppen, E., Jobst, B., & Meinel, C. (2010). Design thinking: An educational model towards creative confidence. In *DS 66–2: Proceedings of the 1st international conference on design creativity (ICDC 2010).*

Roth, B. (2015). *The achievement habit.* Harper Collins.

Royalty, A., Oishi, L. N., & Roth, B. (2012). "I use it every day": Pathways to adaptive innovation after graduate study in design thinking. In H. Plattner, C. Meinel, & L. Leifer (Eds.), *Design thinking research. Measuring performance in context* (pp. 95–105). Springer.

Royalty, A., Oishi, L., & Roth, B. (2014). Acting with creative confidence: Developing a creative agency assessment tool. In H. Plattner, C. Meinel, & L. Leifer (Eds.), *Design thinking research. Building innovation eco systems* (pp. 79–96). Springer.

Saggar, M., Quintin, E.-M., Bott, N. T., Kienitz, E., Chien, Y.-H., Hong, D.W.-C., Liu, N., Royalty, A., Hawthorne, G., & Reiss, A. L. (2016). Changes in brain activation associated with spontaneous improvisation and figural creativity after design-thinking-based training: A longitudinal fMRI study. *Cerebral Cortex, 27*(7), 3542–3552.

Salehi, N., & Bernstein, M. S. (2018). Hive: Collective design through network rotation. *Proceedings of the ACM on Human-Computer Interaction, 2*(CSCW), 1–26.

Simonton, D. K. (1997). Creative productivity: A predictive and explanatory model of career trajectories and landmarks. *Psychological Review, 104*(1), 66.

Simonton, D. K. (2000). Creative development as acquired expertise: Theoretical issues and an empirical test. *Developmental Review, 20*(2), 283–318.

Stanford University. (1962). *Stanford University bulletin. Courses and degrees 1962–63.* Retrieved from https://stacks.stanford.edu/file/druid:cp135qt4613/1962-1963.pdf

Stanford University. (2021). *Stanford bulletin 2020–21.* Retrieved from https://exploredegrees.stanford.edu/

Strauch, T., Hartmann, L., Hilbrich, L., Steigerwald, P., Chafe, C., & von Thienen, J. (2020). *Audible spatialization of EEG data in the context of creativity studies.* Presentation at the MIC conference of creativity, September 14–16, Bologna, Italy.

Szymanski, C., Pesquita, A., Brennan, A. A., Perdikis, D., Enns, J. T., Brick, T. R., Müller, V., & Lindenberger, U. (2017). Teams on the same wavelength perform better: Inter-brain phase synchronization constitutes a neural substrate for social facilitation. *Neuroimage, 152*, 425–436.

Szymanski, C. (2019a). *Social neuroscience and teamwork*. Presentation in the Neurodesign lecture, Hasso-Plattner-Institute at the University of Potsdam, Oct 21, Potsdam, Germany. Retrieved from https://www.tele-task.de/lecture/video/7720/

Szymanski, C. (2019b). *Neural team dynamics*. Presentation in the Neurodesign lecture, Hasso-Plattner-Institute at the University of Potsdam, October 28, Potsdam, Germany. Retrieved from https://www.tele-task.de/lecture/video/7952/

Traifeh, H., Nicolai, C., Refaie, R., & Meinel, C. (2020). Engaging digital engineering students in design thinking. *DS 101: Proceedings of NordDesign 2020, Lyngby, Denmark, 12th–14th August 2020*, 1–14.

von Thienen, J. P. A (2018a). *Design thinking, the body and creativity: Exploring some bridges*. Retrieved from https://www.tele-task.de/lecture/video/7013/

von Thienen, J. P. A. [organizer]. (2018b). *Neuroscience and physiological perspectives on design thinking and creativity*. Symposium chaired by A. Reiss, with contributions from Julia von Thienen, Naama Mayseless, Serena Mastria, Caroline Szymanski, Manish Saggar and Stefanie Faye Frank. September 10, Potsdam, Germany. Recording available at: https://www.tele-task.de/series/1219/

von Thienen, J. P. A. (2020a). *Ethics and human need assessments as fundamentals for the development of worthwhile innovation—introducing design thinking templates for risk-benefit assessments*. Presentation at the research meeting Design thinking—innovation, law and politics, December 3–4, Hasso-Plattner-Institute at the University of Potsdam, Potsdam, Germany.

von Thienen, J. P. A. (2020b). *Creative places. Presentation in the lecture design thinking for digital engineering*. Hasso-Plattner-Institute at the University of Potsdam, Potsdam, Germany. Retrieved from https://s3.xopic.de/openhpi-public/courses/2ChMn3BXUEIjuUEY55thbj/rtfiles/4Z6LYCZXGVumhQPUKCutaJ/creative_places_less_resolution2.pdf

von Thienen, J., Borchart, K.-P., Jaschek, C., Krebs, E., Hildebrand, J., Rätz, H., & Meinel, C. (2021a). Leveraging video games to improve IT-solutions for remote work. In *IEEE conference on games (CoG 2021)*. Retrieved from https://ieee-cog.org/2021/assets/papers/paper_102.pdf

von Thienen, J. P. A., Clancey, W. J., Corazza, G. E., & Meinel, C. (2017). Theoretical foundations of design thinking. Part I: John E. Arnold's creative thinking theories. In H. Plattner, C. Meinel, & L. Leifer (Eds.), *Design thinking research. Making distinctions: Collaboration versus cooperation* (pp. 13–40). Springer.

von Thienen, J. P. A., Clancey, W. J., & Meinel, C. (2019). Theoretical foundations of design thinking. Part II: Robert H. McKim's need-based design theory. In H. Plattner, C. Meinel, L. Leifer (Eds.), *Design thinking research. Looking further: Design thinking beyond solution-fixation* (pp. 13–38). Springer.

von Thienen, J. P. A., Clancey, W. J., & Meinel, C. (2021b). Theoretical foundations of design thinking. Part III: Robert H. McKim's visual thinking theories. In H. Plattner, C. Meinel, & L. Leifer (Eds.), *Design thinking research. Interrogating the doing* (pp. 9–72). Springer.

von Thienen, J. P. A., Ford, C., & Meinel, C. (2016). *The emergence of design thinking in Californian engineering classes: Four historic concepts worth knowing*. Talk at the *MIC Conference: From creative brains to creative societies*, September 14–16, Bologna, Italy.

von Thienen, J. P. A., Kolodny, O., & Meinel, C. (2022). Neurodesign: The biology, psychology and engineering of creative thinking and innovation. In N. Rezaei (Ed.), *Thinking: Bioengineering of science and art*. Springer Nature.

von Thienen, J. P. A., Noweski, C., Meinel, C., & Rauth, I. (2011). The co-evolution of theory and practice in design thinking—or—"mind the oddness trap!". In H. Plattner, C. Meinel, & L. Leifer (Eds.), *Design thinking. Understand—improve—apply* (pp. 81–99). Springer.

von Thienen, J. P. A., Noweski, C., Meinel, C., Lang, S., Nicolai, C., & Bartz, A. (2012a). What can design thinking learn from behaviour group therapy? In H. Plattner, C. Meinel, & L. Leifer (Eds.), *Design thinking research. Measuring performance in context* (pp. 285–302). Springer.

von Thienen, J. P. A., Noweski, C., Rauth, I., Meinel, C., & Lang, S. (2012b). If you want to know who you are, tell me where you are: The importance of places. In H. Plattner, C. Meinel, L. Leifer (Eds.), *Design thinking research. Studying co-creation in practice* (pp. 53–73). Springer.

von Thienen, J. P. A., Szymanski, C., Santuber, J., Plank, I. S., Rahman, S., Weinstein, T., Owoyele, B., Bauer, M., & Meinel, C. (2021c). Neurodesign live. In H. Plattner, C. Meinel, & L. Leifer (Eds.), *Design thinking research. Interrogating the doing* (pp. 357–425). Springer.

von Thienen, J. P. A., Traifeh, H., & Meinel, C. (2018). *Design thinking powered learning experiences*. Invited talk at the Stanford-Potsdam Hasso Plattner design thinking research community building workshop, Stanford, USA, March 14.

Wallas, G. (1926). *The art of thought*. Cape.

Wallisch, P. (2017). The neuroscience of creativity: What we think we know, what we know to be wrong and what we wish we knew. Invited talk at the HPI@NYC inaugural ceremony for Hudson yard 10, September 14–16, 2017, New York.

Weinberg, U. (2015). *Network thinking: Was kommt nach dem Brockhaus Denken*. Murmann.

Xie, H., Howell, A., Schreier, M., Sheau, K. E., Manchanda, M. K., Ayub, R., Glover, G., Jung, M., Reiss, A. L., & Saggar, M. (2019). Finding the neural correlates of collaboration using a three-person fMRI hyperscanning paradigm. *bioRxiv*.https://doi.org/10.1101/782870.

Dr. Julia V. Thienen

Initiator of HPI Neurodesign and Senior Researcher at the Hasso Plattner Institute for Digital Engineering. Photo credit: Kay Herschelmann. Dr. Julia von Thienen studied psychology, neuroscience, computer science and philosophy at the Free University of Berlin. She has taught research methodology at the Free University of Berlin, the University of Chicago and the University of Potsdam. In 2008, Dr. Julia von Thienen joined the Hasso Plattner Institute for Digital Engineering, specifically the Stanford-Potsdam Design Thinking Research Program. Her studies are concerned with design thinking as an approach to creativity and innovation. She specifically seeks to encourage creativity in engineering—all in the service of worthwhile innovation—, and to integrate more body-related perspectives in the process. In design thinking education, one challenge Dr. Julia von Thienen finds important concerns the breadth of approaches taken, so as to orchestrate classes from highly practice oriented approaches to deep treatments of theory and research, from classes on creativity in engineering to innovation projects in all areas of life. Here, design thinking values of diversity, flexibility and collaboration are key. They help to advance rich design thinking programmes, where educators, students and project partners meet in a spirit of curiosity, appreciation and mutual support, so that collaborations emerge naturally.

Dr. Caroline Szymanski Lecturer, HPI School of Design Thinking.

Dr. Caroline Szymanski has 10 years of experience in accompanying organizations through the endeavor of integrating Design Thinking into their strategic innovation practice. She holds a Ph.D. in neuroscience and is interested in how neuroscience can inform Design Thinking and in particular collaboration and team leadership. Caroline is a lecturer at the HPI School of Design Thinking since 2012, was a guest professor for "Design Thinking for entrepreneurs" at Harbour.Space University in Barcelona in 2016 and co-founded the innovation consultancy Kandoee in the same year.

Caroline sees the greatest challenge to using DT in education to balance the expectation for a "That's the way to do it"-lecture-style with the "I don't know how to find the holy grail either"-attitude of a good Design Thinking Coach. And maybe the simplest step to using DT in education is simply bringing more of this very "We are all here to learn and find out" mindset into education.

Her most valuable insight using DT was the realization that there is no single perfect solution to anything and that all humans are on a constant personal transformation journey.

Theresa Weinstein Researcher and Ph.D. Student in Neurodesign, Hasso Plattner Institute.

Theresa J. Weinstein studied neuroscience at the Berlin School of Mind and Brain (Humboldt-Universität zu Berlin). She is currently conducting research at the HPI in the new field of neurodesign on questions related to the biological basis of human creativity and collaborative innovation. Ever since she completed the Basic and Advanced Track of the HPI D-School in 2016/2017, she has been fascinated by the positive impact that Design Thinking has on people's ability to be creative in teams and try out new ways of solving problems. Her aim is to bring a neuroscience perspective to Design Thinking research, practice, and education, and to foster interdisciplinary collaboration among disciplines involved in neurodesign, for example by using new educational formats. Design Thinking methods and mindsets help her achieve these goals.

Dr. Shama Rahman Neuroscientist/Complexity Physicist, Entrepreneur and Interdisciplinary Artist, HPDTRP Researcher, Hasso Plattner Institute. Dr. Shama Rahman has developed a unique conception of neurodesign, which seeks synergies at the intersection of (1) neuroscience, (2) digital engineering and (3) design thinking: creativity , collaboration, innovation and in her first year at HPI she launched a successful lecture series on neuroscience and neurodesign. Shama is the founder of NeuroCreate, a start-up that applies AI and neuroscience in a symbiotic digital design to improve human creativity, performance and well-being. *NeuroCreate* (https://www.neuroc reate.co.uk) has been recognized as Top 100 UK creative technology companies by the Creative Industries Council, featured in Forbes and Thrive Global and been nominated for the RSA Future of Work "Tech for Good" Award. She is a finalist for the "Entrepreneur of the Year" Award from Olympic Legacy.

Prof. Dr. Christoph Meinel (Univ. Prof., Dr. sc. nat., Dr. rer. nat.) is Director and CEO of the Hasso Plattner Institute for Digital Engineering gGmbH (HPI) at the University of Potsdam.

Photo credit: Kay Herschelmann.

Christoph Meinel was born in 1954 and was founding Dean of the Digital Engineering Faculty at the University of Potsdam in April 2017. Currently he serves as Vice Dean. He holds the Chair of Internet Technologies and Systems and is also active in the fields of cybersecurity and digital education, teaching in the bachelor's and master's programs in IT-Systems Engineering and at the School of Design Thinking. Christoph Meinel developed the MOOC platform, openHPI.de, and also provides content on the site. His responsibilities include supervising numerous doctoral students, and he has authored or co-authored more than 25 books, anthologies, and various conference proceedings.

He has published more than 550 peer-reviewed articles in scientific journals and at international conferences and holds a number of international patents. He is a member of the National Academy of Science and Technology (acatech), director of the HPI-Stanford Design Thinking Research Program, honorary professor at the Technical University of Beijing, visiting professor at Shanghai University, professor at Nanjing University, and member of numerous scientific committees and supervisory boards.

Walls, Furniture, People—Theoretical and Practical Aspects of Space in Design Thinking

Martin Schwemmle

Abstract This chapter provides an initial theoretical foundation for a comprehensive understanding of innovation spaces in Design Thinking. It enables the reader to make better informed, concrete decisions for setting up, equipping, and using a space for Design Thinking workshops. Using the metaphor of building a house as a structure, this chapter consists of three main sections. The foundation consists of theories of space and its relevance in the context of Design Thinking (Sect. 2). The blueprint (Sect. 3) outlines a typology of the innovation space in Design Thinking. It is made concrete in the furnishings and utilization in concrete elements of space (Sect. 3) and includes the active design of the space from the perspective of the instructors. The chapter concludes with a brief discussion. Although aspects of Design Thinking are dealt with specifically in some places, the principles presented apply to spaces in general—i.e., from offices to meeting rooms and, if you wish, to your private living room as well. Aspects that are more specific to Design Thinking can often be applied to other forms of innovative, collaborative ways of working. This chapter examines Design Thinking in teaching and how it is used in actual practice, as well as discussing examples of companies and educational institutions that work with Design Thinking.

1 Introduction

Almost 100 years ago, the Hawthorne studies examined the effect of workspace on workers and their productivity, thereby literally shedding light on the subject. In these studies, a team of researchers conducted various experiments on worker productivity under varying conditions at the Western Electric Company's Hawthorne plant in Cicero, outside Chicago (see Sonnenfeld, 1985 for a detailed description). One of the hypotheses investigated was that an appropriate work environment—specifically, higher light intensity in production rooms—would increase workers' productivity.

M. Schwemmle (✉)
HPI School of Design Thinking, Hasso Plattner Institute for Digital Engineering, Campus Griebnitzsee, Prof.-Dr.-Helmert-Str. 2-3, 14482 Potsdam, Germany
e-mail: Martin.Schwemmle@hpi.de

In the illumination studies, which were the first to be conducted, no such correlation between light intensity and productivity was found. Rather, a reduction in light led to productivity gains until workers were sitting in near-total darkness. The research team concluded that lighting was probably not a significant factor and that other more important factors had to exist, but had not been considered in the research design. In short, the researchers were as much in the dark as the workers they were observing. Further studies followed, such as the actual Hawthorne experiments, which examined numerous other influences on the productivity of the Hawthorne workers over an eight-year period.

The "human relations approach" emerged as a key result of these further investigations. It states that productivity is not influenced so much by elements of space, as it is by social factors and relationships in the workplace, such as the need for recognition. Specifically, by being part of a scientific study, the workers enjoyed special attention, were observed, felt appreciated—and worked harder. As a result, they were so radiant with joy at the recognition they were receiving that they did not care whether it was as bright as day or as black as night around them (Carey, 1967).

Had they maintained this interpretation, things would look bleak for the effect of the work environment on productivity, and thus for the relevance of space in general. Many other researchers have revisited the Hawthorne results, sometimes coming to different or at least complementary conclusions (see Franke & Kaul, 1978, for example). And perhaps the work environment did have an effect on performance after all, because the workers were moved to another room for the investigation and no longer worked in the normal production hall. Therefore, this change in space may also have had an impact on productivity (Hatch & Cunliffe, 2006). In the end, as is so often the case, the truth will be in the middle, and both aspects—elements of space and social factors—will have played a role. In any case, scholars continue to debate the results of the Hawthorne study and its interpretation to this day (see Carey, 1967; Hassard, 2012, for example).

The Hawthorne studies with their various interpretations are exemplary for the different perspectives and influencing factors that we must know and observe to be able to seriously engage with the matter of "space" in general, and especially in the context of Design Thinking. Specifically, there are three lessons that can be derived from the Hawthorne studies for this chapter. First, we must always consider physical space together with social aspects—that is, we are dealing not only with the four walls, but also with what happens inside those four walls. Second, things are usually a bit more complex than we think. Simple cause-and-effect chains such as "lights on: productivity up, lights out: productivity down" often do not work, because the space combines a variety of influencing factors. Third, the topic is timeless and still relevant: What used to be the productivity of factory workers 100 years ago is "new work" or simply the space in Design Thinking today. In this spirit: Thank you for your interest—may you become enlightened as you read this chapter!

This chapter highlights space as an element of Design Thinking and bases the outline on the metaphor of building a house. The foundation consists of theories of space and its relevance in the context of Design Thinking (Sect. 2). The blueprint (Sect. 3) outlines a typology of the innovation space in Design Thinking. It is made concrete in the furnishings and utilization in concrete elements of space (Sect. 4) and includes the active design of the space from the perspective of the instructors. The chapter concludes with a brief discussion. Most people find issues relating to the interior more exciting than the calculations done by structural engineers before building the foundation. Nevertheless, this chapter places an emphasis on precisely these bases, as an understanding of these enables the designer to shape and implement plans in a meaningful way. Although aspects of Design Thinking are dealt with specifically in some places, the principles presented apply to spaces in general—i.e., from offices to meeting rooms and, if you wish, to your private living room as well. Aspects that are more specific to Design Thinking can often be applied to other forms of innovative, collaborative ways of working. This chapter examines Design Thinking in teaching and how it is used in actual practice, as well as discussing examples of companies and educational institutions that work with Design Thinking.

2 Foundation: Theoretical Principles of (Innovation) Space

2.1 Understanding and Perceiving Space

As the brief look at the Hawthorne studies has shown, the topic of space is not just a matter of walls, windows, and square meters and is therefore by no means just a matter for architects. If we use a broad understanding of space as a basis, we can find references to space in almost all the scientific disciplines (Günzel, 2008). Perspectives from psychology and innovation management are especially relevant for this chapter, which views space as innovation space in Design Thinking. Some key theoretical foundations from these areas are presented below.

From the wrecking ball to sunglasses: Three perspectives on space

In a meta-study, the English scholars Taylor and Spicer compiled research on the topic of "space" in organizations and summarized it in three categories (Taylor & Spicer, 2007). The first category views space as distance. This perspective has a strong focus on physical factors such as buildings, zones, and surfaces, but also on furniture and how it is arranged, along with the resulting distances between people and objects in space. As every innovation space must ultimately be mapped in a physical space, this perspective is an essential prerequisite when engaging with the matter of space. Ultimately, even virtual innovation spaces need physical spaces in which instructors and students spend time. It is important to note, however, that space as distance represents only one of three categories.

The second perspective views space as the materialization of power relations. The planners of a space—the urban planner for a neighborhood, the architect for an apartment, or the instructor in an innovation space—can exert power over their users through the design of spaces. In other words, they can use the space to exert influence in a very targeted way. The design of supermarkets is a prominent example:

It is not by chance that, shortly after entering, you are first slowed down in the fruit and vegetable department by the floor and temperature, the beautiful display of goods like in a market, and the need to pick them up, put them in bags, and weigh them (Jiménez, 2012). The music that is playing is also intentional: If your supermarket plays French music, the chances are it wants to boost sales of French red wine (North et al., 1999). Just as the planner of a space or the manager of a supermarket influences the behavior of customers through aspects of space, the instructor or coach in Design Thinking can also influence students and participants.

Lastly, the third category considers space as an experience. When you remember your first own apartment, you will probably not think of the floor plan, the defective blinds, or the cemented power of the architect in the kitchen that was much too small, but of the lavish parties you celebrated in that apartment. These experiences that people have in a space—often together with others—also shape our perspective of the space. An innovation space that is associated with positive experiences— such as discovering your own creativity and acting it out—contributes positively to how users understand the space, while creating a positive narrative that can be disseminated throughout the organization.

Distinguishing between these perspectives becomes even more exciting when we put on the construction helmet and set about changing spaces. The strategy for changing a space will vary depending on which of the three perspectives you take, Space as distance: Call in the wrecking ball—or at least roll up your sleeves and move furniture around. Space as an expression of power: Prepare team spaces to your liking or break out of the rules—better not in the supermarket, but who says a table in a classroom cannot be tilted and used as a whiteboard? Space as experience: Celebrate successes or invite people to socialize in the innovation space after work. Having these different perspectives in mind expands the scope of action in room design immensely, as shown in specific examples in the following sections. For one, this also shows that planning a good innovation space requires more than mere calculations of square yards per person and that, instead, a holistic view is needed, worn out though the term may be. For the other, it becomes clear that it is not only the architect or interior designer who can influence the space, but everyone who works in it.

About love and dogs: The gestalt theory

A theory from the field of perceptual psychology underpins this aspect of holistic perception—the gestalt theory (see, for example, King et al., 1994). It is often summarized by the statement: The whole is more than the sum of its parts. The original text is less judgmental: The whole is something else than the sum of its parts. In the end, it is all about the same basic idea: Human perception is holistic and is definitely not an accumulation of individual perceptions. This sounds abstract, but can be explained in simple terms: Why do you actually love your partner or your dog? I assume you are not going to pull out a list of categories, rate individual traits like looks, size, intellect, and smell on rainy days, and then add all the points for an overall assessment. Unfortunately, that kind of calculation only works in the oh-so-rational world of homo economicus. Instead, you will make an overall judgment that reflects all of these individual aspects while going beyond them at the same time. It is the same with rooms: Naturally, you tend to feel uncomfortable in tight spaces and love to spread out on your desk. And of course, you will find a single office perfect, with a door you can pull shut to concentrate in peace. Yet you absolutely enjoy working in the open compartment of a moving German ICE train.

According to the gestalt theory, one should never exclusively consider a single aspect when engaging with the subject of "space," but always consider a space holistically. Even if you make long lists of the relevant factors, chances are you have overlooked one. To make things even more complicated, perception, of course, depends not only on the room itself, but also on the person. This means that experiences, learned behavior—think of the typical classroom situation in school—and even the current mood, also enter into the assessment. But then again, no one said it was easy…!

2.2 Space in Design Thinking

Red couches and runways made of bamboo

Let us set the scene by looking at a situation that occurred on New Guinea during the Second World War. To provide food for the islanders and soldiers stationed there, the American military dropped thousands of cargo packages of food and clothing over the island. From the point of view of the soldiers, this was a legitimate form of supply by means of an airlift, but it bordered on a miracle for the islanders—it rained milk and honey. This miracle came to an abrupt stop when the war ended and the troops were withdrawn. By contrast, the islanders' wish that the miraculous packages would continue to fall from the sky was infinite. Therefore, they imitated the behavior of the soldiers to bring back the miracle: They spoke into specially carved wooden radios, acted like soldiers in the tower, and even recreated entire airplanes and runways out of bamboo. Although this behavior came pretty close to what the American soldiers had done shortly before then, the planes did not return with their supply packages. This incident has entered the history books as "Cargo Cult" and is often used as a metaphor when behavior is unthinkingly imitated without an understanding of the reason behind it (Holmquist, 2005; Lindstrom, 1993).

There is sometimes also the danger of a Cargo Cult when we engage with space in Design Thinking. Simply setting up an innovation room or laboratory does not automatically make a company innovative, no more than the mere purchase of red sofas or whiteboards. Nobody doubts that all these things are helpful, beneficial, or necessary for certain ways of working. However, simply having space and furniture is not enough—you need to understand and use them properly!

As a researcher and coach, I am convinced that the space in innovative teaching and collaborative work is still not used enough, to the effect that lots of potential has not been discovered. Of course, certain basic equipment is required, but it is often the small gestures and interventions that make the difference. The following sections focus on raising awareness of the available tools and making the existing potential usable. Before continuing, though, here are a few concretizing notes on space in Design Thinking.

While all the aspects of the previous section on spaces generally also apply to the spaces in Design Thinking, there are two additional specific aspects resulting from the particularities of the way of working, which are briefly outlined below.

Buttons are for pushing

Design Thinking's ability to invite certain behaviors constitutes an important element of the innovation space. If you see shelves that are full of materials, there is a good chance you will reach in and experiment with the materials. If there is a mobile whiteboard, chances are you will be tempted to move it around. Affordances is the technical term for these "invitations." Put into plain language, affordances are offers made by the environment that users can accept if they see and understand the offers (Chemero, 2003). If an innovation space uses these affordances in a targeted manner, it can communicate permanent invitations to try out something new to its users. And of course, a coach can also specifically create such invitations during a workshop, for example, by preparing the team space (work space of a Design Thinking team) for a particular phase. But be careful! As already stated in the definition of "affordances," the invitation must also be understood. Sometimes, an inviting stack of post-its with pens is not enough to prompt teams to actively jot things down, and a room, unfortunately, does not only have the consciously induced affordances, but also the unconscious ones. For example, an immaculate innovation room with brand-new walls of frosted glass does not necessarily invite active use, because users will not want to get anything dirty. Likewise, post-its that are still neatly wrapped in cellophane tend to say "don't touch" rather than invite people to use them.

Our home is our castle

You have probably heard the saying, "My home is my castle," which may say more about innovation spaces than the cheesy signs it is printed on might suggest. A space has a lot to do with territoriality, that is, the understanding and feeling that it is "my" space and that I am safe here (Brown et al., 2005). This then gives rise to feelings of ownership. Even though few of us will become owners or tenants of the innovation spaces in which we work, it is of key importance for people in general, and course participants in particular, to feel a bit "at home" wherever they are working. The associated sense of security is a prerequisite for thinking in new and unconventional ways, and offsets the many new things that come at participants in a Design Thinking sprint or workshop. As an additional factor in Design Thinking, these spaces are always used jointly with others. A team space should therefore not be the space of just two people on the team, but the home of the entire team. This creates a sense of collective ownership, which has a positive impact on team success (Gray et al., 2020). Accordingly, it is important that teams understand the team space and the entire Innovation Space as *their* space to a certain degree and can develop this feeling of being "at home" together. Strategies for doing so are outlined in Sect. 4.

3   Construction Plan: Typology of the Innovation Space in Design Thinking

3.1   Functions of the Innovation Space in Design Thinking

Based on the concept of "jobs to be done" by Clayton Christensen, we can distinguish between three main tasks (jobs) of space in Design Thinking—functional, emotional, and social (Christensen et al., 2016). Christensen understands a job as the progress a person wants to make in a particular context. According to this view, it is the room's job to support the person in achieving this progress as best as possible.

Functional: The basic requirements

The functional job of a space in Design Thinking is to enable participants to collaborate with others in the Design Thinking mode. Put simply, this requires a place where the team can work, which, first of all, should meet the basic needs of sufficient size, light, temperature, and noise. The latter can definitely be a challenge in a workshop with several teams working close to each other. A basic set of furniture is also required—this normally comprises seating, a table, and a whiteboard; but more on this later. Another functional task of the room is to provide the necessary materials—be it post-its and pens, or extensive prototyping materials. It is important to keep these elements as flexible as possible so that the coaches (while preparing) and the teams (during the workshop) can easily adapt the spatial conditions to their needs or the requirements of the respective phase of the workshop.

Emotional: Curiosity, inspiration, and ownership

Space also has an important emotional function in Design Thinking. First, Design Thinking spaces usually look different from a conventional office workplace or meeting room. This difference alone triggers emotions when you first enter the space—curiosity, joy, or a desire to get down to work in the best case. However, it can also lead to fear of the unknown or a rejection, because writable walls and colorful post-its look more like "kindergarten" than serious work. Second, objects or elements in the space can inspire participants, for example, by acting as affordances—like the aforementioned full shelves of materials, or even empty frameworks on whiteboards that beg to be filled in. The overall atmosphere can also help create the openness needed for inspiration and innovation (Thrash & Elliot, 2004). Third, the space in Design Thinking must allow the participants to feel more or less safe and "at home," i.e., create a sense of ownership (see above).

Social: Collaboration and being human

The social task of the space in Design Thinking consists of supporting collaboration and "being human." In contrast to cooperation, where tasks are solved by using a division of labor, Design Thinking relies on collaboration, and thus on dynamic, joint processing of the issues being engaged with. This means that everyone in the team should be able to participate at any time. The space must reflect this by giving everyone a place with equal rights and not forcing anyone into the second row. More-over, this is one of the reasons why Design Thinking has a preference for whiteboards: While a table usually results in half of the team looking at materials upside down, a larger vertical surface allows everyone to read and write and, if arranged appropri-ately, be the same distance from the whiteboard. The room's task of fostering collab-oration does not only apply to a team, but also to collaboration between teams. Thus, the exchange with a neighboring team can lead to valuable inspirations, provided that the space enables such an exchange or even actively induces it through appropriate meeting areas (those famous chance meetings around the water cooler).

As another social aspect, however, the space must also do justice to each partic-ipant in their role as a human being. That is, the space should support each person as a whole, and not just as a creative team member. This may seem a bit esoteric at first, but spaces wanting to promote a human-centered way of working should, first and foremost, be human-centered themselves and lead by example. Specifically, this means that places to retreat to during breaks and quieter areas should be available as a counterbalance to dynamic teamwork. The iconic red couch as a place to relax, access to fresh air and nature, or an offer of beverages are examples. Of course, there are also numerous individual requirements of certain groups of participants, such as access for people with limited mobility.

3.2   Levels of the Innovation Space in Design Thinking

When discussing space in Design Thinking, we intuitively tend to think of a team space with stools, a table, and whiteboards. Certainly, this is where the most intense part of collaboration in Design Thinking takes place. However, the team space is only the lowest of the three levels of space in Design Thinking, which are described below.

Macro-level: Location, location, location

It is important to develop an understanding of the location of the innovation space in relation to other spaces in the building or the location of the building within the campus. This is irrespective of whether you are free to choose a new appropriate location for the innovation space or whether you have to work with an existing space. An innovation room in the basement of a company's headquarters building is completely different from the hip loft in a big city nearby or the new glass box on the company grounds. Three examples: The conference pavilion of Swiss furniture manufacturer Vitra was designed by Japanese architect Tadao Ando and deliberately built slightly on the outskirts, on the perimeter of the company grounds (Kries, 2020). A winding path leads to the entrance, thus protecting several cherry trees from the chainsaw, and also ensuring to this day that the employees have a few minutes' walk to get to the meeting. At the same time, they are gently slowed down, because they cannot head straight for the entrance (at this point, the inclined reader will most likely have noticed the analogy to the fruit department in the supermarket). This way, the journey to the meeting already becomes part of the spatial experience, and the location of the innovation space influences how the participants arrive at their workshop or training course. Second example: The HPI School of Design Thinking is located in Potsdam, while the majority of students come from Berlin. The train ride and the deliberate departure and journey from the metropolis to Brandenburg are thus already a small part of the spatial experience. In the summer, participants will most likely view this as a country outing, a positive impression reinforced by Griebnitzsee, a lake in the near vicinity. By contrast, they will probably react with the thought of "somewhat remote" in the winter due to Berlin's unreliable commuter trains and the long ride. Third example: In one company, the innovation space is right on the ground floor and next to the entrance to the main building. It has a large window, to the effect that all the employees walk past it and can take a peek inside. A sign next to the entrance door lists the persons to contact if anyone would like to experience working on the other side of the glass firsthand. In the meantime, some of the other companies on the same premises have even started using the space—the location near the entrance makes this convenient.

To sum up, the location of the innovation space and the way to get there constitute an initial influencing factor on the innovation space, one that cannot always be jointly determined, but that can be jointly designed and must certainly be jointly considered.

Meso-level: Being in the zone

The meso-level refers to the innovation space as such in which the actual collaborative work in Design Thinking takes place. Depending on the size, it can be an entire building, a floor or just a single room, possibly with an anteroom. Taken together, it combines various functional areas that are necessary or desirable for working in Design Thinking. These are referred to as "zones" in the following (see also Schwemmle et al., 2018–2021). The zones of an innovation space are:

- Team zones are with team spaces where teams retreat to work. A team space can usually accommodate four to eight people and has a table, seating, and vertical surfaces for writing. The following section deals with team spaces in detail.
- The presentation and plenary zone is where presentations and inputs take place and which should be large enough to accommodate all the participants. Often this zone is also used for lectures and events that are not related to Design Thinking.
- The prototyping zone where, as a minimum, materials are provided and things are permitted to get a bit messy. Depending on the focus of the innovation space, advanced technical equipment, ranging from saws to 3D printers, or a small studio with an edit suite, may also be located here.
- The entrance area, where a wardrobe or lockers are often located. Since this is often the first real impression of the space that participants and visitors get, it is worth investing some work here: Is there a sign that can be used as a background for photographs that may be posted on Instagram? Does the door stick? Does the bell work? Are there boxes or empty crates standing around? Are there signs to help you find your way around?

- The lounge, which invites you to linger before and after the workshop, but also during breaks, or where you can quickly retreat. It also has enough space for participants to have a drink or sit down comfortably.
- The quiet zone where participants can retreat.
- A space for coaches to go for briefings and meetings or to store materials.

Not all the zones are needed in all contexts. At the HPI School of Design Thinking, for example, all of these zones are present. They are supplemented by a prop room with costumes and props, offices for the staff, a workshop for intensive prototyping with saws and similar tools, and a room with virtual/augmented reality equipment (Schwemmle et al., 2018). If the workshop takes place in a hotel, there is usually a single meeting room that houses the team zones and the plenary zone. The lounge is then in the vestibule or in the restaurant. Due to the flexibility of the space and furniture, the zones can be rearranged if there is too little space available. The plenary zone is created by pushing all the team spaces to the edge of the room and then meeting in the center. Rearrangements like that do take some extra time, but can by all means be used actively as an element of the workshop—it is not a bug, it is a feature!

Primary consideration should be given to three factors when arranging the zones in the room: First is the arrangement of the zones beneficial for the flow of a workshop? In other words: Can participants reach the presentation zone quickly, or is it located at the end of the floor? What is the first impression? Do you have to meander through all the team spaces to get to the plenary zone, not to mention the wardrobe area? Second: Is the arrangement appropriate with regard to volume of noise? Putting the prototyping area next to the quiet zone might not be very practical, for example. And third: Can we have a more active formulation? "Will the space also work for other users and use cases?" For example, a number of different events could take place in parallel, or the premises could be used for an evening event with a lecture. If all the people attending the evening event first have to walk through all the team spaces that are still being used by teams or are at least cluttered with paper and other materials, this could cause problems.

Figure 1 uses an example of a schematic floor plan to show how a room can be divided into zones like the ones described and how these zones are frequented during a workshop (the concept was developed together with Carmen Luippold and Claudia Nicolai). The fairly open floor plan with two entrances and two self-contained rooms initially leaves many options open. The proposed zoning takes the aforementioned factors into account: The quiet zone is in a room that can be locked and is as far away from the team spaces and prototyping as possible. The coaches' room is close to the plenary area and the prototyping zone—this ensures short distances and also makes it possible to lock away certain materials or pieces of equipment for prototyping. The plenary area is centrally located and quite easily accessible from all the team spaces. Nevertheless, the zoning is not necessarily perfect: The "top right" team space is remote and difficult to see due to its location; the five team spaces across from the prototyping zone might get quite noisy at times. Figures C through F show how people were assigned to the individual zones during a workshop. Figure G illustrates the flexibility of the space, allowing two different events to take place simultaneously

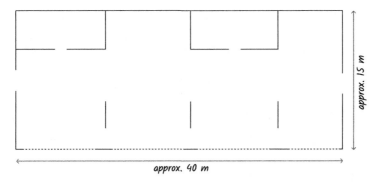

A. The empty floorplan

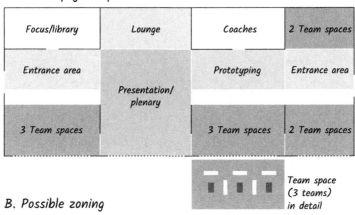

B. Possible zoning

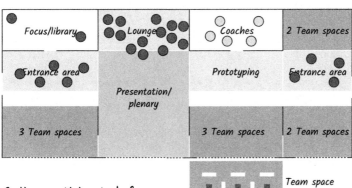

C. Use: participants before
the workshops starts

Fig. 1 Zoning an area for use for design thinking (Author's own image) **a**. Blank floor plan, **b**. Possible zoning, **c**. Use before a workshop begins, **d**. Use during a presentation in a plenary session, **e**. Use during a teamwork phase, **f**. Use for two simultaneous events

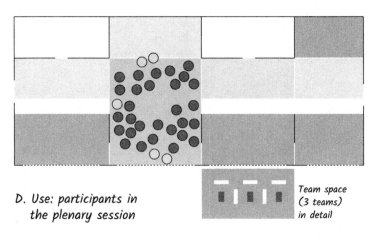

D. Use: participants in
   the plenary session

Team space
(3 teams)
in detail

Focus/library	Lounge	Coaches	2 Team spaces
Entrance area		Prototyping	Entrance area
	Presentation/ plenary		
Team spaces		3 Team spaces	2 team spaces

E. Use: participants in
   the team spaces

Focus/library	Lounge	Coaches	2 Team spaces
Entrance area	Prototyping	Prototyping	Entrance area
Team spaces	Presentation/ plenary	Presentation/ plenary	2 Team spaces

F. Flexible use:
   Simultaneous events

Fig. 1 (continued)

by the use of a spatial and acoustic divider (e.g., curtain, movable walls, whiteboards, foldable wall) and permitting the zones to be adapted by simply moving furniture. Even with the spatial separation, though, it is advisable to coordinate the schedule so that there are not two presentations taking place right next to each other at the same time.

Micro-level: Where the magic happens

The team space is the actual collaborative work space shared by four to eight people who are usually guided or accompanied by a coach. The standard furnishings and equipment in a team space consist of stools, a mobile team table, and two mobile whiteboards. Details of the furnishings and equipment are discussed in the following section. Depending on the length of the formats, participants spend a few hours or, in the case of long projects, several months in "their" team space. It is helpful for the teams to use fixed spaces and not have to clear the space every evening, especially when working on a long project. At the same time, rotating team spaces can add some dynamism to a workshop.

3.3 Users of the Innovation Space

As an approach that is human-centered and user-centered, Design Thinking focuses on the user. Of course, this way of thinking is also beneficial when engaging with the users of the innovation space. We will only sketch an overview of different groups with a few typical needs here to ensure that we do not focus on just a few groups while ignoring those groups that are often neglected.

- Participants in workshops or courses: Where can you safely store jackets and bags? Where can I charge my cell phone?
- Coaches: Where can I have a short private conversation during the break? I need to print something quickly—where can I do that?
- Lead coaches: How are the teams doing time-wise? Do I have an eye on everything?
- Project partners/project sponsors: Where do I have to go? Is there a wardrobe area? Where can I wait? What exactly happens in here?
- Guests: Is there WiFi? Where can I park? What exactly happens here? Are there any written materials available?
- Facilities management: Can the adhesive strips be removed from the wall without damaging it? Is it certain that no one will write on the windows with waterproof pens?
- Fire safety officer: Can you still see where the fire extinguishers are located? Are the rescue and escape routes always clear, or are they completely blocked?
- Cleaning service: Can this be thrown away?

3.4 Typology

If we merge the aforementioned three elements—functions, levels, and users—we obtain a multidimensional matrix of the innovation space. Thus, each of the three levels possesses all three functions, and each user group has functional, emotional, and social demands that it places on the space. Taking all the combinations into consideration would naturally make things far too complex, and many demands may be contrary to each other, so that they cannot be dealt with to the full satisfaction of all the user groups. Nevertheless, it is important to be aware of this complexity and, when making decisions, to perhaps consider the perspective of user groups that may not be given much attention. Especially when designing or redesigning innovation spaces, it is immensely helpful to also enable the designers to understand this. Wherever possible, architects or interior designers should be invited to sit in on a one-day or two-day workshop so they can better understand why certain components are important. Afterward, they will be able to use their expertise in a much more targeted manner and achieve better solutions in the end.

4   Selecting and Using Furnishings and Equipment: Design Elements and the Space as an Instrument in Design Thinking

The previous sections have provided the basic aspects and a structure for the innovation space. Ultimately, this theoretical framework must lead to a concrete setup and workshop design. The following considerations deal with aspects of this implementation. While the sections on furnishings and equipment focus primarily on the specific elements and the process for selecting them, the section on use highlights the active work with the innovation space during a workshop.

If you have read the previous sections carefully, you will probably not expect to be given a specific list of items to order now so you can furnish and equip your innovation room "perfectly." The question of whether you should buy red or green chairs, from which manufacturer, and whether to buy chairs at all is highly individual and dependent on the budget, the objectives, users and use of the innovation space, and corporate culture. This makes it impossible to provide a one-size-fits-all answer. However, the sections on furnishings and equipment aim to accomplish two things: First, it gives you a few methodical suggestions on how you can successfully perform the task of furnishing and equipping. And second, it creates an understanding of what is important and why, so that you can find the specific appropriate elements, taking into account your individual situation.

4.1 A Project in Itself: How to Plan the Space and Select Furnishings and Equipment

Planning a Design Thinking space, including the furnishings and equipment, can be viewed as a small Design Thinking project in itself. In other words: Approach the questions associated with the furnishings and equipment in the Design Thinking mode or conduct a workshop on the topic with a small team! Below are some inspirational ideas and ways of thinking for this purpose.

Get to the bottom of the jobs related to the furnishings and equipment

Earlier in this chapter, you learned about the distinction between the functional, emotional, and social jobs of a space. This distinction also applies to the individual furnishings and pieces of equipment, as many elements do not just have a single functional job or only one emotional or social job. Instead, they have multiple functional jobs and multiple emotional or social jobs (Schwemmle et al., 2020). An example: What is the job of a whiteboard? As discussed earlier, it allows an entire team to work together on one task, everyone can read and write, and you can regroup things, circle things, and simply wipe them away again. If this were the whiteboard's only job, it could also be replaced by writable walls or—Cleaning Staff Members, don't listen!—windows.

A whiteboard can perform even more jobs, though: If multiple teams are working side by side, a whiteboard can serve as an acoustic and territorial partition, as well as a delimitation of the team space. It also allows a team space to be divided into two groups that can work on different aspects in parallel. Mobile whiteboards make it easy to change locations and even move work outside. As a coach, I like to play with the confines of space and, during synthesis, for example, lock the team within their own data by moving the whiteboards to tighten the space. The whiteboard frequently serves as a presentation surface as well or is used in prototyping—whiteboards make excellent houses, buses, trains, and horse carriages!

So, whenever you are planning to purchase individual elements, especially furniture, or just viewing your existing inventory, be clear about the different jobs that the furnishings or equipment are supposed to perform. For one thing, you will save money, and, for the other, they can be used more flexibly. Richard Perez, the founding director of the d-school in South Africa (cf. his Chap. 5 in this book) once summed this up aptly: It is too expensive to not be multi-functional.

Tackle the matter from two perspectives

You can approach innovation spaces from two perspectives—and it does not matter if you are building a space for the first time or preparing an existing space for a workshop. The first perspective should be more functional: How many participants? What kind of workshop? How much room? This can be used as a basis for planning and setting up team spaces or zoning a team space. The other perspective does not use these individual components as a basis, but instead—remember the example with your partner or dog and how they smell when it rains?—the holistic atmosphere of the room. What kind of effect should the room have on the participants? In what mood do you think they will arrive? What do you want the space to represent to the outside world—an iconic lighthouse, an operating room where the big issues are placed on the table, or an artist's studio where you can paint the town red (or any other color) for once? Then, there is the question of how this atmosphere can best be created (see Schwemmle et al., 2020 for specific suggestions on implementation).

You have probably viewed spaces primarily from the first perspective until now. That perspective is certainly important, because, if there is not enough room for half of the participants, or if you have rented a large factory hall for a team of five, that is difficult for many reasons. However, I encourage you to think from the second perspective as well, and then merge both aspects. That starts with a grand gesture: Of course, you can place iconic lamps and armchairs, or objects related to the topic, in the space. But you can also ask yourself some very simple questions: Do I arrange post-its and pens, all sorted neatly by color, on the tables, evoking more of an atmosphere of office supplies, or do I create a chaotic stack with lots of different shapes and colors?

Very important: Do not overdo it! Think about your last visit to a museum: Which wallpaper did you like the most? Probably none at all, because you do not go to a museum to look at the walls, you go to see the artwork. And in the same way, you should not cover every free square inch with pictures, colors, or quotes, but leave enough free surfaces that can be occupied during the workshop. How is a team supposed to acquire ownership if there is no room left for its own creations? That would be like having a fully furnished apartment with no room left for your own furniture.

Take an iterative approach and test

The Design Thinking principles of testing and iterating also apply when working with spaces. That means: Try out different configurations in different workshops and reflect on how certain things in the interior design have worked out. Observe to see whether your actions have led to the desired changes or ask participants directly what their first impression was, for example.

Testing is especially important when furnishing and equipping new rooms: Before buying ten tables and 60 chairs, it would be best to conduct a workshop with one table and six chairs. You will then quickly find out whether the supposedly flexible table actually fits through the door or whether the chairs make annoying noises on the floor.

The iteration still is not over when the innovation space is all set up. Due to the increase in digital elements in workshops, more technology is needed in the team spaces. Certain changes in the space which have been tried out by one team have worked out and should also be used in other spaces. A furniture manufacturer has developed a new product that you want to test. And a change in use, such as a development away from short introductory workshops toward longer projects, may also require spatial adjustments.

4.2   The Fundamentals of Equipment: Elements of the Design Thinking Space

Despite all the attempts not to give you a ready-made shopping list, there are of course some elements that you will need for a Design Thinking workshop or project. They are presented briefly here, but the list does not claim to be final or complete. For illustration purposes, I have presented extreme examples of minimum and maximum furnishings and equipment.

Team space

I consider vertical writable surfaces and a place for depositing materials (pens, markers, and post-its) to constitute the absolute minimum requirement for a team space.

The writable surfaces can be produced by taping a wall with an anti-static adhesive whiteboard film or by using cabinets and windows. If the room has a pinboard, then packing paper (alternatively: flipchart paper) and pins help to turn the pinboard into a whiteboard in no time. Of course, a flipchart can also be used. However, it has the disadvantage that only a few people can work on it at the same time, making it suitable only for small teams. Ideally, each team should have two to three wide mobile whiteboards and a few smaller boards. They can be used to post the agenda, for example, and can easily be transported to other rooms. In hybrid teams, the whiteboard can be replaced by digital solutions, or it can at least be filmed by a webcam for the virtual participants.

The only materials needed are post-its and pens. These can be put into small bags and easily placed on a table or chair. Specifically, you will need: one pad and one pen per team member on a stool that serves as a table and four whiteboard markers. If you use a bistro table instead of a stool, there will still be room for drinks and a few more pens or magnets. A larger table used as a writing surface is usually beneficial when interview transcripts are supposed to be transferred to post-its, or when prototyping. A flexible, smaller mobile team table, at which participants can work while standing, offers enough space for these tasks and can be put away again quickly.

Now let us turn to the seating: I have already conducted workshops where we stood the whole time (the participants were surprised initially, but then loved it). If someone does not want to stand any longer or cannot, they simply lean against a wall or pull up a chair. You will be amazed at how much energy is generated by standing as a team! Do not underestimate the group effect: Participants who are sitting usually get up again quickly, because they notice that it is much easier to participate when standing. Of course, that will only work if you are also standing the whole time yourself and do not permanently exclude anyone (e.g., people with limited mobility). If you want to provide seating in the team space, use stools that make it easy to stand up and move, and also prevent slouching.

So what do you do when you walk into a traditional hotel meeting room? Move all the tables and chairs aside or work in another section of the room. Use bistro tables for each team and convert bulletin boards into whiteboards by using packing paper. Ready!

Last but not least, a timer is very helpful in a team space so that the teams can keep track of their time themselves. Digital solutions can also be used, of course, provided the software or app is permanently visible and not covered by other programs.

Materials

As explained earlier, post-its, pens for writing on the post-its, and markers for the whiteboards are fully sufficient for most phases of a workshop. White paper or notebooks can be helpful when conducting interviews, but often participants are so fond of post-its that they only use their notebook to keep their post-its anyway. I personally prefer post-its in the 76 mm × 127 mm format in different colors to allow color coding. Fatter black pens prevent writing that is too spidery, small, and illegible.

The equipment and materials needed for prototyping vary, depending on the workshop and its focus. A4 cardboard boxes in different colors, empty cardboard boxes, glue, scissors, crayons/colored pencils, modeling clay, pipe cleaners, and LEGOs provide a good basis for introductory workshops and are easy to transport. Open shelves and transparent boxes are well suited for storage. This way, everyone can quickly see where things are, plus the participants will be encouraged to try things out (affordances!). Storage in a mobile cart allows the materials to be rolled to the center for the appropriate phase. The HPI School of Design Thinking uses a workshop cart with office supplies (post-its, various pens, markers, staplers, scissors, glue, etc.) and large shelves with transparent boxes near the team spaces stocked with various materials for prototyping (fabric, cardboard, foil, paper, modeling clay, etc.). There is also a prop room with objects and costumes for role-playing, a room for digital prototyping with a 3D printer, vinyl cutter, audio and video editing software, an area for working with Styrofoam and cardboard boxes, as well as a workshop for wood-working equipped with saws, drills, etc. In addition, a specially prepared room with 3D glasses can be used for augmented/virtual reality prototypes.

Equipment for the coach

Even in small workshops, I always have a small gong with me so I can end work phases with a consistent signal. Of course, you could also play a sound, but a gong can be played at different volumes and seems less technical.

I always bring my own flipchart and whiteboard markers, so I do not have to rely on the almost dried out markers with a limited assortment of colors that are usually available. Your kit should also include a roll of masking tape—you never know what else you might need it for!

Music plays an important role as well. It can influence moods and create an atmosphere without making any major changes to the room. I have prepared or selected diverse playlists to support certain moods with the appropriate music. Electro Swing, for example, has managed to support every prototyping phase so far. I always have a Bluetooth box with me, because not all meeting rooms have good sound systems, and even in the 2020s, it often takes several technicians to operate the building's technical systems. Wireless systems are helpful in workshop rooms where specific zones can be selected or played differently. Playlists for different phases can be provided centrally for all the users.

A projector in the room certainly would not hurt. However, what is true for sound systems is even more true for projectors—so be sure to test connectivity and always have enough adapter cables with you. For smaller groups, a TV or smartboard can also be useful instead of a projector, which is usually permanently installed in a location that is determined by the screen in the room. They are easier to integrate into plenary session scenes and avoid the classic lecture or presentation situation. This also avoids the need for participants to move to a different spot just so they can see the screen. Alternatively, you can exclusively use a (prepared) whiteboard or draw sketches on A2 paper and place them on an easel. The more technology we are used to, the more refreshing and surprising these kinds of analog forms of presentation will seem. But do not underestimate preparation time—it is sometimes easier to prepare a slide deck than to create a well-structured whiteboard.

Making specific suggestions for all the other zones is rather difficult, as the design depends very much on contextual factors. Moreover, these other zones are no longer highly specific to Design Thinking, but tend to follow established spatial concepts (see Schwemmle et al., 2021 for supplementary thoughts and sketches).

4.3 Let us Move It: Space as an Element in Design Thinking

The best concept for a space and the most fantastic mobile table will be useless if the space is not used adequately and the mobile table is not moved. Accordingly, a coach or instructor who works actively with the innovation space and its elements is key to success. To avoid exceeding the scope of this chapter, the following sections contain only selected inputs for the use of team spaces. More in-depth suggestions can be found in Klooker et al. (2019) and Schwemmle et al. (2020, 2021).

The initial situation

The spatial setup that participants find at the beginning of the space already sends important signals or affordances. If there are no chairs in the team space, no one will sit down, and the participants will anticipate certain dynamics. If there are post-its and pens on the stools, people will automatically pick them up before sitting down. You should therefore prepare the team space accordingly at the beginning of a workshop. I personally take at least 10–15 min to do this before the participants arrive. Creating a tidy atmosphere or providing beverages can also contribute to a positive atmosphere.

Transformation of the team space

Unfortunately, experience has shown: Mobile tables and whiteboards are moved too rarely. They are usually only moved when something has to be presented or another team needs the space. One could summarize this as a tendency to react rather than act. It would be better to proactively adapt the spatial environment to suit the next phase in Design Thinking. In the beginning, the coach should most likely assume this role, but in longer projects, the goal should definitely be to delegate this task to the team.

Figure 2 illustrates the transformability of a team space by showing different configurations that can be achieved with the same furniture in the same space—two whiteboards, one table, six stools (A). The elements are shown to scale. The first figures (A–J) relate to phases of the Design Thinking process, while the others illustrate possible applications outside of this field.

Diagram B shows the standard setup: table with chairs between whiteboards. There is usually no need for a table or board for the check-in phase, when the team has an opportunity to get to know each other. Here, the focus should be on the team, which is achieved by arranging a small circle of chairs (C). To move from the check-in to the understand phase, the team only needs to gather in a semicircle around one board (D). It makes sense to work at the table when compiling findings after conducting interviews, so that boards will not be needed in this phase (E). The table can be rolled back to the edge of the space for the synthesis phase. The data is initially analyzed on a whiteboard (F), which is expanded during the process to include the POV statement on a second board (G). It might be useful to move for the ideation phase—there should be at least enough free space to use idea train as a brainstorming method around a whiteboard (H). Next, prototyping will need a table again and possibly a view of a board with the ideas. For the testing phase, a test scenario can be set up with some team members staggered a bit to the back and watching while a tester (gray) is guided through the testing procedure by two team members. Whiteboards serve as partitions or contain information required for testing (J). If the team of six splits into two smaller teams, they can also be accommodated by the existing team space: The two teams can work "back to back" on two boards (K), be separated by two boards (L), or build prototypes at opposite ends of a table (M). For the presentation, the team space can be converted into an exhibition stand with seating for visitors (N) or results can be presented entirely without chairs, as in a gallery (O). All these conversions probably take less than 120 s, but noticeably change the room!

Generation of ownership

As the aspect of ownership has been emphasized at various points in this chapter, you will find below some inspirational ideas for supporting the development of ownership in a targeted manner.

In order to gain ownership of the innovation space, the participants must first become familiar with the space. So, give them time to walk through the space once and take it in, or you can offer a short tour. You should also leave room for setting up the team space or carrying out any planning (reserve time for to-dos, a candy bowl, etc.) during check-in. If you do not reflect actively on the team space, it will be taken as a given. Only by actively engaging with the team space, will the potential for change become visible, thus enabling the team to individualize it. Small things like placing the team's name or a photograph of the team in the space can be helpful here.

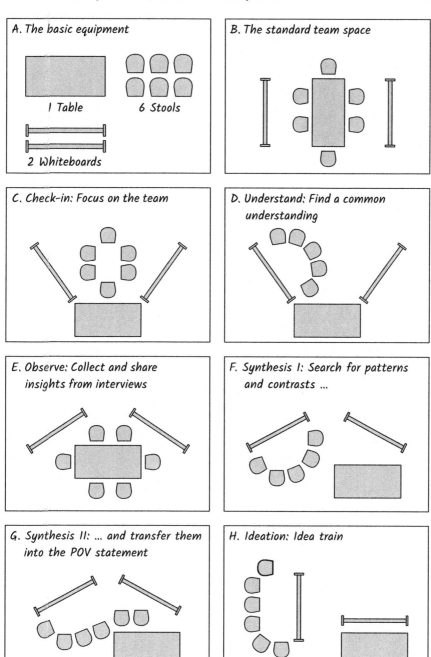

Fig. 2 Different team space configurations in the course of a Design Thinking process (Author's own image)

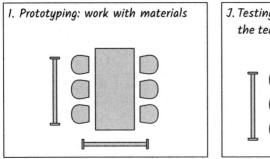

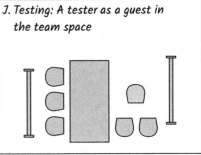

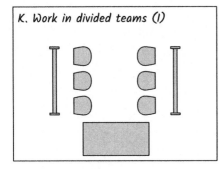

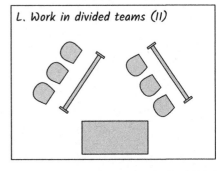

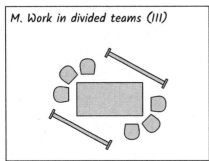

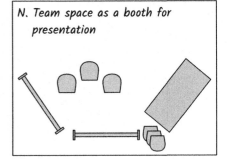

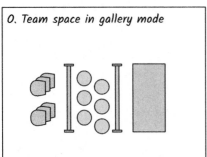

Fig. 2 (continued)

The development of ownership also requires an emotional attachment, not just a rational one (Van Dyne & Pierce, 2004). Capturing pleasant experiences during the project, e.g., photographs of interviewed persons or objects and prototypes, can support this bond. Activities outside of the actual workshop that take place in the space and can be initiated by the participants (a meet-up, a brown-bag lunch, a shared meal) can strengthen ownership with regard to the overall innovation space.

Ownership across the team can only be developed through reflection. During check-out, for example, the team can briefly discuss how they felt about working in the team space, and whether any adjustments were needed. Particularly in longer projects, teams often discover other areas of the innovation space for themselves, where they are more likely to be able to work without disturbances.

Of course, ownership also requires an appropriate protection of space: Teams should respect each other's team spaces and not walk through them unthinkingly. If there are no other workshops taking place, it is beneficial if the teams do not to have to clear their space after working and if the spaces are not changed in the teams' absence. If, for example, an event takes place and the team spaces have to be reduced or moved, the team members may perceive this as an "intrusion" into their team space. It would then be better to ask the teams to reduce their spaces in advance.

Many participants find space to be something abstract, so that the coach's active support is especially crucial at the beginning of a workshop or project. Last but not least, a team must get to know the possibilities offered by a team space first. Merely pointing out and maybe trying different configurations as shown in Fig. 2 can develop ownership and intensify the use of the space by the team.

5　Discussion and Outlook

This chapter has provided an initial theoretical foundation for a very comprehensive understanding of the innovation space to enable the reader to make better informed concrete decisions for setting up, equipping, and using a space. Of course, the amount of time set aside for the space during a workshop depends on many factors. However, I hope that, even if time is short, you will take the opportunity to at least consider the most important aspects of space. Perhaps the thoughts and examples have also inspired you to observe more closely in the future, i.e., how are spaces designed and how are they used by their users—be it in Design Thinking, in a museum, or in a train hall.

Ultimately, technological developments and the consequences of the COVID-19 pandemic have significantly influenced the aspect of space in Design Thinking. For one, workshops are increasingly being held only virtually or in a hybrid format. For the other, onsite workshops require strict hygiene measures. These aspects can only be touched on here, but the good news is: If you understand the fundamentals and implications of physical space in Design Thinking, then you can also design digital spaces! For example, when planning a digital workshop, consideration must be given to the resulting complex concept of space: Each participant has their own physical space and, in addition, works together with others in a shared virtual space. To generate ownership, I therefore usually ask the participants to introduce themselves not only by name, but also by briefly stating their location and giving a glance of their surroundings. This helps provide an understanding of how to create a shared space while respecting the spaces of each individual. Similarly, the theories presented also provide valuable input for workshops that are subject to hygiene regulations. For example, you can consider how the job of a whiteboard or table can be divided among different objects that ensure a minimum distance can be maintained. Clipboards can be used as writing pads, for example.

Regardless of whether physical, virtual, or hybrid: Explore and exploit the potential of space and, when doing so, equally involve walls, furniture, and people!

References

Brown, G., Lawrence, T. B., & Robinson, S. L. (2005). Territoriality in organizations. *The Academy of Management Review, 30*(3), 577–594.

Carey, A. (1967). The Hawthorne studies: A radical criticism. *American Sociological Review, 32*(3), 403–416.

Chemero, A. (2003). An outline of a theory of affordances. *Ecological Psychology, 15*(2), 181–195.

Christensen, C. M., Hall, T., Dillon, K., & Duncan, D. S. (2016). *Competing against luck.* HarperCollins.

Franke, R. H., & Kaul, J. D. (1978). The Hawthorne experiments: First statistical interpretation. *American Sociological Review, 43*(5), 623–643.

Gray, S. M., Knight, A. P., & Baer, M. (2020). On the emergence of collective psychological ownership in new creative teams. *Organization Science, 31*(1), 141–164.

Günzel, S. (2008). *Raumwissenschaften.* suhrkamp taschenbuch wissenschaft.

Hassard, J. S. (2012). Rethinking the Hawthorne studies: The Western Electric research in its social, political and historical context. *Human Relations, 65*, 1431–1461.

Hatch, M. J., & Cunliffe, A. L. (2006). *Organization theory: Modern, symbolic, and postmodern perspectives* (2nd ed.). Oxford University Press.

Holmquist, L. E. (2005). Prototyping: Generating ideas or cargo cult designs? *Interactions, 12*(2), 48–54.

Jiménez, F. (2012). In welche Psychofallen wir im Supermarkt tappen. *Welt Online.* Retrieved from https://www.welt.de/gesundheit/psychologie/article106351705/In-welche-Psychofallen-wir-im-Supermarkt-tappen.html.

King, D. B., Wertheimer, M., Keller, H., & Crochetiere, K. (1994). The legacy of Max Wertheimer and gestalt psychology. *Social Research, 61*(4), 907–935.

Klooker, M., Schwemmle, M., Nicolai, C., & Weinberg, U. (2019). Making use of innovation spaces: Towards a framework of strategizing spatial interventions. In C. Meinel & L. Leifer (Eds.), *Design thinking research. Looking further: Design thinking beyond solution-fixation* (pp. 75–96). Springer.

Kries, M. (2020). *Der vitra campus: Architektur design industrie.* Vitra Design Museum.

Lindstrom, L. (1993). *Cargo Cult: Strange stories of desire from Melanesia and beyond.* University of Hawaii Press.

North, A. C., Hargreaves, D. J., & McKendrick, J. (1999). The influence of in-store music on wine selections. *Journal of Applied Psychology, 84*(2), 271–276.

Schwemmle, M., Nicolai, C., Klooker, M., & Weinberg, U. (2018). From place to space: How to conceptualize places for design thinking. In H. Plattner, C. Meinel, & L. Leifer (Eds.), *Design thinking research. Making distinctions: Collaboration versus cooperation* (pp. 275–98). Springer.

Schwemmle, M., Nicolai, C., Klooker, M., & Weinberg, U. (2020). Overcoming prominent pitfalls of work space (re-)design: Using a theoretical perspective to reflect and shape practice. In C. Meinel & L. Leifer (Eds.), *Design thinking research. Investigating design team performance* (pp. 289–310). Springer.

Schwemmle, M., Nicolai, C., & Weinberg, U. (2021). Using 'space' in design thinking: Concepts, tools and insights for design thinking practitioners from research. In M. Schwemmle, C. Nicolai, & U. Weinberg (Eds.), *Design thinking research. Interrogating the doing* (pp. 123–145). Springer.

Sonnenfeld, J. A. (1985). Shedding light on the Hawthorne studies. *Journal of Organizational Behavior, 6*(2), 111–130.

Taylor, S., & Spicer, A. (2007). Time for space: A narrative review of research on organizational spaces. *International Journal of Management Reviews, 9*(4), 325–346.

Thrash, T. M., & Elliot, A. J. (2004). Inspiration: Core characteristics, component processes, antecedents, and function. *Journal of Personality and Social Psychology, 87*(6), 957–973.

Van Dyne, L., & Pierce, J. L. (2004). Psychological ownership and feelings of possession: Three field studies predicting employee attitudes and organizational citizenship behavior. *Journal of Organizational Behavior, 25*(4), 439–459.

Dr. Martin Schwemmle is a researcher at the HPI School of Design Thinking and part of the Design Thinking Research Program Potsdam-Stanford. His research interests include the innovative capacity of individuals, teams, and organizations, as well as the impact of Design Thinking. He is also a coach in the HPI D-School academic program and shares the findings of his research with companies and institutions in workshops and lectures. In addition to his doctorate at the University of Mannheim, he has a wide range of experience as the founder and managing director of an agency for graphics, communication, and journalism, and has also worked as a trainer and consultant. Martin Schwemmle has authored several books and academic publications. He considers the most difficult step for using Design Thinking in education to be the necessary change from a society and educational system oriented on efficiency to one oriented on impact. That is why he recommends always following Simon Sinek's advice at the start of workshops, initiatives, and meetings: "Start with Why!"

Where Context Matters—Design Thinking in South Africa

Richard Perez

Abstract The Hasso Plattner School of Design Thinking at the University of Cape Town (d-school) first started to teach design thinking courses in the first semester of 2016. One of the first pilot programs that was delivered was a 24-day Foundational Course in design thinking aimed at a diverse cohort of 30 postgraduate students from the university. The program spanned a period of 12 weeks and was modeled very closely on HPI's D-School Basic Track. By 2020, the d-school had taught just under 3500 students in the mind-set and practice of design thinking, varying from short introductions to integrated courses delivered in partnership with various faculties of the university. This chapter outlines some of the contextual factors that have influenced the formative years of the d-school from a teaching and learning perspective. Further, we look at how this influence has manifested itself in the various design thinking programs that the d-school offers.

1 Introduction

The Hasso Plattner School of Design Thinking at the University of Cape Town (d-school) first started to teach design thinking courses in the first semester of 2016. One of the first pilot programs that was delivered was a 24-day Foundational Course in design thinking aimed at a diverse cohort of 30 postgraduate students from the university. The program spanned a period of 12 weeks and was modeled very closely on HPI's D-School Basic Track. By 2020, the d-school had taught just under 3500 students in the mind-set and practice of design thinking, varying from short introductions to integrated courses delivered in partnership with various faculties of the university.

This chapter outlines some of the contextual factors that have influenced the formative years of the d-school from a teaching and learning perspective. Further,

R. Perez (✉)
The Hasso Plattner School of Design Thinking at UCT (d-School), Breakwater Campus, 9 Portswood Road, Green Point, 8002 Cape Town, South Africa
e-mail: richard.perez@uct.ac.za

© The Author(s), under exclusive license to Springer Nature Switzerland AG 2022
C. Meinel and T. Krohn (eds.), *Design Thinking in Education*,
https://doi.org/10.1007/978-3-030-89113-8_8

we look at how this influence has manifested itself in the various design thinking programs that the d-school offers.

2 Framing Design Thinking Within the South African Context

As the first of its kind in South Africa, the local d-school there spent the initial 4 years experimenting and testing a number of different teaching and learning formats aimed at enabling and training students in the mind-set and practice of design thinking. Over this period, a number of key contextual factors emerged which have been instrumental in how we approach, design, teach and deliver design thinking teaching and learning at the d-school. These factors include:

i.   The maturity of the design discipline in South Africa
ii.   Skills of the future
iii. Drive for entrepreneurship within South Africa
iv.   Complexity of local challenges
v.   South Africa's unique cultural diversity.

2.1 The Maturity of the Design Discipline in South Africa

As an emerging market economy and part of the Global South, South Africa's design industry is relatively fragmented, not well positioned and experiences little support and central coordination from a national government perspective. As such, South Africa has a relatively low level of maturity as regards both the appreciation and understanding of the value of design. The value of traditional design disciplines, such as architecture and graphic design, is reasonably understood, but other design disciplines, such as industrial design, service design and experience design, are lesser understood.

To help frame the value of design—and design thinking specifically—the d-school has positioned its method in the context of these traditional design disciplines, which are perhaps more familiar and better understood.

In this way, the d-school makes use of an adaptation of the original Danish Design Ladder[1] to assist in explaining what design thinking is and how design thinking fits into the more traditionally known disciplines of design, highlighting where it has come from and how it can be seen as an enhancement and evolution of its better understood counterparts (Fig. 1).

---

[1] The Design Ladder was developed by the Danish Design Centre in 2001 as a communicative model for illustrating the variation in companies' use of design. https://danskdesigncenter.dk/en/design-ladder-four-steps-design-use.

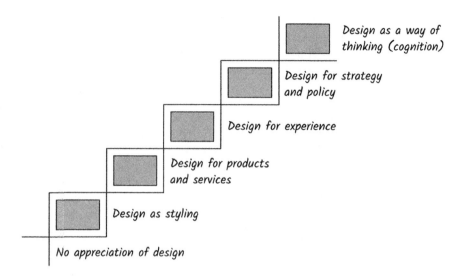

Fig. 1 D-school's adopted version of the Danish Design Ladder

Grounding design thinking relative to other design disciplines enables the d-school to build a narrative around how the design discipline has evolved over time. We see how design itself is disrupted by technology and needs to constantly evolve in order to remain relevant and to have an impact. Key to this narrative is illustrating the real value of design as something that does not lie in the end object or product. The real value of design instead lies in the thinking and doing process (aka design thinking), which is practiced to get to the end object or product.

With this framework in mind, it becomes evident that the design discipline has a role to play in developing new and often abstract outputs beyond the traditional "physically designed object." More precisely, it plays a role in developing experiences, systems, strategies and even policies. Furthermore, design thinking emphasizes that the value of a well-designed solution, and thus one that delivers real impact, sits in the diversity of the thinking that has come to the table. The more diverse the perspectives, the richer the understanding of a given problem and hence the end solution.

Having determined that the value of design sits within its approach, its mind-set, and the way it is structured, we have been able to create an entry point for students who previously may not have recognized their own capability to add value to a design process. These were individuals who had perhaps been told at an early age that they were not creative enough. They had been discouraged from venturing into creative disciplines for lack of ability to articulate their ideas through drawing. The reality is that those who undertook formal training at art and design colleges had their natural creativity enhanced through formal education and those who followed other study disciplines, unfortunately, did not have their inherent human creative talents nurtured.

At the d-school, we develop efficacy and an awareness that we as human beings all have the ability to be creative and contribute to the formulation of new and creative ideas—and this does not mean just those who went to an art and design college. This democratization of design is what lies at the heart of the teaching and learning that we do at the d-school. Our narrative here is often that the challenges we face today are far too complex and important to only be left up to designers to solve and, as such, we all have a role to play.

Anyone who has experienced a design thinking program has also experienced a definite individual growth and evolution when taking a course at the d-school. It has always been our conviction at the d-school that once someone is in our space, we will always be able to build their creative confidence and open their eyes to new and imaginative ways of tackling challenges and designing solutions in our complex world. However, the key challenge is getting the student into the d-school space in the first place. Many young students in South Africa do not see themselves as creative and hence shy away from a d-school environment. To overcome this, many of the programs that have been developed at the d-school are "low barrier to entry" introductory courses. They are aimed at gaining the key attributes and mind-sets of design thinking in as short a time as possible. The d-school has developed a series of introductory courses that vary from two-hour experiences to three-day experiences. These introductory courses are now offered in both in-person and online formats. All of these short format programs are aimed at students who are curious about design thinking but not yet prepared to invest a lot of their time in developing the appropriate skills.

In these short introductory courses, it is fundamental for us to create an experience that surprises and enlightens students so that they want to come back for more. Embedded in these short programs are exercises and experiences that expose students to some of the key mind-sets of design thinking, which include being human-centered, working collaboratively, embracing failure and being visual. In addition to this approach, the d-school introduces students to the elements of the unique ecosystem that enhances the learning journey: the value of working in multidisciplinary teams, the structure of the design process and the experience of working in a physical space that is geared toward fostering the behaviors and social activities needed to practice design thinking.

As part of this initial introduction to design thinking, the d-school provides its students with an overview of the learning journey that it ultimately aims to achieve. This is represented in the diagram below (Fig. 2).

Modeled on the learning ladder, the d-school's short introductory programs focus on exposing students to some of the key tools and methods of design thinking, with the longer courses offering the opportunity to apply these to real-world challenges in more of a project-based environment. However, our primary emphasis in teaching is the mind-set and values that underpin design thinking with the caveat that this takes time and practice. Students find great value in these early introductory courses as they not only provide them with pragmatic frameworks but also with an opportunity to experience what it is like to be creative (again) and to build efficacy and confidence, which is fundamental to the design thinking learning journey.

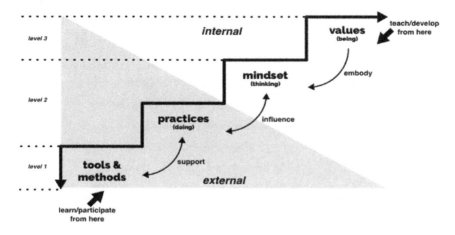

Fig. 2 D-school's learning ladder

2.2 Skills of the Future

A second key frame used at the d-school to attract students is that of bridging the relationship between design thinking and the skills of the future. Every five years, the World Economic Forum (WEF) publishes the *Future of Jobs* report highlighting the most critical skills needed over the next five-year period. This is especially important for students who are moving into the workplace and need to be equipped with graduate skills and experience that prepare them for the complexity and uncertainty of the emerging future. The Fourth Industrial Revolution has brought about an abundance of new opportunities and disruptions, but it has also highlighted the likelihood of redundancy in the future for many of the skills and jobs we are familiar with today. For a graduating student, this is of particular importance as traditional university degrees are generally not aligned to develop or nurture these future-needed skills. The skills outlined in the recent 2020 WEF *Future of Jobs* Report draw direct relationships with the learning outcomes and growth mind-set that many of the d-school's design thinking programs focus on. The list below highlights the top 10 skills that WEF has identified as those that will be needed by 2025 (Fig. 3).

All skills share intrinsic qualities that are essential for humans to remain relevant in the future: the need to refocus on ourselves and rediscover the characteristics that makes us uniquely human. These are skills such as critical thinking and analysis; creativity, originality and initiative; reasoning, problem solving and ideation. They are qualities that artificial intelligence and machine learning struggle to achieve. The d-school has always emphasized the lack of technology needed in teaching design thinking programs, where the deliberate focus is instead given to human interaction, creative thinking and the ability to imagine and enact new futures. At the core of the d-school experience is a mind-set and an approach to working collaboratively in a manner that enables us to unlock our inherent creative potential and to build

Top 10 skills of 2025
- *Analytical thinking and innovation*
- *Active learning and learning strategies*
- *Complex problem solving*
- *Critical thinking and analysis*
- *Creativity, originality and initiative*
- *Leadership and social influence*
- *Technology use, monitoring and control*
- *Technology design and programming*
- *Resilience, stress tolerance and flexibility*
- *Reasoning, problem-solving and ideation*

Source: Future of Jobs Report 2020, World Economic Forum.

Fig. 3 Top 10 skills of 2020 as identified by the World Economic Forum () Source: Future of jobs report 2020

confidence in ourselves. The d-school shows us that we all have the ability to be innovative and add value to the design process.

Over the past four years, the d-school in partnership with a number of faculties at the university has aimed to promote these future-oriented skills by infusing design thinking modules into existing curricula. Most noticeable has been the d-school's relationship with the Engineering Faculty and School of Information Technology, where it has developed a number of partner programs ranging from first-year curricula through to final-year curricula. For example, the Engineering Faculty partnership has focused on enhancing their design curriculum by introducing the design thinking lens as part of the engineer's design journey. This approach provides the faculty with an opportunity to teach students the value of spending more time exploring the problem space, understanding real human needs and questioning design directions rather than rushing into a technical solution that might not finally meet critical desirability aspects of the problem. The engineering students are introduced from the ground up to the concept of "designing the right thing" before "designing the thing right." The design thinking curriculum has also created the opportunity for students to learn how to work effectively in team-based projects in a structured and efficient way.

2.3 Drive for Entrepreneurship Within South Africa

In 2019, South Africa had an overall unemployment rate of 27.6% and a youth (aged 15–24) unemployment rate of 55.2%. Graduating from a university or college no longer guarantees job security in today's world and, as such, the South African government seeks to make entrepreneurship a career choice for graduating students. Through the department of higher education and training, the Entrepreneurship Development in Higher Education Program is intended to develop the entrepreneurial capacity of students as well as academics and leaders. The intention of this program is that students become more successful in terms of becoming active in business during and after their tertiary education. Introducing entrepreneurial activity to students during their studies can enable them to generate additional income and build confidence in starting their own businesses and fast tracking them to becoming economically independent and active. Upon graduation, a student is then better able to consider entrepreneurship as a career, either as a first choice, or as an alternative.

The mind-sets found in both entrepreneurship thinking and design thinking are very closely aligned. Since its inception, the d-school has developed partnerships naturally with existing entrepreneurship programs, both within and outside the university. The d-school currently contributes to a number of programs both formal academic courses and student-run programs. Traditionally, these entrepreneurship courses focused on the business aspects of starting and developing a new idea, and the addition of design thinking has introduced a more structured, co-creative approach to framing opportunities and testing ideas within a human-centered (customer) context. This complimentary approach has enabled design thinking to find its way seamlessly into these curriculums.

2.4   The Complexity of Local Challenges

South Africa is globally known for the complexity of its challenges and holds the highest Gini coefficient in the world. As part of its pedagogy, design thinking uses a project-based approach and, as such, the student teams at the d-school work with real local challenges.

Due to design thinking's emphasis on being human centered, it means that almost every challenge and resulting solution that the students work on exhibits a socioeconomic component. Many challenges the students work on can start off tame in nature, but through the design process, their inherent wickedness reveals itself. Such problems are often complex in nature, operate at a systems level and are generally immune to a single solution.

This means that from a teaching and learning perspective, the d-school needs to pay careful attention to teaching students how to maintain the complexity of a challenge space, which often results in developing a solution that has multiple points of view. Students often feel uncomfortable designing for only a single user and prefer to maintain multiple points of view throughout the design journey.

Furthermore, what makes a design solution truly successful is when the designer (or design team) work on projects and challenges that they are able to relate to and are passionate about solving. This is a key ingredient to the pedagogy of design thinking, and a critical part of the students' learning journey is using challenges

Fig. 4 Typical challenges that students at the d-school work on

that they are passionate about solving. Managing the expectations of the student has been an important lesson for the d-school. This challenge means balancing the learning journey of the student with his or her personal passion for solving a real-world problem. The d-school deliberately chooses challenges at different levels of complexity depending on where the student is in their design thinking learning journey. For the initial shorter programs, the d-school focuses on less complex "tamer" challenges where students can focus more on learning frameworks, structures and mind-sets of design thinking. Thereafter, students are introduced to more complex "wicked" problems that are generally more aligned with their personal interests and where the focus is to apply their design thinking knowledge to develop real implementable solutions.

The types of challenges that the d-school selects for its students are sourced from government, private sector as well as internally at the university itself. The nature and complexity of challenges that are typically found in d-school programs are highlighted in the infographic below (Fig. 4).

2.5 South African Cultural Diversity

South Africa is known globally as the Rainbow Nation, a title that captures the county's rich cultural and ethnic diversity. With 11 different official languages, the population of the country is one of the most complex and diverse in the world.

Fundamental to innovation is the diversity of the thinking that works on a problem. One of the key benefits of design thinking is that it provides structured frameworks that enable collaboration and co-creation within a diverse team. Traditionally, design thinking has embraced the diversity of different disciplines. Here, perspectives from these disciplines come together to challenge other world views and biases in pursuit of new and innovative solutions. At the d-school in South Africa, you will find this diversity as a standard within student teams, but you will also find an additional layer of richness with regard to cultural and ethnic diversity. This additional layer of diversity adds further depth to the students' discussions and framing of challenges. Furthermore, it feeds into the solution space where solutions become multifaceted in encompassing cultural and ethnic awareness.

In South Africa, we also have a value know as Ubuntu that closely aligns with the "embracing diversity" mind-set practiced in design thinking. Originating from the languages of Xhosa and Zulu, this philosophy is not exclusive to these two cultures but instead encapsulates numerous sets of values that have their roots in African cultures. Ubuntu defines togetherness and how all of our actions have an impact on others and on society. There is a commonly known definition of Ubuntu: "A person is a person through other people." This definition speaks to the fact of our universal connection, and that one person can only grow and progress through the growth and progression of others. This spirit is key to the design thinking learning journey of our d-school students where we emphasize the importance of embracing diversity not only from a discipline perspective but also from a cultural and ethnical perspective.

Building onto the value of Ubuntu, we have found limitations with design thinking from an inclusivity perspective. Traditionally, the design thinking approach creates working environments where a team is formed and then tasked with "designing for" another user. This is where they enter the problem space and frame the challenge from their perspective, developing their point of view of a user or a community of users. The user has limited interaction with the design process except in the research and testing phases. This approach often leads to limited buy-in and adoption from end users especially when their own actions and validation are pivotal to the success of the end solution. Within the South African context, we are finding more and more of a need to adopt the "designing with" approach rather than the "designing for" approach. This requires a far more integrated and co-creative approach where the end user is much more integral to the design process and often participates as a member of the design team. From a teaching and learning perspective, the d-school has also developed programs aimed at building implementation and coaching skills. Students are able to steer and guide end users through their own design thinking journey, where the end user becomes the "designer" developing solutions that they themselves will own and implement back into their environments. In this way, individuals are trained and equipped to both understand and develop solutions to their own challenges.

3 Summary

Since its inception in 2016, the Hasso Plattner School of Design Thinking has taught over 3500 students in the practice and mind-set of design thinking.

One of the core challenges that the school faced in its formative years was the need to develop an awareness of the value of design thinking. This was overcome by making use of an adaptation of the Danish Design Ladder. The d-school positioned the value of design not as the end object or service but rather as the thinking and collaboration processes that are followed to get to the end object or service. This framing has created an entry point for students to join programs which they would have not traditionally seen themselves in: as designers or valuable contributors to a design process. Once enrolled in a program, the d-school can further unlock and nurture creative confidence within the students.

The d-school has also found value in aligning the skills and mind-set of design thinking with the critical skills of the future as published every five years by the World Economic Forum. This comparison acts as a further incentive for students to participate in d-school courses to better prepare themselves for the future of work. Furthermore, within the context of South Africa, the need and drive for building entrepreneurship capability as a career alternative have influenced a number of the d-school's courses. Working with many existing programs at the university, the d-school has provided additional structures and frameworks to entrepreneurship curricula introducing core frameworks that enhance team formation, co-creation and a human-centered approach.

The challenges found within the South African context means that many of the projects that the students work on are complex in nature. This contextual complexity has challenged many of the approaches typically found in design thinking. The d-school continuously develops and builds courses and learning experiences that are more relevant in dealing with the complexity of the environment that the school exists within.

The d-school is just starting its journey as a school of excellence in design thinking in South Africa and the African continent. It continues to discover new pedagogies and opportunities of how design thinking can be taught and have impact within the context of the country and continent. This together with the growing demand for design thinking will undoubtedly have a transformative and lasting impact on our future and society as a whole.

Richard Perez Prior to founding the d-school, Richard Perez spent three years as a director at the City of Cape Town where, in a first for a public administration in South Africa, he pioneered design as a strategy and management tool to advance the creation of effective human-centred solutions. Leading a transversal City administration team who were responsible for embedding a culture of design-led innovation, Richard introduced design thinking to unlock collaboration, creative thinking and innovation in response to the needs of local citizens across the socio-economic spectrum. Before his City administration experience, Richard Perez spent 10 years as a partner and director in the award-winning Cape Town based product design agency …XYZ Design, where he managed and developed an extensive and varied portfolio of consumer focused products, services and user-centered research in emerging markets for local and international organisations.

Richard's background includes a Mechanical Engineering degree from the University of Cape Town, a Master of Arts from the Royal College of Art, a Diploma from Imperial College of Science and Technology (London) and an Executive MBA from the University of Cape Town's Graduate School of Business, where his research topic focused on the inter-relationships between constraints and creativity.

Integrating DT and Entrepreneurship: Case Study Universidad Mayor (Chile)

Mario Herane and Ismael Espinoza

Abstract A Design Thinking (DT) approach has the potential to empower young entrepreneurs whose focus is social innovation. DT may serve to help youth move toward efficient and effective action in their environment. Within the scope of the United Nations' (UN) commitment to global youth empowerment, this study is anchored in the Sustainable Development Goals for inclusive growth. We link theory with practice by examining two case studies related to DT as a tool of empowerment. While one case study was conducted in the USA, face-to-face before the COVID-19 pandemic, the other case study took place online, focusing on a young start-up in Kenya. A comparison of these two case studies offers an overview of existing DT principles that are context neutral. In addition, we examine specific characteristics that stem from context (COVID-19) and constellation (online). Taken together, theory and practice lead to a set of recommendations that, if implemented, are conducive to an optimistic outlook for Design Thinking in the UN in general and for youth empowerment in particular.

1 The Latin American Context

The world is in constant change and evolution, and our countries and communities must adapt to these volatile, uncertain, complex, and ambiguous scenarios. The terminology of our times, which seems to resound in every conference, seminar, and conversation, is the reflection of a wave that has been in constant motion over decades and pushed through the force of innovation and technology. This claustrophobic feeling and need for constant reinvention is found everywhere; however, if you add in a little more instability and an additional bit of social inequality, the need

M. Herane (✉) · I. Espinoza
Universidad Mayor, Santiago, Chile
e-mail: mario.herane@umayor.cl

I. Espinoza
e-mail: ismael.espinoza@umayor.cl

© The Author(s), under exclusive license to Springer Nature Switzerland AG 2022
C. Meinel and T. Krohn (eds.), *Design Thinking in Education*,
https://doi.org/10.1007/978-3-030-89113-8_9

and desire to gain traction is stronger. Developing countries suffer most of these symptoms all at once, including many other local conditions.

Let us now focus on Latin America to put things into context. Latin America is an area of the world that is highly rich in natural resources, which at the same time has an ongoing impact on social democracies and definitions of how these countries identify themselves. Latin America shares Spanish as the predominant language, with Portuguese as an obvious and relevant exception in Brazil. Even if these countries share the same language, the difference intonation, slang, and pronunciation reflect the fragmented societies inside and among each country. Each country has a unique history, and to put it in a social constructivist way: our past experiences define our personalities.

Now the story will move into a specific country in this Latin American wilderness. Chile is a long country with the cold Pacific Ocean on the west and the imposing Andes mountains on the east; the driest desert of the world on the north, and Antarctica's ice on the south. These are environmental conditions where the need and desire for progress intersects their local reality. This country, which had almost two decades of economic prosperity and international exposure in the *"Chilean model"* has been in the news and media lately because of the social distress resulting from a push for change. From the outside, this could appear a contradiction. However, if we look closer at the issue, it becomes apparent that two decades of strong expansion have impacted the natural resources, income disparity, the rising cost of living, and much more and led to the current social uprising. These constraints and complexities provide relevant insights and a background context to understand the importance of this chapter's outcome and the impact of Design Thinking on an entrepreneurial mindset.

2   The Entrepreneurial Spirit

During the '80s, Chile was subject to several constitutional modifications to promote the country's development, many of these were a reaction to the first sign of disruption in the technological acceleration. This realization was the source of a generalized urgency to develop new workforce skills and expand the number of productive professionals to confront the new era. This push came from new private actors willing to participate in the higher education sector, and after several rounds of discussion and proposals, new universities came into being. Each institution was founded by people who believed in the value of education as an agent of social movement and transformation; however, the institutional missions, vision, and values were very different. This historical moment was when Universidad Mayor (UMayor) was born in 1988. As a private, non-profit university, it came to the industry to confront the need for qualified professionals in the technological fields. The initial degree programs UMayor were in engineering, architecture, and agronomy, with a declared and unusual focus at that time on science and technology. Over 32 years, the institution has evolved into becoming one of the country's largest higher education institutions, with over 43 undergraduate degrees in almost every field, in four colleges, Arts, Science, Humanities, and Interdisciplinary Studies. The institution has also become strong in research focusing on Life Science, Genomics, Aging, and Social Studies. The institution has accomplished international achievements, including fulfilling the requirements for institutional accreditation in 2010 by the U.S. Regional Accreditation Agency, Middle States Commission on Higher Education.

The previous examples show how for over three decades Universidad Mayor has been a pioneer in developing new initiatives and ideas to promote education and improve the institution's quality. Now, if you ask around about the term *Espíritu Emprendedor* (Entrepreneurial Spirit), no one knows exactly when or how it came to be. Several members and ex-members of the institution declare themselves the owner and originator of the term. Each one declares his own history and reason behind this idea. The most "reliable" history is related to a discussion, which included the founding members and the board, in around 1992 about Chile's complex scenario and how the industry could not hire, retain, and offer good jobs for everyone, including Universidad Mayor graduates. There was a lack of opportunities, which was also heightened by strong fluctuations in the market. It was at this time that the institution realized the need to develop certain characteristics, skills, and competencies to engage the world with a different approach. It was a moment that could be defined as when the Entrepreneurial Spirit was born at Universidad Mayor, and it became part of the logo, slogan, and educational model. These were the early days of entrepreneurship as a word and a concept, which was closely related to the capacity to establish a business. The entrepreneur was not such a well-defined individual. It was more about a way of living and resembling a person who can take risks and pursue dreams. While the institution's objective was to develop certain characteristics in the students' profile and engage in the entrepreneurial initiative; the focus was mostly fixed on generating the "businessperson." This was defined as someone who could successfully set a business initiative and generate opportunity in the challenges of the world. As will be shown, things have changed dramatically since the introduction of Design Thinking into the UMayor educational model.

3 A New Perspective

Before 2020, most traditional institutions of higher education were hesitant about how much technology and online education they could include in their core academic operation—before hitting a wall with academics and students. Today, we know this much better. Universidad Mayor was once again a pioneer, specifically in technology, in having its core operation supported by the world class solution SAP.

It was April 2017, the institution was invited to participate in the SAP world summit for higher education, which was held in Amsterdam. During the meetings, several participants approached the representatives of Universidad Mayor, but one conversation among them was the beginning of a unique journey. A gentleman from a highly prestigious university in Latin America explained how he had participated in an experience that completely changed his perspective and how this was an institutional initiative where all top management was involved. He mentioned the words "transformational" and "mind-blowing." The first impression was between awkward and unusual, but his enthusiasm and the nature of his talk were striking. In particular, he mentioned the need to experience the process to understand its full value and potential and reflect on how you must confront a world full of complex issues to be tackled. To make it clear, one of the Universidad Mayor representatives is one of the authors of this chapter, serving as vice-president for development and management. The idea from this conversation stuck with the VP, which gave way to even more surprise when he learned that the experience was provided by a "cousin" of SAP, the Hasso Plattner Institute (HPI) in Postdam, Germany.

After long conversations with top management, by the end of 2017, the VP joined a cohort at the HPI D-School following the recommendation from a fellow academician at the summit. The second phase of the program at HPI described the interaction with the until then unknown (for him) concept of Design Thinking. The methodology involved several challenges that had to be confronted through Design Thinking as well as finding alternative solutions to solve these issues. The model included the possibility to establish a creative open collaboration, through a highly diverse team to confront issues, where no one person holds the truth. The solution should come from a dialog with the user, and the final product could go back to any previous stage of development without any shame or regret. This was the *AHA* moment for the VP, who saw the potential of this methodology as an opportunity to strengthen the skills of the students at Universidad Mayor and serve the full array of challenges that the country offers to develop new initiatives, services, products, processes, and more. He felt the urge to share this idea with the institution and bring the model to the university and the country.

The institution supported the idea and open to learning more about Design Thinking and if it could be a good fit for the university and the students. From the side of HPI, the idea to establish the first formal D-School in Latin America was also well received; however, many issues remained to be solved before any formal cooperation could be attempted.

4   From the Idea to the Plan

When you think about a trip, you know that it involves much more than just the flight and the hotel: It is about the experience. This was exactly what the HPI team were seeking in the Chilean and Universidad Mayor experience. A small team from HPI visited Chile in January 2018 to get a feeling about the country and the soundness behind the institution's idea of establishing a D-School. The visit was planned; meanwhile, the institution was learning more about what was meant by a "School of Design Thinking," and how such a school (place) could contribute to the university's educational model. During this time, the institutions' evaluation team expanded, and more and more people joined this process of deep reflection. This resulted in a shared opinion of how Design Thinking as a methodology could enable not just the students but the whole community to engage in a collaborative process to confront problems openly and creatively—a great opportunity in a country with many needs.

The HPI team was able to check the country's potential and the desire of the institution to integrate Design Thinking as more than just a methodology. This meant that it should be embedded into the core values of the organization. This effort will require introducing many artifacts, spreading beliefs, and then being fully included in the culture through institutional values. Not an easy task to achieve, including the operational issues about language and cultural localization of the methodology. Chile is clearly not Germany in language and culture.

When the cooperation was fully established, the three-year plan included several stages and milestones before it reached the point where Universidad Mayor was entitled to open the first operational Latin American D-School. The project's first step was the critical mission of defining how we would achieve this objective, the scope, constraints, needs, desires, inspirations, and purpose of this unique initiative. A team selected by Universidad Mayor was sent to Potsdam where the first formal interaction between our organizations took place. The team included the VP of Development and Management, the Director of Entrepreneurship, and a group of academics and researchers who later became the first coaches at UMayor D-School. The team spent a whole week developing the concepts and ideas needed to attach the D-School to the university's core values, which involved a review of the context, profile of the community, and alignment with the institutions' mission and vision. The purpose statement produced for UMayor D-School was the following:

> We believe that design thinking fosters the required character, skills, and motivation to develop an **entrepreneurial spirit** to enable people/students to add value to society by tackling complex problems.

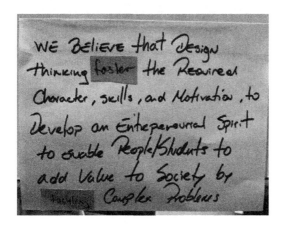

This declaration is the fundamental definition of how Design Thinking would be introduced at Universidad Mayor. The next paragraphs will dig deeper into the who, when, and how the model was integrated with the concept of "entrepreneurial spirit."

5 Our Mindset, the First Design Thinking Coaches and Workshops

As mentioned before, entrepreneurial spirit is part of Universidad Mayor's slogan and therefore its core, so to implement a D-School inside the institution, we had to begin with the alignment of the slogan and the results of a design thinking process.

Historically, education has been approached in a way that knowledge is the focus. The educational system seeks to imbue students with knowledge, but these times, we are living in now need students/professionals who are also confident, creative, and able to work and create with others. Here is when Design Thinking helps us to bring back the focus to the learning individual because by going through a design thinking process, a set of character, knowledge, and capability to learning to learn is developed, consistent with our definition of entrepreneurial spirit which is the expression of a set of skills and attitudes that converge in a professional who is capable of detecting needs and creating innovative solutions that add value to themselves and the environment.

By entrepreneurial spirit, Universidad Mayor understands that beyond offering an education that allows the individual to create a business, the focus must be on developing people to have an entrepreneurial attitude toward the world, who are then able to work with others on a team to be resilient, empathic, and willing to understand failure as a way of learning from mistakes and improving and detecting problems as opportunities and solving them. The implementation of a D-School inside Universidad Mayor allowed the institution to use Design Thinking to generate spaces for the community to experience the mindset and understand how entrepreneurial spirit is developed.

The beginning of the implementation of our D-School started with the first "ambassadors," Design Thinking Coaches who were professors from the Faculties of Science, Humanities, Arts, and Interdisciplinary Studies. An institutional committee was created made of the Dean of Interdisciplinary Studies, the Director of Entrepreneurship, the Director of Educational Innovation, and representatives of the Vice-Presidency of Academic Affairs.

The first cohort was 14 coaches that were trained by the HPI for 3 weeks on a process made of theoretical and practical experiences. Coaching and shadow coaching training was crucial for our coaches and every day ended with reflections and analysis of every participant to assure that they develop the knowledge for the design thinking process and also the mindset of a D-School.

The coaching training process also was used to iterate and define our first workshops; a half-day day workshop and a two-day workshop.

First, the HPI representatives worked with UMayor coaches to create and test a half-day Design Thinking workshop. This workshop aims at providing a short but meaningful exposure for students to the methods and mindsets of design thinking. This exercise was designed to target all incoming freshmen students as part of the existing orientation week at the Universidad Mayor. After completing the workshop, students will be able to say: "I have experienced design thinking and the entrepreneurial spirit."

Second, the work was focused on putting together and test a two-day Design Thinking experience. The objective of this educational offering will be to provide a basic but nonetheless comprehensive introduction to the methods and mindsets of design thinking. The two-day design thinking experience wanted to enable students to experience and explore design thinking by embarking on and reflecting on a design thinking project. After the experience, students should be able to say: "I have understood what design thinking can do for us and how to tap into a business opportunity."

Here was the first link to our Entrepreneurship Programs by applying a design thinking workshop at the beginning of an entrepreneurship process to define a business opportunity based on customers' needs.

6 An Important Step, Institutionalizing D-School Universidad Mayor

After the training of the first cohort of coaches and the definition of the workshops, an important decision was needed: Where was the D-School U Mayor going to be formalized? The answer was under the Faculty of Interdisciplinary Studies due to his mission to train people who integrate creative, scientific, and critical thinking for the generation of interdisciplinary proposals, initiatives, solutions and products in undergraduate and postgraduate degrees at the Universidad Mayor. This, through the creation of academic programs that promote and strengthen entrepreneurship, innovation, and research in conjunction with the Faculties of Arts, Sciences, and Humanities. Within the faculty, the D-School was structured under the Entrepreneurship Department who is responsible for designing and implementing programs that develop creativity, entrepreneurship, and innovation in the Universidad Mayor's community, strengthening its entrepreneurial spirit by positioning a culture of entrepreneurship and innovation.

The D-School's kickoff was in March 2019, where the first workshops were held in a half-day and two-day format for students of different undergraduate levels. On this occasion, HPI Coaches accompanied the D-School which resulted in a resounding success, both from the perspective of the students and from the recently certified D-School Scholars.

Then, in July 2019, HPI Coaches visited the D-School again to train the second generation of D-School Academics and D-School Administrative, who became part of the great D-School family, whose role is to permeate the Design Thinking Mindset into the community of the Universidad Mayor.

Nowadays, D-School of the Universidad Mayor is the first Design Thinking School created in Latin America who seeks to enhance skills such as creativity, leadership, proactivity, resilience, and teamwork.

The user is the main axis of the work, and the results are focused on solving complex problems, creating high-impact solutions.

- Encourages a proactive attitude to solve problems from a creative and sustainable perspective.
- Allows the creation of new products, services, and business models through an innovative mindset.
- Accelerates processes in project development by making progress at work tangible.

The D-School UM functions as a unit with its main headquarters in Santiago, and a headquarters in Temuco. Both venues are governed by the same guidelines and level of certification of their academics. Through its actions, D-School contributes directly to the mission and vision declared by the Entrepreneurship Department.

The main functions of the D-School are:

- Collaborate with the fulfillment of the Universidad Mayor seal by offering its community of students, teachers, and collaborators, through activities based on the Design Thinking methodology, in line with the General Education Model, as well as the Teacher Strengthening Plan declared by Universidad Mayor.
- Promote the development of the D-School Academic Unit through the training of its current academics as well as the certification of future D-School academics.

7   Connection with Universidad Mayor's Academic Model

When D-School UMayor was created, the main purpose was to allow the development of the Entrepreneurial Spirit and therefore becoming part of the Universidad Mayor's DNA. To do so, a university's DNA is their academic curriculum, in this case, called "Curriculum Mayor" an academic structure dictated by the Vice-presidency of Academic Affairs that provides guidelines and conditions for the generation of any study plan and curriculum by a General Education Policy.

UNESCO in 1998 mentions in the World Declaration on Higher Education that if adequate higher education and research institutions are lacking that form a critical mass of qualified people, no country will be able to guarantee an authentic endogenous and sustainable development, and developing countries and poor countries will not be able to bridge the gap between them and industrialized developed countries. As a result of the foregoing, it is understood that the knowledge society is necessarily a teaching-learning society, of the universalization of access opportunities to higher education and of the validation of knowledge through research functions, discovery and innovation, for which the role of universities is very important in the social, political, and economic development of nations, they must demonstrate that it is not only the continuation of basic and secondary education but that their objectives are oriented to full and active participation in development, promoting a social projection. This new scenario generates more competitive work contexts, so twenty-first century professionals must possess a set of characteristics such as leadership, entrepreneurship and management skills, use of ICTs, communication, and collaborative work, among others.

The general education policy of Universidad Mayor expresses as part of the purpose of its mission as the training of people through educational experiences, which highlights among its main among its main areas of importance: ethics, entrepreneurship, innovation, leadership, and respect for cultural and social diversity. In this sense, the educational model of the Universidad Mayor presents guidelines and institutional values that illuminate the task of training students and assume commitments toward the contribution of graduates that allow them to be a contribution to society.

From its foundation until today, the Universidad Mayor has been developing and enriching its educational model, thus, continuously, and consistently seeking fulfillment of its mission. To this end, the "Curriculum Mayor" arises as an educational philosophy, which adjusts the training of professionals to the requirements of an updated and balanced education, while enriching the student's university experience, which coincides with a particularly important stage of its development. The university is convinced that each graduate student is a broadly trained individual, in terms of knowledge and skills, understanding of cultural diversity and attitudes to address problems in the ethical field and at the same time prepared to practice a profession successfully in a global and competitive world.

D-School U Mayor is linked to the "Curriculum Mayor" through two main actions:

- Collaborate with the fulfillment of the competencies declared by the general education policy
- The promotion and development of educational innovation through the continuous improvement of subjects or units.

The general education policy at Universidad Mayor considers that students upon graduation have developed a series of competencies that contribute to their personal development and that of the community in which they are inserted. This is how the five domains have been established that seek to comply with these competencies:

1. Effective communication
2. Self-learning, personal development, and critical thinking
3. Entrepreneurship and management with social responsibility
4. Ethics
5. Scientific Reasoning.

Each domain establishes and defines an associated generic competence, which will be developed by the students through the different study plans. Additionally, the General Education Model establishes the academic units responsible for the fulfillment of each competence at its different levels. For the development of the 3rd

Domain, Entrepreneurship and Management with Social Responsibility, an important academic unit was formed, the "Academic Department for Entrepreneurship and Management," led by one of our coaches and with the purpose of ensuring the correct development of the domain and the curricular incorporation of the programs of the Entrepreneurship Department.

The work of the D-School includes supporting those units responsible for the fulfillment of the declared competencies, at their different levels of escalation. This is how the D-School makes available the activities that have been designed and implemented to collaborate and jointly develop a plan that best suits a specific unit/career it. The offer of Design Thinking workshops and their learning results have been validated by the Vice President of Academic Affairs.

8   D-School Results on Workshops and Curricular Incorporation

Since the kickoff in 2019, D-School UMayor has achieved important milestones and results that position it as an institutional reference in the implementation of methodologies, mindset, and formalization in study plans and academic links:

- Incorporation in the course University Academic Competences in 2019, a course that is on every academic plan, which means that these courses are taken by every freshman student. During 2019, the first project was implemented to incorporate creativity into the DNA of the Universidad Mayor through the Design Thinking methodology. For this, 59 workshops were held in a half-day format, between March and October, gaining the attendance of 1,891 first-year students.
- Incorporation in the course University Academic Competences in 2020: During the first semester of 2020, six modules were introduced, specially designed for students to get to know and experience the design thinking process. The students were guided by professors of the subject, who had previously been trained with fundamental tools, in the Design Thinking in the Classroom course, within the framework of the Teaching Strengthening Program.
- Incorporation into the course University Academic Competences in an online format. During December 2019, an online activity was implemented so that students who could not participate in the face-to-face experience, could experience some of the concepts and fundamentals of Design Thinking in an online format. For this, a virtual classroom was set up with a reading different documents and videos that compiles the main concepts and elements of the Design Thinking mentality and process, and an applied case: a quiz with simple application questions following the dynamic philosophy of the D-School; and finally, an optional activity for those who would like to exercise what they have learned. This is something they (can/) do it in an entertaining and practical way. Under this modality, coverage of 216 students was achieved.

- Redesign of the Business School's course: The D-School and the Business School worked together on the redesign of the subject "Business Games II," based on the Design Thinking methodology, implemented during the first semester of 2020 for the commercial engineering and administration engineering careers.
- Professor Strengthening Program: Design Thinking Course in the Classroom: This course is framed within the guidelines published by the university in The Framework document for Quality Teaching and seeks to contribute directly to some of the criteria that are indicated as priorities. It combines theory with practical spaces, allowing participants (/students) to know and put into practice the six phases of Design Thinking.
- Design Thinking in the "CAU Classroom for Professors": In the context of the redesign of the subject University Academic Competencies (CAU), from March 2020, teachers who complete the course will be able to understand the basis of the methodology and will have the necessary tools to integrate Design Thinking into their subject in an autonomous manner. The course includes the use of the Virtual Classroom for all registered participants. Here, they will be able to access the course material, complementary material, and the format to be used for the final report, which will be evaluated to obtain the approval of the course. In the first version of this course, 14 teachers participated in Santiago and 9 in Temuco.

Design Thinking in the Classroom for Professors (general information): Professors who complete the workshop will be able to count on a battery of tools of this methodology, among which they will be able to select the most pertinent to plan a class or a unit of their subjects. The first version of this course was held on two dates, with the participation of 80 teachers in Santiago and 35 in Temuco. In the period March 2019 to January 2020, a total of 2,728 participants have lived the D-School experience through the different types of workshops:

D-School participants					
First-year students	Undergraduate and graduate students	Students in total	Professors	Administrative staff	Alumni
1.891	369	**2.260**	**175**	**149**	**144**

9 Our Next Steps

After the implementation of our D-School, the next steps were to use the design thinking method, its mindset, and our coaches to explore other areas to improve our Entrepreneurship Programs. For this reason, the Entrepreneurship Department has set up two other programs:

La Fábrica: Entrepreneurship program of the Universidad Mayor since 2017 was responsible for developing solutions to real problems, through its support in the development of projects and access to national and international collaboration networks. La Fábrica has Incubation Processes, Mentor Networks, Coworking Spaces, and different contents for Universidad Mayor's community. After the implementation of our D-School, one of the coaches took charge of these programs to improve most of the activities with the D-School's mindset and workshops.

Protolab: Laboratory of design, experimentation, and materialization of ideas with social impact, which by stimulating creativity and innovation, based on science and technology, allows the generation of functional prototypes. This program was also led by a coach and now links prototyping with design thinking and disciplines like computer programming.

Dr. Mario Herane Vice President of Management and Development at Universidad Mayor.

Mario Herane holds two main responsibilities at the institution. From the management side he is responsible for the overall operation of the institution including the areas of human resources, finances, administration, and infrastructure, and from the development area he is in charge to project the organization into the future through marketing strategies, communications, local and international partnerships, new projects and initiatives, and technological innovation. For over 15 years he has been leading educational institutions in Chile and abroad, with a strong focus on student success and their preparation for the needs of this new era of knowledge. Mario Herane had a first-hand encounter with DT at the HPI in Potsdam, and from then on, he felt in love with this collaborative methodology and its mindset. The greatest challenge of DT is that it can't just be described, you must experience it to understand its potential. A helpful insight is the value of personal relationships and trust to enable organizations and change paradigms, by sharing and inspire others you can distribute leadership and gain traction for change.

Ismael Espinoza Director of Entrepreneurship at the Universidad Mayor.

Ismael Espinoza is responsible for designing and implementing programs that develop creativity, entrepreneurship, and innovation in the Universidad Mayor´s community, strengthening its entrepreneurial spirit by positioning a culture of entrepreneurship and innovation. For over 10 years he has gained experience in entrepreneurship by developing different programs that aim to promote the generation of Business. After becoming a design thinking coach at HPI he started to work in education by co-designing with Schools the different approaches to link design thinking with the academic plans. The greatest challenge to using Design Thinking in education has been to translate the methodology in ways a professor could understand and appreciate their impact and results. A value insight through this journey has been that human-centeredness approaches should first be lived and then learned/applied because the Mindset needs to be appreciated and understood before the theory.

Towards a Culturally Responsive Design Thinking Education

Mana Taheri

Abstract The demand for teaching and learning DT has been on the rise. The number of educational institutions around the world that are offering DT training is growing every day. Considering that the majority of educational offerings are still in Western Europe and North America, involving DT educators from the West has become a popular format in setting up new programs. Since the DT education as we know it today originated in the Silicon Valley context, the questions that arise are: what happens as it travels across the globe? Are the methods, tools, and mindsets of DT replicable in a new context? Are the pedagogical approaches used to teach DT, effective around the globe? This chapter explores these questions.

1 Introduction

The last decade has witnessed an upswing in Design Thinking (DT) across an array of disciplines. The demand for teaching and learning DT has been on the rise. The number of educational institutions offering DT training is growing every day. New offerings come in different shapes and forms: from programs that solely focus on teaching DT over several semesters, to university seminars and workshops within an already existing curriculum.

The Stanford d.school and HPI School of Design Thinking were among the pioneering educational institutions that contributed to teaching and research in DT. In response to the global rise in learning DT, both HPI and Stanford have been involved in creating new programs internationally; whether through sending experienced educators to host countries or training future educators at home. Considering that the majority of educational offerings are still in Western Europe and North America, involving DT educators from the West has become a popular format in setting up new programs.

M. Taheri (✉)
Hasso Plattner Institute for Digital Engineering, Campus Griebnitzsee, Prof.-Dr.-Helmert-Str. 2-3, 14482 Potsdam, Germany
e-mail: Mana.Taheri@hpi.de

© The Author(s), under exclusive license to Springer Nature Switzerland AG 2022
C. Meinel and T. Krohn (eds.), *Design Thinking in Education*,
https://doi.org/10.1007/978-3-030-89113-8_10

However, practices that are effective in one context may not prove as effective and appropriate in another context (Brannen, 2004; Värlander et al., 2016). Some scholars argue that practices that are more social (e.g., involving much social interaction) are more likely to be influenced by the cultural context, and more likely to be re-contextualized when transferred to a new country (Yu & Zaheer, 2010; Brannen, 2004). Considering the high level of social interactions in DT classrooms, it is safe to assume the need for proper contextualization.

In this work, however, my focus will be on the teaching and learning of DT. Since DT education as we know it today originated in the Silicon Valley context, the questions that arise are: What happens as DT travels across the globe? Are the methods, tools, and mindsets of DT replicable in a new context? Are the pedagogical approaches used to teach DT effective across the globe?

In their literature review of research on cross-border educational partnerships, Waterval et al. (2015) highlight that "simply copy-pasting a curriculum is generally considered to be destined for failure." They suggest that as established academic institutions engage in cross-border partnerships, they need to create awareness about differences in learning behaviors among their teachers and adapt their curriculum accordingly.

While there are some studies that explore the intersection between DT and orga-nizational culture (e.g., Elsbach & Stigliani, 2018; Prud'homme van Reine, 2017; Buchanan, 2015), the impact of national culture on DT education has been under-examined. My aim for this chapter is to explore DT education through the lens of cultural diversity and to examine the effectiveness of the common approaches in teaching DT with regard to diverse cultural contexts.

At this point, it is relevant to mention my own connection with the topic at hand. I have been working as a DT educator in various international contexts for over seven years. Throughout my studies, I have been exposed to a number of educational systems with sometimes stark differences, such as in Tehran, Berlin, Havana, and Istanbul. As a student, I experienced my fair share of cultural shocks and mismatches. At times, I felt confused and uncomfortable. Later on, as I began working as an educator, I recognized the same look of confusion and discomfort on some of my students' faces in different parts of the world. I have witnessed firsthand, how some methods, tools, or teaching strategies that are synonymous with DT may not always resonate with the cultural context of our learners. I became curious about creating learning experiences that account for the socio-cultural context. I turned this fasci-nation into my thesis project, where I look into two DT educational institutions—namely d-school at University of Cape Town (UCT), South Africa, and Genovasi in Kuala Lumpur, Malaysia—to learn about the practices and strategies that local educators apply to adapt DT education to their own unique context.

The chapter in hand provides a glimpse into some of the questions I have been engaged with. My hope is that it will give the reader food for thought in reconsidering some of the teaching practices in DT education and its relevance for different contexts. A more comprehensive research will be published in my thesis.

2 Culture and Design Thinking

Culture is omnipresent in all aspects of our lives. It affects what we deem appropriate in different contexts, our values, interactions, and our attention to our surroundings (Nisbett et al., 2001). Despite its crucial role in an individual's life, the definition of culture has been long debated by scholars across different fields. Widely cited frameworks such as Hofstede's *Cultural Dimensions* (1986) and the famous GLOBE study by House and his colleagues (2004) show the long desire for operationalizing culture.

Despite their popularity to this date, such works have been heavily criticized, especially by scholars with a postcolonial sensibility (e.g., Joy & Poonamallee, 2013; Yeganeh & Su, 2006; Kwek, 2003; Goodfellow & Lamy, 2009; Fougere & Moulettes, 2007). Some of the critics argue that these frameworks try to simplify and reduce a complex and multilayered concept of culture into measurable dimensions (Yeganeh & Su, 2006; Tayeb, 1994) as well as implying a static view on culture (Signorini et al., 2009). Kwek (2003) argues that Hofstede's work "must be viewed in the context of the historical power-relationships that existed between East and West during colonialism, and that [this] allowed the East to be defined by the West." Moreover, Fougere and Moulettes (2007) criticize Hofstede's work for its "western-based, ethnocentric perspective." I also share these critiques and tend to agree with scholars who have a more dynamic view of culture and see it as a complex set of practices and values that are not necessarily limited to geographical boundaries (e.g., Goodfellow & Lamy, 2009; Jung & Gunawardena, 2014; Signorini et al., 2009).

Gay (2002) argues that some aspects of culture such as traditions and values, as well as communication and learning styles, have direct implications for learning and teaching and are thus very important for educators to pay attention to. Joy and Kolb conducted one of the first studies on the implication of culture on learning and suggest that culture significantly influences learning styles (Joy & Kolb, 2009).

The relationship between design and culture has been under-researched (Hinds & Lyon, 2011). However, design and its practices are not free from cultural influences. Hinds and Lyon (2011) explore the relationship between culture and design practices through a series of observations and interviews with designers across the globe. Chavan et al. (2009) explain the limitations of using conventional design methods in different cultural contexts. In designing for different cultures, they advise designers to be sensitive to the context of their users and to be open to unlearn "what they have been doing for decades."

Despite its sharp rise in popularity, a limited understanding of how DT is taught in different cultural contexts remains. To my knowledge, one of the only studies that have explicitly dealt with culture and DT education was conducted by Thoring et al. (2014). Comparing Hofstede's cultural dimensions with criteria they deem crucial for DT, the authors suggest that some cultures may deal with DT better than others. Their goal is to help educators to anticipate potential challenges of cultural differences. Apart from the above-mentioned critiques of applying "essentialist" frameworks, such as Hofstede's (Jung & Gunawardena, 2015), I do not share the notion that some cultures are "better suited" to DT than others. I believe that it is our responsibility as educators to adapt our teachings and create learning experiences that are contextually appropriate and resonate with our learners.

After over a decade of teaching and learning DT, it is time to examine different aspects of DT education and their effectiveness in meeting the needs of diverse learners. In the following, selective aspects of DT education including coaching, language, and pedagogical approach will be discussed.

3 Culturally Sensitive Coaching

The need for a teacher's sensitivity to cultural diversity and its implications for teaching and learning has increased in the field of education. The rise of globalization, diverse classrooms, and international educational cooperation require educators to embrace cultural diversity and adopt teaching practices that address the needs of learners from diverse cultural backgrounds.

Culturally relevant education, culturally responsive, inclusive, or sensitive teaching are some of the keywords that can lead us to research on teaching and education that strives to accommodate cultural differences. Chen et al. (1999) name cultural inclusivity as one of the crucial pillars of a student-centered learning environment. van Boeijen et al. (2017) argue that teachers' awareness and reflection on their own cultural background is an important step towards developing design education that is culturally sensitive.

With the increase in cross-border DT educational cooperation, the need for educators that are sensitive and responsive to their learners' context becomes clear. DT educators, often called coaches, play a crucial role in any effective DT training. Coaches accompany teams through the learning experience, support them with tools and methods of DT, and help them to get inspired. They remain sensitive to team dynamics and help teams overcome challenges in project work. Despite their important role, research on DT coaching is scarce. Tschepe (2017) conducted a study that explores the requirements for a successful DT coach through qualitative interviews with experienced coaches. He suggests five qualities (e.g., being empathic, appreciative, and reflective) and eleven capabilities (e.g., acting flexibly and intuitively, knowing when to intervene, and being sensitive to convergence and divergence) for a successful DT coach.

I would argue that being culturally sensitive is a much-needed quality for DT coaches, especially in international settings. Diversity in teams goes beyond disciplinary differences. Potential power dynamics, social justice issues as well as racial, gender, linguistic composition, and socio-economic gaps, may play into the classroom and team spaces. Therefore, the coach needs to pay attention to the socio-cultural context of learners.

Our teaching practices are culturally influenced. It shouldn't come as a surprise that replicating the same teaching strategies from home may not yield the same results in other contexts. We may need to adopt different teaching strategies to accommodate learners from different cultural backgrounds. If we insist on teaching the same way across the board, we are not only deviating from the empathetic and human-centered principles that we advocate, but we may also fall into the trap of what Bennett (2004) calls "ethnocentrism", meaning "to refer to the experience of one's own culture as 'central to reality'," as "just the way things are."

Being open and flexible to doing things differently and having an appreciative attitude towards cultural differences—rather than a deficit view—can help coaches to be more culturally sensitive. The following quote from one of the programs managers I interviewed at the d-school at UCT, sums it up well:

> In the spirit of design thinking, I would suggest to anyone who goes to a different context that [you] try to empower yourself with a little bit of knowledge about the context. This doesn't mean that you should be an expert, but at least have a little bit of knowledge about the nuances.

4 Language

As in any educational experience, language plays an important role in teaching and learning DT, where English is often the language of instruction. Many DT coaches may speak English as their first language or be professionally fluent in it. However, this may not always be the case for the students in the host country. Difficulties with language can complicate learning (Dobos, 2011). Briguglio (2000) suggests that often the challenges that students face in adapting to a new learning methodology is more due to their level of language proficiency than the teaching and learning styles.

"Designers are notorious for using expressive words specific to their trade" write D'souza and Dastmalchi (2017), who have explored slangs and jargons in the design process. Design jargons (e.g., point of view and pain point) and US American slang influenced by the Silicon Valley tech scene (e.g., disrupt and MVP) have become part of the DT teaching language. While learning a new methodology may be already challenging, picking up new jargons on top of that can be overwhelming.

The important role of language in teaching DT was highlighted by coaches and program designers in both d-school at UCT and Genovasi. Whether it was code-switching in Kuala Lumpur or simplifying or choosing better fitting replacements for some of the jargon in Cape Town, language was named as one of the first aspects of designing a learning experience that resonated with the audience.

In addition, the choice of words and adjectives matters. Using hyperbolic language to spark motivation and creativity is common in teaching DT; phrases like "game changing solution," "radical innovation" or "wild idea" are just some examples. While a North American audience may relate to using hyperbole in language, it may not yield the same resonance in other places. In one workshop, for example, describing a potential solution as "game changing" proved to put undue pressure on my German students, rather than encouraging creativity because their understanding of the expression was almost entirely in a literal sense. We iterated our framework and ended up changing the wording.

To my surprise, teaching DT in my mother tongue of Farsi in Tehran proved to be one of my most challenging teaching experiences to date. Throughout the training, I often struggled to find fitting translations for common DT terms and to convey the right message.

In short, keeping the language as simple as possible and highlighting the intended outcomes of each method and tool, instead of emphasizing terms and names which may feel distant to the audience, can go a long way.

5   Learning by Doing, or One-Size Fits All?

Learning by doing has become a mantra in teaching DT. We often warn our learners that we are going to "throw them into the deep end." We encourage them to avoid over-discussing and to "jump right in" and "get their hands dirty." But is this emphasis on experimenting effective in every context?

Although DT education is relatively new, there are some parallels to other long-established student-centered and constructivist approaches, such as Problem-Based-Learning (PBL), or Kolb's (1984, 2014) Experiential Learning Theory (Beckman & Barry, 2007). Some of the similarities include minimal guidance (Kirschner et al., 2006), short lectures, and strong emphasis on collaboration.

I suggest that learning by doing may not be the only way to teach DT effectively. Prior educational experiences do matter. Learners who have been socialized in educational systems that promote critical thinking or collaborative project work may have an easier time adapting to the DT way of working. They have "been there, done that." On the contrary, if the educational system is hierarchical and teacher-centered, with an emphasis on knowledge acquisition and rote learning, one simply cannot expect fast adaptation to this new way of learning and working.

It is easy to assume that student-centered educational approaches will be accepted by students from all backgrounds. However, in a study of cross-border educational partnerships, scholars have reported that students in host countries with "spoon-fed" educational approaches face difficulties adapting to a student-centered approach to imported curricula (Briguglio, 2000; Castle & Kelly, 2004; Heffernan, et al., 2010; Wilson, 2002). In this light, as educators, we need to adapt our teaching strategies in consideration of the education system our learners have experienced. Contrary to the famous saying "learning happens outside of one's comfort zone," too much discomfort may actually have an adverse effect on an individual's learning.

The following is an example of the impact of preferred learning/teaching strategy on DT training. I was responsible for designing and delivering two successive DT introductory workshops for two different cohorts. One group was comprised of managers from China, the other of managers from Nordic countries. The client persisted in delivering an identical curriculum for both cohorts. At the end of the first day with the Chinese cohort, I could sense the discomfort and the hesitation towards "trying things out" as we encouraged them constantly. The coaches also confirmed this observation. We realized that learners wished for more guidance and wanted to know more before trying things out. We decided to respond to their needs and adapt the schedule on the go. One of the coaches offered an hour-long lecture on the state-of-the-art research on DT in organizations, which although lengthy for a typical introductory workshop, was appreciated by the audience.

I have seen similar reactions in Iran, Cuba, and Malaysia, where the focus of education systems is on acquiring knowledge and rote learning instead of experiential learning. This quote by one of the coaches in Genovasi describes the tension between the dominant education system and the common experiential approach in teaching and learning DT:

> We need more guidance. Our education system is designed in such a way that the more you memorize, the cleverer you are. The smarter you are. The more you can score in an exam. So, there's really not much effort needed in terms of creative thinking, we are all spoon-fed … So, when it comes to here [Genovasi], everything is so unstructured, it's so ambiguous. You have absolute freedom, and it scares them [the participants]. And so, then they get paralyzed by so many [*sic*] choices, so much … suddenly they have no direction to go.

Informing ourselves about the prevailing education practices in other countries may provide us with insights into how students have been socialized to learn. It tells us whether individuals have been trained to voice their opinions or not, whether there is a strong teacher-student hierarchy, and whether critical thinking and experiential learning are commonplace. At times, we may need to balance our minimal guidance approach with more hand-holding and gradually expose our audience to the mindset and principles we wish to see.

6   Conclusion

As DT educators, we are faced with the exciting opportunity to promote human-centered design across disciplines and countries. However, we are also confronted with the responsibility to create learning experiences that resonate with the needs of our diverse learners. After all, we are a product of our context and influenced by our own culture and values. In order to create truly learner-centered DT education, we need to reflect on our teaching practices and, at times, question their effectiveness for our diverse learners. We need to be cognizant of the context we are teaching in and be willing to adapt ourselves if necessary.

Although DT seems like a unique learning experience and far from any conventional classroom, it is, after all, still about teaching and learning new skills, methods and mindsets. Therefore, we can benefit from good practices in the field of education and instructional design.

Without the curiosity and will to learn about and from other cultures and adapt if needed, our expertise in the methods and tools of DT may not suffice for teaching in different contexts. Luckily, we have the DT principles of user-centricity, empathy, and iteration to help us design learning experiences that resonate with our audience in different contexts.

References

Bennett, M. J. (2004). Becoming interculturally competent. Toward multiculturalism: A reader in multicultural education, pp. 62–77.

Brannen, M. Y. (2004). When Mickey loses face: Recontextualization, semantic fit, and the semiotics of foreignness. *Academy of Management Review, 29*(4), 593–616.

Briguglio, C. (2000). Language and cultural issues for English-as-a-second/foreign language students in transnational educational settings. *Higher Education in Europe, 25*(3), 425–434.

Buchanan, R. (2015). Worlds in the making: Design, management, and the reform of organizational culture. *She Ji 1*(1), 5–21. https://doi.org/10.1016/j.sheji.2015.09.003

Castle, R., & Kelly, D. (2004). International education: Quality assurance and standards in offshore teaching: Exemplars and problems. *Quality in Higher Education, 10*(1), 51–57.

Chen, A.-Y., Mashhadi, A., Ang, D., & Harkrider, N. (1999). Cultural issues in the design of technology-enhanced learning systems. *British Journal of Educational Technology, 30*(3), 217–230.

D'souza, N., & Dastmalchi, M. (2017). "Comfy" Cars for the "Awesomely Humble": Exploring Slang and Jargons in a cross-cultural design process. In *Analyzing Design Thinking: Studies of Cross-cultural Co-creation* (pp. 311–330). CRC Press.

Dobos, K. (2011). "Serving two masters"–academics' perspectives on working at an offshore campus in Malaysia. *Educational Review, 63*(1), 19–35.

Elsbach, K. D., & Stigliani, I. (2018). Design thinking and organizational culture: A review and framework for future research. *Journal of Management, 44*(6), 2274–2306.

Fougère, M., & Moulettes, A. (2007). The construction of the modern west and the backward rest: Studying the discourse of Hofstede's culture's consequences. *Journal of Multicultural Discourses, 2*(1), 1–19.

Gay, G. (2002). Preparing for culturally responsive teaching. *Journal of Teacher Education, 53*(2), 106–116.

Goodfellow, R., & Marie-Noëlle Lamy (eds.) (2009). *Learning cultures in online education.* A&C Black.

Heffernan, T., Morrison, M., Basu, P., & Sweeney, A. (2010). Cultural differences, learning styles and transnational education. *Journal of Higher Education Policy and Management, 32*(1), 27–39.

Hinds, P., & Lyon, J. (2011). Innovation and culture: Exploring the work of designers across the globe. In *Design thinking* (pp. 101–110). Springer.

Hofstede, G. (1986). Cultural differences in teaching and learning. *International Journal of Intercultural Relations, 10*(3), 301–320.

House, R. J., Hanges, P. J., Javidan, M., Dorfman, P. W., & Gupta, V. (eds.) (2004). *Culture, leadership, and organizations: The GLOBE study of 62 societies.* Sage.

Joy, S., & Poonamallee, L. (2013). Cross-cultural teaching in globalized management classrooms: Time to move from functionalist to postcolonial approaches? *Academy of Management Learning & Education, 12*(3), 396–413.

Joy, S., & Kolb, D. A. (2009). Are there cultural differences in learning style? *International Journal of Intercultural Relations, 33*(1), 69–85.

Jung, I., & Gunawardena, C. N. (eds.) *Culture and online learning: Global perspectives and research.* Stylus Publishing, LLC.

Kirschner, P. A., Sweller, J., & Clark, R. E. (2006). Why minimal guidance during instruction does not work: An analysis of the failure of constructivist, discovery, problem-based, experiential, and inquiry-based teaching. *Educational Psychologist, 41*(2), 75–86.

Kwek, D. (2003). Decolonizing and re-presenting culture's consequences: A postcolonial critique of cross-cultural studies in management. In *Postcolonial theory and organizational analysis: A critical engagement* (pp. 121–146). Palgrave Macmillan.

Kolb, D. A. (2014). *Experiential learning: Experience as the source of learning and development.* FT Press.

Nisbett, R. E., Peng, K., Choi, I., & Norenzayan, A. (2001). Culture and systems of thought: Holistic versus analytic cognition. *Psychological Review, 108*(2), 291.

Prud'homme van Reine, P. (2017). The culture of design thinking for innovation. *Journal of Innovation Management, 5*(2), 56–80.

Signorini, P., Wiesemes, R., & Murphy, R. (2009). Developing alternative frameworks for exploring intercultural learning: A critique of Hofstede's cultural difference model. *Teaching in Higher Education, 14*(3), 253–264.

Tayeb, M. (1994). Organizations and national culture: Methodology considered. *Organization Studies, 15*(3), 429–445.

Tschepe, S. (2017). Was sind die wichtigsten Eigenschaften und Fähigkeiten von Design Thinking-Coaches? Master's thesis, Humboldt-Universität zu Berlin.

Thoring, K. C., Luippold, C., & Mueller, R. M. (2014). The impact of cultural differences in design thinking education. In *Proceedings of the DRS 2014: Design's big debates*, Umea, Sweden, 16–19 June 2014.

van Boeijen, A., Sonneveld, M., & Hao, C. (2017). Culture sensitive design education–the best of all worlds. In *DS 88: Proceedings of the 19th International Conference on Engineering and Product Design Education (E&PDE17), Building Community: Design Education for a Sustainable Future*, Oslo, Norway, 7 & 8 September 2017, pp. 643–648.

Värlander, S., Hinds, P., Thomason, B., Pearce, B. M., & Altman, H. (2016). Enacting a constellation of logics: How transferred practices are recontextualized in a global organization. *Academy of Management Discoveries, 2*(1), 79–107.

Waterval, D. G. J., Frambach, J. M., Driessen, E. W., & Scherpbier, A. J. J. A. (2014). Copy but not paste: A literature review of crossborder curriculum partnerships. *Journal of Studies in International Education, 19*(1), 65–85.

Wilson, M. (2002). Transnational nursing programs: Models, advantages and challenges. *Nurse Education Today, 22*(5), 417–426.

Yeganeh, H., & Su, Z. (2006). Conceptual foundations of cultural management research. *International Journal of Cross Cultural Management, 6*(3), 361–376.

Yu, J., & Zaheer, S. (2010). Building a process model of local adaptation of practices: A study of Six Sigma implementation in Korean and US firms. *Journal of International Business Studies, 41*(3), 475–499.

Mana Taheri is a researcher at the HPI- Stanford Design Thinking Research Program and has been working as a DT educator for over 7 years in different international settings. She has been part of the teaching team at the HPI d-school and has worked with HPI Academy on various programs. As part of her research project, together with her team, she has designed and run three MOOCs on topics around human-centered design with over 20,000 participants from all around the world. Her research interests lie in the field of cultural inclusivity and MOOCs, and the impact of the socio-cultural context on DT education (PhD thesis). Mana believes that the biggest challenge in using DT in education, considering the global popularity in teaching and learning DT, is failing to create culturally responsive learning experiences. An insight that can help us overcome this challenge is to dare to deviate from common DT practices and to be open to adapt to the socio-cultural context of our learners, using DT principles such as empathy, human-centeredness, and iteration.

Design Thinking in Professional Education
and Organizational Contexts

Design Thinking for Leaders—Made Possible by Innovation and Agility

Selina Mayer, Flavia Bleuel, and Christina Stansell

Abstract Education neither begins nor ends with formal schooling. Learning is an ongoing process. Leadership is an ongoing learning process—as are the values and skills that underpin them. Over the years, we have worked with a variety of leaders from a wide range of industries. Despite the differing contexts, we have found many commonalities when considering the issues of innovation, transformation, and agility within organizations. In this chapter, we describe four key practices that leaders apply to foster innovation and agility: create and communicate a clear vision, build systems to learn and experiment, enable autonomy, and foster psychological safety. Furthermore, we give a brief overview of the Design Thinking mindset and how the mindset elements are connected to the four practices. We then provide a starting point for practitioners to apply these insights in their own contexts by posing questions that trigger self-reflection, as this lays the foundation for changing how we behave. Overall, this chapter can help leaders take the first actions towards agility and innovation.

1 Introduction

Education neither begins nor ends with formal schooling, as we see in the other parts of this book and as we know from our lived experience. Our sense of ourselves is learned. Creativity is learned. Leadership is learned—as are the values and skills that underpin them. Warren Bennis, a pioneer of the contemporary field of leadership studies, writes: "In fact, the process of becoming a leader is much the same as the process of becoming an integrated human being." (Bennis, 2009, p. Xxxii). Leadership competencies are something we can develop over time, especially if we

---

S. Mayer (✉)
HPI School of Design Thinking, Hasso Plattner Institute for Digital Engineering, Campus Griebnitzsee, Prof.-Dr.-Helmert-Str. 2-3, 14482 Potsdam, Germany
e-mail: Selina.Mayer@hpi.de

F. Bleuel · C. Stansell
Hasso Plattner Institute Academy, August-Bebel-Str. 88, 14482 Potsdam, Germany
e-mail: Flavia.Bleuel@hpi-academy.de

157

do so deliberately. At the same time, it is important to pay attention to our underlying assumptions and mental models and challenge them when needed, so that we can develop into effective leaders. This enables us to bring out the best in ourselves and in our organizations, especially in times of great uncertainty and change.

Approaching leadership from the perspective of Design Thinking and agility is a powerful way of growing effective leaders and empowered organizations, especially in turbulent contexts (Schumacher & Mayer, 2018). This view builds on a slow decades-long shift in the understanding and practice of leadership away from the command-and-control models of the past. In its best incarnations, leadership should echo key values of the Design Thinking mindset.

As the executive education arm of the HPI family, we at the HPI Academy have been supporting leaders from all over Germany and the world for a decade in their innovation journeys. As a result, we experience firsthand the challenges and the opportunities that our dynamic world presents to them. Intrapreneurs are increasingly demanding new ways of leading and are searching for approaches like Design Thinking for the orientation they need. By supporting them on their development journeys and letting ourselves be guided by Design Thinking as our core orientation, we have developed four practices to help leaders increase their effectiveness in the area of innovation and agility.

This chapter provides a brief overview of the Design Thinking mindset and describes the four leadership practices along with practical first steps for each, that support direct application. The focus here will be on questions that trigger self-reflection, as this lays the foundation for changing how we act.

2   Design Thinking Mindset

Due to the multitude of available definitions, there is still a lively discourse on the properties of Design Thinking (DT) today (see Micheli et al., 2019 for a review). Recent publications have referred to mindset as "one of the most crucial elements in the Design Thinking approach" (Dosi et al., 2018, p. 1991). The importance of the DT mindset as found in academia is also reflected in practice. For example, the HPI Academy demonstrates the importance of the role of mindset by including it as an integral part of DT coach training and certification (Fuchs & Graves, in press).

Managers are becoming less and less involved in actual project work as their responsibilities increase. This makes internalizing and exemplifying the DT mindset even more important for them than applying specific methods they have learned. At the HPI Academy, we have identified six elements of the DT mindset that form a foundation for our leadership training (HPI Academy, 2020).

It is probably not surprising that the first element relates to the human-centered nature of DT: *Think and act in a human-centered way*. This refers to the desire to understand human needs, emotions, behaviors, and values as a basis for gaining inspiration for one's own work. For leaders, this means being aware of the needs of their customers, users, stakeholders, employees, and even organizational needs, and acting accordingly.

This human-centered approach is also reflected in the second element where the focus is on collaboration in different teams (e.g., *collaborate in diverse teams*). As important as it is to listen to customers and users, it is equally important to introduce this open and reflective attitude in your own team. This will make it possible to harness the power of diversity in order to understand complex problems from different perspectives, and thus create innovation. For a leader, this means allowing a diversity of opinions in the team and creating a culture in which disagreement is constructive and different perspectives are valued.

The third mindset element relates to DT's holistic and open approach: *Explore the problem space.* This is about questioning your starting point and exploring a topic from multiple angles to discover your own blind spots and decide what the most promising focus point is. For leaders, this means allowing resources to be used for exploration with unknown outcomes, but also balancing this with the question of when to move on from exploration toward implementation.

This exploratory nature is supplemented by the creation of solutions in compact cycles that are integrated into the corresponding elements of mindset: *Learning through experimentation.* This element emphasizes the need to learn by developing experiments and the tendency to act and try things out in order to learn early on what works and what may not. Leaders are invited to support this approach to learning by establishing systems that reward learning and by creating an atmosphere that allows for failure.

DT is often oriented to complex issues in dynamic environments. Being comfortable with diverse opportunities and changing conditions is therefore part of the mindset: *Embrace uncertainty.* This means seeing ambiguity as an opportunity rather than a threat, and yet still being able to act. After all, complete information will likely never appear in complex and ambiguous situations, and no solution is final. For a leader, this means accepting on a personal level that you cannot always be the expert nor always have all the answers.

Last but not least, the sixth element of the mindset, *envision a radically new future,* is about optimism. It is about believing in a better future and believing that you, as a leader and with your team, can actually help change things despite all the challenges. A leader must therefore be able to think beyond a single solution and envision how entire systems will function in the future.

These elements of mindset already provide many clues as to how DT can help lead innovation and agility. In the next section, we will describe in more detail four leadership practices that we consider fundamental to successful leadership in today's world.

3   Leadership Practices

Over the past few years, we have worked with a variety of leaders from a wide range of industries. Despite the differing contexts, we have found a lot of commonalities when considering the issues of innovation, transformation, and agility within organizations. The view of leadership has also changed significantly. Historically, leaders were praised primarily for their management skills, including timely planning, management of resources and manpower, and the orientation of planned tasks. However, these behaviors are not compatible with the changing ways of working that we can observe in agile teams. We have therefore identified four key practices that leaders implement in order to foster innovation and agility (see Fig. 1).

The first practice is: *Create and communicate a clear vision.* The vision is based on an understanding of the needs of individuals, the market, and the organization, which a leader must communicate and constantly adapt.

The second practice is situated inside the organization, but has points of overlap with the outside: *Build systems to learn and experiment.* This refers to the development of processes and structures, but also to networks and a culture that enable learning and experimentation. It additionally refers to the balance between different work modes, such as exploring new markets and opportunities, as well the optimization of existing business areas and processes which can be adapted within teams or between them.

Within the team, a leader must implement the third practice: *Enable autonomy.* Leaders must enable flexibility and ownership in the team; i.e., they must allow a certain level of autonomous decision making to promote self-organization.

The fourth and final leadership practice is: *Foster psychological safety.* This is a critical foundation for building high-performing teams.

In the next section, we will look at the four practices in greater detail, each followed by one practice you can try out as a leader tomorrow.

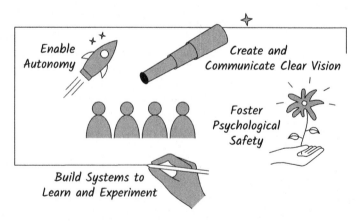

Fig. 1 Four leadership practices to foster innovation and agility (author's own figure)

3.1 Create and Communicate a Clear Vision

Regardless of whether we consider leadership in its new forms or traditional ones, it is clear that leaders have a special role to play when it comes to vision (Fig. 2). A vision is what gives us and our organizations a north star. The vision provides the direction that the strategy aims to achieve. "Visionary" is a favorite adjective our society bestows upon leaders who are considered truly exceptional in their sphere of influence, be they CEOs, politicians, or artists.

So, what is special about considering vision from the perspective of Design Thinking and agility? First, people should be at the center of this vision. It is based on a deep understanding of the needs of customers, stakeholders, and employees. Leaders can use the methods from Design Thinking to gain insights into the needs and opportunities within the marketplace and then develop innovative solutions to current—and even future—needs, thereby creating added value. For example, the Design Thinking methods based on empathy can assist in gaining these insights. Afterward, prototyping can help create better solutions faster.

However, the vision is just as much related to the inner workings of the company as it is to what happens externally in the market. This same human centeredness can be focused internally to better understand the strengths and needs of employees and stakeholders. This enables leaders, first of all, to better align value-creation opportunities with the skills and needs of the employees, and secondly, to be more sensitive and effective in communicating with employees and engaging them on an ongoing basis.

In addition, Design Thinking offers *co-creation tools* that can be used to collaboratively develop and harness an organization's vision—turning stakeholders, employees, and even customers into co-creators alongside the "users" of an organization's vision and impact. The benefit of this approach is twofold: gathering collective knowledge on a broad basis helps an organization identify potential blind spots or undiscovered potential, and the insights thus gained are integrated into the visioning process from the beginning.

Here, too, we draw on another element of the Design Thinking mindset: *Envision a radically new future.* This means that you, as a leader, look ahead with an open

Fig. 2 Create and communicate a clear vision (author's own figure)

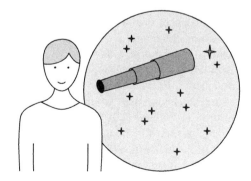

mind and try to proactively create a future that is different from what we see now. This attitude is the opposite of that of a reactionary who only responds to threats in order to survive in a saturated market. As a visionary, you therefore see uncertainty as an opportunity, actively search for innovations and, if necessary, create new markets.

One Thing to Try Out Tomorrow

Have an informal conversation with your employees about the shared vision. Above all, make sure to listen! Then reflect on what you have heard using the following questions:

- What does the vision mean to the employees and what is important to them?
- How does their view differ from your understanding of the vision—or that of the board/top management?
- Do the employees find it difficult to answer this question, e.g., to recall or connect to the organizational vision?
- Dig deeper whenever you find inconsistencies. Are inconsistencies rooted in simple errors in communication or deeper contradictions between what is said or lived as a vision and the values in your organization?

3.2   Build Systems to Learn and Experiment

Our business environment is becoming ever more complex. As a result, leaders and their team members are not always able to immediately answer all questions. The subject of lifelong learning is thus becoming increasingly important. For a long time, a leader was expected to provide answers, no matter what the question. The leader was often the only "source of wisdom" for many employees. Today, this image is undergoing significant change. It is no longer the leader's job to always have answers at hand, but rather to set up a system that focuses on learning and trial and error for themselves and their teams. Therefore, the goal now is to *build systems to learn and experiment*, as shown in Fig. 3. This requires a balancing act between setting up structures and allowing flexibility. Accordingly, the leader's task is to build a structure rather than a turnkey house, while the team members are responsible for furnishing the house and moving in. Here, the leaders should set an example by demonstrating *learning through experimentation.*

Building a system also means paying attention to its different levels, since these are inherent in every system (Heifetz et al., 2009). Continuing our metaphor of a system as a house, there would be the dance floor in the living room, which is always bustling and where daily business is taken care of. But there is also the balcony higher up, from which you have a view of the dance floor and yet can also see other areas of the house as well as the outdoors. So, leaders need adaptive systems where they can step onto the dance floor whenever necessary, to be involved in day-to-day

Fig. 3 Build systems to learn and experiment (author's own figure)

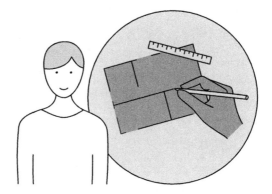

operations and experience their team's daily work up-close. It is just as important, though, that leaders be able to take a step back and have the view from the balcony, enabling them to see the big picture. If we want to be able to switch between these levels quickly and efficiently, we need a system that permits all of this, but goes a step further by also supporting leaders in taking the time and flexibility for these different levels and the associated tasks.

Another aspect of the system concerns the different work modes (i.e., *exploration* and *exploitation*) in which employees and teams can operate (O'Reilly & Tushman, 2011). For example, there is the *explore mode,* which we especially find in in the area of innovation. It is an investigative mode of working in the early phases of a project where the aim is to gather and explore all kinds of different perspectives. Then, there is the *exploit mode*, in which the focus is on maximizing and optimizing the insights and value gained once an innovation project has been completed and integrated into the operational business of a company. It is therefore the leader's task to keep an eye on the system as a whole and to consider the interfaces and overlaps of these modes of working. This includes the interactions within a team and between the individual employees and projects that are operating temporarily, or even simultaneously, in the different modes of work. However, it also includes collaboration between different teams, where some of the teams have their long-term focus on exploring new opportunities and others on maintaining the competitiveness of current day-to-day business through optimization.

Learning and experimentation are especially crucial in the exploratory approach. Short cycles, in which teams try out new solutions and quickly learn what works and what does not, make it possible to achieve better results in the long term.

Leadership is needed and wanted today, even in teams with flat hierarchies that are largely autonomous. A leader's presence can improve the results of the entire team. When leaders build such systems with a focus on learning and experimentation, this effect is likely to be maintained during their absence as well.

One Thing to Try Out Tomorrow

The next time you have to make a decision, consider alternatives and test what the "better" option is.

- What cheap and quick experiment can be used to obtain more information? Reflect on the results.
- How can you ensure that what has been learned is fed back into the organization?

3.3   Enable Autonomy

An agile organization aims to continuously optimize its core business while exploring new business opportunities to stay relevant in the market in the future. When complex challenges need to be resolved, agile teams take on more (decision-making) responsibility so they can react quickly and accurately to changes or advance these changes themselves.

A leader must aim to enable (cross-functional) teams to make decisions within their defined area and without friction from the "silo mentality," while finding a balance between freedom of decision and accountability (Fig. 4). Leaders should often practice applying the *embracing uncertainty* mindset to deal with this situation! The highest level of autonomy is achieved when teams can make the following decisions themselves (Hackman, 2002):

(a)   Define the objective or main task of their project work;
(b)   Determine the composition of their team themselves: These teams can dismiss team members and hire new ones;

Fig. 4 Enable autonomy (author's own figure)

(c)   Determine the reporting structures themselves: In some cases, autonomous teams also have decision-making authority with regard to the reporting structures within the team and those involving individuals outside the team;

(d)   Manage processes and decisions regarding ways of working themselves: This may include whether they will use the agile approach (or not).

At first glance, it seems paradoxical for a self-organized team to require leadership. However, leadership skills have a direct impact on the success or failure of such a team. Although leaders may not always be intensely involved in the actual project work, as the project progresses, there will be issues and requirements that cannot be planned and that the team will not be able to resolve on their own. In these cases, they will need to rely on the leader for support. Then, the leader can send strong signals by responding flexibly to the requests and leading the team by asking questions or offering them a strategic perspective. Enabling autonomy and self-organization therefore does not mean that all the responsibility is delegated to the teams and that there is no longer a need for leadership. Teams work in faster cycles and thus have to make decisions more quickly. When they do, waiting until the next meeting or postponing decisions until the information has traveled through several hierarchical levels is often not an option. The leader is responsible for all the decisions that are strategically relevant, such as which projects are placed in which areas of opportunity or how a team's results fit within the organizational strategy and the bigger picture. The leader should also support their team with advice on trends, regulations, competitors, or stakeholders.

One Thing to Try Out Tomorrow

If you want to practice enabling autonomous decision-making, you should pay attention to your leadership language and ask your teams what they plan to do to solve the problem, rather than telling them what to do.

- When are you really needed in the project?
- Who made the last 10 decisions?

3.4   Foster Psychological Safety

When teams are challenged to take on more responsibility, to experiment, and to adapt to change, work culture has a critical impact on the behavior of the team and the individual team members. What risks are individuals willing to take, how are mistakes communicated, how are lessons learned, and who is willing to address problems directly? People are often reluctant to experiment or take risks for fear of being evaluated negatively or as less competent by others. Although this form of self-protection is a natural human strategy, it also gets in the way of effective teamwork. Google scientifically followed 180 teams over several years in a large-scale study to analyze the factors that foster high-performance teams (Rozovsky, 2015). A psychologically safe work environment turned out to be a surprising factor in the study (*psychological safety*). Psychological safety is described as the feeling that people will not be shamed or punished if they speak up (Frazier et al., 2017).

In a meta-study, Frazier et al. (2017) investigated which conditions have a particularly strong effect on the individual, as well as on the psychological safety of the team. According to their findings, the following factors are key to psychological safety: role clarity, peer support, interdependence, learning orientation, and positive leader relations. Accordingly, the direct positive consequences of psychological safety are information sharing, higher job satisfaction, proactive learning behaviors (seeking information, experimenting, and reflecting), commitment, and improved task performance.

Therefore, it is up to the leader to create a work environment that is psychologically safe for interpersonal risk-taking (Fig. 5). This requires an environment that allows team members to feel safe with each other, admit mistakes, acknowledge each other as partners and equals, and have the courage to take on new roles. Concrete rituals can help here, such as a *failure Friday* (i.e., discussing mistakes, and especially what was learned from them, every Friday). The Google study shows that individuals in teams with higher psychological safety are less likely to leave the organization. They build on the diverse ideas of their teammates, generate more revenue and are twice as likely to be rated as effective by executives (Rozovsky, 2015). Especially when using and accepting different ideas and perspectives, the mindset element of *collaboration in diverse teams* is essential.

One Thing to Try Out Tomorrow
Ask yourself the following questions to assess the level of psychological safety and learning culture in your organization:

- If you make a mistake at work, will it be used against you?

Fig. 5 Foster psychological safety (author's own figure)

- Are employees allowed to address problems directly?
- Are unique skills and talents valued?
- Is it safe to take a risk?
- Is it difficult to ask other people for help?
- Would someone in the team/department intentionally act in a way that undermines the efforts of others?
- As a leader, what rituals do you cultivate to foster an open culture of learning and error?
- This exercise is inspired by Edmondson (1999).

4   Summary and Outlook

In this chapter, we have shown how the Design Thinking mindset can help leaders foster innovation and agility in themselves and their employees. Based on this, we have presented four leadership practices: *Create and communicate a clear vision, build systems to learn and experiment, enable autonomy,* and *foster psychological safety.* These can help a leader take the first concrete steps toward agility and innovation.

As noted in the beginning, learning outside of formal schooling is also a central building block for being and staying successful in our dynamic world. The World Economic Forum has published a study on which 10 skills will be most important by 2025 (Whiting, 2020). These include, for example, active learning, complex problem solving, developing innovations, building resilience, and flexibility. This underlines how the practices we have described here will continue to become more relevant in the future. Innovation can be learned. Agility can be learned. Leadership can be learned.

References

Bennis, W. G. (2009). *On becoming a leader.* Basic Books.

Dosi, C., Rosati, F., & Vignoli, M. (2018). Measuring design thinking mindset. *Proceedings of International Design Conference, DESIGN, 5,* 1991–2002.

Edmondson, A. (1999). Psychological safety and learning behavior in work teams. *Administrative Science Quarterly, 44,* 350–383.

Frazier, M. L., Fainshmidt, S., Klinger, R. L., Pezeshkan, A., & Vracheva, V. (2017). Psychological safety: A meta-analytic review and extension. *Personnel Psychology, 70*(1), 113–165. https://doi.org/10.1111/peps.12183

Fuchs, J., & Graves, M. (in press). Teaching the design thinking mindset A practitioner's perspective. In I. Schmidberger, S. Wippermann, T. Stricker, & U. Müller (Eds.), *Design thinking im bildungsmanagement. Innovationen in Bildungskontexten erfolgreich entwickeln und umsetzen.* Springer

Hackman, J. R. (2002). Why teams don't work. In R. S. Tindale, L. Heath, J. Edwards, E. J. Posavac, F. B. Bryant, Y. Suarez-Balcazar, & E. Henderson-King (Eds.), *Theory and research on small groups* (pp. 245–267). Springer. https://doi.org/10.1007/0-306-47144-2_12

Heifetz, R. A., Grashow, A., & Linsky, M. (2009). *The practice of adaptive leadership: Tools and tactics for changing your organization and the world.* Harvard Business Press.

HPI Academy (Ed.). (2020). *Design thinking mindset for innovation.* https://hpi-academy.de/des ign-thinking/design-thinking-mindset-for-innovation.html

Micheli, P., Wilner, S. J. S., Bhatti, S. H., Mura, M., & Beverland, M. B. (2019). Doing design thinking: Conceptual review, synthesis, and research agenda. *Journal of Product Innovation Management, 36*(2), 124–148.

O'Reilly, C. A., & Tushman, M. L. (2011). Organizational ambidexterity in action: How managers explore and exploit. *California Management Review, 53*(4), 5–22. https://doi.org/10.1525/cmr.2011.53.4.5

Rozovsky, J. (2015, November 17). *The five keys to a successful Google team.* Google rework. https://rework.withgoogle.com/blog/five-keys-to-a-successful-google-team/

Schumacher, T., & Mayer, S. (2018). Preparing managers for turbulent contexts: Teaching the principles of design thinking. *Journal of Management Education, 42*(4), 496–523.

Whiting, K. (2020, October 21). *These are the top 10 job skills of tomorrow—And how long it takes to learn them.* World Economic Forum. https://www.weforum.org/agenda/2020/10/top-10-work-skills-of-tomorrow-how-long-it-takes-to-learn-them/

Selina Mayer has spent the last five years guiding clients all over the world in learning and applying Design Thinking in her role as Program Lead at the HPI Academy. This includes everything from small methodological introductions and long-term project support to strategic and cultural change processes. One example of her work was her aid in establishing a D-School in Chile. Prior to that, she gained experience with transformation and innovation in both a digital start-up and a large multinational corporation. She is currently also conducting research in the Hasso Plattner Design Thinking Research Program on the topic of the "Impact of DT in Organizations." Selina Mayer believes a major challenge of Design Thinking in education is transferring what is learned in the "classroom" to real-world applications. Blended learning formats, individualized learning content, and in-situ guidance can especially help companies and their employees achieve sustainable learning success.

Flavia Bleuel Over the past 15 years, Flavia Bleuel has guided organizations from various industries and of different sizes in their transformation towards human-centered innovation, agile leadership, and cross-functional-collaboration. She is responsible for designing and running leadership development formats like Leadership for Innovation and Agility, Navigating Uncertainty—Personal Leadership Compass or Design Thinking and Organizational Implementation. Furthermore, she leads cooperation formats with well-known Business Schools like HEC Paris, London Business School or ESMT. Flavia has helped shape the curriculum of the HPI School of Design Thinking in Potsdam and coached students from around the world. Prior to this, she worked as user researcher, lecturer, and innovation coach at the University of the Arts Berlin. There she built a user research lab from scratch together with her team. She founded a network for innovation experts and published in the field of Design Thinking, Agile Innovation Management and Leadership.

For her, Design Thinking is rooted in the mindset, and mindset is something people rarely change in their lifetimes, as it involves changing behavior. But change and innovation are our constants in life. Transformation does not end after one educational session, but is an ongoing process. Inspiring people with suitable formats, challenging them, and tapping into their potential is the essence of excellent professional education.

Christina Stansell Through her work in the #SmartDevelopmentFund at GIZ, Germany's leading provider of international cooperation services, Christina Stansell supports the development and scaling of innovative ideas, technologies and approaches to tackling pressing global challenges in low-resource environments. Prior to this, she spent six years as a Program Lead for Leadership Experiences and Corporate Innovation at the HPI Academy and as a teacher at the HPI D-School, where she designed, led, and coached programs that brought Design Thinking to real world challenges. She previously worked at the Institute of International Education in the USA, managing leadership and capacity-building programs, specializing in the field of global women's health.

Christina Stansell has coached hundreds of professionals and students in their Design Thinking journeys over the years, in addition to applying the method and mindset in her own global program work. One of the greatest challenges—and opportunities—she sees with Design Thinking is for leaders to leverage and adapt it effectively to foster agility and innovation, while also taking into account the unique realities of their institution and their broader context. Some helpful insights for doing that can be found here, in her and her colleagues' chapter on "Design Thinking for Leaders."

Human-Centeredness in Professional Education – On the Use and Application of a Human-Centered Approach in the Field of Professional Education

Jan Koch

Abstract This chapter will reflect on several examples from the field of professional education how a human-centered approach can be of value for both the conceptualization of professional education formats as well as the further development of existing tools, working materials, or exercises. It also demonstrates how more tailored ways of knowledge transfer and application can be created based on a human-centered approach and how this can contribute to the continuous advancement of a format.

> "One of the greatest strengths of Design Thinking is its focus on people. This means, firstly, wanting to understand human needs, behaviors, emotions and values. Secondly, it means using this understanding to inspire and shape your own work".

HPI Academy—Design Thinking Mindset for Innovation

This chapter will reflect on several examples from the field of professional education how a human-centered approach can be used both for program development itself and for the further development of existing tools, working materials, or exercises and thereby contribute to an effective knowledge transfer into organizations.

The HPI Academy's long-standing *Professional Track* will serve as an illustrative example of this, as it has formed a large knowledge base over time. In addition, it vividly demonstrates how a human-centered approach can benefit the program development by considering the requirements and needs of course participants (in this case from the executive levels of organizations).

J. Koch (✉)
Hasso Plattner Institute Academy, August-Bebel-Str. 88, 14482 Potsdam, Germany
e-mail: jan.koch@hpi-academy.de

© The Author(s), under exclusive license to Springer Nature Switzerland AG 2022
C. Meinel and T. Krohn (eds.), *Design Thinking in Education*,
https://doi.org/10.1007/978-3-030-89113-8_12

1   Human-Centered Approaches in Professional Education Program Development: Experience—Apply—Transfer

Since 2014, the *Professional Track*—developed by Professor Ulrich Weinberg and Annie Kerguenne—addresses as an independent course the great demand from the private sector for a training concept related to the HPI School of Design Thinking's educational program for students. Besides some organizational differences, such as a course structure in block format to enable participants to fit the program more easily into their everyday professional lives, the *Professional Track* also aims to support and guide participants as they transfer what they have learned into their respective context or organization.

For this purpose, the individual course blocks are each divided into three days with different focal points:

Day one (*Experience*) consists of experiencing individual elements of Design Thinking by means of in-depth exercises (*deep dives*). Participants also develop an understanding of how the principles of human centeredness impact ways of working on innovation topics.

Day two (*Apply*) focuses on the concrete application of these principles as part of an exemplary project. The question (*challenge*) to be worked on in each case comes from a real company and deals with specific questions on organizational topics or developing offers or portfolios, for example. With this *challenge* as a starting point, the course participants go through all the phases of Design Thinking as multidisciplinary teams.

Working on the issues of real project partners increases the relevance for the course participants, as there are often overlaps with issues from the participants' organizations. The sample project thus simultaneously serves to prepare participants for the transfer tasks on the third day of the blocked course.

The focus of the third day (*Transfer*) is on transferring and adapting what has been learned into the participants' respective professional context or organization. For this purpose, all participants are asked in advance of the course to provide a question (*challenge*) that originates from within their own organization so they can directly apply the approach learned in the course to this *challenge*.

In contrast to the teamwork in the first two days, the third day is characterized more by individual support for the participants in their own project work. Experienced coaches address the specific difficulties participants face in working on the *challenges* they have brought with them. These range from putting together a project team and defining the initial question to issues of empathy work and synthesis, idea generation, prototyping, and testing.

From the very beginning, the program design, therefore, provides for individual reflection and knowledge acquisition using applied exercises—and this is also done with special consideration to the respective conditions of the participants' organizational and work situations.

The individual support on day three enables the coaching team to better understand the participants' primary challenges and to jointly develop approaches for finding solutions. This approach also improves understanding of user needs and perspectives with each program cycle, therefore allowing for a continuous improvement of the program itself.

How these developments take place and in what form they are integrated into the program can be illustrated through examples of so-called *"hacks"* that were created as part of the *Professional Track*.

This chapter thereby focuses on examples of *hacks* that were developed as a part of efforts to better convey human-centered innovation work.

2 The Concept of *"Hacks"*

Within the *Professional Track*, the term *"hack"* has established itself for small, specific adaptations of work materials, work steps, or exercises in response to specific questions or difficulties that participants have faced as part of the projects (*challenges*) they have brought with them. These little adaptations were always made with the objective of introducing the principles of Design Thinking as precisely and effectively as possible into the participants' specific organizational context, thus making these principles more tangible and communicable.

At the same time, developing these adaptations was in itself a human-centered approach, as a *hack* took into account the particular characteristics of teams or organizations when designing ways to introduce them to a Design Thinking work mode.

As part of a regular exchange among coaches and participants between the blocked events or during *hacking jams* (short presentations during the blocked courses), the participants shared their experiences with the *hacks*.

Participants appreciated this exchange so much that the *hacking jams* have now become a regular part of the alumni events and form a lively knowledge network for the context-specific application of Design Thinking in the professional field.

3 The *Cardboard Cut-Out Persona*—An Example of the Creation and Application of a *Hack*

A challenge that arose while transitioning from the synthesis to the idea generation phase led to the first *hack* example.

3.1   Problem Description

Despite a comprehensive database resulting from the empathy phase, individual teams in the synthesis phase did not sufficiently discuss possible user groups and their needs. This resulted in a lack of shared understanding, which proved problematic in subsequent phases.

For example, individual team members saw very different characteristics as being central to the user group even though the team had previously jointly developed a *Point of View* and a *Persona* and documented these in the provided working materials (*templates*).

In other teams, the ideas developed seemed only marginally inspired by the user group and only tangentially addressed the user's problems or needs. Instead, ideas appeared to be more guided by technological developments or possibilities.

3.2   Approach to Finding a Solution

Based on these problems, the following requirements for an approach to finding a solution arose:

(1)   Supporting a more extensive exchange within the team on understanding the needs and characteristics of the user group as part of the synthesis phase.
(2)   Finding a way to keep the change in perspective in terms of a user-centered way of working at the forefront of the team's mind over a longer period of time.

3.3   *The* Hack

The solution approach developed referred to the principle of prototyping and consisted of designing a complementary small exercise—a *hack*—to encourage the team to engage in an understanding of the user group that was both playful and more in-depth.

For this purpose, the worksheet (*template*) for the *Persona* description was supplemented by an approximately 30 cm-tall, unlabeled cardboard figure (*Cardboard Cut-Out Persona*) (Fig. 1), which could be positioned as a three-dimensional display in the team's work area (*team space*). The team's additional task besides filling out the regular working materials was to also make the central characteristics and needs of the user group visible on the figure by applying details, accessories, or speech bubbles. The *Cut-Out Persona* therefore complemented the visualization that was already part of the *Persona* worksheet, but transferred it into a haptic form.

The goal of the *hack* was to create a physical reference to the user group for the team during the creation process in addition to a more extensive team discussion.

Fig. 1 Cardboard Cut-Out Persona

The hack was also intended to serve as a visible reminder of the insights gained from the empathy work.

In terms of fostering exchange and maintaining a reference to the user, this, therefore, aligns with the broader concepts of Alan Cooper in the development of the *Persona* as a tool for Interaction Design (Cooper, 1999; Cooper et al., 2007).

Accordingly, the *Cut-Out Persona* remained in the team space for the following phases even after the exercise was completed.

3.4 *Observed Effects of the* Hack

The following observations were made while testing the *hack*:

- Designing the *Cut-Out Persona* allowed more easily to involve several team members at the same time in contrast to filling in a worksheet.
- Because of the limited space on the figure, a natural discussion developed among the team members about what the most important features and characteristics were that needed to be incorporated.
- The speech bubbles attached to the figure helped to additionally describe the *Point of View* from the user's perspective, therefore making it even more memorable for the team. Here, too, the limited space had a positive effect on the intensity of the discourse within the team.

As hoped, the *Cut-Out Persona* also turned out to be a useful tool for teamwork in the subsequent work phases:

- During the idea development process, teams used the *Persona* as an "additional team member" in the process of selecting the ideas by having the cut-out at the table with them and discussing from the cut-out's point of view when evaluating possible solutions.
- During the test phase, new insights about the user group were added to the design of the *Cut-Out Persona* and relevant information about the context of the *Persona* was also incorporated using further elements.
- When onboarding additional team members, the *Cut-Out Persona* was used to present the synthesis results.

Overall, from the observations on the use of the *Cut-Out Persona*, it could be concluded that this *hack* contributed to the two desired goals: It encouraged exchange within the team to form a shared understanding of the user group and reminded team members to keep the user perspective in mind even beyond the synthesis phase.

The *Cut-Out Persona* was therefore added to the *Professional Track's* repertoire of available working materials.

Even more so, this *hack* also represents an example of the aforementioned claim that a human-centered approach contributes to program advancement.

3.5 *Further Iterations and Applications of the* Hack

The deliberate designation as a "*hack*" was also intended to indicate that the current adaptation is not necessarily final and to invite further experimentation with possible applications and improvements.

For example, the author also used the *Cut-Out Persona* in project work with a team of students at the HPI School of Design Thinking. This showed that the figures could be useful even early in the synthesis phase due to their rapid and easy reproducibility:

The team created a figure for each relevant perspective as part of their joint review of the research results, illustrating the patterns and viewpoints they found relating to the project topic. This created a gallery that was used in the subsequent establishment of the *Point of View* to find a project focus that suggested a relevance even to other user groups in addition to the primary selected user group.

Several students iterated the idea of a haptic manifestation of the *Persona* within their own design agency after completing the HPI School of Design Thinking and developed a much more professional version made of a sturdy, lightweight foam core with a plastic coating. This allowed the figures to be written on and wiped off like a whiteboard, making them even more flexible in use and enabling faster revisions. Supplemented by visualization aids and attachable speech bubbles, this version is now successfully marketed as a product under the name *Pop-Up Persona*.

This higher-quality model also replaced the first generation of handmade *Cut-Out Personas* in the *Professional Track* as part of its further development, and in turn, enabled new ways to apply the *hack* in conveying a human-centered way of thinking and working into organizations:

For example, the more professional design of the *Pop-Up Persona* encouraged course participants to also use the figure as an element in project presentations outside of their core project team. They reported that the physical representation of the user group positively influenced the subsequent discussion in terms of a human-centered perspective.

In addition to using the figure in the synthesis phase, individual course participants also used it as an introductory exercise (*warm-up*) for the subsequent phases of the Design Thinking process. Jointly crafting and designing the figure prior to developing ideas again reminded the team of the user group and, at the same time, prepared them for the subsequent phase of physical prototyping.

A final example shows the use of this *hack* beyond its application in the Design Thinking context and in terms of a general human-centered way of thinking and working:

One course participant subsequently used the *Pop-Up Personas* to prepare important presentations within her organization. In other words, in contrast to the described use as a presentation *element* and reference to the user group, the course participant used the figures to collect the participants' expectations, requirements, and perspectives. In this way, she was able to take central user perspectives into account when designing the presentation and to relate these perspectives to each other.

This approach of specifically looking at the user perspectives of the presentation participants in advance and displaying them by means of the *Pop-Up Personas* has since been used with great success many times.

These types of examples and experiences from using the *hacks* were shared during the *hacking jam* sessions, helping other course participants to develop a specific introduction and delivery strategy for Design Thinking within their organization and likewise helping the program team to continually refine and adapt the course format.

4   Further *Hacks* Related to Introducing Human-Centered Innovation Work

Of course, *hacks* on other challenges in conveying a human-centered way of working were also created in the *Professional Track* together with the course participants.

Two more examples shall be mentioned briefly here as well. Both of them dealt with conveying and communicating aspects of the user perspective to stakeholders or third parties outside the project team.

The first hack aimed to provide non-team members with an understanding of empathy work in the most time-efficient way possible. For this purpose, participants developed various *hacks* in which they recreated typical environments or life situations of the *Persona* in their team spaces, into which the guests of the team could then enter and thus "immerse" themselves.

In contrast to the *Cut-Out Persona*, it was not the representative of a user group who was designed, but rather his/her environment. The scope of the work and effort that the teams put into it ranged from partly recreating the home furnishings as they had experienced them in the users' homes during the empathy phase all the way to smaller and often mobile variants of these scenes, e.g., in the form of a suitcase with things that had a connection to the *Persona* and contributed to a better understanding of these users' realities and daily lives. In this way, the teams managed to give their guests a better understanding of the function and importance of empathy work.

The second hack aimed to provide a team's guests with the possibility to engage with the content and results of the synthesis phase in a more interactive way. Here, the hack consisted of having a team member take on the role of the *Persona* and be available for some sort of "interview" or "conversation with the user group" for the team's guests. This person's task was to revisualize all the results of the empathy phase again as comprehensively as possible in advance in order to be able to answer questions as authentically as possible from the *Persona's* perspective. This variant also gave third parties a better experience surrounding the role and relevance of empathy work in a project.

5   Summary

In this chapter, illustrative examples were introduced to provide insight into how a human-centered approach can be applied concretely both in the conceptualization and further development of professional education formats. Likewise, the concept of *hacks* demonstrated one way in which a human-centered approach can serve as the basis for more tailored adaptations of knowledge transfer and application of Design Thinking in organizations.

References

Cooper, A. (1999). *The inmates are running the asylum.* SAMS/Macmillan.
Cooper, A., Reimann, R., & Cronin, D. (2007). *About face 3: The essentials of interaction design.* Wiley.
HPI Academy. (2020). *Design thinking mindset for innovation.* https://hpi-academy.de/en/design-thinking/design-thinking-mindset-for-innovation.html

Jan Koch Design Thinking Strategist, HPI Academy.

With his background in communication research and media management as well as his interest in information technology, Jan Koch initially worked as a project lead and an intermediary between management and IT departments within strategic development and implementation projects. Since 2009, Jan Koch has been engaged in educating students at the HPI School of Design Thinking while also actively supporting companies and organizations in conceptualizing and guiding human-centered ways of working and in establishing innovation units.

One of his insights from conceptualizing professional courses and workshops is to include a human-centered perspective already very early on in the process. Taking into account the participants' expectations, prior knowledge, goals, and challenges allows to design an optimal learning path that enables them to successfully transfer and apply the acquired knowledge to their respective contexts or organizations.

Strategic DT as a New Instrument for Leadership in Digital Transformation

Annie Kerguenne

Abstract The Harvard Business Review headline from 2015: "Design Thinking Comes of Age" marked a milestone in the widespread integration of user-centered thought and the participatory implementation of digital transformation. Obviously, Design Thinking identified at times since its inception as the "esoteric hippie method," had reached a new stage of development. That is, evolving from a method whose roots go back to the Bauhaus movement, to an approach on how to tackle complex tasks, to a strategy that made possible the promotion and development of an innovative and adaptable corporate culture. Strategic Design Thinking encompasses both the application of the method and the fundamental mindset of the transformational pioneers, as well as principles that can be derived for the implementation of specific transformation strategies. The article presents a brief, albeit greatly reduced, outline of the history of design thinking, and develops connections to the constructivist learning theory. References to research findings in neuroscience are made and, based on application examples, the leveraging power of strategic design thinking is shown in the context of digital transformation. The reflection closes with the elaboration of an answer to the question **"How can strategic design thinking help to guide the implementation of an agile transformation strategy?"**.

The Harvard Business Review headline from 2015: "Design Thinking Comes of Age" (Kolko, 2015) marked a milestone in the widespread integration of user-centered thought and the participatory implementation of digital transformation. In addition to the participation of executives from innovation departments, managers from human resources, corporate strategy and IT were increasingly attending design thinking workshops at Hasso Plattner Institute. This school of thought and craftsmanship, identified at times since its inception as the "esoteric hippie method," had reached a new stage of development. That is, evolving from a method whose roots go back to the Bauhaus movement, to an approach of how to tackle complex tasks, to a strategy

A. Kerguenne (✉)
Hasso Plattner Institute for Digital Engineering, Hasso Plattner Institute Academy, Campus Griebnitzsee, Prof.-Dr.-Helmert-Str. 2-3, 14482 Potsdam, Germany
e-mail: Annie.Kerguenne@hpi-academy.de

that made possible the promotion and development of an innovative and adaptable corporate culture. It was an evolution that could be explained with findings from the theory of learning and neuroscience.

In reflecting on strategic design thinking here, we do not mean strategic design for creating a visual corporate identity—but rather the application of this method in the entrepreneurial field of action involving the planning, management, implementation, and long-term anchoring of transformational activities. Strategic design thinking encompasses both the application of the method and the fundamental mindset of the transformational pioneers, as well as principles that can be derived for the implementation of specific transformation strategies. We explore operative design thinking in the sense of its methodical application for the development of innovative solutions (products, services, processes) and we reflect upon its significance in the transformation process.

The following article presents a brief, albeit greatly reduced, outline of the history of design thinking, and develops connections to the constructivist learning theory. References to research findings in neuroscience are made and, based on application examples, the leveraging power of strategic design thinking is shown in the context of digital transformation.

1   How Has Design Thinking Evolved from an Innovation Method to a Strategy for Cultural Transformation?

"The method is based on common sense",

said Hasso Plattner, co-founder of the software company SAP and founder of the Hasso Plattner Institute, when asked by a journalist to explain design thinking. Plattner thus sums up the essence of design thinking, and what has been the driving force behind the discipline from its start until today: people. People as the starting point for innovation and a unit of measure for conceptual design. The roots of which can be found, among other places, already in the Bauhaus movement and the motto, "Form follows function." It was a principle that bore fruit far beyond German borders, as seen in such creative influencers as interior architect and designer Charlotte Perriand or her business partner, architect Le Corbusier. "Modulor," the system of proportions developed by Le Corbusier, radically placed people as an objective unit of measurement in the center of interior design and architecture (Le Corbusier, 1950). In the 2000s the triumphant advance of the "Design Thinking Mindset" began in earnest (i.e., the basic principle of discovering an innovative solution to complex problems). The founder of the American innovation and design agency IDEO, engineer, product designer, and Stanford professor David Kelley brought about widespread media awareness with a sensational innovation project and the implementation of the three fundamental parts of the innovator's mindset. These areas, "user-centeredness," "multi-perspectivity," and "learning through experimentation," served from then on to shape the basic attitude toward work on innovation projects.

Posters in creative spaces and innovation labs of companies soon expressed messages such as "FOCUS ON HUMAN VALUES," "RADICAL COLLABO-RATION" or "EMBRACE EXPERIMENTATION." On Dec. 2, 2009, the ABC program "Nightline" (ABC Nightline, 2009) showed how the multidisciplinary IDEO team developed by way of fast prototype simulation a modern, modular shopping cart within only five days—while having fun at the same time. The user-centered shopping cart made shopping at various grocery store stations easier and reduced the risk of injury to a minimum for children sitting in a cart. This marked the visible beginning of the design thinking mindset era. With this new approach toward complex problems and with the help of precise processes, new products, new services, new processes, and entirely new business models could be successfully designed. For example, magnetic resonance tomography transforms this tedious procedure into an adventure-like experience for children. Or a banking service, which, in small steps, makes saving easier by rounding up daily purchase amounts. Or a warming bag created for prematurely born babies in developing countries, to prevent hypothermia on the long trip to the next hospital, which has evolved into a successful startup (https://www.gehealthcare.com/products/acc essories-and-supplies/adventure-series-for-ct, https://www.bankofamerica.com/dep osits/keep-the-change/, https://www.embraceinnovations.com).

The dissemination of the innovation method grew, and, at the same time, the mindset associated with it. This was reflected in the success of a new generation of entrepreneurs at the top of startups like Google, Apple, Airbnb— but also at established companies such as Bank of America, GE Healthcare, or Bosch. Today, design thinking is considered among the core qualifications of top executives so that they can not only successfully lead in the area of conception but also in the planning and implementation of digital transforma-tion processes (https://www.mckinsey.com/business-functions/organization/our-ins ights/unlocking-success-in-digital-transformations). The strategic use of design thinking makes two things possible: first, the fast learning and integration into dynamically-complex contexts, and, second, the derivation of principles that are effective in a specific context for transformation. It is precisely for this reason that the method has proven its usefulness: the context of the transformation in each organization is so different that the "best case" strategies cannot simply be copies. The Cynefin Framework (https://www.cognitive-edge.com) of English scholar David Snowden is, among other things, based on the theory of complex systems and offers a helpful categorization of different contexts and appropriate strategies. Snowden differentiates clear situations, characterized by simple causal relationships, as well as complicated situations, which combine a variety of these causal relationships and complex situations with high dynamics that make it impossible to determine in advance how a result can be achieved. The strategy in these complex situations must therefore be based on a policy of small steps in which one moves forward while learning. Which is one of the core elements of the design thinking mindset (Fig. 1).

The leverage of the strategic use of design thinking is also documented in the above-mentioned Mc Kinsey study concerning the technologies and methods used by companies with successful transformation activities. Design thinking is the only

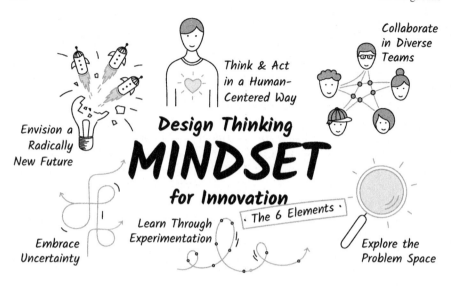

Fig. 1 Design thinking mindset

method to stand alongside technologies such as cloud-based services, mobile internet technologies, Big Data, Internet of Things, or artificial intelligence instruments. It can be considered belonging to the basic equipment for digital transformation.

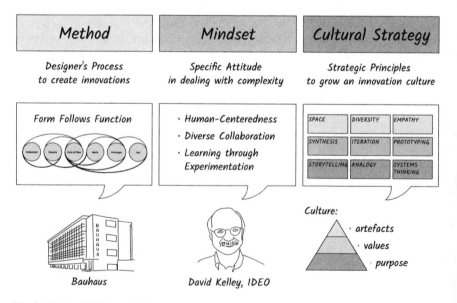

Fig. 2 Design thinking evolution

2   Which Findings from Learning Theory Help Users to Understand the Benefits of Strategic Design Thinking?

Design thinking can become the basic principle for re-orientation of our organization in the future.

Thus, the assessment of Uwe Raschke, managing director of Robert Bosch GmbH (https://hpi-digitalblog.de/interview_post/uwe-raschke-about-design-thinking-and-its-implementation-at-bosch/). How is it possible for an innovation method to qualify as the basic principle for the development of an innovative corporate culture? A look at the topic concept of "experience-based learning" (Kolb and Frey 1975) helps to explain this.

The model is based on the assumption that the effectiveness of learning will rise parallel to the level of practicality with which the subject is dealt with.

In other words, if I drive a car myself, driving skills are better anchored in my mind than if I just attend theoretical lessons. The "learning by doing," which appears so logical in practical skills, also applies, in experience-based learning, to abstract learning elements such as teamwork, empathy building, or the iterative development of solutions. The model distinguishes four learning phases that build on each other in cyclical organization and form, as such, a permanent learning cycle (Fig. 3).

The experience: Transformation Pioneers experience the value of direct discussions with users. They ask open questions, inquire about good and bad experiences on a topic, ask about the reasons for positive or negative emotions and, perhaps—make a discovery. For instance, that a young person does not enjoy doing schoolwork when it is parent-monitored—because this would give her a defeating feeling of not being taken seriously. This surprised the researchers who had assumed students would more likely view such monitoring as a way to establish orientation and structure.

The reflection: When compared to the usual batteries of closed questions used in

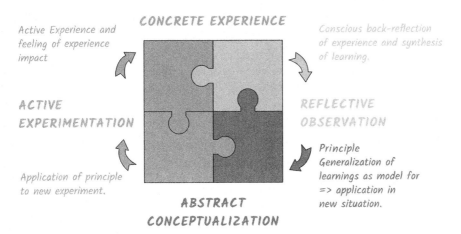

Fig. 3 Model of experienced-based learning

classic market research, the empathic technique of placing oneself in the user's shoes through open questions and follow-ups allows a deeper dive into unknown motifs—as well as a way to track them. These new findings offer good starting points for innovative, user-centered solutions. **The concept formation**: A principle or concept is derived from the reflection that serves as a concrete guideline in other situations. Whenever it is a matter of exploring the deeper reasons for certain behavior in order to find new solutions to problems (whether with colleagues, family members, or criminal offenders) the principle of empathy offers a successful formula. **Experimentation**: Other related questions are now dealt with and problems solved with this principle. These mark the beginning of the learning cycle as concrete experience. In this way, strategic principles for acting in new contexts are gradually developed over time.

The direct experience as a basis for learning and the active role of the learner are two principles that are deeply anchored in the design thinking approach. The innovators themselves go into the field to research the needs of the users. They analyze what they have found in a team and develop solution hypotheses, which they test as quickly as possible with the users as rough prototypes. From the users' reactions, they learn how the solution should be further developed in order to finally give a valid answer to a real user after several iteration loops. The design thinking process can thus also be described as an experience-based learning process. But it is not just about learning by doing, it is the concept formation phase that enables the learners in design thinking to make their experiences translatable for themselves and their situation. The development of these transfer principles can be strengthened in design thinking training through the integration of research knowledge, which illuminates the various aspects of the agents behind the method. The principle of creative space design to support higher team performance can be better validated if, for example, one knows from neuroscientific research that the design of a space has a significant impact on human self perception and that a change of perspective can influence the anchoring of what has been learned to a large degree (Proulx et al., 2016).

In addition to cognitive (theoretical) knowledge and affective (motivational and approach-based) knowledge, transformation pioneers can build the application-based knowledge necessary to implement the transformation processes (Taheri et al., 2016). Accordingly, the design thinking practitioner can exploit the approach to its fullest potential—as a method, as a mindset, and as a cultural strategy (Fig. 4).

3 How Can Any Innovator Derive Specific Strategic Principles from the Method Application?

How do I find the right strategic principle for my own transformation situation?

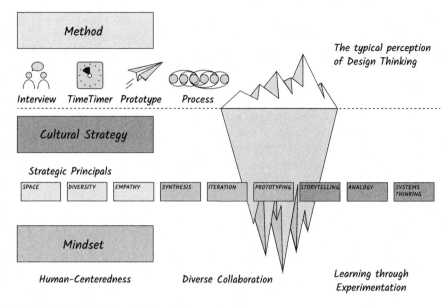

Fig. 4 Design thinking method—mindset—cultural strategy

This is the key question for many design thinking course participants. In other words, how exactly does a person get from the mindset to the behavior that is goal-oriented for the specific situation? What works for one company cannot simply be copied for another; the systems are just too complex and different. The simple answer: "apply design thinking in order to be able to implement design thinking in every context." A comparison with an analogy field can help to clarify the necessity of principle derivation (Fig. 5):

Fig. 5 Application of a principle

If I am convinced that making and repairing things in life makes more sense than buying and throwing them away, I have a DO-IT-YOURSELF mindset. All sorts of tools and methods are available to me to put this attitude into practice. Therefore, I don't hire service people from the furniture store to put the mirror on my wall, but instead, I pick up a hammer, and a strong enough nail, to hold the mirror. But what happens if I have misplaced my hammer? Because I am not having the "hammer experience" for the first time, but have already hammered a lot of nails of different sizes into different surfaces, I know the underlying principle. Hard objects can selectively bundle and increase my physical strength in such a way that nails can be driven into various surfaces. This principle enables me to, for example, simply use the heel of a shoe with properties that are similar to a hammer. If I know the principle of a hammer's effect, then I can also apply this principle when I find myself in a different situation where no hammer is available. What is obvious for the DIY sector can also be applied to fields such as team-building, internal communication or user needs research.

Once I have understood the principle behind the method, I can adapt this principle to my specific context and develop or adapt my own, appropriate tools and methods to implement the transformation.

The so-called "design thinking hacks," meaning selective design thinking interventions with adapted—"hacked"—methods and tools, play a role because of their strong leverage effect. With the development of design thinking principles, everybody is able to develop their own individual "hacks" for use in everyday life. Using the principle of rapid prototyping, for example, to accelerate the decision of investment in 50 "time timers" was made by a management consultancy company. By way of a demonstration, using fast constructed prototypes made of cardboard, everyone involved could experience the benefits directly. Another principle, based on quick learning, works through the open communication of mistakes. On monthly "Failure Fridays," project teams of a national bank put the focus of discussions on the mistakes they have made during the project work. Thus, the entire department can learn from them. The principle of regular, short feedback with high frequency, (i.e., the comparison of expectations and behavior in a multi-perspective team), found its implementation in an unusual feedback ritual: every time the team rode together in the (very slow) elevator, a (very short) exchange took place focusing on the question: "What is currently going well in the team, and what can be improved on?" Feedback was, therefore, recast from a taboo subject to an integral part of the project work, with its firmly established place. These examples of daily interventions have been developed by the protagonists themselves and can function positively as transformation signals. Rather than replacing transformation strategies, they set the stage for the perception that "something is changing here and—it seems to be fun."

4 Design Thinking "Hacks"—Why Does It Make Sense to Think Big and to Start Small in the Processes of Digital Transformation?

In Systems Engineering, a hack is an "inelegant solution to a specific computer problem" and hackers are "all talented computer experts who use their technical knowledge to overcome a problem." (Wikipedia).

Hacks in design thinking are not about the perfect reproduction of, or adherence to, methods, but about the translation of underlying principles into simple interventions with great leverage in the respective system. The strategic planning and networking of these selective, system-adequate interventions for a human-centered digital transformation can create a domino effect, and lead to a—positive—guerrilla effect.

This phenomenon can be illustrated using the culture model of system theorists and organizational psychologists Karl Weick and Edgar Schein (Schein 2003). According to them, culture can be described in terms of three dimensions. The first is artifacts. These are the visible expressions of company culture, such as objects, processes, structures, narratives, and rituals—that is, everything that can be touched and seen. Supporting them is the "currency" of the culture: rules, philosophies, and strategies that justify and legitimize the artifacts. Both dimensions are manifestations of a culture's learned systems of beliefs or the premises of a culture: its world views, basic attitudes, and the often unconscious and emotional perspectives of reality. All dimensions interact and are interdependent. The attitude influences the values, which in turn brings forth the artifacts. The potential problem can be found at the base of the pyramid—the fundamental attitude. "If people are missing, and the fundamental inclination for change and the current practices in an organization are broken, then digital technologies will only serve to strengthen these defects (Tabrizi et al., 2019). The changing of mindsets—of basic attitudes—is, however, the most difficult and tedious undertaking in cultural change. How can design thinking have a positive effect here? In brief, this can be done by creating artifacts that represent—in the sense of a human-centered digital transformation—an orientation and model of an altered basic attitude.

The interrelationship of the three dimensions of culture described above also work in the opposite direction: namely, with the artifacts as the starting point, which can then recharge existing values, and consequently provide new impulses to the basic attitudes. The following presents a practical example of this approach.

We have to become more networked when working together if we want to keep on being successful on the market in the future.

The goal of a globally operating company in the pharmaceutical branch was formulated in just this way. The company's mission was clearly laid out: join forces in working together to help people cope well with the challenges of their illness. The core values for the way of working as anchored in the corporate strategy are "teamwork," "diversity of cultures and perspectives," and "responsibility." For example, the top management at a branch office decided to introduce an app with which the employees could meet at random during their lunch break in order to informally exchange their expert knowledge. The response to the implementation turned out to be mixed. While some tried out the app, most employees had reservations. Question arose such as: "Who defined the algorithm that brings us together?", "Should we now also sacrifice our lunch break for the job?", "We already have enough digital tools, so why now an additional app on top of it?" As a result, the transformational activity is relatively slow on the grounds of acceptance. At the same time, at the company's headquarters, the issue of collaborative work is pursued in other ways. Solutions are developed in an internal idea competition based on the design thinking principle of participation and self-organization. The teams conduct interviews, explore user needs, define the problem from a human perspective—and develop an idea with name "Lunch Wiki." Colleagues with the need for knowledge on a subject-specific topic can turn to an internal "Wiki team" who recommends an appropriate internal specialist for lunch. A prototype is quickly tested, first in the department—and it is successful. Knowledge is exchanged in a way that is fast, pragmatic, and with the personal benefit of network development.

At the company's annual national conference, two colleagues from the headquarters and branch meet by chance and engage in the topic of "collaboration." In doing so, they find that they have essentially implemented the same core idea—independent of one another. In one case it was a purchased app and in the other a self-developed idea that was initially analog. Solution: the Wiki Lunch concept was then digitized with the help of an app development company to fit the specific needs of users, and it was implemented.

This example shows us how design thinking interventions can help in providing the planning and implementation of digital transformation projects. In a participatory way of working, artifacts are created that are based on user needs. Aided by digital technology, they also offer positive leverage in the organizational system. Abstract value concepts such as "team", "diversity" or "responsibility" can be positively filled with life- and utility value through small solutions with practical value. In the case described, this is the "swarm knowledge" that is available within the company. Corporate values made tangible in this way, reinforce the overarching corporate promise and shape the perceived basic attitude—both internally and externally.

Strategic design thinking helps us to apply design thinking hacks in a targeted manner at the leverage points—the so-called "Levers and Hubs" (Boehnert, 2018). These can mobilize the transformational processes in complex systems that can be understood as system components, which due to their function in the structure, or their connection, have a disproportionate influence. For example, neuralgic points in information flow, multipliers ("community champions"), system rules (e.g., incentives), or the above-mentioned superordinate mission or moral right of a system to exist.

5 How Can Strategic Design Thinking Help to Guide the Implementation of an Agile Transformation Strategy?

"Participants in design thinking workshops want to learn how innovations are developed. In the end, the ability to innovate essentially determines an organization's survival and success. What organizations ultimately need, however, is the knowledge of how to deal with the complexity inherent in the transformation processes." (Ney & Meinel, 2019)

The social scientist and designer Steven Ney explain the challenges and opportunities in the transformation processes. It's all about the inherent "wicked problems" (translatable as "tricky problems") that accompany transformation projects. Examples of wicked problems could be challenges like the interplay between corporate value creation and ecological sustainability, the balancing of unequal income structures, or the conflict that arises between efficiency and innovation. The tight interweave of psychological, social, economic, and ecological causal strands make simple "right" or "wrong" solutions impossible.

Ney references the "Cultural Map," developed by British social anthropologist Mary Douglas. The map describes different cultural strategies of an organization that are only effective in solving wicked problems when taken as an integrated, whole strategy. In a nutshell (and very simplified): transformation succeeds when the plurality of all four cultural strategies are united. This means a clear target orientation with credence given to the classic leader strategy as well as the performance-oriented individual view of solutions, together with the collaborative intelligence of an egalitarian perspective and finally the inclusion of the "fatalistic" strategy, which opens up the possibility for chance and puts the unforeseeable into its proper place in the change process.

Strategic design thinking makes it possible for all actors in the changing organization to pursue their own strategies through derivable strategic principles. In this way, the canteen chef can contribute his expertise in more efficient and employee-friendly processes, in the same way as the head of the IT department can contribute her solutions toward the development of technological sovereignty for all employees. With principles that can be derived for both, the chefs in their daily work and the CEOs in their function as managers of an organization, participation in the change processes can go from being a title in a transformation conference into reality. Because design thinking is based on common sense.

References

ABC nightline—IDEO shopping cart (2009, February 12). https://www.youtube.com/watch?v=M66ZU2PCIcM

Beispiele für die frühen, klassischen Desing thinking cases: ge healthcare adventure series: https://www.gehealthcare.com/products/accessories-and-supplies/adventure-series-for-ct. Bank of America keep the change: https://www.bankofamerica.com/deposits/keep-the-change/. Embrace innovations: https://www.embraceinnovations.com

Boehnert, J. (2018, November). *EcoLabs*. Researchgate, https://www.researchgate.net/public
ation/328723690_THE_VISUAL_REPRESENTATION_OF_COMPLEXITY_Definitions_E
xamples_Learning_Points

https://www.cognitive-edge.com

https://hpi-digitalblog.de/interview_post/uwe-raschke-about-design-thinking-and-its-implement
ation-at-bosch/

https://www.mckinsey.com/business-functions/organization/our-insights/unlocking-success-in-
digital-transformations

Kolb, D. A., & Fry, R. (1975). Toward an applied theory of experiential learning. In C. Cooper
(Ed.), *Theories of group process*. Wiley.

Kolko, J. (2015, September). *Design thinking comes of age*. Harvard Business Review

Le Corbusier "Le Modulor". (1950).

Ney, S., & Meinel, C. (2019). *Putting design thinking to work—How large organizations can
embrace messy institutions to tackle wicked problems*. Springer.

Proulx, M. J., Todorov, O. S., Aiken, A. T., & de Sousa, A. A. (2016). Where am I? Who am I?
The relation between spatial cognition, social cognition and individual differences in the built
environment. *Frontiers in Psychology*

Schein, E. H. (2003). *Organisationskultur*. Weltbild Verlag.

Tabrizi, B., Lam, E., Girard, K., & Irvin, V. (2019). *Digital transformation is not about technology*.
Harvard Business Review.

Taheri, M., Unterholzer, T., & Meinel, C. (2016, August). Design thinking at scale: A report on best
practices of online courses. In *Design thinking research*.

Annie Kerguenne   Design Thinking Strategist and Master
Coach for Digital Transformation, HPI Academy.

Photo credit: Kay Herschelmann.

Since 2013, Annie Kerguenne has been supporting the HPI
in the development of training formats for executives and in
implementing Strategic Design Thinking in organizations. At
the HPI, she heads the "Professional Track" and "Leading
Digital Transformation & Innovation" (in cooperation with
Stanford University) programs, as well as the online course
"Strategic Design Thinking for Every Day," all of which she
designed with her team. They were conceptualized for all three
key areas of stakeholders of digital transformation in organizations: the basis, the management and the top executive level.
Annie Kerguenne has launched new collaborative platforms for
professional alumni such as the Design Thinking Hacking Jam
and Connect & Do Day to strengthen the sustainability of
learning outcomes in the organization. Previously, Annie has
served as executive managing director, creative director, and
strategy planner for innovation consulting firms and creative
agencies. She sees her challenge in translating Strategic Design
Thinking for different corporate cultures as well as for the
diverse players in digital transformation. Her guiding principle for mastering complex tasks is: "Think big and start
small." As a strategic consultant and coach, Annie Kerguenne
supports both established companies and start-ups in Germany
and France as they develop and sustainably integrate a collaborative, innovative culture in their daily work. She is co-author
of the book "Design Thinking. Die agile Innvovationsstrategie"
(Design Thinking. The Agile Innovation Strategy), which was

published by Haufe Verlag in 2017, and author of numerous articles on the topics of "user-centered innovation" and "digital transformation." Annie Kerguenne was born and raised in France. She studied business economics, psycholinguistics, and sociolinguistics in Germany, laying the groundwork for her multidisciplinary work.

The Certification Program for Design Thinking Coaches at the HPI Academy

Steven Ney

Abstract The chapter describes the history, principles and underlying structure of the Certification Program for Design Thinking Coaches at the HPI. The program, founded on 2015 as the first of its kind in Germany and Europe, aims to provide high-quality instruction and training for professionals seeking to lead innovation teams and design effective innovation interventions. Targeted at people who have had no prior in-depth education in the methods and mindsets of Design Thinking—so-called Design Thinking Immigrants—the Certification Program is based on the following three principles: Certification is always connected to training, Certification requires hands-on training in practice, and Certification needs to be flexible and user-centered. The chapter then reviews how the three basic building blocks—Training, Practice and Transfer—put the principles to work to create a balanced and high-quality training program for Design Thinking Coaches.

1 Introduction

The certification program for Design Thinking coaches at the HPI Academy is one of the first training courses of its kind in Germany and Europe. Practical courses, workshops and projects provide participants with a space to experience DT, thereby learning how to coach Design Thinking teams in different organizational contexts and on different problems.

Since December 2015, when the program's pioneers gathered for the first train-the-trainer workshop, approximately 25 prospective coaches have been welcomed to the HPI Academy in Potsdam each semester. In the first five years, 250 participants successfully completed the program. Like the HPI Academy and the HPI School of Design Thinking, the certification program has a global footprint: today, someone in need of a design thinking coach can find HPI-certified coaches in Austria, Belgium, China, France, Hungary, India, Morocco, Russia, Saudi Arabia, South

S. Ney (✉)
Hasso Plattner Institute Academy, August-Bebel-Str. 88, 14482 Potsdam, Germany
e-mail: steven.ney@hpi-academy.de

Africa, Switzerland, the UK and the USA. The professional and occupational background of these coaches is as diverse as that of the participants in other HPI Academy formats, who come from various walks of life. They range from managers of global corporations to professors in academia or specialists from mid-sized businesses and to self-employed consultants and entrepreneurs.

Prospective coaches are supervised by a small and competent certification team, now consisting of five HPI Design Thinking and coaching experts. The certification program is additionally backed by a global network of experienced DT experts. Over the past five years, the certification team has developed a unique expertise in Design Thinking coaching based on their intensive work with coach candidates and consistent development of the program.

The following chapter provides a brief overview of the certification program for Design Thinking coaches. It describes the motivation for the program, discusses the target group and the vision and outlines the program's basic principles and structure.

2 Motivation for the Program—Quality Ensures Acceptance

The methods and mindsets of Design Thinking have rapidly gained popularity in business and society over the last ten to fifteen years. While using the term "Design Thinking" in 2010 still drew questioning looks, the terminology and the underlying concepts are now commonplace in large parts of the business community and society as a whole. Although the HPI School of Design Thinking has done much to popularize the approach in the academic world—and the HPI Academy has done the same in the business world—the ideas, mindsets and methods of Design Thinking have found their way into companies and organizations through a variety of actors without any discernable structure or method. On the one hand, the increasing interest in and improved knowledge of Design Thinking is to be welcomed. On the other hand, this "viral" spread also poses quality assurance challenges for those who seriously apply and develop DT. Sometimes, much of what is considered Design Thinking is difficult to recognize as such. As a consequence, Design Thinking is often only experienced in abbreviated form (e.g., DT as brainstorming with post-its or "playing" with Legos), creating a misleading perception of the methods, practices and mindsets.

Part of the problem is undoubtedly the nature of Design Thinking itself. In many ways, Design Thinking can also be understood as a participatory method. You do not have to be a DT expert to work successfully on innovations in a Design Thinking team. In addition, the threshold for first applying DT methods can be very low: Usually, a few core methods, some material and a little time are enough for initial, successful experiences with the DT method. The danger here is that these DT users very quickly reach the limits of their DT skills and then blame the approach itself for perceived lack of progress or success. In this way, incomplete application of DT methods based on an insufficient understanding has contributed to discrediting DT in many businesses and organizations.

The continued acceptance of DT in companies and organizations therefore crucially depends on the quality of the experience and results of a DT project. Designing DT engagements so that people with little or no prior knowledge can successfully engage in innovation work requires coaches with in-depth methodological expertise and sufficient experience in applying DT. The certification program for DT coaches is designed to ensure the acceptance and legitimacy of the DT approach through quality assurance—that is, high-quality training that sets the standard for DT coaching.

3 Target Group and Vision

After the decision to establish a certification program for Design Thinking coaches was made, the question arose as to the program's target group.

3.1 Who is the Target Group? DT Natives Versus DT Immigrants

In Design Thinking, similar to digitization, people can be classified as *DT natives* or *DT immigrants* on the basis of their access to DT. The group of DT natives includes graduates of the HPI D-Schools (in Stanford, Potsdam and Cape Town), as well as similarly intensive and immersive trainings in Design Thinking. Students who have attended these courses have spent two or more semesters exclusively studying the many facets of Design Thinking. In addition, they have not only grasped these working methods academically, but have also applied and experienced them in project teams on a daily basis. DT natives have profound DT methodological knowledge, as well as practical experience in DT working methods. In this regard, they are a unique, if quite small, group.

In contrast, the significantly larger group that we can call "DT immigrants" are people who come to DT from other areas of the working world. In this group, the motivation for learning and applying DT in a professional context is as heterogeneous as the educational profiles, the wealth of professional and occupational experiences and the sociocultural resources that each of the "immigrants" brings to the DT community. DT immigrants' access to and prior knowledge of the DT methods and ways of thinking and working also vary widely. Some have attended introductory courses (such as the HPI Academy's three-day Design Thinking Introduction); others have taken company training courses in agile methods; still others have taught themselves DT.

DT natives and DT immigrants therefore have different demands on a training and certification program for coaches. In general, DT natives have in-depth knowledge and a practical understanding of the DT ways of working and thinking, but they tend to have little direct experience in occupational, professional and organizational settings. This group would need a program that supports them in applying their in-depth DT knowledge to various professional contexts and organizational realities. In short: DT natives understand DT through and through, but need contexts in which they can gain professional and life experience.

With the DT immigrants, the situation is reversed. Both as a group and as individuals, DT immigrants can usually draw on a wealth of knowledge, professional practice and general life experience. This group tends to have gaps in their basic understanding of Design Thinking, as well as in transferring these mindsets and practices to their work environments. DT immigrants differ from DT natives in terms of depth and confidence in applying DT knowledge. What is more, levels of DT knowledge and practical experience diverge greatly within the group. Thus, in addition to providing a basic understanding of DT, a coaching program needs to help identify and fill existing knowledge gaps.

Since the two groups' needs for a certification program differ so greatly, it was necessary to focus on one group. The decision was based on which focus would best contribute to the goal of effectively assuring the quality of DT practice. This question does not arise when it comes to training at renowned educational institutions, whether specifically for DT (such as Potsdam, Stanford or UCT) or design in general (such as TU Delft or Parsons School of Design). Indeed, critical reflection of principles and practices within these institutions significantly contributes to setting standards in these fields. It is not a putative lack of knowledge or skill on the part of DT natives that potentially undermines the legitimacy of the approach. Rather, their DT competencies are often dismissed as "purely theoretical," and therefore largely impractical. Conversely, due to the divergent level of knowledge and expertise of DT immigrants, there is a danger that DT mindsets and practices will be used in an abbreviated way without the underlying DT principles taking effect. As an example, DT is often reduced to brainstorming with colored post-it notes.

Accordingly, a training program would serve quality assurance well for two reasons: First, a certification program would equip DT immigrants with the methodical and coaching skills to effectively implement DT practices and mindsets in different organizational contexts. Second, a program for DT immigrants would also enhance the practical relevance of the generic, "purely academic" teaching of DT. Many DT immigrants in the program have had valuable experiences with DT in various work and professional contexts. Some of the participants have—mostly on their own—successfully adapted DT methods and mindsets to specific industries, sectors and organizations. Some have even invented their own methods. This is why the certification program never aimed at harmonizing the various experiences to an HPI-defined canon. Instead, from the very beginning, the certification program focused on mutual learning and discussion.

3.2 What is the Vision of a DT Immigrant Coach?

The certification program aims to train "outstanding" coaches. For this reason, the certification team very quickly abandoned the idea of aligning the program to a notion of an "ideal" coach. Such an ideal type would have presupposed teaching a (more or less) comprehensive canon of methods prescribed by the HPI Academy. Quite apart from the fact that such a canon is difficult to define, this teaching approach would have been incongruous with what we believe constitutes outstanding coaching. Good DT coaches are not so much those who follow an external standard—which consists of a catalog of methods, rules of conduct and design principles.

Outstanding DT coaches support DT teams by skillfully balancing each team's needs, the design challenge and the organizational situation. While this undoubtedly requires methodological competence, it also calls for the ability to define, open up and shape a free space for innovation, based on the situations and materials at hand. The best DT coaches create this freedom by applying DT methods individually and creatively to situations as they arise.

Accordingly, the certification program focuses on participants learning to assess and judge coaching situations. When it comes to the pragmatic application of DT mindsets and ways of working, coaches are given a great deal of leeway for shaping the situation individually. Instead of restricting this by prescribing standardized rules of method and conduct, the certification program explicitly aims to enable creative use of the possibilities. In this manner, DT methods and practices are vehicles and tools for individual design possibilities. Good coaches have methodological expertise; outstanding coaches use these methods individually and creatively to produce innovative open spaces for DT teams.

4 Principles of the Certification Program

Training outstanding coaches involves applying the following basic principles.

4.1 Certification Requires Training

Many certification programs in executive education and professional development focus exclusively on the formal aspects of a qualification. Here, certification consists of an examination that tests a previously defined catalog of knowledge and skills. The certification of the "*Scrum*" agile method is a prominent example of a similar qualification with the *Scrum Alliance* acting as the central global certification body. Similar to obtaining a driver's license, candidates must attend a course accredited by the *Scrum Alliance* and pass a specified exam in order to obtain the certificate of a *Scrum Master* or *Product Owner*, for example.

The HPI Academy decided against this model for the DT certification program for two reasons. The first reason is mainly practical: There is simply not enough teaching capacity outside the HPI Academy to allow certification and training to be separated. This is also related to the second, more substantive, reason. Educating not merely good coaches, but outstanding coaches, requires explicit training as well as a great deal of mentoring. Honing the situational judgment of a coach calls for practice as well as the critical feedback of peers and experienced coaches. As already noted, certification is not limited to successfully transferring knowledge about processes and methods. Rather, HPI-certified coaches have applied this knowledge to real-world work settings in order to exercise situational judgment and to find and foster their individual coaching style. For this reason, training cannot be separated from certification.

4.2 Certification Requires Practical Experience

Training to become an HPI-certified coach is extremely hands-on. In the HPI Academy certification program, participants learn by actively and passively experiencing the DT mindset and approach to working. From the very start, participants explore Design Thinking's methods and mindsets in different practical contexts. The basic learning principle of the certification program is to provide brief methodological preparation, followed by participants actively experiencing the Design Thinking approach and Design Thinking coaching. Participants then reflect critically on what they experienced together with the HPI coaches and peers in the program. This pattern of experiencing, reflecting and learning runs through all elements of the certification program (see next section).

Of course, this does not mean that the certification program is entirely devoid of theory or methods. In fact, quite the opposite is true. The logic of many courses is often to first give participants a comprehensive overview of the entire methodological and theoretical landscape and then to underpin this overview with practical examples. The certification program turns this logic on its head: Here, methods and theory are a means to practically experience and explore the participants' situational judgment. Participants in the program are therefore given a basic but functioning methodological toolkit. However, the primary purpose of this minimally functional toolkit of methods is to serve as a compass for the individual exploratory journey into the landscape of DT coaching. By applying the toolkit as well as employing systematic reflection of that practical application, participants discover their strengths and weaknesses, their likes and dislikes and new areas of activity and interest.

4.3   Certification Needs User-Centeredness

The program's third basic principle is user-centeredness, a key value it shares with Design Thinking itself. Recall that the certification program focuses on the needs and demands of professional and occupational DT immigrants. For this reason, the program is designed to be as flexible as possible, both in terms of organization and in terms of content.

The emphasis on practice and reflection also means that program participants need to actively attend a range of DT engagements. This is true for both face-to-face and virtual coaching. The certification team therefore designs the program calendar to largely accommodate the participants' scheduling needs. In practice, this means providing many alternative dates for mandatory elements (sometimes at different locations) in order to reconcile the DT coach training with professional commitments.

The program's user-centeredness at the content level is even more important than organizational flexibility. The program supports participants in discovering and developing their own authentic coaching style. To facilitate this, the certification team works with individual participants to design a learning journey to identify and explore their individual potential, interests and talents in DT. The direction and course of this journey are reflected on at each stage and, if necessary, adjusted.

5   Structure of the Certification Program

The certification program for Design Thinking coaches comprises 20 days of coursework. These 20 days are made up of three interrelated elements. The first element contains the three workshops of the certification program. In these workshops, participants are provided with a basic toolkit—both in coaching and in the working methods and techniques of DT. These three workshops each last three days. The second element consists of the practice days: participants are required to complete at least nine practice days to qualify for the certificate. Here, the participants take the tools they learned about in the workshops and use them in Design Thinking projects. The third element—the Design Thinking master classes—provides the prospective DT coaches with specialized insights into the practical application of DT in various fields. To earn the Design Thinking Coach Certificate, participants in the program are to complete these 20 days within one year.

5.1   The Workshops: DT Mindset and Train-The-Trainer

The HPI Academy is characterized by high-quality courses and workshops in the field of executive education. Whether in methodological training sessions such as the Design Thinking Introduction, targeted workshops with customers, or specialized courses such as "Agile Meets DT": The HPI Academy offers professionals sustainable learning *experiences*. It should therefore come as no surprise that the certification program for Design Thinking coaches relies on this core competence in order to provide program participants with a basic toolkit in Design Thinking as well as coaching.

The workshops aim to enable participants to use DT in professional situations in a very short time. As with many other DT trainings (including the HPI Academy), methods are of course one of the topics. Yet, over and above the methodological toolkit, the workshops also teach the mindsets and, more importantly, the particular practices of Design Thinking. In particular, the aim is to encourage prospective coaches to use methods in a situational and creative way right from the start. The workshops primarily involve reading coaching situations, embedding those situations in the larger project or organizational context and adapting methods to best support the team members in their innovation work. In accordance with the fundamental principle of practical orientation, the workshops focus on applying the approach.

The starting point of the certification program—*Understanding the DT Mindset*— concentrates on the mindsets and practices of Design Thinking. In this phase, the focus is not yet on coaching. Rather, the group of aspiring coaches is encouraged to discuss their understanding of Design Thinking. Participants come to the program with widely divergent background knowledge and experience. Many may have attended an introductory event—such as the Design Thinking Introduction— and have not engaged with DT since. Others may have already taken more advanced courses, such as the ProTrack, and are applying the mindsets and working methods of Design Thinking on a daily basis. Still others may be self-taught and have acquired aspects of DT coaching from books and their own experience. Although these different approaches and levels of knowledge certainly pose a challenge for the certification team, this first workshop is not about resetting DT knowledge to align with a canon set by the HPI Academy. Instead, participants should assess where gaps remain and, almost more importantly, how they can contribute to the group's learning experience.

With the second workshop, *Train-the-Trainer Basic,* participants dive into DT coaching in earnest. The three-day workshop focuses on the methods, mindsets and practices of a **team coach**. Team coaches, as opposed to lead coaches (see below), up sport individual Design Thinking teams. They are responsible for the day-to-day implementation of a DT project or workshop plan. They structure each phase of the DT process, manage team dynamics and coordinate the team's activities with other team coaches as well as lead coaches.

The smallest working unit of a team coach during a DT project or workshop is the preparation, implementation and follow-up of a *project phase* defined in the DT process. *TTT Basic* provides a safe space for program participants to explore, observe and experience for themselves the methods, practices and tasks of a team coach. After a brief theoretical introduction, participants are given the opportunity to prepare, lead and reflect on several phases of the DT process with the other participants. Thus, participants in the program are in both an active and an observational role. Veteran DT coaches from the certification program observe and comment on the experiences.

The final workshop event of the certification program revolves around the activities of a **lead coach**. Unlike team coaches, lead coaches are not responsible for DT teams, but rather for supporting teams of team coaches. This task includes customer communication, DT project design and coordination and coach support. In turn, coach support includes both content-related support (e.g., of a methodological nature) and organizational and logistical support (e.g., providing an appropriate workplace and a constructive working atmosphere).

As in *Train-the-Trainer Basic*, the tasks and responsibilities of a lead coach are not only taught theoretically. The exercises in the *TTT Advanced Workshop* enable participants to actively experience the tasks together with the associated methods, mindsets and working practices and to reflect on these experiences with the other participants and HPI coaches. In the practical part of the program, participants work on DT workshop and project design, practice recognizing team dynamics and dealing with difficult workshop situations and try their hand at designing and delivering unique workshop and learning experiences.

With the three workshops, the participants have the resources necessary to

- understand and practically implement the DT mindsets and practices (*Understanding DT*),
- support a Design Thinking team, i.e., prepare phases of the DT process, guide the team through the phases and follow up on the results for further use (either during the process or beyond) (*TTT Basic*),
- plan and design a DT project while supervising the coaching team during the project (*TTT Advanced*).

5.2 Practice Days

As we have just learned, the certification program workshops are extremely hands-on. Participants learn through practical application of methods and ways of working as well as through systematic reflection on what they have experienced and applied. Despite all this, the knowledge and skills acquired in this way form only an initial, rudimentary outline of a DT coach's skill profile. First, knowledge and skills are to be developed until the participants feel confident applying them, and in a second step, the participants integrate these competences into their own individual, authentic coaching style. To do this, prospective coaches have to develop these skills under realistic conditions, that is, in real Design Thinking projects and workshops. This part of the program not only aims at consolidating the knowledge and skills acquired in the workshops. Over and above, the practice days allow prospective coaches to discover and critically confront their own strengths and weaknesses as well as methodological likes and dislikes.

The certification program therefore offers participants two practice modes in three application contexts. In what is known as *shadow coaching*, aspiring DT coaches learn by shadowing experienced DT coaches in *coaching sessions*. In theory, shadow coaching is limited to observation of the experienced coaches; in practice, the prospective coaches are often included in the process by their experienced colleagues. Subsequently, participants in the program must also apply the knowledge and skills themselves in a workshop or project context: As team coaches, they coach a team through an entire workshop or (co-)design and lead the workshop as lead coaches. If possible, the prospective coaches work in tandem, as is customary at the HPI Academy. Besides the support (moral or practical) in the face of a potentially intimidating situation, it is very important for participants to prepare and execute a DT project as a team. A key feature of these projects is the joint preparation and reflection of the practical work as well as sharing the experiences gained in the workshop.

The certification program offers three different application contexts with various challenges for the practical days of the prospective coaches. One such context is the student program at the HPI School of Design Thinking. Although student DT training may not be applicable to most participants' future daily DT lives without significant transfer, the D-School experience is valuable for several reasons. First, the HPI D-School is an ideal type of DT practice in some ways. From the resources to the coaches to the project parameters, the conditions at D-School are excellent: The D-School shows prospective coaches what is possible. The second setting consists of the *Pop-Up Workshops*. These are one-day to three-day workshops—often, but not exclusively, methodological in nature—that are usually conducted with organizations from the NGO, education or public sector. Third, the certification program offers participants the opportunity to join in the HPI Academy's professional development projects and workshops, both as a *shadow* and as an active coach. These coaching days are carefully prepared with the participants. The experiences and results are reflected on together with other participants and the HPI coaches in the certification program.

5.3   Master Classes

The *master classes* represent the final element of the certification program. They are, so to speak, the "elective subject" of the certification program. During each semester, members of the DT community offer workshops and classes on specific topics. For example, these topics may consist of applying DT in a specific area (e.g., DT in social entrepreneurship); they may relate to a specific phase or methodological approach (e.g., digital prototyping); or they may address a horizontal issue (e.g., team dynamics). The master classes are open to all DT coaches in the DT community. To obtain the certificate, participants must have attended at least one master class.

The master classes pursue two objectives. The first is that they often give critical insights into the practical application of DT in particular sectors or professions, and the second is that they give participants access to the DT community.

6 Conclusion

The certification program for Design Thinking coaches is one of the first programs of its kind in Germany and Europe. It arose out of the tremendous growth in interest and the viral spread of DT ways of working and thinking. Although the growing popularity of the approach is encouraging in principle, qualitatively questionable practices threaten the long-term legitimacy and acceptance of DT. To counter this, the HPI Academy established the Certification Program for Design Thinking Coaches in December of 2015. The program is aimed at a group referred to as DT immigrants, that is, people who have found their way to DT from their occupational and professional context. The certification program provides these individuals with flexible training that is very much hands-on and designed to identify, explore and develop each participant's individual coaching style. By training "outstanding" coaches who create innovative freedom in companies and organizations using their situational judgment, the certification program contributes to long-term quality assurance.

Dr. Steven Ney Director of Education, Hasso Plattner Institute Academy. Steven Ney completed his doctorate in the policy sciences at the Department of Comparative Politics in the University of Bergen. Trained as a policy analyst at the University of London, Steven Ney has worked on a wide range of policy issues in a number of research institutes including the LOS Center in Bergen, ICCR in Vienna and the International Institute for Applied Systems Analysis in Laxenburg. After spending four years from 2005 as an Assistant Professor of Political Science at Singapore Management University, Steven Ney took up the Chair of Social Entrepreneurship at Jacobs University, Bremen in August 2009. From 2014-2018, Steven Ney designed, led and implemented continuing education formats at the HPI Academy and the HPI School of Design Thinking in Potsdam. In November 2018, Steven joined T-Systems International, a subsidiary of Deutsche Telekom. Working with both internal and external T-Systems customers, Steven designed and delivered co-creation processes to help develop innovative digital products, organizational strategies, and new business models. In April 2021,Steven joined the HPI Academy as Director of Education. His responsibilities include supporting the education team, the development of new formats and new customer segments as well as the forging of an extended innovation ecosystem.

Outlook: Design Thinking in Education for the Big Picture

Beyond Brainstorming: *Introducing medgi, an Effective, Research-Based Method for Structured Concept Development*

Jonathan Edelman, Babajide Owoyele, and Joaquin Santuber

1 Introduction

In this chapter, we introduce **medgi**, an effective, research-based method for structured concept development. "**medgi**" is an acronym for **mapping, educing, disrupting, gestalting** and **integrating**. The **medgi** method is the result of observation and video analysis of interaction patterns of high-performance design teams at work.

Research has indicated that traditional brainstorming methods yield inconsistent results. Furthermore, a critical examination of the so-called rules of brainstorming reveal unexamined assumptions and flaws in respect to brainstorming as a serious methodology that yields consistent results.

Dedicated to translational research and development funded by the Hasso Plattner Design Thinking Research Program (HPDTRP), the Research to Impact (R2I) Group has conducted video analysis of high-performance teams at work. Video and transcript analyses of team mechanics suggests that high-performance teams iteratively engaged in a set of interactions that yielded new possibilities to explore and to expand upon. **medgi** is one of several performative patterns that the Research to Impact Group has uncovered. The Research to Impact Group has developed a collection of highly effective performative patterns which, like **medgi**, are grounded in new knowledge about how teams work. This work, along with other work funded by the HPDTRP, has produced rigorous insights concerning team mechanics and

J. Edelman (✉) · B. Owoyele · J. Santuber
Hasso Plattner Institute for Digital Engineering, Campus Griebnitzsee, Prof.-Dr.-Helmert-Str. 2-3, 14482 Potsdam, Germany
e-mail: Jonathan.Edelman@hpi.de

B. Owoyele
e-mail: Babajide.Owoyele@hpi.de

J. Santuber
e-mail: Joaquin.Santuber@hpi.de

© The Author(s), under exclusive license to Springer Nature Switzerland AG 2022
C. Meinel and T. Krohn (eds.), *Design Thinking in Education*,
https://doi.org/10.1007/978-3-030-89113-8_15

how new concepts are developed in teams. **medgi** is the practical application of but one of these insights that have resulted from HPDTRP research. This paper presents a distillation and operationalization of key interactions and mechanisms observed from hours of video recordings and transcripts in the framework and performance of **medgi**.

medgi can be effectively taught to teams and results in improved team performance. Through the performance of **medgi**, teams are able to craft new concepts through an informed, structured method. **medgi** makes it possible for team members to interact with a common framework of micro-interactions upon which they can radically and rigorously distribute the work of exploring new possibilities.

As a performative pattern (Edelman, 2018, 2019), the steps of **medgi** can be instantiated as roles or parts that the team members perform. One advantage of the **medgi** approach over traditional brainstorming is that team members explicitly understand what role they are playing, or that their team members are playing, and how their interactions move along an arc of concept development that begins with a clear articulation of the state of affairs, proceeds to open up the possibility space, and then concludes with a new state of affairs that is once again clearly articulated. The analog to this in sports is players on a football field, each knowing their role and how that role moves the ball down the field to a score a goal. In this case, the goal is a new product–service–system concept.

The **medgi** framework and exercises have been tested in numerous academic environments (Stanford University, the Hasso Plattner Institut, Politecnico di Milano, the Royal College of Art, London, SRH Hochschule Berlin, Bucerius Law School, Hamburg, LUISS University, Rome, Italy) and professional engagements (SAP, the HPI Academy, African Health Research Institute, EIT Climate KIC, Munich Legal Tech Association, LegalID Professional Education, Bogotá, Colombia).

2   The Problem with Brainstorming

Brainstorming found its way into the world when Alex F. Osborn posited an approach to improving unproductive meetings. Osborn was a marketing executive and needed meetings to produce better ideas for marketing campaigns and solutions to customer problems. In his book, *Applied Imagination* (Osborn, 1953), the author introduces brainstorming in this way:

"Idea-producing conferences are relatively fruitless unless certain rules are understood by all present and are faithfully followed. Here are four basics:

(1)   *Judicial judgment is ruled out.* Criticism of ideas must be withheld until later.
(2)   *"Free-wheeling" is welcomed.* The wilder the idea, the better; it is easier to tame down than to think up.
(3)   *Quantity is wanted.* The greater number of ideas, the more the likelihood of winners.

(4) *Combination and improvement are sought.* In addition to contributing ideas of their own, participants should suggest how ideas of others can be turned into *better* ideas; or how two or more ideas can be joined to still another idea."

In all fairness to Osborn, it is important to note that he introduces these four basics *at the end of his book*, on page 300 of a 307-page publication. Prior to that, Osborn details a virtual compendium of "principles and procedures of creative thinking" which include experimentation, education, association, processes, analysis, synthesis, emotions, luck, tools, frameworks, teams and more. Each chapter of *Applied Imagination* concludes with a series of questions to support reflection and critical thinking, exercises for practice, and references for further investigation. Only after detailing all these subjects and providing exercises for mastery, does Osborn give his "four basics." *Applied Imagination* is truly a prodigious work, written in the spirit of making the world a better place. It is curious that what appears to be the legacy of this work has been reduced to four rules.

Over time, the original four rules have taken on new forms and new rules have been added, though little has changed Osborn's fundamental approach of relying on *collecting lots of ideas without impediment.* What is missing, however, in much of the current discourse and education regarding Osborn's method of idea generation are all the techniques that come in the 299 pages that precede the rules.

As much as we admire Alex Osborn and his work, there remain several problems with brainstorming, whether the rules are four or seven. We will address two classes of issues that point to the ineffectiveness and inconsistency of brainstorming as a concept development tool. First, we will consider research examining the effectiveness of brainstorming. Next, we will offer a brief, critical examination of the rules themselves.

There has been copious research on Obsorn's method since he published *Applied Imagination* in 1953. Representative papers have found conflicting results: Some papers have found that brainstorming is fruitful (Isaksen, 1998), and some have found it inhibiting (Feinberg & Nemeth, 2008; Mullen, 2010; Kohn & Smith, 2011). Some papers have focused on the rules of brainstorming, while others have examined whether teams are better or worse for idea generation (Isaksen, 1998). Some research has suggested that the benefits of brainstorming are negligible in terms of idea generation, but significant in terms of their positive impact on an organization (Sutton & Hargadon, 1996).

Supporters and practitioners of brainstorming sometimes dismiss negative research findings which question the effectiveness of brainstorming by claiming that participants simply do not know how to brainstorm the right way. Our research findings (Edelman, 2011) suggest that when brainstorming is done effectively, the mechanisms of what makes successful outcomes are not in keeping with the rules of brainstorming. That is, participants may think that they are following the rules, but analyses of video recordings and transcripts reveal other mechanisms at work that lead to successful outcomes. For example, a common practice in brainstorming, suggested by Osborn to support the activity of coming up with as many ideas as possible, is to create an associative list. Our findings indicate that associative lists of nearly any length do little or no apparent work in making change to existing products, services or systems.

A critical examination of the rules of brainstorming reveals questionable assumptions and several flaws contained in Osborn's rules of brainstorming. We will examine each of Osborn's four rules in turn.

Osborne's Rule 1.

(1) *Judicial judgment is ruled out.* Criticism of ideas must be withheld until later.

This rule is sometimes rephrased as "Defer Judgment," the sense remains the same as the original, though somehow the redacting of the original seems like a commandment from a higher authority rather than an advertising executive. This rule has expanded to include statements such as, "creative spaces are judgment free zones" (IDEO, online resource)—a judgment that itself ignores not only the history of creative teams (Farrell, 2001), but also ignores contemporary research in team dynamics and new product development (Edelman, 2011; Sonalkar, 2011; Verganti, 2017).

Verganti (2017) argues that the practice of criticism is essential to not only refining ideas, but to generating robust ideas. Historically, the "crit" has been a mainstay of art and design education in the world's leading institutions and communities for years. The "crit" not only gives immediate feedback about an artist's or designer's work, which leads to making changes to the work, but it cultivates the ability to see from others' points of view and thus is the ground for changing how we see our own work and the world. Thus, critique serves as a foundation for at least two kinds of transformation: One in the work itself and the other in the designer. This practice stands in stark contrast to the practice of "post-it voting," in which there is very little time for transformative discourse surrounding an idea or the mind of a designer.

In his excellent book on the work of creative teams, *Collaborative Circles: Friendship Dynamics and Creative Work*, sociology professor Michael P. Farrell (2001) presents a compelling account of the complex dynamics of successful teamwork across creative domains. In his study, Farrell presents evidence about leading creative teams in art, psychology, social change and literature. Farrell unpacks how criticism and challenges have been essential components of team dynamics.

Furthermore, instructing designers to rule out judicial judgment (or to defer judgment) is the equivalent to a swim coach instructing swimmers, "don't drown." Standard coaching practices make a clear effort to dissuade coaches from making these kinds of directives as they have been found to put athletes' attention on the wrong thing (in this case, drowning) and not on implementing and performing methods that do the work of making change.

Osborne's Rule 2.

(2) *"Free-wheeling" is welcomed.* The wilder the idea, the better; it is easier to dame down than to think up.

While there is a lot of sense in "it [being] easier to tame down than to think up," it is not clear why "the wilder the idea the better." To be sure, this rule sounds exciting, yet there is little evidence that "wild ideas" do any real work of transforming a product-service-system into something useful. In fact, our observations regarding the use of "wild ideas" have repeatedly shown that they do not work in developing new concepts or new concepts that are relevant (Edelman, 2011). Often wild ideas are not relevant and do not yield applicable insights to the problem at hand. We have also observed that most team members do not know how to integrate a wild idea into the conversation. Wild ideas get stated and then drop like a lead balloon because in practical terms it is hard to float them. Furthermore, if we as educators are to encourage "wild ideas" there must be some metric for assessing "wildness." The authors are not aware of such a metric in common use. In fact, experience in teaching at both art colleges and in engineering departments suggests one person's wild idea is another person's everyday notion and vice versa. "Wild" is very subjective and as such provides little solid ground to stand on in respect to understanding how new concepts are developed. Finally, "encourage wild ideas" contains the assumption that ideas arise solely from one person's head, rather than being collaboratively built by a team.

Osborne's Rule 3.

(3)   *Quantity is wanted.* The greater number of ideas, the more likelihood of winners.

Rule three represents a dogma that has been hard to shake in the design world. However, there is little evidence that having many ideas is a cause of successful outcomes rather than many ideas being an outcome of a robust process.

Furthermore, a tacit assumption that underlies the third rule is that each member of a team contributes *whole ideas*, rather than contributing meaningful parts of a concept that become a new whole in the work of building a new concept. Our research (Edelman, 2011) suggests that while expert designers may *believe* that they are generating a large number of ideas, their *behavior* reveals a different mechanism at work which involves radically distributed cognition (Hutchins, 1995). In the framework **medgi**, the generation of new concepts is broken up into steps that are performed by individual players.

Additionally, it is not clear whether having a lot of ideas to choose from leads to a greater chance of having a winner. It may be that having a lot of poorly crafted ideas leads to a greater chance of having a loser. Verganti (2019) presents evidence showing it is not always the case that the greater number of ideas means the greater chance of a winner. Verganti argues that often a small number of well-crafted ideas are more beneficial to new product development and the development of new product meanings.

Our experience of teaching concept development to designers suggests another more fundamental problem: the majority of neophyte designers do not know how to craft new concepts, let alone generate a lot of new ideas in either a brainstorming session or outside of one. When we have taught **medgi** and related material to neophyte designers, their ability to develop new concepts is greatly enhanced, as is their creative confidence (Edelman, 2019).

We have observed that even many experienced designers rely on intuition alone rather than having a structured approach that serves as a container for previously undefined content, or that they enlist tacit structures that they are often unaware of. When we have introduced **medgi** and related materials to experienced designers, we have overwhelmingly received positive feedback (Edelman, 2019).

Finally, the third rule is like a sports coach telling an athlete "score more." Most athletes want to "score more." At the same time, if they are in a role that requires scoring, they simply either do not know how to score more, or have not practiced the skills necessary to achieve this aim. Best practices in coaching demonstrate that effective coaches provide instruction in body mechanics and skill development that promote scoring; scoring follows the mastery of concepts and skills.

Furthermore, not all positions on a team require scoring, nor is it desirable for some positions to score at all. An example of this is the goal tender in many field sports or mid-field players whose responsibilities include setting up conditions so that forward players can score. Osborn's third rule assumes that all members of a brainstorm are organized horizontally and that they all play the same role in coming up with lots of individually generated ideas. Our research (Edelman, 2011) has shown that individually generated whole ideas do not necessarily lead to better outcomes. In fact, a radically distributed development of new concepts—when players tacitly or explicitly understand their unique role in the enterprise of transforming a state of affairs—leads to better outcomes.

Osborne's Rule 4.

(4)   *Combination and improvement are sought.* In addition to contributing ideas of their own, participants should suggest how ideas of others can be turned into *better* ideas; or how two or more ideas can be joined to still another idea.

Our own research supports Osborn's fourth rule, in that combining different notions and improving them has been observed to be an effective practice. Nonetheless, the fourth rule is another instance of a goal disguised as a process. The directives of how to combine and what constitutes an impactful combination, as well as the directives of how to make improvements and of what constitutes improvement are absent. In all fairness to Osborn, clues to these issues are indicated in the preceding three hundred pages of *Applied Imagination*. The problem here is that those techniques are not taught in the majority of cases, the fourth rule is taught as a stand-alone principle and is often elaborated on as an afterthought, instead of the other way around, meaning that the rule is an afterthought to understanding the mechanisms of making change.

However, a greater problem exists in the fourth rule. As in the case of the third rule, "*quantity is wanted*," the fourth rule elides the process of generating new concepts. It asks that designers come up with complete concepts on their own to either be combined with other full-blown concepts or to be material for improvement. As mentioned in the critical examination of the third rule, we have found that this notion does not match the profile of the behaviors of high-performance teams.

In short, while Osborn's rules of brainstorming and its subsequent versions look good at first glance, they do not hold up under a critical eye. Unfortunately, Osborn's

Fig. 1 Black-boxing the new concept development process (author's own image)

legacy is not based on the compendium of techniques in his book *Applied Imagination*, but rather that he did an impressive job of creating compelling slogans to engage people. The "four basics" seem to have provided none of the sound logic and robust mechanisms that would lead to a deeper understanding and a sound and consistent practice. Osborn's rules of brainstorming effectively black box the process of developing new concepts (Fig. 1).

It must be said that we have come a long way in understanding teams and how teams generate new concepts in the years since Alex Osborn wrote *Applied Imagination*. An enormous amount of research has been done on creativity, and new understandings of cognition that have resulted in new cognitive models upon which to understand team behaviors. New research and teaching tools, such as video recordings and computer-aided analysis, have made it possible to see mechanisms that had until the introduction of these tools and techniques remained hidden.

To conclude, research regarding the effectiveness of brainstorming suggests a weak correlation between the common use of the method and its successful outcomes. If a method yields wildly varying results, it is possible that a mechanism other than the assumed method was responsible for achieving these results. Another explanation could be that the brainstorming training is at fault, either in communicating the rules themselves or how to carry out the rules to cultivate the skills necessary for consistently successful outcomes. Research done in the context of the Hasso Plattner Design Thinking Research Program at Stanford's Center for Design Research and the Hasso Plattner Institute indicates that both explanations are in play and that both the rules and the practical application of brainstorming are at fault.

3   medgi in Depth

The central function of **medgi** is to *un-black box* the concept development process; **medgi** does not rely on individual designers who magically come up with lots of linguistically based ideas to throw into a pile from which to choose. Instead, **medgi** leverages extended cognition (Clark & Chalmers, 1998; Hutchins, 2005; Tversky & Suwa, 2009; Kirsh, 2010, 2011; Becvar et al. 2005) by enlisting gesture and objects

old

object

interaction

new

object

interaction

Fig. 2 Un-black-boxing: the five steps of **medgi** (author's own image)

to communicate and create legible offers for other team members to pick up and transform. Furthermore, **medgi** radically distributes cognition through the team (Hutchins, 2005). Both extended and distributed cognition are proven hallmarks of high-performance teams (Fig. 2).

We have found that teams enlist **medgi** in different ways. Sometimes they enjoy keeping to specific roles. Team members often find a role that resonates with them, for example disrupting or a **gestalting**. Other teams can be observed as being more fluid in their roles, much like basketball players. In **medgi**, with practice, the fundamentals of each role can be mastered by design team players. Working knowledge of the five roles helps players situate themselves in the flow of making change.

It is important to note that each step of **medgi** serves as an offer to be picked up and transformed by the next step. This radical distribution may seem difficult or cumbersome at first, but with practice, it leads to superior team interactions and outcomes. The sports analogy in football helps us here. When beginners are learning to play a game, they tend to want to run the ball down the field and attempt to score. Often one can observe neophytes crowding around the goal, trying to score. While professional football players sometimes run the ball down the field and score, this is a rare and celebrated occurrence. Instead, professional players *pass the ball* and receive it according to well-practiced routines. These routines serve as a repertoire of possible interactions that can be changed as conditions change on the field. With **medgi**, team members learn to pass and receive concepts in the same way that high-performance design teams do; instead of trying to transform the state of affairs all at once, which—like in sports—rarely occurs and is worthy of celebration, design teams distribute the activity of transformation though a series of hand-offs, of ***offers*** and ***pick-ups*** that lead to new ground of possibility. Mapping is the first move that provides the foundation for the rest of the **medgi** cycle.

The Five Behaviors of **medgi**.

Mapping.

Mapping consists of describing what exists in respect to a product or service to be redesigned and interactions that users have with it. Mapping can be very simple, for example, "it is a hand-held selfie camera." Mapping can also be complex, including timelines and various interactions between stakeholders. The key concept in **mapping** is that team members state what is there.

A helpful analogy in understanding **medgi** comes from the world of jazz improvisation. With respect to **mapping**, players in a jazz ensemble will typically begin with all members playing the "head," which is the melody and harmonic progression of the piece upon which they will improvise. Jazz musicians are schooled in understanding the conventions of music in respect to genre, harmonic changes and melodic structures. Players will pay careful attention to the head, in order to create a shared ground for exploring the melodic, harmonic and genre possibilities of the piece. This is the musical equivalent of **mapping**.

When **mapping** is done effectively, it presents the next player ample opportunities for their pick-up or response. It gives the next player, who performs **educing**, the ability to focus on what works and what does not work, the pain and pleasure points and plenty of thematic material to work with.

Educing.

Educing consists of pulling out and highlighting what works and what does not, as well as identifying pain and pleasure points. This step focuses the team on relevant changes that will be explored in the following steps of **medgi**. In the case of what works and pleasure points, it may be that the design team explores amplifying these aspects of the object interaction. In the case of what does not work and pain points, it may be that the design team explores how to repair and reduce pain points. In either case, the step of **educing** makes public the areas for the team to investigate. Like **mapping**, the key concept in **educing** is that team members state what is there, the state of affairs.

Back to our analogy with Jazz. When Jazz musicians hear something in the head, for example a set of chord changes or a melodic phrase, they often find a part of that offer particularly moving (either a pain or pleasure point, depending on the emotional content), or they find something that is perplexing and needs to be worked out. An illustrative example from classical music is that from JS Bach's Goldberg Variations, where Bach pulls out and highlights moments in the aria for material to explore and develop in respect to several dimensions, including genre, harmony and melodic variation (Dreyfus, 1996; Edelman, 2015, 2016). This is the musical equivalent to **educing**.

Disrupting.

Disrupting consists of making a proposition about a change that could be made, without reference to either how that could be accomplished or what a solution would look like. **Disrupting** takes the form of a question, for example "What happens if…?" Generally, **disrupting** takes one of four possible lines of inquiry: changes of form, material, process or the reason for the state of affairs (e.g., the intent of the product, service or system, the user or the situation). Thus, a **disrupting** proposition could be formulated as, "What happens if we change the user?" Or "What happens if the product is larger?" Or "What happens if we break it into two pieces?" Note that **disrupting** differs from the previous two steps or roles in that it proposes making a change to the current state of affairs. The form of question that characterizes **disrupting** was discovered by Dr Ozgur Eris (Eris, 2003), who examined the kinds of questions that high-performance teams ask and their impact on outcomes. Eris calls this kind of question a "Generative Design Question" or GDQ, because this kind of question affords opening the discourse to many possibilities rather than a single answer.

Disrupting can stem from two different sources, intentional and serendipitous cues. Intentional disruption occurs when the player makes a proposition based on a planned or commonly shared set of disruptions. For example asking a question like: "What happens if we make the product bigger?" Serendipitous disruption takes place when a mistake, a word misspoken, a misunderstanding or an unexpected event occurs and is used as a disruptor. For example, when a player accidentally turns a product backwards or upside down. It takes skill for the players to embrace the mistake and see where it could lead, both in **disrupting** and in **gestalting**.

A well-known example of a serendipitous disruption and a masterful response in the world of musical improvisation is recounted by pianist Herbie Hancock (Hancock, 2014). Hancock was playing with Jazz legend Miles David, and—during Davis' solo on "So What"—Hancock played what was obviously the wrong chords. The chords were neither intentional, nor part of the basic repertoire of chord changes that the ensemble had been accustomed. They were just plain wrong. This meant that the cues Hancock was sending Davis were out of place. Hancock recounts that Davis waited a moment and then incorporated the new serendipitous material into his solo. For Davis, Hancock's offer was just something that happened, and then, it became Davis' responsibility to find something that fit.

> What I realize now is that Miles didn't hear it as a mistake. He heard it as something that happened. As an event. And so that was part of the reality of what was happening at that moment. And he dealt with it.... Since he didn't hear it as a mistake, he thought it was his responsibility to find something that fit.

Hancock's serendipitous offer was simply more ground from which to explore the musical and emotional possibilities of "So What."

Miles Davis has been widely quoted saying, "When you hit a wrong note, it's the next note that you play that determines if it's good or bad." Davis' extension of this dictum to others when they hit the wrong note, and his masterful integration of Hancock's mistake, is testimony to his understanding of how to integrate new and often unexpected material into one of his own trademark musical pieces. In product–service–system design, **medgi** offers a context and method for attaining this kind of understanding. The next step or role, called **gestalting**, offers insight into how to gain proficiency in transforming disruptions.

Gestalting.

Gestalting consists of roughing in the implications of **disrupting**. Rather than bringing the transformation of the state of affairs to a new and tidy bundle, **gestalting** asks the design player to work in broad strokes. Specifically, **gestalting** challenges the designer to consider the implications of the disruption in respect to use-case scenarios, major formal elements and/or functional changes. **Gestalting** is not concerned with important specifications like the exact kind of button or adjustor to be used, the textures of surfaces, legibility or making something precise. **Gestalting** is concerned with proposing the *general notion* or a *"sketch"* of a new state of affairs.

For example, if a **disrupting** team member made the offer, "What if the camera could be used under water?"(which indicates a change of the "why" as a new situation or a new use-case scenario), the **gestalting** team member could propose something like, "Then it would have an underwater housing, and you would swim along snapping photographs…".

In reference to musical improvisation, listeners can hear performers "working out" new musical material in the form of experiments with chord substitutions, melodic variation or even genre. Often these experiments begin as the equivalent of a rough sketch in the hands of visual artist. Over time and upon iteration, the musical sketches begin to take form and something new comes into being—something that is no longer a sketch but a well-formed musical experience that has transformed the head into something well defined and complete in its own right, in other words the performers have **integrated** it.

Gestalting, when effectively performed, provides an offer for the next and final step: **integrating**.

Integrating.

Integrating consists of picking up on the offers made by **gestalting** and refining them. Generally speaking, **integrating** entails considering surfaces and touch points, such as *exactly* what kind of button or adjustor and detailed characteristics of these touch points (e.g., color, texture), as well as usability and legibility issues, which will be enlisted to allow access to functions and use-case scenarios. Often, giving a new name to a product–service–system occurs when **integrating**. **Integrating** signals a return to *what is,* meaning a new and transformed state of affairs. No longer a sketch or a notion full of different potentials, the product–service–system is now redefined with the intention of making the claim that a single new object interaction has crystalized.

To follow with the sports analogy, **integrating** is the equivalent to scoring. It is important to note that while not every play in sports leads to scoring, through practice and drilling plays scoring becomes more likely and predictable. **Integrating** is when a new musical experience crystalizes, and takes on a new complete form, and becomes something other than a collection of disjunctive excursions into new genres, harmonic chunks or melodic fragments. A new piece has been brought into the world with new meaning.

4   Training for medgi

medgi is best performed iteratively in the same way that plays in sports are performed iteratively or that improvisation in jazz is performed iteratively.

There are several ways that **medgi** iterations can be performed, the most important of which are ***medgi star*** and ***medgi chain***. ***medgi star*** occurs when players return to the original product–service–system for each iteration of **medgi**.

The Research to Impact Group at the Hasso Plattner Institute has modeled **medgi** training after proven training approaches in sports (Porter, 1974) and music (Harnum, 2014). While some common approaches to design instruction are biased towards affective outcomes, such as so-called creative confidence, **medgi** relies more strongly on creating cognitive and skill-based outcomes. We have found that this approach produces equivalent or better ***affective*** outcomes than focusing on affective outcomes alone (Edelman et al., 2021). Let us draw an analogy to sports training, in this case high diving. All the encouragement in the world ("You can do it, you go!") without an understanding of body mechanics and a breakdown of the high dive into manageable and practiceable chunks, will not give an athlete the confidence they need to perform well, let alone win medals in a competitive environment. Without knowledge of body mechanics and sufficient practice to develop the skills needed for successful execution, the diver will likely leave the board with little control and splash awkwardly on the water and perhaps get injured as well. The end result would likely be one of discouragement, rather than a confidence boost.

medgi training has three components:

- Warm-ups
- Individual skills
- Team drills.

Each of the three components is designed to cultivate fluency in making explicit and useful hand-offs and subsequent pick-ups. Great concept and experience development are more than simply a matter of trading words. Using language alone as a tool for concept development has been shown to be less effective than multi-modal communication that includes gesture and shared media. Utilization of the three elements of language, gesture and media help develop an awareness of extended cognition. **medgi** training promotes keen observation in the context of team interactions and reinforces radical distributed cognition in that the warm-up breaks the activity into smaller components. With **medgi** training, design performers learn and practice the critical skill of making small meaningful moves, rather than attempting to black box the whole process of transformation.

medgi Warm-Ups

medgi warm-ups have been designed and selected to reinforce specific skills that reinforce each **medgi** behavior (Talbot, 2020). Thus, each of the five **medgi** behaviors has their own warm-up. The practice of task-specific warm-ups is grounded in the training regimens of top-level sports teams and music conservatories.

For reasons of economy, we present a single, whole **medgi** warm-up below which serves to illustrate our approach to warm-ups in general. **medgi** warm-ups are designed to promote extended cognition (language, physical tools or media and gesture, each as a means of cognition) and distributed cognition (breaking the cognition into smaller chunks that are sequentially taken up by each player). With this in mind, please note that while some **medgi** warm-ups are more linguistically weighted, or weighted towards working with media, the warm-up below focuses on gestural enactment, interaction and communication.

medgi Warm-Ups

Copy-Extend-Combine

Copy-Extend-Combine is a team warm-up that makes explicit useful hand-offs and subsequent pick-ups. Copy-Extend-Combine emphasizes the gestural vector of extended cognition as gestures are proposed and then modified in several understandable and manageable small steps. Copy-Extend-Combine is best performed with three to five players.

> Step 1: Team member 1 repeatedly makes a gesture as an offer to the other design performers. The other team members watch carefully and…
>
> Step 2: **Copy** the gesture, repeating this same gesture, until the all team members are able to replicate the gesture to a high degree of accuracy and synchronously with one another. Accuracy matters. This warm-up is designed to cultivate keen observation and replication.
>
> Step 3: Each design performer **Extends** the gesture in some way. Enacting the extension should last long enough for every team member to observe other team members' extension.
>
> Step 4: Each team member now **Combines** their own gestural extension from Step 3 with the extension of another team member.

medgi Individual Skills

medgi Individual Skill 1: Sketching medgi

Sketching **medgi** prompts a design performer to go through each step of **medgi**, making quick sketches for each step. This exercise not only develops expertise in each step of **medgi**, but also develops facility in non-linguistic visual analysis and expression of new possibilities. *Sketching* **medgi** also trains designers to stay focused on issues that have been identified as areas that need to be addressed as reducing fail points or increasing successful aspects of the state of affairs.

Step 1: Mapping (the state of affairs)

The designer creates an interaction timeline/map of an existing product-service-system, noting what happens, where and when in the object interaction. This is effectively performed with a *fat-tipped* (so not too much detail is recorded), black or gray marker on large sheets of paper (to allow plenty of room to unpack the object interaction on a timeline. Visualization of time, place, touch points, scenarios and networks are essential in *Sketching* **medgi mapping**, as is embodied enactment of those moments in the form of shorthand gestures called "marking" (Kirsh, 2011).

In our classes and workshops, we ask that as players go through their day, they take dedicated time to look at their surroundings and practice **mapping** products, services and systems with various **mapping** frameworks, such as Edelman's Dimensions of Engagement (Edelman, 2011), Donella Meadows' Leverage Points (Meadows, 2008), or Aristotle's Four Causes (Aristotle 350 B.C.E). Mapping practice can also be a group activity with two or more designers practicing together, calling out and noting what they perceive.

Step 2: **Educing (what works and does not work, pain and pleasure points)**

The designer now pulls out and highlights what works and what does not work, the pain and pleasure points on the timeline/map. It is effective to do this with a *fat-tipped, bright and saturated color marker* to clearly signal that these notations mark places of interest to be explored. In performing **educing**, a designer will find it useful to enact the pain and pleasure points. In this phase, the designer may find that it makes sense to redraw some aspects of the timeline/map to emphasize and make evident the observations realized through **educing**. Redrawing is an important step as it gives designers practice in creating clear and explicit offers for the next step: **disrupting**.

In our classes and workshops, we often practice **educing** as a group exercise. Designers will detect and speak about different moments of what works and what does not work and of pain and pleasure points. What is striking about this group practice is that one designer's pain point can be another designer's pleasure point. Another benefit of group practice is that different designers will often look at an object experience through different lenses, some concentrating on the characteristics of the state of affair, while others will concentrate on the mechanisms and structures that lie under the surface. Group practice not only benefits the team through the generation of more data, but opens designers to see, experience and benefit from other points of view.

Step 3: **Disrupting (what happens if…?)**

Picking up on the brightly colored notations of what works and what does not work, or the pain and pleasure points on the timeline/map, the designer now proposes questions for each of the notations. Questions regarding amplification are in order for what works and pleasure points; for what does not work and pain points, questions regarding how to reduce or eliminate them are in order.

The questions must take the form, *'What happens if…?*
For the purpose of this exercise, players should get familiar with the four kinds of questions that, based on our observations, are asked by high-performance teams (Eris, 2003). These are questions we can ask about changes to a product-service-system pertaining to:
form ("What happens if… we make it bigger?", "What happens if… we make it flexible?").
material ("What happens if… we change the material?").
process ("What happens if… we change the steps?", "What happens if… we add a feedback loop?").

reason ("What happens if… we change the user?", "What happens if… we change the use-case scenario?", "What happens if… it is for preventive medicine?").

In our classes and workshops, we ask that designers practice **disrupting** by examining many situations throughout their day and asking disruptive questions. It is helpful to have a cheat sheet at hand with Edelman's *Dimensions of Engagement* (Edelman, 2011), Donella Meadows' *Leverage Points* (Meadows, 2008), or Aristotle's *Four Causes* (Aristotle 350 B.C.E.) in the form of "What happens if…?" questions.

One of the essential aspects of this practice is that it builds an awareness and fluency for opening up the *possibility space* without reflexively jumping to a solution or an idea. Collectively and sequentially opening up the *possibility space* is a critical skill for radically distributing cognition through a team. Here, the analogous situation in sports is again worth mentioning. While scoring is the objective of the game, scoring is more successful when the activity is a shared activity. In simple terms, if one player is doing all the scoring, it will eventually alienate other players, not to mention exhaust the single player who is compelled to carry the burden of scoring alone.

Disrupting with the four classes of questions serve as clear and potent offers to be picked up in the next step of the exercise, **gestalting**.

Step 4: **Gestalting ("sketching")**

With **gestalting**, the designer considers possible implications of the disruption made in Step 3. As described earlier, **gestalting** is similar to creating a rough sketch. This could be a gestural sketch, a physical sketch (with a large felt tipped pen), a sketch made in language or a combination of the three. Importantly, the sketch performed in **gestalting** is made in direct response to the preceding disruption. It is crafted to be the reciprocal of the disruption. There are four fundamental ways to change the camera (form, material, process or the "why" (which includes the user, the scenario and the goal). While **disrupting** only **asks** about one of the changes, **gestalting** "sketches" one or more of the remaining three.

For example, while redesigning a point and shoot camera, if **disrupting** asks for a change in **form, such as** "What happens if we make the camera bigger?" **gestalting** might entail sketching a **use-case scenario** in which the bigger camera was being used, a new **material**, a new **process** or new **reason** for the camera. Another example would be if in redesigning the point and shoot camera **disrupting** asks for a change in the *reason* or "why" for the camera, "What happens if we wanted to take a photograph of a big group of people?", **gestalting** might entail sketching changes in *form, material* or *process* or a combination of the three. For example, a camera for photographing a group might entail a change in form (making it bigger), a change in material (it might need to be lighter) or a change in process (it is difficult to get a large group to look good all at once, so multiple images could be rapidly shot and then composited so everyone looks good in the photograph—think a photograph like Rembrandt's *The Night Watch*, in which everyone in the frame is rendered in an iconic pose and expression).

It is important to note that **gestalting** is concerned with broad sweeps of general changes to form, material, process and the "why" to the current state of affairs and not to specifics like surfaces, adjustors and usability. This is because **gestalting** serves as an offer for **integrating**—the phase in which these crucial fine points are addressed. Too often, we have found that designers conflate a sketch with a finished outcome and do not understand the underlying product–service–system architecture that distinguishes the specifics of surfaces, adjustors and usability from broad formal elements, functionality and use-case scenarios. **Gestalting** is fundamentally a speculative behavior and does not seek to make something seem real.

In our classes and workshops, we ask that participants practice **gestalting** as an activity in itself. Sketching in the graphic arts and marking, sketching's equivalent in dance, theater and athletics are key behaviors that lead to mastery. It takes practice to sketch or mark well, just as it takes practice to create finished drawings or perform sports routines. Sketching and marking provide a context for exploring, learning, experimenting and working out parts of a whole, rather than having to get the whole right all at once.

Step 5: **Integrating**

When performing integrating, the designers refine the sketch created in **gestalting** through a combination of one or more of several moves. A central theme of **integrating** is to make the new concept concrete. **Integrating** can take the form of detailing the surfaces, buttons, adjustors and enacting the usability of them. It can take the form of creating a new name of a product.

As in the other steps of **medgi**, we ask designers to practice **integrating** as an activity in itself. Dr Ade Mabogunje, working at Stanford University's Center for Design Research found that teams that created new names, called "noun phrases" were one characteristic of high-performance teams (Mabogunje, 1997). In respect to creating noun phrases and their impact on developing a new concept, we gratefully credit Dr Mabogunje with coining the term "**medgi**" in a research meeting. Dr Mabogunje began his critique of our work with the statement, "So you have '*medgi*'…". Previous to Dr Mabogunje's creation of a noun phrase, we had been listing the five steps without a single name for the collection of them. At that moment our thinking changed, we realized that we had a single thing with five parts, and we were able to communicate the new method with greater clarity. We are happy that the lineage of the name "*medgi*" was a gift from the father of noun phrases.

medgi Individual Skill 2: medgi Walk About

Individual **medgi** Walk About is an exercise in which a designer practices the individual the steps of **medgi** as stand-alone exercises. This exercise promotes depth in each of the steps of **medgi**. Rather than simply making mental notes or keeping written notes, we strongly suggest that designers make graphical representations and enact what they perceive and what they propose.

medgi Team Drills

medgi Team Drill 1: Group medgi Walk About.

Similar to Individual **medgi** Walk About, Group **medgi** Walk About is an exercise in which two or more designers practice the individual steps of **medgi** as stand-alone exercises through acting out, speaking out and sharing their notation. This exercise promotes depth in each of the steps of **medgi**, as well as externalizing their perceptions and insights regarding the state of affairs, and this entails how to deconstruct it, how to intervene and how to rebuild it. Group **medgi** Walk About is literally performed "on your feet." It is terrific practice for building proficiency in analysis and synthesis. Because this exercise emphasizes acting out and sharing notation, it serves to cultivate awareness of extended cognition; because it engages more than one player, it cultivates awareness of distributed cognition, both of which are hallmarks of high-performance team behavior.

medgi Team Drill 2: Fast medgi

This instance of a **medgi** team drill follows the same form as the **medgi** individual skill, above; however, it is more concise and cultivates the facile performance of **medgi** on a team. Designer expertise in all five **medgi** skills, which have been honed with individual skill development, are extended to working in specific roles on a team. In **fast medgi**, designers are challenged with taking on one role, performing hand-offs and pick-ups in (eventually) rapid succession. It has proven successful to run **fast medgi** several times with each player keeping the same role and then switching roles until each player has gotten practice in each of the five **medgi** skills. Each of the steps below is to be performed by an individual player, and thus, this exercise works best with at least five designers. If there are less than five designers, then some of the designers can take on two roles. If there are more than five designers and less than ten designers (in which case it would make sense to form two teams for the purpose of this team drill), then **fast medgi** can be extended through the group, the sixth player taking on the role of **mapping**, the seventh player taking on the role of **educing** and so forth (Fig. 3).

Step 1: **Mapping**
The first player **maps** or *describes* what is there in no more than few brief and concise sentences (this is **fast medgi**: in this exercise being brief is a requisite).

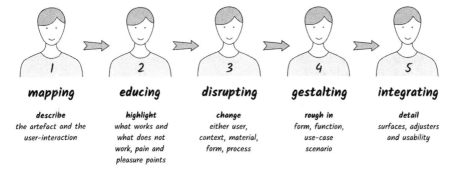

Fig. 3 Fast **medgi** (author's own image)

Different rubrics can be used as a basis for the description, each of which will have a different impact on the following steps. Describing user experience, or the interaction timeline, materials, formal elements, process or reason are good places to start. Taking elements from more formal mapping techniques like *Leverage Points* (Meadows, 2008) or the *Dimensions of Engagement* (Edelman, 2011) presents a more coherent offer for the next step, **educing**.

Remember, a key behavior for practice in each step is *creating hand-offs* that can easily be picked up by the next player. In the same way that effective passing in ball sports are directed to a zone which makes it easy for the receiver to catch the ball, design performers should strive to make their hand-off land in a zone that fosters a successful transformation in the next step.

Step 2: **Educing**

The next player *pulls out* and *highlights* a single aspect of the previous player's brief description of the state of affairs that is either something that works or does not work—this is a pain point or a pleasure point. In this step, it is important for the player to practice the discipline of only **educing** and not suggesting any kind of solution.

Step 3: **Disrupting**

The third player addresses the opportunities contained in Step 2, by asking "What happens if...?" in order to amplify what works or a pleasure point, or conversely reduce what does not work or is a pain point. It often makes sense for the **disruption** to follow on the rubric presented in Step 1, picking up on and continuing with the "play" that the player performing **mapping** has offered. Thus, if the **mapping** took the form of describing the *form* of the state of affairs, the player performing **disrupting** would pose a question about making changes to material, to process, or to the reason (users, use-case scenarios, or the goal of the product, service and/or system).

Step 4: **Gestalting**

The fourth designer sketches in the major formal elements, the functions, or the use-case scenario in response to the "What happens if we change...?" question posed by **disrupting**. For example, if the question is, "What happens if the camera can be used under water?" appropriate **gestalting** could include responses that relate to questions like, "It would have an underwater housing..." or "That way you could photograph the amazing things you experience when snorkeling..." or "You could send images back to shore in real time..." Note that **gestalting** responses do not try to get to the finished concept; **gestalting** sets the stage for **integrating**, in which the finished concept can emerge.

Step 5: **Integrating**

The fifth designer now sets about **integrating**, in response to the previous "sketch" created in **gestalting**. While **gestalting** is concerned with use-case scenarios, functions and general notions of form, integrating is concerned with detailing surfaces like screens and textures, buttons, adjustors and usability, as well as giving a compelling name to the new object interaction. An example of this could be, "It would have large, brightly colored buttons that would go here so they could be seen in low light and easily pressed with gloves on, just below the screen, which would right at eye level so you could look at a fish and the screen pretty much at the same time... we could call it the 'Snorkel-Cam'...".

The reader may be thinking that performing **medgi** is more difficult than following the rules of brainstorming, and they would be correct. Indeed, **medgi** is more difficult, in the same way that being an Olympic athlete is more difficult than being a casual sports player, or in the same way being an accomplished jazz pianist is more difficult than making noise on a piano. Mastering **medgi** takes effort, time and practice. Like performance in sports and music, the pay offs are commensurate with the dedication of the player to a deeper understanding and practice. In this respect, the question we often ask our students is, "How good do you want to be?".

Players may find that they are inclined to work in one of the five **medgi** skills, and either they enjoy performing the skill or they find it challenging. We have also observed that players may find themselves enjoying changing roles depending on the demands of the team and situation.

medgi Team Drill 3: medgi Star

medgi Star is an iterative variation of **Fast medgi. medgi Star** is comprised of the same steps as in **Fast medgi**, though the steps are done iteratively. The starting point of each iteration is the same: the mapping of the state of affairs to be redesigned (Fig. 4).

Ideally, in each iteration of **medgi Star,** designers perform **mapping, educing, disrupting, gestalting** and **integrating** on a different aspect of the original state of affairs. In this way, as the players create the arms of star around the same

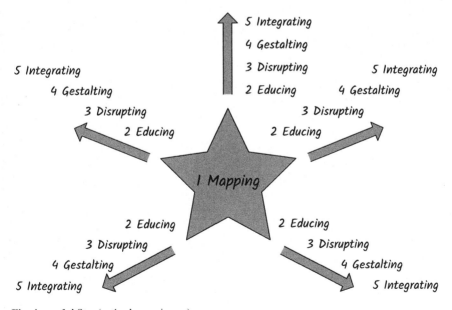

Fig. 4 **medgi** Star (author's own image)

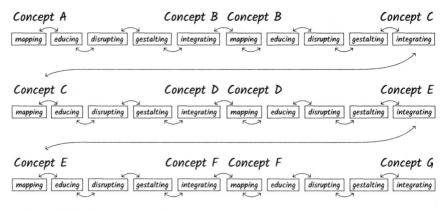

Fig. 5   **medgi** Chain (author's own image)

state of affairs, new possibilities are revealed and are brought to the shared field of exploration.

medgi Team Drill 3: *medgi Chain*

Like **medgi Star, medgi Chain** directs designers to perform **medgi** iteratively. Unlike **medgi Star**, **medgi Chain** begins each new iteration where the last iteration left off, thus building a chain of **medgi** iterations. Because each iteration begins where the last one left off, new radical possibilities emerge, which are clearly traceable to the original state of affairs (Fig. 5).

5   Conclusion

medgi method is a research-based method for generating new concepts. **medgi** training promotes high-performance team behavior through performing explicit steps that lead to a new concept, rather than relying on chance or talent alone. Because **medgi** un-black-boxes the concept development process, it does not depend on teams relying on individual designers who magically come up with a lot of linguistically based ideas to throw into a pile from which to choose. Instead, **medgi** leverages extended cognition, develops experiences and radically distributes cognition through the team, which are proven hallmarks of high-performance teams.

The Research to Impact Group has developed unique warm-ups, individual skills and team drills for each of the behaviors in **medgi**. We have created these in order to facilitate and cultivate more robust team performance. Additionally, **medgi** is one of many **highly effective performative patterns** that the Research to Impact Group has developed and tested in academic and professional settings. It is beyond the scope of this chapter to include these exercises in the current publication, though the authors look forward to sharing them with a broader audience in the near future.

The authors would like to thank the Hasso Plattner Design Thinking Research Program for their generous and continued support of the research that serves as the foundation for the approach presented in this paper, as well as the development of highly effective performative patterns, warm-ups, individual skills and team drills. We would also like to thank Professor Christoph Meinel and the Hasso Plattner Institute in Postdam, Germany, and Professor Larry Leifer of Stanford University, Stanford, California, for their dedication to understanding and improving design practice and education. We would like to thank Professor Cabirio Cautela and Fabrizio Pierandre for their contributions to this work, both in the development of theory and practice. Thank you to Stanford's Professor David Beach and Craig Milroy of the Product Realization Lab for their significant support and deep knowledge of teaching design and design practice. Thank you to William Burnett and Michael Barry from whom we have learned so much. Thank you, Ade Mabogunje, for giving this process a worthy name. Thank you to our colleagues in design research and practice, the participants in our studies of what makes great teams work, and our students who provided valuable feedback about the warm-ups, individual skill exercises and team drills. The work that is presented in this chapter is truly a result of many teams working together toward a previously undefined outcome.

References

Aristotle (350 B.C.E.), and Hippocrates George Apostle (1969). *Aristotle's physics*. Indiana University Press.

Becvar, L. A., Hollan, J., & Hutchins, E. (2005). Hands as molecules: Representational gestures used for developing theory in a scientific laboratory. *Semiotica, 2005*(156), 89–112.

Bloom, B. S. (Ed.). (1987). *Taxonomy of educational objectives. The classification of education goals; handbook. 30th print*. Longman Group.

Clark, A., & Chalmers, D. (1998). The extended mind. *Analysis, 58*(1), 7–19. Available online at http://www.jstor.org/stable/3328150

Dreyfus, L. (1996). *Bach and the patterns of invention*. Harvard University Press.

Edelman, J. A., Owoyele, B., Santuber, J., & Talbot, A. V. (2021). Designing as performance: Bridging the gap between research and practice in design thinking education. In: C. Meinel, & L. Leifer (Eds.) *Design thinking research*. Understanding Innovation. https://doi.org/10.1007/978-3-030-62037-0_3

Edelman, J. A., Owoyele, B., Santuber, J., Talbot, A. V., Unger, K., & Von Lewinski, K. (2019). *Accessing highly effective performative patterns in design thinking research*. Springer.

Edelman, J. (2019). *Accessing highly effective performative patterns in team-based design*. Lecture, Dartmouth College, 2019. Available online at https://engineering.dartmouth.edu/events/accessing-highly-effective-performative-patterns-in-team-based-design, checked on 18 February 2019.

Edelman, J. (2016). *Learning from bach: Musical rhetoric as creative paradigm*. Lecture Pratt Institute, Brooklyn.

Edelman, J. (2015). *Learning from bach: Principles and practices of design thinking*, Keynote address on the occasion of the first graduating class from the new food innovation program. Future Food Institute, University of Modena and Reggio Emilia.

Edelman, J., Agarwal, A., Paterson, C., Mark, S., & Leifer, L. (2012). Understanding radical breaks. In H. Plattner, C. Meinel, & L. Leifer, (Eds.) *Design thinking research. Studying co-creation in practice* (pp. 31–51). Springer (Understanding innovation).

Edelman, J., & Currano, R. (2011). Re-representation: Affordances of shared models in team-based design. In H. Plattner, C. Meinel, & L. Leifer (Eds.) *Design thinking. Understand improve apply* (pp. 61–79). Springer.

Edelman, J. (2011). *Understanding radical breaks: Media and behavior in small teams engaged in redesign scenarios.* Doctoral Dissertation, Stanford University http://purl.stanford.edu/ps394d y6131

Edelman, J. A., Leifer, L., Banerjee, B., Sonalkar, N., Jung, M., Lande, M. (2009). *Hidden in plain sight: Affordances of shared models in team based design, Proceedings of the 17th international conference on engineering design (ICED09).* Stanford University.

Eris, O. (2003). *Asking generative design questions: A fundamental cognitive mechanism in design thinking.* Springer.

Farrell, M. P. (2001). *Collaborative circles: Friendship dynamics and creative work.* University of Chicago Press.

Feinberg, M., & Nemeth, C. (2008). The "Rules" of brainstorming: An impediment to creativity?. *UC Berkeley: Institute for research on labor and employment.* Retrieved from https://escholars hip.org/uc/item/69j9g0cg

Hancock, H. (2014). *Norton lectures,* Harvard University. https://mahindrahumanities.fas.harvard. edu/search/site/hancock?&solrsort=%20

Harnum, J. (2014). *The practice of practice.* [Online content edition]. Sol UT Press.

Hutchins, E. (1995). *Cognition in the wild.* MIT Press.

IDEO U. *7 Simple rules of brainstorming.* https://www.ideou.com/blogs/inspiration/7-simple-rules-of-brainstorming

Isaksen, S. C. (1998). *A review of brainstorming research: Six critical issues for inquiry.* Creative research unit, creative problem solving group, Buffalo.

Kirsh, D. (2010). Thinking with external representations. *AI and Society, 25*(4), 441–454.

Kirsh, D. (2011). *How marking in dance constitutes thinking with the body* (pp. 183–214). The external mind.

Kohn, N. W., & Smith, S. M. (2011). Collaborative fixation: Effects of others' ideas on brainstorming. *Applied Cognitive Psychology, 25*(3), 359–371.

Mabogunje, A. (1997). Noun phrases as surrogates for measuring early phases of the mechanical design process. In *The proceedings of the 9th international conference on design theory and methodology.*

Mullen, B., Johnson, C., & Salas, E. (1991). Productivity loss in brainstorming groups: A meta-analytic integration. *Basic and Applied Social Psychology, 12,* 332–340. https://doi.org/10.1207/ s15324834basp1201_1Taylor&FrancisOnline

Meadows, D. H. (2008). *Thinking in systems: A primer.* Chelsea Green Publishing

Osborn, A. F. (1953). *Applied imagination; principles and procedures of creative problem-solving.* Scribner.

Porter, P. (1974). *Judo from the beginning* (Vol. 1). National Coaching Standards, Zenbei.

Putman, V. L., & Paulus, P. B. (2009). Brainstorming, brainstorming rules and decision making. *The Journal of Creative Behavior, 43,* 29–40.

Sutton, R., & Hargadon, A. (1996). Brainstorming groups in context: Effectiveness in a product design firm. *Administrative Science Quarterly, 41*(4), 685–718. https://doi.org/10.2307/2393872

Talbot, A. (2020). *Improvisation as the foundation for teaching the fundamental skills of design thinking in education.* Design thinking in education management—Successfully developing and implementing innovation in educational contexts. Springer.

Tversky, B. (2019). *Mind in motion: How action shapes thought.* Basic Books.

Tversky, B., & Suwa, M. (2009). Thinking with sketches. In A. B. Markman & K. L. Wood (Eds.), *Tools for innovation: The science behind the practical methods that drive new ideas* (pp. 75–84). Oxford University Press.

Verganti, R. (2017). *Overcrowded: Designing meaningful products in a world awash with ideas.* The MIT Press.

Dr. Jonathan Edelman Dr. Edelman is founder and head of the Digital Health Design Lab and leader of the Research to Impact Group at the HPI. Before his appointment at the HPI, Dr. Edelman was Head of Programme for Global Innovation Design at the Royal College of Art, London. Prior to that, Dr. Edelman was the Director of Interdisciplinary Design at Stanford University's Product Realization Lab and Consulting Assistant Professor in Mechanical Engineering at Stanford University.

His research and teaching at the HPI focuses on Human Centered Design in Digital Health, with a special interest in Human Centered Machine Learning, Digital Transformation and Design Team Dynamics. He also serves as a Visiting Professor in Design at Politecnico di Milano. Dr. Edelman is also founder of the Center for Advanced Design Studies, the objective of which is to explore and communicate cutting edge innovation processes in a wide spectrum of creative and scientific domains, and is the COO of Health Innovations.AI.

Dr. Edelman has been involved with design thinking since 2004, when he attended Stanford's Joint Program in Design. He attended some of the first classes in design thinking given at Stanford. Dr. Edelman has the honor of being in the first cohort of researchers to receive funding from the Hasso Plattner Design Thinking Research Program for his work on understanding the affordances of shared media in team-based design. He has lectured on several continents about research-based design practice. A helpful insight is to use your body and tools to do some of the thinking for you.

Experience with DT: 16 Years.

Greatest challenge and simplest step to use DT in education: Understanding that cognition doesn't happen in the brain alone, cognition happens in the body and the tools we use as well.

Most valuable insight/result: Through DT Research, DT education has evolved from rules of thumb to a robust practice of behaviors.

Babajide Owoyele As a member of the Research to Impact Group of the Hasso Plattner-Stanford Design Thinking Research Program, Babajide Owoyele is developing evidence-based Design Thinking teaching materials in collaboration with Dr. Jonathan Edelman and Joaquin Santuber. He was a researcher at the Wuppertal Institute, Germany, and the European Institute for Innovation and Technology Climate Knowledge and Innovation Community; Babajide Owoyele holds a master's degree in Global Production Engineering (Solar Technologies) from the Technische Universität Berlin. He has been involved in DT education in undergraduate and postgraduate level courses, such as Digital Health Design and Business Model Design. Babajide Owoyele is also an alumnus of the School of Design Thinking in Potsdam and advises the HPI Academy. He believes applying DT in education is challenging because topics such as food, healthcare, law, and energy are very different, and each domain requires careful and iterative adaptation of DT tools and methods. In the academic setting, teaching with domain-specific cases is both a challenge and an opportunity for the DT community. DT can be made more accessible, however, by using and reflecting on digital tools and platforms to create experience maps, generate concepts, and prototype ideas. Just trying out templates in MIRO provides a lot of hands-on practice for DT. Especially in the current Covid-19 era, evaluating DT training outcomes will require multimodal analysis of DT trainers and student interactions in digital environments. DT is already demonstrating promising approaches in healthcare as it helps physicians, researchers, and students co-create better patient experiences using digital video prototyping. In these types of projects, modern DT techniques can radically improve learning and communicating.

Joaquin Santuber Joaquin is a researcher and practitioner working at the intersection of Law, Design, and Digital Transformation. Together with being a researcher at the Hasso-Plattner-Institute, he is the Head of Design --and one of the founders-- of This is Legal Design GbR a creative consultancy firm and Think Tank based in Berlin where he applied design approaches (such as DT) working with Law Firms and Legal Departments. As a design researcher at the HPI-Stanford Design Thinking Research Program, he is part of the Research2Impact group looking at team dynamics to create educational material for high-performing design teams. Joaquin applies these novel training packages in the context of legal professional education, as well as in Law Schools. From this experience, he sees Design Thinking as powerful tool to put traditional skills from a profession or practice to work on new challenges.

Joaquin learnt Design Thinking at the School of Design Thinking, HPI, and was part of the teaching team. Before that, he worked at a legal tech startup in Berlin, in innovation consulting industry in Panama and Turkey, and of course, working as a Lawyer. He has also been a Research Fellow at the Humboldt Institut für Internet und Gesellschaft (HIIG - Humboldt University).

Design Thinking and the UN Sustainable Development Goals: Design Thinking and Youth Empowerment Case Study ForUsGirls (US) and Start-up Africa (Kenya)

Joann Halpern and Cornelia Walther

Abstract A Design Thinking (DT) approach has the potential to empower young entrepreneurs whose focus is social innovation and may help them move towards efficient and effective action in their environment. Within the scope of the United Nations (UN) commitment to global youth empowerment, this study is anchored in the Sustainable Development Goals for inclusive growth. We link theory with practice by examining two case studies related to DT as a tool of empowerment. While one case study was conducted in the US, face-to-face before the COVID-19 pandemic, the other case study took place online, focusing on a young startup in Kenya. A comparison of these two case studies offers an overview of existing DT principles that are context neutral. In addition, we examine specific characteristics that stem from context (COVID-19) and constellation (online). Taken together, theory and practice lead to a set of recommendations that, if implemented, are conducive to an optimistic outlook for Design Thinking in the UN in general and for youth empowerment in particular.

1 Issue

Today there are 1.8 billion people between the ages of ten and twenty-four, the largest generation of youth in history. Close to ninety percent live in the Global South, where they make up a large proportion of the population, and their numbers are expected to grow. Between 2015 and 2030 alone, it is projected that about 1.9 billion young people will turn fifteen years old. (UN SDG. Retrieved Sept., 2020).

COVID-19 has put the jobs of millions among this cohort at risk. Those who had worked in the informal sector are especially affected. Estimates suggest that

J. Halpern (✉)
Hasso-Plattner-Institut, New York, 10 Hudson Yards, 48th Floor, New York 10001, USA
e-mail: Joann.Halpern@hpi.de

New York University, New York, USA

C. Walther
POZE Space, New York, NY, USA

C. Meinel and T. Krohn (eds.), *Design Thinking in Education*,
https://doi.org/10.1007/978-3-030-89113-8_16

more than one in six young people has stopped working due to the pandemic. It is critical to accelerate the four Es that matter for youth today—Education, Employment, Entrepreneurship, and Empowerment. To support short-term recovery from COVID-19 while boosting longer term resiliency to external circumstances, the United Nations together with researchers and practitioners from private and nonprofit sectors seek to create employment opportunities and foster entrepreneurship.

Among the many questions at stake are the need to revive small and medium-sized businesses, increase private sector engagement while leveraging new digital job opportunities, and improve access to online education for those who are most at risk of falling through the cracks. Young people from marginalized families, in particular those who live in countries that suffocate under the compounded burden of COVID-19, chronic poverty, fragile governance, and overall insufficiency of social services, are particularly at risk. The present chapter hones in on the best of all worlds—helping social enterprises created by young people to solve problems in their environment. Defined as a private sector entity that generates resources while furthering a social cause, social enterprises have expanded massively over the past years in the West. We are looking at the Global South and in particular Kenya, where *Startup Africa* is coaching young entrepreneurs to translate their business ideas into practice. The practical manifestation of such high-level ambition is direly needed.

While recent decades have witnessed advances in terms of human development, major challenges remain. Progress has been uneven, and millions of young people across the globe remain locked in interconnected forms of discrimination, social and political exclusion, chronic poverty, and limited access to health systems, educational opportunities, and decent jobs. The goals and targets of Agenda 2030, the official document that summarizes the SDGs, have interconnected benefits. The aim was to integrate three dimensions of sustainable development: economic, social, and environmental. (UN SDG Official site, Retrieved Sept 2020). This is in line with the four principles that underpin human existence—Change (everything evolves), Connection (everything is linked to something else), Continuum (everything is part of a whole), Complementarity (everything is part of something that renders it complete). (Walther, 2020). The experience, expertise, and expressions of young people are essential to finding and implementing innovative solutions that will realize these ambitions in the aftermath of COVID-19.

Much of the current global and local attention is geared towards overcoming the social and economic conundrum that has arisen from the COVID-19 pandemic. Even though tackling these issues with and for youth is crucial, it is not enough. We must be aware of the transformative potential of youth. Connected to each other, young people can and want to be part of social change that matters beyond the here and now. Indeed, many of them already contribute to the resilience of their communities, proposing innovative solutions, driving radical social progress, and inspiring political disruption. They are agents of change on the ground. Moving from paper to practice, they are translating the Sustainable Development Goals (SDG) by improving the lives of individuals and the health of Planet Earth. When they are provided with the necessary space and support to see and reach their full potential, young people can be catalysts of shared prosperity and social peace. Stronger youth-led organizations, which act as conveners and intermediaries between young people and politicians, have the potential to translate Agenda 2030 into local, national, and regional policy.

The organizations play a significant role in the implementation, monitoring, and review of the SDGs. They can hold governments accountable. Today's youth are the partners of older and future generations. In order to overcome the fallout of COVID-19 and build a society that is fair and cohesive, all sectors, ages, and socio-economic spheres must work together.

The following section looks at youth empowerment in the UN's move towards the SDGs, and the role that Design Thinking (DT) can play in moving youth empowerment plans beyond the abstract into action, and from desire for change to hands-on transformation.

a. An overview of the current focus on youth empowerment in the United Nations

The 2030 Agenda for Sustainable Development, adopted in 2015, is the international community's response to the most pressing global development challenges. It is meant to guide the UN's development priorities for an entire generation. One-third of the 169 SDG targets refer to young people explicitly or implicitly and focus on empowerment, participation, and/or well-being. There are 20 youth-specific targets spread over six key SDGs: Goal 2 (hunger), Goal 4 (education), Goal 5 (gender equality), Goal 8 (decent work), Goal 10 (inequality), and Goal 13 (climate change). Youth involvement is also critical if the call for participation, inclusion, accountability, and revitalized global engagement embedded in Goals 16 (peaceful, just, and inclusive societies) and 17 (partnerships and implementation) is to be achieved. (UNDP, 2017). Young people were involved in shaping this agenda. This involvement is a step in the right direction for three reasons: Relevance of Agenda 2030—the document seeks to address many issues that youth experience first-hand; Inclusiveness—youth must be given space to be heard; Sustainability and Scale—plans made without those who are supposed to benefit from them are unlikely to succeed.

Building on its global convening role, the United Nations is uniquely suited to act as a source of protection and support for young people. It is a platform through which their needs can be addressed, their voices amplified, and their engagement advanced. The UN has a large variety of bodies, programs, and committees. Most of these have embraced youth as a topic on their agenda, directly or indirectly, seeking to address them through their activities. The form that these approaches take varies, depending on the overall mandate and priorities of each agency. Broadly, the approaches can be broken down into the following four categories:

Policy: The UN is accompanying governments as they integrate the SDGs into their national and local strategies while supporting young people by creating formal spaces for their engagement, e.g., as national youth platforms, to provide viable opportunities for young women and young men to participate, to provide evidence, inform decisions, and influence development priorities as well as budget allocations. Within the scope of their respective mandates, UN agencies may help to identify obstacles, such as discrimination, and promote enhanced youth participation and civic engagement.

Monitoring & Accountability: The UN supports government and other stake-holders' efforts to produce quality data needed to capture the underlying development realities of youth. At times, it also works with parliaments and relevant institutions, supporting oversight and accountability.

Research: As a global convener, the UN often partners with academia and civil society organizations to produce fresh research and insights connecting local, national, and global knowledge to address gaps in emerging areas of youth partici-pation and development, such as research on financing for youth and on youth and peacebuilding. Among the regular reports are, e.g., UNICEF's State of the World Children and UNDP's Human Development Report on Youth.

Advocacy: The UN creates space for international and local dialog. Increasingly, the complementarity of online and offline consultations and campaigns is sought to reach the most marginalized young people. It is critical to hear their voices and make them heard. Participation in the online and offline space is a way to help young people step into their roles as advocates and partners in the implementation of the SDGs.

Overall, the aim of investments in youth empowerment at the UN is to provide effective, demand-driven, context-specific and evidence-based policy advice and technical assistance, drawing on the depth and breadth of knowledge and experi-ence across the world. To embrace diversity, the UN is advocating for approaches that reflect diversity. In line with the UN Charter of 1945, the ultimate aim is to ensure that young people everywhere, independent of race, gender, location, and (dis-) ability can live up to their potential.

Within the context of this chapter, we define empowerment as the identification and pursuit of inherent human potential and the sense of purpose that derives from it (Walther, 2021a, b).

The UN recognizes young people as rights holders and promotes and facilitates transparency, accountability, and responsiveness from governments, international organizations, and others towards young people. However, the path from theory to practice remains long and, at times, the gap that separates ambition from facts is wide. This is where DT comes into play.

b. Design thinking supports local and cross-border empowerment through partic-ipatory development

DT in the context of the UN's ambition of Youth Empowerment can be seen as a form of participatory development (PD), which has been around since the 1970s.[1] While in its classic form, the latter seeks to engage local populations in development projects, the present experience with *Startup Africa* illustrates that DT expands PD

---

[1] Since its emergence in the 1970s, *public participation* in development was mostly approached as a means to "give the poor a part in initiatives designed for their benefit." (Cornwall, 2002). Often presented as an alternative to mainstream top-down development, it has become an accepted method of development practice, which is now employed by a variety of organizations, including the UN. (Mohan, 2008). The most common definitions of participatory development are the 'Social Movement Perspective' and the 'Institutional Perspective'.

beyond this local aspect to embrace the empowerment of youth as agents of change for others, locally and regionally.

Before we look at the characteristics of DT that make it an interesting tool for youth empowerment, let us look briefly at the logic of participatory development. The latter matters due to the preponderance of social issues in low-income countries, and the fact that *Startup Africa* intervenes in one of those countries, Kenya.

The four stages of the "institutional perspective" on participatory development (Tufte & Mefalopulos, 2009) are in harmony with the logical phases of the DT processes: (1) The Research Stage is where the development problem is accurately defined, including relevant stakeholders. Research around the development problem can include previous experiences, individual and community knowledge and attitudes, existing policies, and other relevant contextual information related to socio-economic conditions, culture, spirituality, gender, etc. (2) The Design Stage defines the actual activity, while helping to secure the ownership and commitment of the communities involved. (3) The Implementation Stage relates to the actual activation of the planned intervention. (4) The Evaluation Stage ensures that the most significant changes are voiced, brought to everyone's attention, and assessed. For a meaningful evaluation, indicators and measurements should be defined in a participatory process at the very beginning of the initiative and involve all relevant stakeholders. While PD misses out on the prototyping phase, both approaches share the overall ambition of inclusive co-creation, referring at the same time to a shift in mindsets and a set of solution-based practices.

What follows is a review of four aspects that make DT relevant to youth empowerment and the UN's ambitions in that regard: *Empathy* is central to human-centered programming. It puts the spotlight on the emotions, motivations, and functional needs of users; *Multidisciplinary Ideation* generates solutions via cross-disciplinary teamwork and collaboration; *Experimentation* refers to rapid prototyping and the iterative testing of products or services with an ongoing feedback loop that associates target users before and during the development and implementation phase. Finally, *Open-Mindedness* implies that neither the outcome nor the processes itself are contained within a blueprint that derives from preceding experiences.

The philosophy of both Design Thinking and participatory development, are in sync with the POZE-model that understands human existence as a composition of four dimensions—soul, heart, mind, and body, expressed as aspirations, emotions, thoughts, and sensations; and addresses the decision-making processes within these four dimensions. (Walther, 2020a). The schema below illustrates the ongoing interplay of the four stages that complement each other (Fig. 1).

While it is relevant to community development and youth empowerment anywhere and in all institutions, it is worth outlining the distinctive differences that DT brings to Youth programming in the UN.

Fig. 1 Participants aspire to a solution (aspiration); adopt the perspective of those whom they seek to help through empathy (emotion), think about a large variety of possible options (thought), and test the outcomes hands-on (sensation). The results of that experience are fed back into the process until the result corresponds to the desired solution. [*Source* Walther, 2020]

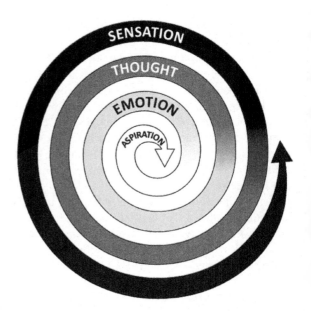

Empathy-driven design seeks to optimize user engagement, immersion, and motivation. As such, it has the potential to address key limitations of classic aid schemas. The usual premise of input a + input b = output c which leads to outcome d is replaced with an open-ended question. Empathic design is grounded in the ambition of helping a specific population solve a problem they have, rather than applying a blueprint solution to a problem that appears at first sight. It thus helps practitioners expand beyond the limited focus of sectorial programs (i.e., education, protection, employment—what do we know) towards user concerns (i.e., needs, desires, and habits—what do they need).

Beyond understanding the demographics, personalities, and preferences of individual users, empathic design shifts the focus from inputs/outputs to understanding the whole end-to-end user *experience*. An empathy-driven approach is anchored in *participatory design*. A key shift for the UN and its implementation partners is the understanding that programs that are conducive to youth empowerment must not merely be designed *for* young people but *with* them; and that this integrated codesign must happen from the very beginning of an intervention. Over the past decade, researchers from various disciplines have addressed the importance of recruiting young people in the development process. This practice has been referred to as participatory design, participatory research, codesign, user-centered design, etc. (Fleming et al., 2016).

In the context of aid programs in general and within the UN in particular, the greatest barrier to participatory approaches is the implicit paternalistic mindset to which certain aid practitioners may have become accustomed. Since the Grand Bargain in 2016, researchers, practitioners, and local civil society have repeatedly called for the localization of aid. However, critics of the vertical design and implementation of aid predate the Grand Bargain.[2] They received fresh wind during COVID-19, which placed a spotlight on lingering social issues in low-, medium- and high-income countries alike, while adding to the burden carried by the most marginalized parts in every society. At the core of localization is the question of participatory design and decision-making.

Multidisciplinary Ideation emphasizes cross-sectoral and interdisciplinary cooperation based on the understanding that genuine innovation arises only through the complementarity of multiple diverse perspectives (Duncan & Breslin, 2009). A central piece of DT practice is the generation of large quantities of ideas. As these are not evaluated for veracity or relevance in the initial phases, this leads to the broadest possible range of creativity. This approach stands in contrast to the conventional aid approach, which starts from a place of established principles and evidence-based techniques. While much can be discovered from best practices and lessons learned in related programming contexts, we argue that the potential for new opportunities must be allowed to breathe, especially in the area of youth empowerment. To attract and engage young people, they must be compelled to explore options outside the known territory of the past and beyond empirically established methods. Broad exploration is much more likely to yield genuinely novel design possibilities when diverse perspectives are encouraged, even if many will be subsequently discarded due to pragmatic constraints. As we will see in Sect. 2, the reframing of the issue to be tackled may shift the approach significantly. As seen in this case study, the observation and define phases led the participants to reverse the scope of their immediate efforts from a programmatic focus (delivery of supplies/cash to students) to a fundraising initiative. For DT methods to work for youth empowerment, a maximum of relevant stakeholders must be involved, e.g., teachers, community workers, parents, peers, and siblings.

The prototyping phase in DT refers to a set of processes and practices built around creating a prototype, which is a simplified version of a product, or part of a product, that is created in minimal time with minimal cost. It is used to test the validity of ideas or design assumptions. Despite its low-cost implications, this step is often skipped in the case of classic aid approaches. Locked into a 'know it all, done already' perspective, many development professionals are not sufficiently open-minded to put the planned approach to the test. The reasons for such reluctance may include worries about delays in delivery connected with donor demands for quick results, and the looming risk to discover a need to reverse course altogether.

---

[2] The Grand Bargain, launched during the World Humanitarian Summit in May 2016, is a unique agreement between some of the largest donors and humanitarian organizations who have committed to getting more resources into the hands of people in need and to improve the effectiveness and efficiency of the humanitarian action. Initially thought of as a deal between the five biggest donors and the six largest UN Agencies, the Grand Bargain now includes *63* signatories (25 states, 11 UN Agencies, 5 inter-governmental organizations and Red Cross/Red Crescent Movements, and 22 NGOs) which represent around 84% of all humanitarian contributions donated in 2019 and 69% of aid received by agencies.

Prototyping may take various forms (e.g., paper-and-pencil games, whiteboards with sticky notes, storyboards to illustrate a user's end-to-end experience, and presentation mock-ups). Applied iteratively with a small number of target users, they are tangible artifacts that offer hands-on experience and evaluation before the actual programming starts. Prototyping does not replace baselines, nor quantitative evaluation and monitoring. Rather, it addresses specific design questions before the implementation begins, yielding insights about the actual feel and usability of a product. Often, it triggers 'creative serendipity' and unanticipated insights. (Scholten & Granic, 2019).

The open-minded logic of DT and participatory development stand in direct opposition to development approaches that are cast in blueprints. DT starts with a fresh slate and an open attitude towards potential inputs and outcomes. Most people, especially those who suffer from deprivation, are aware of their needs and the support that is required to overcome them (Robertson et al., 2012). The key barrier to improving outcomes for those in need is thus not their own ignorance of whether they need help or even the kind of help they need, but their ability to find the resources and services that will support and train them in a way that speaks to their preferences and modes of learning (Robertson et al., 2012). Working with young people who are familiar with the target program context from the outset of the design process, offers valuable insights—and opens up the mindset of the aid practitioner, which maximizes the chance of relevant interventions. As seen in the case of *Startup Africa*, the young entrepreneurs were experts in their area of intervention; DT helped them distill and use this knowledge for their project.

In sum, DT is a subjective practice that focuses on discovering the emotional needs of users, their idiosyncratic contexts, their motivational concerns, and other related entities. (Scholten & Granic, 2019). It aims to build a practical product or service that serves a specific need. It is not a stand-alone practice to empower young people. However, in complementarity with other methods and high-quality data, its multidisciplinary scope offers much added value to UN programs that are geared towards youth. (Brown, 2008). The next two sections offer an illustration of the use of DT with young people, covering on the one hand ForUsGirls (Sect. 2), and *Startup Africa*, a youth-led startup incubator in Kenya, which is followed by an overview of the compounded challenges that derive from distance design and COVID-19 (Sect. 3).

2   Approach

The following pages link theory with practice, by examining two case studies related to DT as a tool of empowerment. The first example was conducted in the US, face-to-face before the pandemic. The second took place online amid COVID-19, focusing on a young Startup in Kenya.

a.   Case study DT for ForUsGirls

In 2019, the ForUsGirls Foundation approached the Hasso Plattner Institute (HPI), New York to conduct a Design Thinking workshop for young women, ages 11–18 from underserved populations in New York City and New Jersey. According to its website, the ForUsGirls Foundation "creates safe spaces for marginalized girls to be their authentic selves and to live their full potential. [They] work within a feminist, inclusive, sustainable framework and value teamwork, creativity, and innovation as strong pillars of women's and girls' empowerment."

The Design Thinking workshop focused on the following areas:

- Introducing young women to Design Thinking while simultaneously addressing an aspect of UN Sustainable Development Goal #11 that affected their communities
- Developing the participants' leadership and socio-emotional skills
- Empowering the participants to have an impact in their own underserved communities.

The Design Challenge

After reading numerous articles, interviewing individuals who were conducting research on air quality in cities, and speaking with individuals from underserved urban communities, HPI New York created the following design challenge: *How might we reduce traffic-related pollution in cities?*

Preparation

Prior to the Design Thinking workshop, HPI New York sent the coaches background information about the workshop, the agenda, and links to several articles about air pollution that provided a context for the design challenge. During an in-person coaches meeting prior to the Design Thinking workshop, we reviewed the agenda, elicited ideas, and explained a leadership exercise we had developed especially for this workshop. This exercise, "Changemakers," is described in detail later in the chapter.

The Workshop

After welcoming the participants and introducing all of the coaches, the two lead coaches provided a contextual background for the workshop, including a brief explanation of the UN Sustainable Development Goals (SDGs), with a focus on SDG 11.6, in particular. Afterward, the coaches at each table conducted an ice-breaker with their groups followed by a large group reflection on the purpose of the ice-breaker, highlighting concepts and mindsets that the groups would be using throughout the workshop, such as empathy.

The lead coaches then introduced "Changemakers," a leadership and confidence-building activity developed specifically for this workshop. One of the goals of the workshop was to help the students recognize when they were exhibiting specific leadership qualities. Taking the time to identify leadership qualities among their peers was also a valuable part of this exercise.

"Changemakers" Exercise

Each table had a sheet of paper with the same list of seven leadership qualities. These included patience, flexibility, positivity, as well as the ability and willingness to empower others, foster teamwork, take risks, and listen to ideas. The coaches and their groups were asked to select four qualities they would like to practice throughout the workshop. The team members circled the four qualities they selected, wrote those qualities on the right side of the sheet, and assigned a different colored "dot" (round sticker) to each of those qualities. See diagram below. Subsequently, throughout the workshop, every time a member of the team demonstrated one of these qualities, she would receive a sticker from the person in the group who observed the individual demonstrating that quality. The individual would then stick the dot onto her name badge. This practice not only built up the confidence of those receiving the stickers and called their attention to their own strengths, but it also taught the group members to observe and reward the behaviors of their peers—an important leadership quality as well. As the young women became more confident and empathetic, they started to give their coaches dots as well (Fig. 2).

Upon completion of the "Changemakers" exercise, the groups transitioned back to the lead coach, who gave a brief overview of Design Thinking and then introduced the Design Challenge: "How might we reduce traffic-related pollution in cities?".

The teams approached the design challenge by implementing HPI's six-phase Design Thinking model. See diagram below. The coaches explained the "Understand" phase to the students at their tables and reviewed articles about pollution in cities to help them understand the challenge's context and history. There were also several

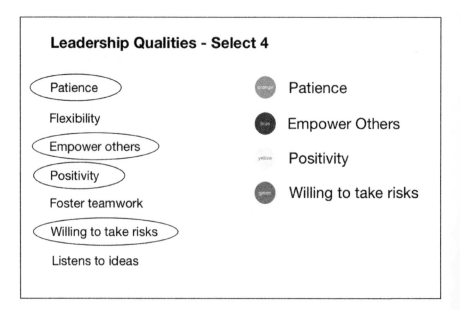

Fig. 2 "Changemakers" exercise

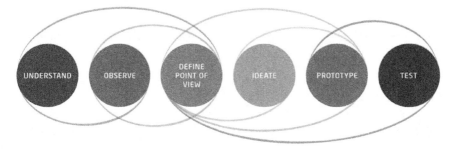

Fig. 3 Six phases of the design thinking process (HPI image)

articles that focused on individuals who lived in areas that were affected by high rates of traffic-related pollution. Each group also had an A3 piece of paper taped onto one of its whiteboards with bullet points summarizing the main points of the articles HPI New York had sent to the coaches prior to the workshop. The group discussions about the articles helped the students develop empathy by better understanding the perspectives of the people for whom they would be "designing" and why such a project was relevant. The coaches and their teams also deconstructed the design challenge through a variety of methods, including a semantic analysis[3] of the question, group discussion, drawings, and more. The goal was to make sure that every person at the table understood the challenge (Fig. 3).

Upon completion of the Understand phase, the coaches checked whether the participants at their tables had given dots to other people in their group based on the leadership qualities they had displayed.

The lead coaches then transitioned the teams into the Observe phase by conducting an abbreviated interview in front of all of the participants and asking the participants to write down their observations. After the interview was completed, the coaches and their groups discussed what they had observed and posted their observations on their whiteboards. The coaches also added techniques they deemed important that the students might have missed.

Some of the observations made by the students included establishing a connection with the interviewee, asking open-ended questions, eliciting stories, and asking "why" questions to dig deeper, rather than moving quickly from one question to the next. The coaches noted any surprises or contradictions and discussed the importance of paying attention to non-verbal cues. Writing direct quotations rather than summarizing an interviewee's answer could be useful as well. In addition, some of

---

[3] A semantic analysis of a design challenge is conducted to make sure the entire group understands the challenge. One approach involves asking group members to specify any words/phrases they might not understand or words that might be understood differently by different members of the group. Some coaches will then have the group members write down or draw images they associate with the words or phrases that have been mentioned. The group members share and discuss their results, and the outcome is often a richer and more in-depth understanding of the design challenge. This experience also enhances empathy among group members, helping them realize that others might have a completely different understanding of the same word or phrase.

the coaches mentioned that there might be pauses during the interview and it was important to give interviewees time to respond, which had the potential to generate deeper insights. They also emphasized the importance of having at least two interviewers—one to take notes and pay attention to non-verbal communication and one to ask questions. These interview techniques as well as the interviews themselves help the designers develop empathy with the interviewee.

After the coaches further explained interviewing techniques to their teams, the group members prepared some interview questions. We then had an expert on air pollution from Columbia University give a presentation to the students on some of her research findings. Following her talk, the students asked numerous questions. They also conducted interviews in smaller groups.

After the interviews were completed, the students made sense of the data by "downloading" their findings. A template had been designed for them, which made it easier to organize and interpret the information they acquired through the interviews. During this phase, participants usually create "How might we questions" to define the problem followed by ideation in which they can come up with many different ideas, a few of which will be prototyped and tested.

To address time constraints, an abbreviated "Define" phase was introduced. After downloading their findings onto the template we had provided, each group was asked to prepare a five-minute presentation in which they explained one or two things they had learned as well as how they envisioned utilizing this knowledge and their leadership skills to make a difference in their communities.[4]

The students left the workshop in high spirits, confident that they could have an impact on their communities. During our debriefing with the coaches, they said that the young women, most of whom had not known each other before the workshop, started to bond during the group exercises. The coaches also spoke about the cooperative and supportive atmosphere in which most of the participants, even the youngest ones, opened up and were not afraid to speak.

Developing trust and a safe space is integral to the success of a Design Thinking workshop. Participants need to feel comfortable taking risks, working outside of their comfort zones, and coming up with "wild" ideas without being judged. Based on the presentations and our coaches' comments, our in-person workshop with the ForUsGirls Foundation achieved these goals.

This case study illustrates that much can be achieved in a short timeframe, in terms of interesting results (mind), confidence building (emotion), and personal empowerment (aspiration). However, the human connection that was established through face-to-face engagement turned out to be essential.

---

[4] The following "results" were repeated most frequently by participants during the presentations: Awareness of their own leadership skills—Motivation to use leadership skills to make a difference in their communities—Understanding of how traffic-related pollution can affect their health—Developing empathy before trying to solve a problem—Interviewing strategies—Motivating others—Listening to their peers—"really listening"—Learning how important it is to encourage others—Building on each other's ideas rather than judging—Understanding that young people have the ability to make a difference in their families and communities—Becoming more curious about their surroundings—Empowering themselves and others—Adopting a beginner's mindset being curious.

The COVID-19 pandemic has disrupted our "normal" way of functioning, forcing unprecedented numbers of people to shift their lives online, many working remotely 100% of the time. Tools and activities that support youth empowerment, including Design Thinking, have had to be modified to serve their target audiences. The following case study is an example of DT online, which illustrates some of the challenges that arise when face-to-face interactions are replaced with various levels of separation through time and space.

b.　Case study Startup Africa

Online Design Thinking workshops have the potential to empower young social entrepreneurs, helping them develop leadership skills and acquire a better under-standing of the structures within their communities.

During our online Design Thinking workshop with a small startup in Kenya, Leveraging Africa's Education Initiative (LAE), the Design Thinking approach facil-itated interactions between the entrepreneurs and a variety of individuals within their community, helping them hone their interviewing skills, build their networks, better understand individual needs and different structures within society, e.g., how schools interact with the local government. They also started to understand how they could have a greater societal impact despite limited resources.

LAE was founded in 2019, with the goal of increasing retention in schools located in Kericho County, the Londiani sub-county region of Kenya. Specifically, the team was interested in addressing the following challenge: "How might we increase retention among students in Londiani County schools?".

Our first step in the Design Thinking process, after getting to know each other, was to learn more about the context in which LAE was working. The LAE team had been donating their own money to the schools in Londiani County to help the schools pay for textbooks and other learning materials. Some of the money they donated was also used to help students and their families cover education costs, but the team wanted to have a greater impact. At the time of the workshop, they were not working with any other donors.

After conducting a semantic analysis of the design challenge and gaining a deeper understanding of the problem, the students prepared for the interviews, which would help them empathize with those affected by the problem they were trying to solve. The interviewees included school principals, teachers, current students, parents, alumni, and students who had dropped out of school. Prior to the interviews, the coaches and the team discussed interview strategies.

The interviews helped the students understand the problem from different perspec-tives, practice interviewing skills, and connect with different members of the community, thereby enhancing their visibility among their stakeholders.

After the LAE Team had conducted the online interviews, they reconvened. It was then time to share their findings and download their interview results. Most of the results pointed to financial constraints, but one of the findings they found particularly compelling was a comment made by a college graduate who now works in the community. He stated that high school and college graduates were providing essential services to the community, for example, doctors, journalists, teachers, and architects.

This comment motivated the LAE team to reframe its approach and shift its focus. Educated high school and college students were more likely to become valuable assets to the community than those who dropped out of school. With this insight, LAE now saw one of its roles as helping community leaders truly understand the value that educated students provide. Recognizing the imitation effect that ensues when individuals mirror behavior that they observe among others in their environment (Biccheri, 2017), they assumed that recognizing the important contributions educated individuals made to the community would motivate community members to donate money or other resources to help students finish high school.

Accordingly, the team reframed the initial question to, "How might we motivate the community in Londiani County to provide more financial support to High School X to increase student retention?".

The students revised the above question several times. In all versions, the accountability shifted from the LAE team, as the central actors, to the surrounding community, which would benefit from having a better-educated population. This reframing also created a more inclusive approach to the problem. The LAE members had been the primary donors until this point, and now they were going to involve their communities, taking on more of a leadership role and assuming a greater social engagement.

The students also decided that it would be useful to focus their energy and resources on one school initially, which would make it easier to demonstrate their impact and increase their chances of success, rather than dividing and diluting their efforts over many different schools. This would also allow them to prototype and test their strategy in one location.

One of the many advantages of the testing phase is the contact with the community. Community members are being included in the design process, which makes them more likely to contribute, either financially or intellectually as this process develops. In addition, the LAE team is building its network within the community and gaining valuable experience as community organizers. The results of this phase are yet to be assessed. As the number of Covid-19 infections started to decrease in Kenya, the participants' schedules changed and it became increasingly difficult to find a time when the entire team could meet. The seven-hour time difference between Kenya and the East Coast of the United States exacerbated this issue.

Despite these contextual challenges, the participants' expanded ability to communicate with confidence has proven to be a significant positive outcome of the workshop. The exercises familiarized them with new tools and strategies to revamp and develop their startup scope and strategy. Not only have they gone through several iterations since the workshop ended, former participants are bringing their community together in pursuit of a common goal. Though it was limited in time, space and scope, this Design Thinking experience helped them recognize leadership skills in themselves that they had been unaware of, such as communication, listening, motivating others, risk taking, and patience, to name a few.

In the following section, we look at the lessons learned and conclude with perspectives and a way forward to apply DT as a tool of empowerment beyond borders.

c.   Lessons learned

Design Thinking is a process that thrives on the creation of a safe space, a shared context in which to work effectively, interpersonal interaction, trust, engaged participants, and regularly scheduled sessions. Having every participant working remotely presents a unique set of challenges and distractions: unstable internet connections, untimely mail deliveries, background noise, and disruptive family members, to name a few. These distractions can affect an individual's level of participation in the Design Thinking process. As a facilitator or coach, it is therefore especially important to create an online environment that encourages active participation by building trust, establishing rapport, creating transparency, and ensuring that participants feel comfortable sharing their ideas.

During our Design Thinking workshop with the LAE team from Kenya, we focused on creating a virtual space in which the team members felt comfortable sharing ideas, asking questions, and moving outside of their comfort zones. As coaches, we strove to provide encouragement and support as well as regular status check-ins to include individuals who were not speaking or participating as frequently.

One of the greatest challenges we faced, which affected the quality of the workshop, was the different levels of internet connectivity among the participants. The success of a workshop truly depends on all of the participants being well connected, virtually and mentally. Some of the team members had very low bandwidth and others lost their internet connection frequently. This affected the communication flow as well as the comfort level of all participants. In this kind of environment, it is challenging to build trust and create a safe space, and even more challenging to engage in a collaborative project. Yet the team was persistent. Although we had to adjust throughout the workshop, using the chat function and whiteboards more than we had anticipated, the students were very patient. These disruptions did affect the working atmosphere, e.g., during the ideation phase, the idea flow was sometimes interrupted.

In contrast to the young women we worked with in person in New York City, we noticed a hesitancy among the LAE team to venture far outside of their comfort zones, especially during the ideation phase. Beyond factors of cultural caution and trust, the environment had an impact on their thinking. There were numerous distractions, such as poor bandwidth and loss of internet connectivity, which affected the communication among the participants and between the team and the coaches. The inability to build a safe, close-knit environment without distractions had a strong effect on the outcome of the workshop.

The young women, unlike the members of the LAE team, had not yet actively engaged in solving problems within their communities when they came to the Design Thinking workshop. The workshop provided them with motivation, confidence, and an awareness of their ability to make a difference in their communities. They also learned about different Design Thinking mindsets and activities that they could use to recognize and approach challenges within their own communities. The constant, interpersonal interaction, the colored "dot" reward system, and the in-person encouragement they received from coaches and peers contributed to a safe, supportive atmosphere. This kind of atmosphere is critical when you are trying to encourage individuals to generate wild, unconventional, or innovative, ideas.

In order to create a similar atmosphere online, it is essential to engage participants in relevant warm-up activities that help them connect with the other participants and coaches. Other strategies include leaving extra time in your agenda to account for glitches, such as poor internet connectivity; testing the technology with participants in advance; introducing the tools/platforms you will be using prior to the workshop and providing engaging practice exercises to help the participants learn how to use the tools before the workshop begins.

The comparison of these two case studies illustrated the significance of specific characteristics that stem from context (COVID-19) and constellation (online). Building on these, we conclude with a set of recommendations that, if implemented, will be conducive to an optimistic outlook for Design Thinking in the UN in general and for youth empowerment in particular.

3   Perspectives and Way Forward

Compared to traditional forms of development, participatory development and, by extension, Design Thinking may be criticized for being more time consuming and more costly than conventional approaches. A project may take longer if one must engage, work, and come to a consensus with local communities, than if one did not have to do these things (Jennings, 2000). This may also lead to higher startup costs than traditional development. In addition, one might criticize participatory design and development for reaching a smaller population than traditional development blueprints, since community dialog and youth design may initially involve only a few individuals, whereas vertical aid reaches hundreds of people.

Furthermore, some of the concerns regarding a systematic inclusion of women in local aid projects may apply to the inclusion of young people. Even though many organizations acknowledge the importance of inclusive development, the history of success has been limited (Mayoux, 1995). Potential causes include a focus on immediate needs, which leave out the underlying aspects of subordination, restricted mobility, violence, lack of autonomy, etc. Similar criticism may apply to youth.

Participatory approaches have also been accused of inadequately addressing deeper inequalities, such as class and caste (Mohan, 2007). In trying to give voice to communities, the UN and its implementation partners may connect only with the (children of the) elites of a group, thereby re-enforcing local inequalities. Finally, participatory design may, under certain circumstances, enable tokenism, where a few handpicked local (youth) voices are allowed to speak and are used as proof to show participatory credentials. This view suggests that organizations only include local voices to improve their image, without really seeking to engage the population with which they are working. (Mohan, 2008).

Because and despite these supposed weaknesses ascribed to participatory development approaches, the core strengths of DT are worth the caveats. The criticism summarized above illustrates another perspective of the central benefit of co-creation: empowerment. The latter necessarily involves slower-paced, creative, multidisciplinary scoping and implementation. In line with the *Purpose for Power* (P4P) methodology, which pursues collective transformation via individual change (Walther, 2020), DT hones in on individual needs and ideation to design solutions that serve the collective. To conclude, we look at possible entry points and necessary conditions to scale DT within the UN context, and in particular regarding its aim for youth empowerment in the context of the SDGs.

a.   Potential for integration in UN empowerment programs

The UN's work for children is enshrined in the Convention of the Rights of the Child (CRC) of 1989. The latter has four pillars—Education, Protection, Participation, and Health. DT for youth empowerment clearly matches the first three and may contribute significantly to the last. The UN is thus fertile territory for the use of DT. There are additional areas within which participatory problem scoping, inclusive design, implementation, and monitoring could have substantial benefits without drastic changes to the existing programming structure. These include: gender programs, which are, by definition, cross-sectoral and multidisciplinary; peacebuilding—due to the strong mark left by youth manifestations and the stronghold of under-18-year-old civilians involved in political unrest in recent years; employment—young people represent the bulk of the present and future active workforce. Their voice, vision, and skills are vital for any program that seeks to be relevant in the short and long run.

As for other changes to the status quo, the integration of DT within existing UN programs does not derive from external constraints, but from the internal institutional set-up.[5] Assuming that Youth Empowerment has been agreed upon as a shared priority, as widely acknowledged within the UN SDGs and other international declarations, using DT to make true on this commitment still requires the three other pieces of the *P-Puzzle* to undergo drastic change—people, positions, and programs. A word on each.

Existing and future *Programs* must be (re)designed to replace vertical approaches with empathy-driven design. Intra-disciplinary planning must be combined with multidisciplinary thinking and implementation. Experimentation must find a firm place in the process that leads from planning to implementation. Finally, short-term results-based monitoring must see the value of open-minded scoping and measuring. *Positions* relate to the formal script of how an institution proceeds. If this script is based on a top-down, blueprint, quantifiable, sector-specific input versus outcome

---

[5] Four components constitute any institution—priorities, people, positions, and programs. Priorities are what matter most for the organization. They guide People/staff, who work along formal Positions, such as rules and regulations to manifest the institutional Priorities in the form of Programs. The *P-Puzzle* must be solved to optimize an institution, and introduce changes in its *modus operandi* (Walther, 2020b).

logic, a shift is needed to mainstream DT. While *Priorities* represent the big picture vision—the purpose of the institution, Positions rule staff on a day-to-day basis. Changing how an institution works entails a modification of these all-pervasive everyday procedures. *People* are the vagus nerve of the institutional setting. They are the DNA and the embodiment of the organization. Thus, incorporating DT within the UN in general, and applying it as a generalized approach within youth empowerment efforts starts with people's mindsets and skills. DT requires a shift in both areas—expertise and expectation. It is a choice to be made. To conclude, we look at a set of recommendations to facilitate the best outcomes if this choice were to be made.

b.   Recommendations for next steps

We will concentrate on four points that are particularly relevant when it comes to working with young people in a highly connected multi-stakeholder environment— Vision, Marketing, Technology, and Inspiration.

Vision—The UN requires an inclusive vision for youth empowerment that goes beyond agency agendas. The UN Children's Fund (UNICEF), the UN Population Fund (UNFPA), the UN Development Program (UNDP), the Secretariat of the UN, including its special Youth Envoy, and many other UN entities all have a vision for youth empowerment and a set of programs and staff to place their respective priorities front and center. While it is encouraging that the issue of youth is recognized as a priority, it is not enough. A shared vision that leaves behind labels and logos to focus on the outcome for young people is needed to sway citizens in general, and youth in particular.

Marketing—If scalability and broad impact are the aims, marketing, and business experts may be key to developing optimal models of service delivery. The range of stakeholders must be expanded beyond the usual suspects (UN officials, policy-makers, program specialists) to consider, on the one hand, local experts (teachers, psychologists, journalists, youth associations) and on the other, the unique expertise of marketing experts, business leaders, technical support teams—and unlikely allies, such as artists.

Technology—The potential of technology to improve the effectiveness, efficiency, cost, reach, personalization, and appeal of empowerment interventions for young people is immense. However, it is not a magical potion. Challenges include initial engagement, retention, fidelity, lack of personalization, and cognitive load in a virtual space that is loaded with commercial offers. The four characteristics of DT (empathy, multidisciplinary ideation, experimentation, and open-mindedness) come into play yet again. (Berger, 2010). They must serve not only within the design of the youth empowerment programs themselves but also inform the development of online and offline outreach interventions to make these programs known, desirable and accessible to a maximum number of individuals.

Inspiration—COVID-19 has revealed a status quo that is marked by inequity. Individuals around the world, beyond age and gender, culture, and socio-economic standing feel that change is overdue. The United Nations may play a central role in inspiring people, younger and older, to join hands. Genuine empowerment begins with the aspiration of meaning. The call for a common cause can unite individuals and institutions. The UN can be a catalyst to spark a global dynamic with and for young people. For this to happen, the UN must recognize the four principles that underpin the environment in which it operates—Change, Connection, Continuity, and Complementarity, and capitalize on them. It must change its own *modus operandi* and connect with likely as well as unlikely allies within a continuum of shared needs and complementary resources.

References

Berger, W. (2010). *The four phases of design thinking*. Retrieved October, from Harvard Business Review. https://hbr.org/2010/07/the-four-phases-of-design-thin

Biccheri, C. (2017). *Norms in the wild: How to diagnose, measure, and change social norms*. Oxford University Press.

Brown, T. (2008, June). *Design thinking* (Vol. 86, no. 6, pp. 84–92, 141). Harvard Business Review.

Charter of the United Nations. (1945). Retrieved from https://www.un.org/en/charter-united-nat ions/index.html

Cornwall, A. (2009). Locating citizen participation. *IDS Bulletin, 33*. i–x. https://doi.org/10.1111/ j.1759-5436.2002.tb00016.x

Duncan, A. K., Breslin, M. A. (2009, February 27). Innovating health care delivery: the design of health services. *Journal of Business Strategy, 30*(2/3), 13–20.

Fleming, T. M., Bavin, L., Stasiak, K., Hermansson-Webb, E., Merry, S. N., Cheek, C., et al. (2016). Serious games and gamification for mental health: Current status and promising directions. *Front Psychiatry,7*, 215.

Jennings, R. (2000). Participatory development as new paradigm: The transition of development professionalism. *Community based reintegration and rehabilitation in post-conflict settings conference* (p. 4).

Mayoux, L. (1995). *Beyond naivety: Women, gender inequality and participatory development* (p. 242). Institute of Social Studies.

Mohan, G. (2008). *Participatory development. The companion to development studies* (p. 45). Hodder Education.

Mohan, G. (2007). *Participatory development: From epistemological reversals to active citizenship* (p. 784). Geography Compass.

Robertson, I. (2012). *The Winner Effect*. New York: Bloomsbury Publisher

Scholten, H., & Granic, I. (2019). Use of the principles of design thinking to address limitations of digital mental health interventions for youth: Viewpoint. *Journal of Medical Internet Research,21*(1), e11528.

Sustainable Development Goals. *Youth*. (2020). Retrieved from https://www.un.org/sustainabled evelopment/youth/

Tufte, T., & Mefalopulos, P. (2009). *Participatory communication a practical guide* ([Online-Ausg.] ed.) (pp. 5–6). The World Bank.

UN Convention of the Rights of the Child. (1989). Retrieved from https://www.ohchr.org/en/profes sionalinterest/pages/crc.aspx

UNDP. (2017). *Fast facts. Youth as partners for the implementation of the SDGs*.

Walther, C. (2020a). *Development, humanitarian aid and social change. Social change from the inside out*. Palgrave.

Walther, C. (2020b). *Development and connection in times of COVID. Corona's call for conscious choices*. Palgrave

Walther, C. (2021a). *Technology, human behavior and social change. Influence for impact*. Palgrave.

Walther, C. (2021b). *Leadership for social change and development. Inspiration and transformation.* Palgrave

Joann Halpern, Ph.D. is the director of the Hasso Plattner Institute New York (HPI) and an adjunct professor of international education in the Department of Applied Statistics, Social Science, and Humanities at New York University.

Prior to joining HPI, she was the founding director of the German Center for Research and Innovation (DWIH), which was created as a cornerstone of the German government's initiative to internationalize science and research. In addition to teaching and administrative assignments at universities in the United States and Germany, Dr. Halpern co-founded Knowledge Transfer Beyond Boundaries, an NGO with projects in Cameroon, Nigeria, Yemen, and Antigua. She received her B.A. from Dartmouth College, her M.A. from Harvard University, and her Ph.D. in International Education from New York University. She runs Design Thinking workshops at HPI in New York City and has found new ways to integrate leadership training as well as socio-emotional skill development into the Design Thinking process while working with underserved communities from New York and New Jersey. She is a recipient of the Harvard University Award for Distinction in Teaching as well as scholarships and fellowships from the Fulbright Association, German Academic Exchange Service, Robert Bosch Foundation, and the National Endowment for the Humanities. Dr. Halpern serves on the advisory boards of the German Center for Research and Innovation, Technical University of Dortmund, Charité Entrepreneurship Summit, University Alliance Ruhr, and the External Advisory Board of the Tandon Institute for Invention, Innovation, and Entrepreneurship. Photo credit: Nathalie Schueller.

Cornelia C. Walther, Ph.D. Creator & Catalyst POZE, Author and Advocate.

Cornelia C. Walther, Ph.D. combines praxis and research. As a humanitarian practitioner, she worked for nearly two decades with UNICEF and the World Food Program in large scale emergencies in West Africa, Asia and Latin America. As lecturer, coach and researcher, Cornelia collaborates with various universities, including the Center for Humanitarian Leadership at Deakins (Australia), the Fachhochschule Muenster (Germany), the University of Palermo (Argentina) and Aix-Marseille's Law Faculty (France). Cornelia holds a doctorate in Law and is a certified yoga and meditation teacher. Recent books include 'Development, humanitarian action and social welfare'; 'Humanitarian work, social change and human behavior'; 'Connection in times of Covid'; 'Technology, Behavior and Social Change' and Leadership for Social Change and Development. Inspiration and Transformation [Macmillan Palgrave/Springer, New York].

LinkedIn   Profile   https://www.linkedin.com/in/corneliaw
alther.

Aside from her interest in the multiple shapes of influence, Cornelia's focus is on social transformation from the inside out, looking at individual aspirations as the point of departure. Her objective is to refine a methodology that influences people towards wanting to get involved in social change processes, rather than obliging them to act for the sake of others. In 2017 she initiated the POZE (Purpose—Optimization—Zenith—Experience) dynamic in Haiti, offering individuals tools to identify and pursue their aspirations. The network is now expanding into the Americas, Africa and Europe.

Website https://www.poze.cc.

Contextualizing Design Thinking With Multiple Intelligences: The Global SUGAR Program as a Case

Falk Uebernickel and Christine Thong

Abstract In a rapidly changing world, there are various socio-technological challenges such as globalization, digitalization, and climate change, which lead to a shift in consumer behavior. Individuals must therefore constantly acquire new skills and improve their competencies for collaboration to solve complex problems while being creative and empathetic. The education sector has the responsibility to impart the building blocks for reskilling and relearning in their students at a young age to prepare the next generation of talents. This article presents the case of the SUGAR Network, a global network of universities, that enables its students to solve wicked problems of their corporate partners using the design thinking paradigm. The article further elaborates on how the network's design thinking mindset and its structured activities have resulted in its students launching several successful startups and generating new product ideas for their corporate partners. While in the past and present, design thinking focused exclusively on empathy towards humans and their collaboration, the future of design thinking shall also focus on empathy towards the world by integrating environmental intelligence, global intelligence, and digital intelligence into its pedagogy.

1 Motivation

The world has massively changed over the last ten years. Under the umbrella of Digital Transformation (Vega & Chiasson, 2019) and Digital Innovation (Nambisan et al., 2020), new technologies have arisen in the past decade. Information is available at our fingertips via a Smartphone, which has led to a new communication culture between people and organizations. Artificial intelligence is becoming a mature technology that not only influences standardized work routines in daily life but also adds

F. Uebernickel (✉)
Hasso Plattner Institute at the University of Potsdam, Potsdam, Germany
e-mail: Falk.Uebernickel@hpi.de

C. Thong
Design Factory Melbourne at Swinburne University of Technology, Melbourne, Australia
e-mail: cthong@swin.edu.au

255

value through the ability to identify patterns that have been invisible to humans in large data sets (Haefner et al., 2021).

As part of this transformational process, firms have changed their business models from a product-driven approach towards a service-driven one, digital platforms, and even digital ecosystems (Anthony et al., 2019). For example, Netflix revolutionized the movie and TV industry by introducing the most famous cloud-based video broadcasting platform. As a global motor vehicle manufacturer, Tesla redefined the future's mobility by focusing on autonomous and purely electrical cars while traditional car manufacturers still lag behind in this area (Tesla, 2018). Facebook shaped communication among people of all cultures through its messenger applications in unforeseen ways.

This new generation of companies consistently reshapes business from a national and continental focus towards a global claim. In such multinational organizations, employees work more and more in intercultural and interdisciplinary teams (Molinsky & Gundling, 2016). Further, the time for developing new products and services is getting faster as well (Smith & New Product Dynamics, 2000). While in the past, typical development cycles took months or even years, today technology enables cycle times of days or weeks shaping and responding to increased digital services in the global economy.

Along with these developments, society has changed as well. Although these trends have already existed for decades, sustainability and ecology are of increasing global importance (Neshovski, 2021; NZZ, 2021). As a result of industrialization, climate change progresses much faster than centuries ago (UN, 2021). The effects are becoming visible in our daily lives, such as global warming causing economic damage in unforeseen ways (WWF, 2021). Change has also happened in the educational sector (Govindarajan & Srivastava, 2020). The balance of teaching has evolved from a largely analytical approach to one that incorporates emotional and social intelligence (Miller, 2015). Due to globalization and the increasing role of technology, children and young adults have to acquire early in life skills to be able to socialize with others (Miller, 2015). Especially artificial intelligence technology will compete with humans on highly standardizable activities and tasks in the future. Scientists predict that the ability to socialize and be creative is a competitive advantage of humans over machines. Starting in kindergarten, kids and young adults learn besides foundational courses, like math, physics, and languages, soft skills in teamwork, collaboration, and communication. The same is observable for life-long learning trajectories.

Due to the recent global pandemic crisis, all of these developments have accelerated. In schools and universities, the adoption of online teaching formats happened virtually "overnight" (Anbarci & Hernando-Veciana, 2020; Govindarajan & Srivastava, 2020). The business world responded similarly in a reaction never seen before: online and home office work has become ubiquitous. Many experts argue that this change will last forever, altering our ways of working and knowledge acquisition permanently (Fogarty et al., 2021).

As a consequence of this change, the educational sector, including kindergartens, schools, high schools, and higher education institutes, must address society's evolving needs for future work skills. The World Economic Forum predicts that 50%

of all employees will need reskilling by 2025 (Whiting, 2020). Our next generation of talent must be fit for global collaboration, readily trained for new work paradigms, and have a high intelligence for emotion and resilience (Davies et al., 2020). At the forefront will be training in critical thinking, problem-solving capabilities, and solving complex problems while being creative (Whiting, 2020). By 2030, our future workforce must be able to tackle mostly non-repetitive, cognitive, and highly skilled tasks (Willcocks, 2020) since machines will progressively take over repetitive activities. Due to workforce specialization, new capabilities also need to be consistently developed, via continuous learning, and this will require tolerance for ambiguity, self-motivation, and the ability to collaborate.

The following article will focus on the SUGAR network (*SUGAR* Network, 2015). SUGAR network is based on a global Design Thinking program where high standing universities, their students, and corporate partners collaborate to solve complex challenges set by the corporate partner. Part of the network's mission is to educate students beyond the corporate challenge of addressing the mega-trends mentioned. The article will highlight the different development stages of the network (and will take) to educate people with intelligence needed by the world—through design thinking.

2 The SUGAR Program for Design Thinking Education

SUGAR's current quest is *SUGAR wants to create impact by uniting universities and industries across the world to promote an alternative education, where students have ownership of the projects and are encouraged to be passionate about learning. SUGAR provides a platform to share knowledge and empowers students to solve real-world problems based on human-centered, conscious [[,] and responsible design.* (SUGAR Network, 2015). The shared vision of all participating faculty members can be framed as a "mission-based learning" approach (Shih & Chen, 2002). Students of all disciplines work together on existing and real problems and thereby discover and apply appropriate science theories. As stated by Shih and Chen, mission-based learning approaches embrace risk-taking, persistence, and learning by error (Shih & Chen, 2002).

In the following, we will briefly describe the SUGAR network's historical roots, including its members. Further, we will describe SUGAR's Design Thinking approach that guides all participating members and the global network's organizational structure. Finally, we will show three concrete project examples of the past.

2.1 Historical Roots and Members

The SUGAR network established itself in 2010 as a "sister program" to the famous Mechanical Engineering 310 (ME310) program at Stanford University (Carleton,

2019; Carleton & Leifer, 2009). Among the first participating universities were the Hasso Plattner Institute in Potsdam (Germany), the University of St. Gallen (Switzerland), Javeriana University in Cali (Columbia), and Aalto University in Helsinki (Finland). The mission was twofold. The first aim was to manifest a new educational paradigm among the participating members. The second objective was to grow the network (if possible) to all continents to reach out to as many students as possible. The network grew to 18 core university members on all continents except Africa in the subsequent years. The wider network counts more than 25 members (*SUGAR* Network, 2015), brought together by shared values in design thinking pedagogy. Part of SUGAR's philosophy is that member universities do not have to belong to a specific scientific discipline. Instead, the network is open to facilitate every scientific direction like computer sciences, mechanical engineering, business administration, design, and architecture (Wiesche et al., 2018).

Thereby, the network has collaborated on more than 220 projects with industrial partners from all industries globally over the last ten years. Our analysis revealed that the top four sectors are automotive and mobility, software, consumer products, and pharmaceutical. Such well-known organizations as Takeda (pharmaceutical industry), BMW (automotive industry), SAP (high-tech), Electric Mobility Norway (utility), and UBS (financials) have participated.

2.2   SUGAR's Approach to Design Thinking

SUGAR's pedagogical approach roots back to the Design Thinking teaching philosophy at Stanford University (Carleton, 2019; Uebernickel et al., 2020). While it seems complicated to conceptualize what Design Thinking is in general (Micheli et al., 2019), the SUGAR approach has two distinct dimensions that are characterizing: (1) the mindset and cultural understanding of Design Thinking and (2) the activity/process layer of Design Thinking (curriculum) (Brenner et al., 2016).

By looking at the first dimension, "mindset and cultural understanding", the SUGAR approach is based on six principles partially described by Micheli et al. (2019) in their seminal work.

Human-centeredness: Being human-centered is interpreted in the SUGAR philosophy to mean that the human being, as the receiver of innovation outcomes and person affected them has to be at the center of all design considerations. Many authors such as Brown (2008) support is the most essential feature of design thinking. The Design Thinking project team should anticipate the individual's full context and surroundings by involving the human being in all design considerations. A clear distinction between a human and a user or customer is essential to make. The notion of a user provides a limited view of a human that is willing to use a dedicated product or service, while the human itself is not constrained by this. In SUGAR projects, this opens the possibility to anticipate a more extensive problem space for identifying new opportunities and designing comprehensive solutions. Qualitative field research is a standard methodology to realize human-centeredness through common techniques like interviews, observations, or self-immersion sessions.

Iteration and experimentation: SUGAR projects are iterative and foster experimentation throughout the process (Uebernickel et al., 2020; Wiesche et al., 2018). As part of the curriculum, each SUGAR project has to go through at least seven iteration phases. Each iteration cycle takes approximately 3–4 weeks (Uebernickel et al., 2020). The first three iteration cycles aim to expand the problem scope and deepen the problem understanding, while the last four iterations focus on developing a solution.

Ambiguity and failure: Solving wicked and complex problems requires dealing with ambiguous situations (Buchanan, 1992) and failures in between. SUGAR teams experiment and iterate often with a "trial and error mentality" (Micheli et al., 2019) to gain insights into the "real" problem and to identify valuable solutions. Failing in each project's context is seen as an active engagement in learning. The faculty regularly initiates reflection sessions with each team to facilitate the learning. The explication of failure situations in these sessions helps gain valuable insights into the project.

Prototyping: "Ideas are not real, be real. Prototypes allow you to get in touch with your reality."[1] Prototyping stands in SUGAR projects for doing and thinking simultaneously. Building solutions in the form of prototypes offers the team the possibility to explore ideas, communicate solutions, test them with people, and refine them on the go. Since SUGAR project teams deal with complex problems, it is often difficult to share ideas across team members or potential users and customers. In such situations, materialized ideas in the form of prototypes, can help overcome these barriers. Furthermore, prototyping is facilitating a process of thinking at the same time. While building a prototype, people think about their doing simultaneously, which helps to see flaws and potential improvements early in design development. On average, each team is building up to 40 prototypes as part of their project (Uebernickel et al., 2020).

Interdisciplinary collaboration: The complexity of today's problems requires diverse disciplinary expertise and perspectives to analyze the solution's situation and development. Therefore, SUGAR project teams are always composed of team members with diverse educational backgrounds (Carleton, 2019). Interdisciplinarity ensures different angles on the problem like a business, technical, or marketing view. Typically, the participating universities are providing this dimension.

Intercultural collaboration: The SUGAR network believes in the power of intercultural collaboration (Brenner et al., 2016). By their nature, most challenges are complex and require consideration from different perspectives. Thereby, people with diverse cultural backgrounds help analyze problems more thoroughly with a "360-degree" approach. In some situations, teams might perceive these different views as contradictions and cumbersome to talk about, but the cultural-based differences help to understand and explore the problem with greater depth and comprehension.

---

[1] Reference: slide deck from Alexander Grots.

Secondly, the SUGAR network curriculum follows a semi-standardized process model (Carleton, 2019; Uebernickel et al., 2020; Wiesche et al., 2018). Each of the seven phases represents one iteration. The process model enables the network to collaborate across universities, faculties, countries, and language borders. It synchronizes all participating universities' main activities throughout the nine-month program. Furthermore, it provides a clear structure for the engaged corporate partners too. While the core activities are defined, the outcomes and methods are not. These depend on every phase and the specific corporate design challenge. Moreover, the particular educational background of each student matters. The stages are as follows:

Design Space Exploration Phase: As part of the design space exploration, the Design Thinking team focuses on the problem context and design challenge provided by the corporate partner. The aim is to gain a profound understanding of essential project stakeholders, relevant technological and societal trends, as well as existing knowledge through a process called "instant-expertise". This approach involves activities of need finding, benchmarking, and problem framing, and draws on methods such as observation, interviews, and data mining.

Critical Function Phase: In this phase, the project team approaches the first insights and opportunity fields gleaned from design space exploration through prototyping. The team is pushed to think about specific functions or features of a design idea instead of focusing on larger systems. Each specific feature represents a critical function addressed by at least one prototype that is simple and quickly created. The simplicity is essential because most prototypes will fail. Why? Because in this early project stage, the Design Thinking team is mostly basing its knowledge on assumptions that are challenged by these prototypes. A careful analysis of the failures will eventually lead to meaningful learnings for the project team to align designed outcomes with human needs.

Darkhorse Phase: The darkhorse phase challenges existing project boundaries that might limit the Design Thinking team in finding creative solutions. It aims to foster potentially groundbreaking solutions by pushing the team to think about the unthinkable. The guiding motto is dissent and not consent within the team and potential customers. This stage's outcome is usually several futuristic prototypes that challenge the status-quo and contain insightful elements for a possible design solution.

Funky Phase: The funky phase intends to lineate the previous three stages' results into a few general solution concepts. The most promising critical function and darkhorse prototypes are selected and inform the development of larger systems and concepts based on user testing and feedback. This stage further marks the inflection point between the diverging and the converging phase in a Design Thinking project.

Functional Prototyping Phase and X-is finished Phase: Both stages aim to refine the system solutions from the Funky prototyping phase. Generally, the Design Thinking teams increase the funky prototypes' resolution and fidelity. Frequent user testing happens during these phases, but with the intention directed largely towards feasibility and viability testing rather than desirability testing.

Final Prototyping Phase: The final iteration of a SUGAR project is the final prototyping phase. This phase aims to use a high fidelity prototype to see the most relevant functions and features. Part of the prototype is technical systems, such as computer programs and mechanical components, as well as the business model, form and interface designs, and marketing details.

Across these seven phases, SUGAR curriculum follows a standard Design Thinking routine that is typically described in an iterative process of five steps (Brown, 2008; Wiesche et al., 2018)). The process starts with the problem definition. As part of this, students explore the boundary conditions of the given challenge, which can involve constraints and assumptions. Typically, the teams use standard mapping techniques to gain a comprehensive overview. The Need finding and Benchmarking follow this step. The focus shifts towards achieving empathy for the environment, users, and stakeholders to gather real data (Köppen & Meinel, 2015). Students conduct field research techniques such as interviewing, observation, and immersion sessions. These sessions happen in the field, whether the needed participants are located in the neighborhood or other regions and countries.

Combined with the Need finding and Benchmarking, teams conduct regular synthesis sessions. The aim is to distill new knowledge from the gained data pool. Typically, students search for new insights, opportunities, or contradictions. As part of the third step, the teams turn the outcomes into several "how might we questions" (HMW) (Berger, 2012) for the ideation step. By considering all the knowledge, each team conducts intensive ideation sessions to find potential solution ideas for each outcome of the synthesis step. The number of proposed solutions can easily exceed several hundred for average projects. Exciting or useful ideas are prototyped as part of step four by the student team. The notion behind the prototyping step is to make ideas tangible. This tangibility aspect helps communicate the results with their group and test them through prototypes. Finally, the student team tests selected prototypes with users and stakeholders. The aim is to verify or falsify the design team's underlying assumptions. Testing failures are opportunities to change existing beliefs and help the design team to learn and reflect.

2.3   Organization of the SUGAR Network

The SUGAR network is a global movement. Rather than the lead being taken by a designated institution, the network itself takes this position. The network trusts in its self-organizing capability. Each participating university is responsible for acquiring corporate partners to get involved in the Design Thinking program. Contracts between the network entities, like corporate partners and universities, are organized decentrally.

A team of students consists of 6–8 students who join from two universities on a micro-level (Carleton, 2019). Such a team collaborates with a corporate partner on a given design challenge. Each team is supported by a teaching team (usually two faculty members) every week.

Enablement, enactment, and communication are the three underlying teaching principles. Large group meetings (LGMs) are conducted once or twice per week at every university. The intention of such meetings is to enable the student teams to understand the given problem space and solve it later as part of the design process, by means of methods, tools, and theoretical knowledge. LGMs aims to teach students the essentials of Design Thinking. Small group meetings (SGMs) strongly focus on coaching and enactment by supporting the teams to overcome any mental barriers of the knowing-doing gap. In each SGM session, specifically adopted techniques are practiced together with a faculty member for a given design challenge. Lastly, slightly unorganized design sessions (SUDS) aim to build an open-innovation mindset among the entire student group at each university. These sessions promote social and agile interactions, where strong bonding between students, faculty, and corporate partners can grow over time.

Besides the project outcome in the form of a prototyped solution to address the given problem, students have to provide two other main deliverables as part of the curriculum. The first deliverable is the documents. The documentation consists of a final report and one or two reports on the work in progress at key milestones. The intention is threefold. First, the documents validate the project's progress and its final state. Second, students demonstrate their expertise in writing scientific-based documents with high quality. Third, students use the reports to reflect on their learning progress. While bringing the project into a sequence, students think about their doings and can draw additional learnings.

The second main deliverable is presentations. Students have to present verbally and visually to an audience their project progress three times throughout the course of the project. Typically two of the three presentations happen in an international setup where students from all SUGAR member nations meet together and exchange through a presentation on their project progress. This format, somewhere between a hackathon and a symposium, sharpens the students' presentation and communication skills.

2.4   Project Examples and Successes

Since the SUGAR network's foundation, companies and student entrepreneurs have brought 44 successful products and 131 service innovations into the market.[2] Table 1 shows the four different project outcomes and implementation results.

In the following, we briefly describe three exemplary product and service innovations from the first and second category: Flemo/Vimcar, IRIS/Visense, and Yanmar. The interested reader can find more projects on www.sugar-network.org.

---

[2] Based on internal analysis.

Table 1 SUGAR network outcome types (author's own figure)

Outcome type	Description	Examples[3]/industries
Startups	Startups are freshly established organizations based on the SUGAR project outcome. Either set up together with the corporate partner or entirely funded by a third party. Students are usually involved to some degree in the startup	• Vimcar • Visense • Swissify • Mimi
Corporate products or services	The SUGAR project outcome is translated into a corporate product or service offering. Often student team members get hired by the corporate partner to drive further implementation	• Wheeboo • Miira
Non-for-profit products or services	Similar to the previous category, SUGAR project outcomes are transferred into a non-for-profit product offering	• Resilyou[4]
Influence products and services	The majority of SUGAR project outcomes influence existing corporate products and services by either enhancing particular product features or adding new product components	• Software • Banking and insurance • Automobile • Lighting • Utility

2.5 Flemo/Vimcar (Startup)

The project Flemo was initiated in 2011 by the Universities of Modena and Reggio Emilia (Italy) and St. Gallen (HSG) (Switzerland) together with a corporate partner from the automobile industry. Together, they defined the following design challenge for the student team *"Redesign the user experience for current and future automobile customers in the context of mobility and connectivity."*[5] The project team invented a modern and fully digital car sharing and fleet management solution for private and professional customers in 2011—called Flemo. At this time, the group decided to implement the fleet management component for small and medium-sized enterprises (SME) as a startup in Germany. The two founders' conviction and passion for revolutionizing SMEs' market drove the decision. The value proposition of Flemo is helping SMEs manage carpooling more effectively and efficiently by saving operational costs and potentially even state taxes.

---

[3] Vimcar (www.vimcar.de), Visense (www.visense.io), Wheeboo (www.wheeebo.com), Miira (www.miira.ch).

[4] A project with the protestant church in St.Gallen (Switzerland).

[5] Based on internal documents of the University of St.Gallen and University of Modena and Reggio Emilia.

Today, Vimcar has established itself in Germany and the United Kingdom. The company manages more than 100,000 cars every day. According to Vimcar, more than 160 employees of 26 nationalities work at their Berlin headquarters (Vimcar, 2021). Interestingly, the first part of their initial idea—the sharing of private cars within a city—is independently and successfully realized by getaround.com in the United States of America (Getaround, 2021).

2.6   IRIS/Visense (Startup)

Visense started as a SUGAR project in 2019 as a collaboration between the Hasso Plattner Institute (HPI) at the University of Potsdam (Germany) and the University of St. Gallen (HSG) in partnership with the automobile manufacturer BMW Group. The interdisciplinary team of computer scientists (HPI) and business students (HSG) started with the design challenge to establish a data-driven working model in BMW's factories (Haskamp & Uebernickel, 2020). The aim was to further reduce machine downtimes at the production floor. As Haskamp and Uebernickel state, such a downtime can cost up to the US $22,000 per minute (Haskamp & Uebernickel, 2020).

Applying the SUGAR network's Design Thinking process helped the interdisciplinary student team investigate BMW's factory's many reasons for machine breakdowns and the opportunities to prevent and/or fix them. Based on more than 60 interviews, 15 company visits, and over 30 prototypes, the team invented a new, fully automated monitoring solution, to detect quickly repetitive failures at the production floor (Haskamp & Uebernickel, 2020). The production engineer and production quality manager benefit greatly from this invention, as they usually have great difficulties in comprehending intricate failure patterns in automobile production. The product consists of specially designed high-resolution cameras combined with a secure artificial intelligence module to detect failures visually and based on machinery data.

Nowadays, Visense operates in Germany (Potsdam) and Switzerland (Schaffhausen) as a newly founded startup. The three founders are former students of the SUGAR project at the HPI and HSG.

2.7   Wheeebo (Corporate Product)

The project Wheeebo started as a SUGAR network project in 2016/2017 as a collaboration between the Kyoto Institute of Technology (Japan), Swinburne University of Technology (Australia), and the engine manufacturer Yanmar (Japan). As a design prompt, the student received the following "*Explore new opportunities for products and/or equipment relating to water leisure that provides a 'wow' experience for the user.*" Guided by the Design Thinking process and mindset, the team did comprehensive field investigations in Australia and Japan. The intercultural and interdisciplinary design team analyzed several opportunity fields through intense prototyping and testing.

After numerous iterations, water sports seemed to be the field with the most potential for innovation. In both countries, the team quickly identified that surfing on the water is naturally only possible if the wind is blowing. Furthermore, people need a lot of practice in windsurfing. As part of their ideation and prototyping sessions, the team invented Wheeebo (Picture 1) (*Wheebo*). Wheeebo is a surfboard that does not require wind. A small water turbine below the disc propels the board. A sensor array can detect shifts of the user's center of gravity and drives the board in the desired direction. With Wheeebo, users are able to drive approx. 3–4 h around without additional power charge (*Wheeebo/Yanmar*, 2020). Yanmar implemented this idea immediately after the final prototype was finished. The product is now available in Asia.

Picture 1 Wheebo
(Author's own image)

3   The Evolution and Revolution Stages of the SUGAR Program

While the SUGAR network's genesis happened two years before the network was founded in 2010, the roots of the movement reach much further back in history. The engineering curricula, including the design practices, was likely put into practice during the 1960s (Carleton & Leifer, 2009). A constant cycle of evolutionary and revolutionary phases has taken place in Design Thinking development since then. In general, prolonged growth periods that are usually "quiet" and with "modest adjustments" are defined as evolutionary stages ("Evolution and Revolution as Organizations Grow," 1998). Evolutions stand for stability. According to Greiner, such a phase lasts between 6 and 8 years ("Evolution and Revolution as Organizations Grow," 1998). In contrast, revolutionary stages require effective teaching and curriculum adjustments. External factors are triggering revolutions and force us to change beyond the obvious and ordinary ("Evolution and Revolution as Organizations Grow," 1998). Such external triggers include growth of the network with the addition of new universities, the availability of new digital tools (like Slack and Miro), or global trends such as those described in the introduction (Fig. 1).

We will describe the evolution and revolution stages of the SUGAR network in the following. The starting point for our analysis is the year 2008. The "past" represents the time between 2008 and 2012 (5 years), the "present" stands for the period from 2014 until today (7 years) as the future defines the year 2023 and onwards. The transformations in between will be described as revolution phases.

Our focus is primarily on students' learning objectives as part of the curriculum. In analogy to Gardner's multiple intelligences (Gardner, 2011), we define each evolution phase of the SUGAR network with its respective, intelligence types to focus our

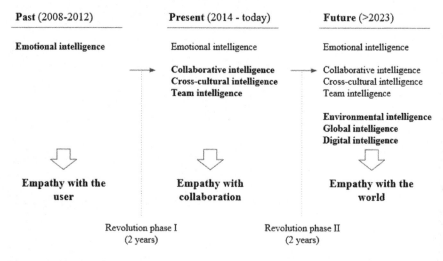

Fig. 1 Modes of intelligence as part of the SUGAR program (author's own figure)

teaching efforts. Each intelligence type requires a set of skills and capabilities for students to learn. In this context, we understand intelligence as the individual's ability to adapt effectively to the environment (Ang et al., 2013). We explore the past, the present, and the future of the SUGAR network through dedicated lenses of different and multiple intelligences.[6] Table 1 summarizes our rationale. In the following, we will elaborate on the three evolution stages.

3.1   The Past—Empathy with the Human

In the early phase of the SUGAR network, the responsible faculty of the participating university was highly focused on the program's core. This focus meant developing and implementing the necessary infrastructure—like processes—in the organization and curriculum. From a pedagogical perspective, the aim was to focus on the design mindset and build our students' emotional intelligence at that time. In the context of a Design Thinking program, we define emotional intelligence (EI) in a similar way as Salovey and Mayer: *"the ability to monitor one's own and others' feelings and emotions"* (Salovey & Mayer, 1990). The development of the individual student was the center of our efforts.

3.1.1   Emotional Intelligence (EI)

The observation of students guided the thinking and rationale of the faculty. For example, often new students were not aware of their surroundings, such as team members and users, or they were poorly equipped with learned techniques to be mindful of their own biases. This led to the development of a first generation curriculum that targeted the students' EI.

With Need finding techniques, including an Empathy Map or Persona, we helped students become aware of users, team members, and other stakeholders' emotions. Through early prototyping and fast testing techniques, students learned the benefits of an iterative Design Thinking process to quickly uncover their own biases and incorrect assumptions. The Design Thinking process's fast-paced iterations led to accelerated learning within the teams and the individual. Students who had no prior knowledge in the challenge domain became instant experts.[7] Regular reflection sessions helped both the faculty and the students talk about (personal) emotions and increase EI.

---

[6] Klein discusses and elaborates on some of Gardner's multiple intelligence theory shortcomings' (Klein, 1997). We are aware of this discourse in science, nevertheless interpreting the "multiple intelligences" as a lens to help us structure the development of the SUGAR movement.

[7] We are aware of an enlarging and critical discussion about the "rise of the instant expert" (*The Dangerous and Inexorable Rise of the Instant Expert*, n.d.). In this context, the "instant expert" is framed differently so that experts are still consulted as part of the project, but team members are still gaining a certain level of know-how that is novel and relevant to the project.

Furthermore, regular ideation sessions with team members, faculty and corporate partners, and sometimes externals increase critical and creative thinking abilities and improve interpersonal skills that require sensing others' feelings and motives. A large number of teaching and coaching faculty members paired with smaller-sized classes (usually between 8 and 20 students per class), provides intensive learning opportunities and motivation to students to learn, participate and perform. By looking at the top 10 skills of 2025 according to the World Economic Forum (Whiting, 2020), the SUGAR program of 2008–2012 already addressed six of ten skills through its educational program.

The first turning point and revolution phase of the network started in 2012–2013. Because of the network's intense global growth (from 10 to around 30 projects) and evolving framework, including internationalization, the program realized a need for change. Besides this, the core faculty got smarter throughout the first phase too. One of the colleagues said, *"We got better to play coaches:"* What sounds amusing today was a reality at that time. The faculty and their designated teaching teams emancipated themselves from traditional teaching hierarchies and moved towards a coaching approach. They started to practice what they preached by displaying greater emotional intelligence in their modality. This meant the need for greater soft skills to optimize the hard skills being taught. The difference between teaching and coaching does not sound like much, but it is. As a coach, the faculty accompanied and developed the students as learners to achieve their personal and team goals. A disintegration of hierarchy between faculty and students started to happen. The entire group learned that everyone is in the same boat. Consequently, the faculty and students felt emotional to be in the same team, with the same goals. The faculty became a partner to the students and corporate partners.

3.2   The Present—Empathy to Collaboration

The present stands in the light of collaboration—collaboration between people, collaboration within the design team, and collaboration across cultures. The need for emphasizing collaboration as part of the curriculum arose from the insight to better support the increased diversity featured in SUGAR to solve complex and wicked problems. We split them into three intelligence types again to address the different forms of collaboration, namely, collaborative intelligence, team intelligence, and cross-cultural intelligence.

These three forms of intelligence types complement emotional intelligence. While emotional intelligence is primarily focusing on the individual and one's capability to empathize with others and itself, the intelligence types mentioned above focus on the collaboration of the individual with other people and groups.

3.2.1　Collaborative Intelligence (CI)

We defined collaborative intelligence "*as the ability to think with others on behalf of what matters to us all*" (Markova & McArthur, 2015). It expresses the need that today's problems are generally not solvable by individuals anymore, but rather by groups and teams. Being innovative demands different interpretations, views, and opinions about topics to understand challenges in-depth and find comprehensive solutions.

Therefore, the SUGAR network intensified coaching students to think about collectives of people working together, not just others as individuals. It meant that the faculty had to prepare the students for understanding and incorporate different views on a given problem. "Understanding" in this context refers to the capability to listen first and judge someone's comments later on. It usually comes with a culture of acceptance, openness, and tolerance: in recent years the expression of mindfulness was coined. As Martini et al. write, it is "a state of being present in the moment and leaving behind a tendency to judge" (Martini et al., 2020). A study at the MIT Center for Collective Intelligence showed that specific training in being mindful increased the CI by almost 13% (Martini et al., 2020).

The ability to "incorporate" different views in one's thinking requires the ability to be open-minded and willing to change a personal standpoint—if necessary. Further, it requires communicating one's own perspective clearly and neutrally to others, with attention to fact. Especially if the student's counterpart is starting to change their opinion, students need to create enough "mental freedom" to let this change happen with respect. Being a "know-it-all" is not helpful in these situations.

Lastly, CI demands abilities to analyze and solve complex problems together. The togetherness requires transparency, openness, and willingness to exchange personal information with your teammates. Egoistic mechanisms of knowledge accumulation hinder the progress and performance of such groups. Effective collaboration can only happen if the students share their knowledge proactively. Regular team coaching sessions help students reflect on their own and group behavior (Tables 2 and 3).

3.2.2　Team Intelligence (TI)

As part of the development of the SUGAR network, we further intensified the focus on the team and its intelligence structures. While collaborative intelligence focuses on the individual's ability to incorporate different views of group members, team intelligence targets the ability to effectively and efficiently act as a homogenous group. Certainly, the team has always been there as part of the SUGAR network, but we started to learn as faculty that further teaching and coaching are required to improve team intelligence within the students' minds. In this context, we define team intelligence (TI) as "... *a team's capability to use information processes through project-related activities that achieved a desired end or performed a particular function or value activity during the project.*" (Akgün et al., 2008).

Table 2 Intelligence types and capabilities of students (author's own figure)

Time	Intelligence type	Definition	Student skills and targeted capabilities by the SUGAR Network
Past	Emotional Intelligence (EI)	*"We define emotional intelligence as the subset of social intelligence that involves the ability to monitor one's own and others' feelings and emotions, to discriminate among them and to use this information to guide one's thinking and actions."* (Salovey & Mayer, 1990)	• Ability to engage with others • Ability to monitor one's own and others' feelings and emotions (Salovey & Mayer, 1990) / being self-reflected / showing empathy • Aware of own biases (Liedtka et al., 2021) • Curious and creative thinking (Liedtka et al., 2021; Salovey & Mayer, 1990) • Motivated to learn (Salovey & Mayer, 1990) and seeking knowledge • Critical thinking and willingness to challenge
Present	Collaborative Intelligence (CI)	*"Collaborative intelligence addresses problems where individual expertise, potentially conflicting priorities of stakeholders, and different interpretations of diverse experts are critical for problem-solving."* (Wikipedia contributors, 2021) in this context it is defined according to Markova and McArthur as *"[The] ability to think with others on behalf of what matters to us all."* (Markova & McArthur, 2015)	• Ability to think with others on behalf of what matters to the group (Markova & McArthur, 2015) • Ability to understand and incorporate different views on a problem • Ability to deal with complexity and ambiguity in problem-solving situations • Paying attention to someone else's opinion and integrating team members' diversity (Martini et al., 2020) • Analyzing and solving complex problems as a group

(continued)

Table 2 (continued)

Time	Intelligence type	Definition	Student skills and targeted capabilities by the SUGAR Network
	Cross-cultural Intelligence (CCI)	We define cross-cultural intelligence as the cognitive, motivational, and behavioral capacity to understand, and effectively respond to the beliefs, values, attitudes and behaviors of individuals from other cultures. (adopted from (Ang et al., 2013))	Based on (Ang et al., 2013) work: • Ability to acquire and understand cultural knowledge sometimes through "experimentation" • Knowledge about cultures and cultural differences • Ability to direct and sustain efforts towards functioning in intercultural situations • Empathy in cross-cultural interactions
	Team Intelligence (TI)	Team intelligence is defined in accordance to (Akgün et al., 2008) as *"...a team's capability to use information processes through project-related activities that achieve a desired end or perform a particular function or value activity during the project."*	Based on the work of (Akgün et al., 2008): • Information acquisition capability of the team to conduct primary and secondary research with relevant stakeholders • Information dissemination ability as the team's capacity to diffuse and transmit information among relevant members of the team • Information utilization ability to use information directly and indirectly as part of the project • Ability to create and share information within a team

Table 3 Intelligence types and capabilities of students (author's own figure)

Time	Intelligence type	Definition	Student skills and targeted capabilities by the SUGAR Network
Future	Environmental Intelligence (EvI)	In our context, we define environmental intelligence based on (*Environmental Intelligence*, n.d.) as the anticipation of human behavior causing environmental changes by integrating "… *environmental and sustainability research with data science, artificial intelligence and cutting-edge technologies to [create meaningful insights] to mitigate the effects of environmental change.*"	• Ability to acquire and interpret knowledge about the environment and environmental change • Knowledge about the impact of today's decisions on the future of the environment • Ability to steer design decisions towards the improvement of the environment in the future
	Global Intelligence (GI)	*"The ability to understand, respond to and work towards what is in the best interest of and will benefit all human beings and all other life on our planet"* (Spariosu, 2004)	• Ability to understand the interrelationship between humankind, and nature • Capability to abstract from local thinking to global thinking • Ability to act in the best interest of society
	Digital Intelligence (DI)	*"Digital intelligence is the sum of social, emotional, and cognitive abilities that enable individuals to face the challenges and adapt to the demands of life in the digital world."* (Wikipedia contributors, 2020; Yildiz, 2019)	• Ability to apply multiple intelligences in digital languages • Algorithmic and Artificial intelligence thinking (Zeng, 2013) capabilities • Ability "…to convert or represent the physical world in digital format." (Yildiz, 2019)

The faculty intensified sessions on team dynamics and proper project planning. In focus are students' abilities to disseminate information adequately to team members and project stakeholders. Teaching about project plans, Jour-Fixe meetings, project progress reports, inclusive language, and clear communications practices are just a few things incorporated. Activities such as sharing hopes and fears and personal motivations are used to assist functioning team dynamics. Further, the faculty focused on utilizing available information within the team. Young and newly formed teams can struggle to digest the sheer amount of data they have gained from their field research activities. To improve knowledge utilization, we focused specifically on the synthesis sessions as part of the Design Thinking process. Students learn how to collect, analyze and interpret all gathered data together. Before the Covid19 crisis, these activities happened physically on the whiteboard with post-its and digitally on platforms like Miro. Since Covid19, the use of physical whiteboards has disappeared and the digital space has fully absorbed these group techniques.

Furthermore, TI's essential aspect is the ability *"to learn in teams."* While most students are trained in learning individually, we focused our efforts on enabling them to learn together as a group. As a group, with diverse characters and diverging views on the problem and solution space of the design challenge, we often observe the phenomenon of "accelerated learning" on the project when teams work effectively. To enforce this behavior, we usually assign group tasks to each team they have to accomplish together.

3.2.3   Cross-Cultural Intelligence (CCI)

Cross-Cultural Intelligence (CCI) increased its importance for the SUGAR network as we grew across countries and continents. Student teams started to work more frequently together across cultural spheres like Germany (Europe)—China (Asia), Australia (Australia)—Japan (Asia), or Poland (Europe)—Columbia (Latin America). Adopted from Ang et al., we define Cross-Cultural Intelligence (CCI) as the cognitive, motivational, and behavioral capacity to understand and effectively respond to individuals' beliefs, values, attitudes, and behaviors from other cultures (Ang et al., 2013).

To strengthen the CCI muscle within our students, we, as SUGAR network, introduced as part of our global kick-off week several workshops, speeches, and reflection sessions to raise the awareness and importance of these differences across cultures. These sessions usually cover the basics like meeting culture, cultural heritage, organizational culture, preferences with conflict, and communication barriers because of language. For example, even for countries within Europe, it turns out to be essential to raise the awareness of cultural differences as early as possible. This awareness creates the possibility for the individual to compensate and adjust to the new circumstances.

Part of CCI is the ability to be flexible in cross-cultural interactions—when you don't know what you don't know. Students need to find consensus and common ground between the different cultures. Even more, they need to be able to realize and understand differences to turn them into advantages! Potential team conflicts arise because of a lack of understanding of the opposite culture. Students can only mitigate negative team conflicts if the participants on all ends show willingness, openness, empathy, and respect to negotiate these cross-cultural interactions.

3.3 The Future—Empathy to the World

What will be the future development steps of the SUGAR network? The next revolution phase is becoming visible on the horizon and might have started already. Our world continues to change with various techno-cultural, socio-political drivers, shaping our direction. Climate change, a massive acceleration of digital technologies' progress, and ongoing globalization, to name a few, will push us and the next generation of students to adapt again. Schemel et al. (2019) provide clear insight into how future scenarios might look based on the behaviors and decisions we take today. Moreover, the recent pandemic has increased the speed of introducing digital technology in almost all parts of our lives.

In particular, the United Nations have envisioned the change needed for our environment and its global inhabitants as part of their 17 sustainability goals (*THE 17 GOALS*, n.d.). The SUGAR movement should anticipate this change early enough to prepare future students and participants.

Robust foresight techniques guide our thinking. Indeed, no one will be able to foresee the future precisely. However, with intelligent methods, we can still make predictions of specific life scenarios in the future, to provoke discourse and action to guide desired futures. To guide our thinking about the future, we base our assumptions on the UN sustainability goals and the foresight of the report by Schemel et al. from 2019 (2019; *THE 17 GOALS*, n.d.). We hope to achieve a positive future, like the "Post Anthropocene" described in detail by Schemel et al. (2019), who postulate "... *a shared consciousness and an understanding of Earth's limited resources.*" Part of this future scenario sees the economy shifting into a fully circular model supported by smart computer technologies like Artificial Intelligence to optimize our ecological footprint permanently. Citizens are globally well-educated, and most people have sufficient access to educational resources.

Educating people on eco-design has been going on already for decades. Victor Papanek wrote his seminal book on *Design for the Real World: Human Ecology and Social Change* in the 1970s (Papanek & Fuller, 1972). McDonough and Braungart followed Papanek with their groundbreaking book *Cradle to Cradle* in the early 2000s (Braungart & McDonough, 2010) and many more followed on similar topics, including *Circular Economy* (Kirchherr et al., 2017; Korhonen et al., 2018).

Looking backward in time it feels that so far ecology has been a topic that has been "in and out of fashion" in society. But by looking into the future, scientific studies about the environment and climate change show us clearly, that with the new drivers coming into place environmentally responsible behavior can no longer take a backseat. Accelerating population growth, increasing inequality, the recent pandemic, and more factors call for change. As an international community, we have to take responsibility and enfold action for the design outcomes we imagine and realize to protect our planet earth.

From our perspective, and by incorporating the insights about desirable futures into our thinking, we propose the SUGAR network integrate environmental intelligence, global intelligence, and digital intelligence into design thinking pedagogy as a next step. As with the previously discussed intelligence types, these three future intelligences are additional to the existing set of intelligence types and combine to form a new "version" of the Design Thinking mindset. All seven intelligence types together will shape Design Thinking of the future.

3.3.1 Environmental Intelligence (EvI)

While there are many definitions out there already, we define environmental intelligence as the anticipation of human behavior causing environmental changes by integrating "... *environmental and sustainability research with data science, artificial intelligence, and other cutting-edge technologies to mitigate the effects of environmental change.*" We want to sharpen our students' skills and capabilities to acquire and interpret accessible knowledge about upcoming environmental changes and challenges. Having soft skills such as the ability to conduct proper primary and secondary research is one part. The other part is enabling the students to utilize modern or cutting-edge technologies to analyze large data sets of our environment.

Additionally, we want to strengthen our education in forward-thinking techniques to empower all SUGAR members to think about desirable futures. Exploring desirable futures will help students be ready to shape today's solutions in a direction that is responsible for environmental sustainability. Design leadership and taking the right design decision can only unfold its potential with a robust understanding of systems and futures thinking.

3.3.2 Global Intelligence (GI)

Global intelligence is seeking to improve students' capabilities in grasping and understanding global phenomena. We believe that people need to make decisions that incorporate every human's well-being in tomorrow's world. This decision making behavior requires a broad understanding of humanity, considering constructs across Social, Technological, Economic, Environmental, Political, and Ethical (STEEPLE) domains Empathy is required to anticipate needs, wishes, desires, challenges, and problems of different cultures and societies. Our students must learn how to abstract from a local thinking style into a global thinking style. The health of our planet is a highly complex challenge and will more than ever need capable, responsible, and diverse expertise to collaborate and innovate in response. GI implies a broad set of capabilities to enable us to empathize and be open-minded towards complex systems.

Students have to seek patterns and understanding by navigating perhaps seemingly different opinions and learn integrative thinking styles to develop appropriate solutions that address our society's challenges.

3.3.3 Digital Intelligence (DI)

As our future will become much more computerized, we firmly believe that digital intelligence is necessary for our students. We define it as "... *the ability to adapt to the demands of life in the digital world.*" Recent examples show that people need to learn to address to the digital world fundamental questions of life. For example, ethical and moral questions are just two examples of free speech, democracy, and privacy in the digital space that need to be thought about. The digital space will require new sets of capabilities in the future: that people become better designers and better design thinkers in the future. Students in this program must learn to interpret better existing and newly created data, leverage AI and develop digital business models. Furthermore, students must be able to effectively use digital mediums and language to enhance collaboration.

4 Conclusion

The Design Thinking mindset space has grown over the last 13 years of development within the SUGAR network. It started with a narrow view of a design mindset as a key element and extended to emotional intelligence. In recent years the emphasis has shifted and increased towards collaboration—collaboration between people, within a team, and across cultures. For the future, we foresee at least three additional intelligence types as relevant for extending the Design Thinking mindset: the focus on the environment, the extended view on global citizenship, and the anticipation of the fast-growing digital world. As shown in Fig. 2, the future Design Thinking mindset is, for us, the convergence of the Design mindset and the seven types of intelligence.

To conclude, today's and tomorrow's challenges require an even stronger focus on planetary health and the living beings who inhabit earth. Design Thinking, in our view, offers an approach to tackle these areas of life efficiently and effectively.

5 Disclaimer

This article includes a fact-based report describing the SUGAR network and proposes strategic visions about this incredible movement's future. As authors, we know that our vision has to be shared and developed with all SUGAR movement members, which is still in progress. Therefore, this report reflects the authors' opinions and beliefs and does not represent everyone's SUGAR views.

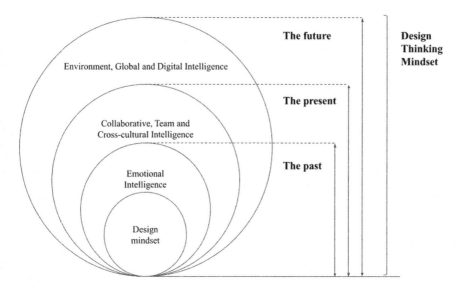

Fig. 2 The composition of the Design Thinking mindset (of the future) (author's own figure)

Acknowledgments We are grateful to Carolin Marx, Thomas Haskamp, and Tomás Gamboa for their insightful and constructive comments throughout writing this article. Thank you to Dr. Sharon Nemeth for language support. Further, we thank Associate Professor Sushi Suzuki and Prof. Dr. Matteo Vignoli for their inspiring interviews. Lastly, we appreciate the work of Maia Kuhnen as head of the strategy and operations of the SUGAR network every day. Thank you.

References

Akgün, A. E., Dayan, M., & Di Benedetto, A. (2008). New product development team intelligence: Antecedents and consequences. *Information & Management, 45*(4), 221–226.

Anbarci, N., & Hernando-Veciana, A. (2020, December 18). The pandemic is a chance to rethink education, not settle for online lectures. *The Guardian.* http://www.theguardian.com/education/2020/dec/18/the-pandemic-is-a-chance-to-rethink-education-not-settle-for-online-lectures

Ang, S., Van Dyne, L., & Rockstuhl, T. (2013). Cultural intelligence. In *The Encyclopedia of cross-cultural psychology* (pp. 310–313). Wiley, Inc. https://doi.org/10.1002/9781118339893.wbeccp130

Anthony, S. D., Trotter, A., & Schwartz, E. I. (2019, September 24). The top 20 business transformations of the last decade. *Harvard Business Review.* https://hbr.org/2019/09/the-top-20-business-transformations-of-the-last-decade

Berger, W. (2012, September 17). The secret phrase top innovators use. *Harvard Business Review.* https://hbr.org/2012/09/the-secret-phrase-top-innovato

Braungart, M., & McDonough, W. (2010). *Cradle to Cradle (Patterns of the Planet) (English Edition).*

Brenner, W., Uebernickel, F., & Abrell, T. (2016). Design thinking as mindset, process, and toolbox. In *Design thinking for innovation.* https://link.springer.com/chapter/https://doi.org/10.1007/978-3-319-26100-3_1

Brown, T. (2008). Design thinking. *Harvard Business Review, 86*(6), 84–92.

Buchanan, R. (1992). Wicked problems in design thinking. *Design Issues, 8*(2), 5–21.

Carleton, T. (2019). *ME310 at Stanford University: 50 years of redesign (1967–2017)* (Illustrated Edition). Innovation Leadership Publishing.

Carleton, T., & Leifer, L. (2009). Stanford's ME310 course as an evolution of engineering design. In *Proceedings of the 19th CIRP Design Conference—Competitive Design*. https://dspace.lib.cranfield.ac.uk/handle/1826/3648

Davies, A., Fidler, D., & Gorbis, M. (2020). *Future work skills 2020*. https://www.iftf.org/uploads/media/SR-1382A_UPRI_future_work_skills_sm.pdf

Environmental Intelligence. (n.d.). Retrieved February 6, 2021, from https://www.exeter.ac.uk/research/environmental-intelligence/

Evolution and Revolution as Organizations Grow. (1998, May 1). *Harvard Business Review*. https://hbr.org/1998/05/evolution-and-revolution-as-organizations-grow

Fogarty, P., Frantz, S., Hirschfeld, J., Keating, S., Lafont, E., Lufkin, B., Mishael, R., Ponnavolu, V., Savage, M., & Turits, M. (2021). *Coronavirus: How the world of work may change forever*. https://www.bbc.com/worklife/article/20201023-coronavirus-how-will-the-pandemic-change-the-way-we-work

Gardner, H. E. (2011). *Frames of mind: The theory of multiple intelligences*. Hachette UK.

Getaround. (2021). https://www.getaround.com/

Govindarajan, V., & Srivastava, A. (2020, March 31). What the shift to virtual learning could mean for the future of higher ed. *Harvard Business Review*. https://hbr.org/2020/03/what-the-shift-to-virtual-learning-could-mean-for-the-future-of-higher-ed

Haefner, N., Wincent, J., Parida, V., & Gassmann, O. (2021). Artificial intelligence and innovation management: A review, framework, and research agenda☆. *Technological Forecasting and Social Change, 162*(120392), 120392.

Haskamp, T., & Uebernickel, F. (2020, November 18). *The value of design thinking in solving complex problems for industrial manufacturing*. The Future Factory®: Business Transformation Training. https://www.thefuturefactory.com/blog/66

Kirchherr, J., Reike, D., & Hekkert, M. (2017). Conceptualizing the circular economy: An analysis of 114 definitions. *Resources, Conservation and Recycling, 127*, 221–232.

Klein, P. D. (1997). Multiplying the problems of intelligence by eight: A critique of Gardner's theory. *Canadian Journal of Education/revue Canadienne De L'éducation, 22*(4), 377–394.

Köppen, E., & Meinel, C. (2015). Empathy via design thinking: Creation of sense and knowledge. In H. Plattner, C. Meinel, & L. Leifer (Eds.), *Design thinking research: Building innovators* (pp. 15–28). Springer International Publishing.

Korhonen, J., Honkasalo, A., & Seppälä, J. (2018). Circular economy: The concept and its limitations. *Ecological Economics: THe Journal of the International Society for Ecological Economics, 143*, 37–46.

Liedtka, J., Hold, K., & Eldridge, J. (2021). *Experiencing design: The innovator's journey (English Edition)*.

Markova, D., & McArthur, A. (2015). *Collaborative intelligence: Thinking with people who think differently (English Edition)*.

Martini, J.-P., Stephan, L., & Tamdjidi, C. (2020, February 5). *Tap your company's collective intelligence with mindfulness*. BCG Global. https://www.bcg.com/publications/2020/tap-your-company-collective-intelligence-with-mindfulness

Micheli, P., Wilner, S. J. S., Bhatti, S. H., Mura, M., & Beverland, M. B. (2019). Doing design thinking: conceptual review, synthesis, and research agenda. *Journal of Product Innovation Management, 36*(2), 124–148.

Miller, C. C. (2015, October 16). Why what you learned in preschool is crucial at work. *The New York Times*. https://www.nytimes.com/2015/10/18/upshot/how-the-modern-workplace-has-become-more-like-preschool.html

Molinsky, A., & Gundling, E. (2016, June 28). How to build trust on your cross-cultural team. *Harvard Business Review*. https://hbr.org/2016/06/how-to-build-trust-on-your-cross-cultural-team

Nambisan, S., Lyytinen, K., & Yoo, Y. (2020). *Digital innovation: Towards a transdisciplinary perspective*. Edward Elgar Publishing.

Neshovski, R. (2021). *17 goals to transform our world*. https://www.un.org/sustainabledevelopment/

NZZ. (2021, January 19). *WEF mahnt: Trotz Pandemie bleibt Klimawandel das grösste Risiko*. https://www.nzz.ch/wirtschaft/wef-mahnt-trotz-pandemie-bleibt-klimawandel-das-groesste-risiko-ld.1597212

Papanek, V., & Fuller, R. B. (1972). *Design for the real world*. Thames and Hudson London.

Salovey, P., & Mayer, J. D. (1990). Emotional intelligence. *Imagination, Cognition and Personality, 9*(3), 185–211.

Schemel, S., Simunich, J., Luebkeman, C., Ozinsky, A., McCullough, R., & Bushnell, L. (2019). *Four plausible futures—2050 scenarios*. Arup.

Shih, Y.-C., & Chen, N.-S. (2002). Mission-based learning model and its instructional activity design. In *International Conference on Computers in Education, 2002. Proceedings* (Vol. 2, pp. 943–944).

Smith, P. G., & New Product Dynamics. (2000). *Fast-Cycle Product Development. 2*(2). https://doi.org/10.1080/10429247.1990.11414568

Spariosu, M. I. (2004). *Global intelligence and human development (MIT Press): Toward an ecology of global learning*.

SUGAR Network. (2015). https://sugar-network.org/

Tesla. (2018). Tesla. https://www.tesla.com/

THE 17 GOALS. (n.d.). Retrieved February 8, 2021, from https://sdgs.un.org/goals

The dangerous and inexorable rise of the instant expert. (n.d.). Retrieved February 7, 2021, from https://www.msn.com/en-gb/news/other/the-dangerous-and-inexorable-rise-of-the-instant-expert/ar-BB19HAaP

Uebernickel, F., Jiang, L., Brenner, W., Pukall, B., Naef, T., & Schindlholzer, B. (2020). *Design thinking: The handbook*. WS Professional.

UN. (2021). *Climate change*. https://www.un.org/sustainabledevelopment/climate-change/

Vega, A., & Chiasson, M. (2019). A comprehensive framework to research digital innovation: The joint use of the systems of innovation and critical realism. *The Journal of Strategic Information Systems, 28*(3), 242–256.

Vimcar. (2021). *Vimcar—About us*. https://careers.vimcar.com/en/aboutus

Wheeebo/Yanmar. (2020). https://www.yanmar.com/au/news/2020/01/07/67221.html

Whiting, K. (2020). *These are the top 10 job skills of tomorrow—And how long it takes to learn them*. https://www.weforum.org/agenda/2020/10/top-10-work-skills-of-tomorrow-how-long-it-takes-to-learn-them/

Wiesche, M., Leifer, L., Uebernickel, F., Lang, M., Byler, E., Feldmann, N., Garcia-Cifuentes, J. P., Höltää-Otto, K., Kelly, K., Satzger, G., Suzuki, S., Thong, C., Vignoli, M., & Krcmar, H. (2018). Teaching innovation in interdisciplinary environments: toward a design thinking syllabus. In *Proceedings of the AIS SIGED 2018. AIS SIGED International Conference on Information Systems Education and Research*. San Francisco, CA. https://www.alexandria.unisg.ch/id/eprint/255309

Wikipedia contributors. (2020, November 28). *Digital intelligence*. Wikipedia, The Free Encyclopedia. https://en.wikipedia.org/w/index.php?title=Digital_intelligence&oldid=991097521

Wikipedia contributors. (2021, January 10). *Collaborative intelligence*. Wikipedia, The Free Encyclopedia. https://en.wikipedia.org/w/index.php?title=Collaborative_intelligence&oldid=999536967

Willcocks, L. (2020). Robo-Apocalypse cancelled? Reframing the automation and future of work debate. *Journal of Information Technology Impact, 35*(4), 286–302.

WWF. (2021). *Impacts of global warming.* https://www.wwf.org.au/what-we-do/climate/impacts-of-global-warming

Yildiz, D. M. (2019, December 21). *Digital intelligence.* Technology Hits. https://medium.com/technology-hits/digital-intelligence-for-entrepreneurs-bfd8c917ee3a

Zeng, D. D. (2013). *From Computational Thinking to AI Thinking, 28*(6), 2–4.

Prof. Dr. Falk Uebernickel worked as a professor specializing in strategy and design at the University of St. Gallen before moving to his current position at the HPI. He is co-president of the global network SUGAR, which brings together students, universities, and companies for sustainable innovation using a new learning experience and introduces young people to human-centered design.

Prof. Christine Thong Ph.D. is a member of the SUGAR board, bringing 18 years of experience in design education programs. At Design Factory Melbourne, Christine Thong oversees all interdisciplinary, design thinking student programs as Academic Director. She specializes in design-inspired innovation for science and technology and is currently a Principal Innovation Fellow at the Australian Nuclear Science and Technology Organisation (ANSTO).

IQ Grows in WeQ Mode

Ulrich Weinberg

Abstract The education landscape is facing major changes, and not just since the Corona crisis. The step from an industrialized to a digital, increasingly networked world is understood by many companies and organizations as a fundamental process of change, combined with a change in perspective toward the customer. The world of education is undergoing a similar process of change. Here, the focus is increasingly on learners and the competencies required to survive in a rapidly changing world. While traditional learning apparatuses such as schools and universities still focus heavily on imparting knowledge and assessing individual performance, learning programs such as those offered by the HPI School of Design Thinking allow learners to develop skills such as critical thinking and complex problem solving, to learn as part of a team and to develop entrepreneurial qualities through real-life projects. Ulrich Weinberg describes in his article "IQ grows in WeQ mode" why such innovative programs need to be taken to a wider audience, in which direction the change of perspective should take place and how we can inspire a rethinking of the educational landscape.

1 Not Only Learning from Crises

One of the most impressive encounters in 2020 was a virtual one. In early September, I was invited by the Bertelsmann Stiftung to a small roundtable with the Digital Minister from Taiwan, Audrey Tang. Video conferencing had become a regular occurrence for me since March 2020, so there were six more digital meetings on my calendar that day, but this early morning encounter left a lasting impression on me. "Digital Democracy—What Europe can learn from Taiwan" was the topic for this hour and it was extremely impressive to hear the 39-year-old talk about what Taiwan is doing to constructively engage the population in complex decision-making processes through collaborative meetings using the latest digital technologies.

U. Weinberg (✉)
HPI School of Design Thinking, Hasso Plattner Institute for Digital Engineering, Campus Griebnitzsee, Prof.-Dr.-Helmert-Str. 2-3, 14482 Potsdam, Germany
e-mail: Uli.Weinberg@hpi.de

The minister spoke about "crowdsourced agenda setting," "collective intelligence," and "data collaboratives," areas in which work is being done in the Social Innovation Lab in Taipei. But what really made a lasting impression on me was her statement on the education landscape in Taiwan. Audrey Tang reported on the curriculum revision for Taiwanese schools and kindergartens that had taken place the year before and in which she had been involved. The essential point: With a view to the necessities of a modern knowledge society, it had been decided to replace the term "literacy," which is used throughout, with "competence." In other words, the Taiwanese education system is no longer primarily concerned with teaching basic skills, such as writing, reading, arithmetic, and the collection and retrieval of as much knowledge as possible; instead, the focus is on developing competencies while strongly activating the individual's personal capacity for action. In the words of Audrey Tang, "make people feel as producers and co-creators."

Is this a specifically an Asian way of thinking about the future of education? We in Europe, and in Germany in particular, still find ourselves engaged in wide-ranging discussions about whether to add more subjects to the curriculum in schools that teach digital and media skills. We launch a digital pact in which hardware investments are to be financed but investments in software and, above all, in continuing education have been left out. Asia is already one step ahead. They have understood that a digital future shaped by new machines requires a fundamental rethink and that this must begin as early as kindergarten. Or as Jack Ma, founder and CEO of the largest Chinese IT group Alibaba, aptly put it at the World Economic Forum 2018 in Davos: Schools should no longer focus on teaching knowledge and skills that machines will be able to do better, faster, and more thoroughly in the future. Students need to learn "to recognize values, to believe in themselves, to think independently, to work in teams, to care about others, and to do a lot more sports, music, and art." This means to, above all, never stop learning. Mr. Ma likes to refer to himself as the CEO "Chief Education Officer."

The COVID-19 pandemic has been like a magnifying glass in exposing the shortcomings of our education system, especially its poor learning capacity. As the father of an elementary school student, I have witnessed firsthand how children have been completely neglected by these very schools overnight in one of the few countries in Europe with compulsory school education. Why? Not even the simplest digital skills can be demonstrated by a sufficient number of teaching staff. Additionally, learning materials are not available in digital form and the technological equipment is reminiscent of pre-digital times, not to mention new thought processes, which are rarely found in the education policy arena. Even after 30 years after the launch of the World Wide Web, it is hard to comprehend how little the digital knowledge society, has arrived in our education systems. While industrial companies are using digital infrastructures and new participative, agile and team-oriented methods to keep themselves fit for work even in pandemic times, educational institutions are still stuck in traditional patterns of thought and action. The supposedly relevant educational content does not allow them to adapt to rapidly changing circumstances in order to even maintain the operation of essential functions.

2   The Learning World Needs Change

The head of the OECD Education Directorate, Prof. Dr. Andreas Schleicher, known as "Mr. Pisa," speaks of key competencies for 2030. He targets systemic thinking, critical thinking, creative thinking, design thinking, digital competencies, information and communication competencies and global competencies. The aggregation of knowledge and the corresponding processing of curricular learning requirements, which still dominate the everyday learning of students in Germany, play only a minor role for him. If you look at the curriculum in German schools, you will find hardly any evidence that this change in thinking has taken hold there. The focus is still on the retrieval of prefabricated knowledge packages and the corresponding assessment of the replication quality.

The World Economic Forum published a list of the "Top 10 Skills of 2025" in October 2020. Again, the focus is on problem-solving skills, self-management, leadership, and development skills, rather than knowledge acquisition.

Here is the list:

- Analytical thinking and innovation
- Active learning and learning strategies
- Complex problem solving
- Critical thinking and analysis
- Creativity, originality, and initiative
- Leadership and social influence
- Technology use, monitoring, and control
- Technology design and programming
- Resilience, stress tolerance, and flexibility
- Reasoning, problem-solving, and ideation.

With a view on the rapidly changing job market, and the shifting, disappearing and emerging career fields, the WEF calls for a focus on the skills that will help us navigate better and more sustainably in a fast-changing world.

3   Networked Thinking and Acting

These skills require new patterns of thinking and acting that do not play a role in the traditional education systems or play a role only in an incidental way. The world of schools and universities is characterized by thinking in terms of subject competencies and disciplines, hierarchies and priorities, knowledge accumulation and retrieval, testing and assessment. Following a general pattern, after a completed learning period

ends a work period begins. It is a separative way of thinking that focuses on the
measurable performance of the individual. Having this mindset means spending a
large amount of time fabricating exercises, tests, and assignments on which learners
can be individually measured and assessed. After a few years, however, learners
can lose their feeling of individuality—meaning as self-effective personalities with
their own ideas, potentials, desires, abilities, preferences, ideas, and visions. The
experience of individual measurement and the reduction of feedback to a grade or
score changes self-perception in such a way that I place myself in this set of criteria
that the school teaches me. I have poor grades in mathematics and thus categorically
exclude myself from anything related to math in the future. My life path ends up
seemingly defined by areas that do not have much to do with math. However, this
catalog of criteria—defined by curricula and study and examination regulations—is
only a vanishingly small section of the possibilities available to us in the twenty-first
century.

In my book "Network Thinking," I describe these traditional patterns of thought
and action from the pre-digital age as "Brockhaus Thinking." The Brockhaus, the
best-known German encyclopedia and its history, is a beautiful metaphor for the
analog age. It is the period we are all moving out of as we enter a new, self-created
digital world that is completely different from anything we have known before. It
is a world that can no longer be safely entered with the old thought patterns. The
200-year-old idea of collecting the everyday knowledge of humankind in the form of
a many-volumed encyclopedia remains with us today. And the encyclopedia is still
to be found on the bookshelves of many people's homes.

While the desire for knowledge aggregation still exists, the digital version has
taken a form entirely foreign from its analog counterpart. No longer printed linearly
from A to Z in separate volumes, the encyclopedia of today is not separated anymore
with cross-references, which must be laboriously searched. The user is no longer
confronted with expensive leather volumes that take months to be delivered. And it
is no longer an illustrious group of buyers who can gain access to 300,000 keywords
and 40,000 illustrations by purchasing the 30 volumes. The digital version of the
knowledge aggregation, "Wikipedia" has been available to everyone free of charge
on the Internet since 2001. Kept up-to-date on a daily basis by a host of volunteers,
it is available in about 300 languages. The German edition alone has more than 2.5
million articles and lives from the cross-references that can be reached by simply
clicking on a link. The printed version of the Brockhaus was discontinued in 2014,
more than 200 years after the first edition was published. This is an example of
traditional, tried-and-tested methods that were unique in the analog age and which
are now irrevocably coming to an end in the digital age.

The sheer numbers alone illustrate how, within a short time, a tradition developed
over centuries has been fundamentally transformed by digital technologies. The
essential thing is that it is no longer the sorting criterion of the initial letter that leads
me in the search to find what I am looking for in the 70 kg compendium, but the
term itself. It is the searched term itself that makes further contexts accessible almost
effortlessly in real time, and usually freshly updated through the connecting links.

However, even 80 years after Konrad Zuse introduced the first computer, the educational landscape is still in Brockhaus mode. The tentative attempts to go digital in an increasingly globally networked world are more reminiscent of a desperate attempt to sort Wikipedia from A to Z than a spirited departure into a new era. Yet schools and universities, in particular, should boldly move forward in using their creative, largely publicly funded capacities to explore this new world and set an example by pointing out new paths for society.

4 Why Bologna Must Be Reformed

The digital world brings us linking, networking, and context. At the separation and division, which still dominates much of our educational reality, is no longer an absolute. With human knowledge doubling approximately every 5–10 years, the Brockhaus mode now makes us more than a bit nervous. However, the fundamental change of pattern has not yet arrived in many people's minds, and therefore, even courageous reform projects turn into a pipe-burst.

If we take a look at the Bologna Process of 1999, for example, which successively replaced the previous *Diplom*-titled degree programs with bachelor's and master's study programs in Germany starting in 2006, it becomes clear that this reform was still carried out completely in the old thought patterns. Whereas in 2006, at the start of the reform, there were around 1500 Diploma courses at German universities, today there are around 18,000 bachelor's and master's courses to choose from. It was as if an attempt had been made to control the information and knowledge explosion by increasing the number of Brockhaus volumes tenfold. It is not surprising that the reform has achieved a partial goal: namely to create degree formats that are internationally comparable. Due to the specifically German way of interpretation, the course of study of the bachelor's and master's degree programs is significantly more over-schooled and regimented than before the Bologna Process. A fundamental reform is still pending.

This reform then no longer becomes about comparable degrees and evaluation systems, but about fluidity, agility, adaptability, and resilience. These are qualities that are no longer possible to achieve in the rigid Brockhaus structures. On the contrary, the old structures prevent the necessary adaptability, as we could see very well during the Corona pandemic. It was significant with which priorities the Standing Conference of the Ministers of Education and Cultural Affairs the KMK, presented to the public in spring 2020 during the first lockdown period. Their concern was *not* primarily about protecting the health of teachers and students and transferring learning formats from lecture halls and seminar rooms to virtual spaces as quickly as possible. The discussion was dominated by the question of how examinations could still be held deception proof, and whether examinations could still be held at all. The question was raised as to whether it would be better to skip entire semesters or school years because individual examinations could no longer be conducted in a safe manner. It was less a question of the learning content of the pupils and students and the material they had missed. The central question became more one of checking and evaluating the learning successes of the individual regarded as essential for the further course of life.

However, if we look at the list of competencies deemed forward-looking by the OECD or the WEF, and if our education system had been oriented toward what learners actually need in the twenty-first century, then we would have proceeded with a completely different set of priorities. Problem-solving skills, self-management, leadership, and development skills can also be acquired without a lecture hall, seminar room, or classroom. With these skills in mind, elementary school students who are used to teamwork would have organized themselves into small learning groups on social media and video conferencing platforms. The project tasks would have been available on digital learning platforms, and the learning groups could have arranged to meet in a virtual workshop to work together on solutions, to look for new tools, or to develop them themselves.

In the university, the cross-disciplinary teamwork, which forms the basis for tackling complex issues, would not have taken place in the seminar room or lab but in a digital chat room. Such chat room would be organized by the team members, who would be joined by their teachers, who are in the role of learning companions or coaches. Here, too, people would have met as a team in a virtual lab or chat room; become acquainted with a complex, not completely familiar toolset; started collaborative learning processes; and spent the time for the learning process in a meaningful way. Assessment, grading, and examinations would have played a secondary role. Since only teamwork is usually graded now (if at all), questions of cheating security would have been superfluous and the focus could have been on collaborative work while providing proactive support to the university in meeting the challenges posed by the pandemic.

Of course, this approach also requires a technological infrastructure that is not yet available in many educational institutions or is seriously underdeveloped. Even more we need a change in thinking; that is, an awareness that in the twenty-first century in a globally networked world, we can no longer work with thought patterns from analog times. We must come to the realization that "learning" no longer involves a period of legally prescribed school years that then comes to an end after training or study, but it must be learned as a lifelong task in the rapidly developing information and knowledge society we live in.

5   Rethinking Education Means Changing Perspectives

What must we do to achieve an up-to-date educational landscape that does not systematically detract from our young people's desire to learn and obstruct their future? It must be a landscape that provides them with the opportunity to become professional learners who deal with the challenges of a rapidly changing world in a fun, responsible, and proactive creative manner.

The first thing necessary is a change of perspective—the learner needs to become the focus of interest, not the teacher, the subject matter or the educational institution. This sounds simple, but it is a great challenge, in a similar way as it is difficult for large companies to focus on the customer rather than on the products or services they offer. If we place the learner at the center of the educational landscape, then what we know about the human learning process suddenly becomes relevant. That is, the role of extrinsic motivation and the much greater role of intrinsic motivation. This is a view of learning as a social process that needs inclusiveness and a trusting and inspiring environment. That on the other hand, an individual assessment turns any teamwork into a farce and reduces the quality of the results rather than increasing them. We must ask ourselves whether we want to continue to use individual assessments to increase the competitiveness of learners while decreasing their ability to collaborate? We need an appreciation of collaborative qualities, and with that a complete redesign of grading systems.

We must also question traditional roles. Teachers have to stop treating learners as objects, and instead recognize them as learning subjects—on par with themselves—always ready and open to learn. We also know how important context is in learning. Context can best be created in the form of long-term projects—not in 45-min lessons. These will be projects that are best developed by a team of teachers and worked on by a team of learners. The self-organizing powers of small teams ensure that a number of organizational activities which were previously carried out by administrative individuals are now handled by team members.

A change of perspective is also necessary with regard to learning content. A traditional curriculum is often oriented on a canon of tasks presented by the teacher, consisting of ready-made questions—with answers to be found by the learners. In the future, the focus will be on the complex question for which there is not yet an answer defined in the curriculum, and the solution of which will be a challenge addressed in a team effort.

6   The Learning World of the Twenty-First Century

For many years now, the HPI D-School in Potsdam has been a kind of prototype for the learning world of the twenty-first century and enjoys a lively popularity among students, teachers, and project partners from all over the world. Every semester, a small unique group gathers here, with 120 students from about 70 disciplines: sociologists, mechanical engineers, computer scientists, sports scientists, physicians, business economists, etc. Participants come from 60 universities and 20 nations and work in small teams on complex problems two days a week. They also come from large corporations, medium-sized or small companies, NGOs, cultural institutions, and administrations.

There is no one main topic, indeed every topic is welcome—the trickier the better. The questions for this additional study program come from the areas of mobility, health, energy, security, logistics, etc. The challenges are developed in an intensive coordination process by the D-School team together with project partners.

There is also no curriculum in the classical sense instead there is a project portfolio of about 16 projects which the students can apply for, depending on their focus of interest. In this way, teams of 5–6 students are formed. They work on the solution collaboratively. The learning environment is not the classic lecture hall or seminar room, but a kind of laboratory with highly flexible team furniture developed in collaboration with the Berlin furniture manufacturer System 180 in 2007, when the D-School began. The students are accompanied by a coaching team of about 40 coaches. The role of the coach is one of a learning companion, who supports the teams in words and deeds and supports them methodically, but does not lead them. The focus is on the self-organization of the teams, which define and distribute their roles internally as they see fit and as is appropriate for the project or project partner.

Individual grading is not carried out either, rather the focus is on collaboration. Individual grading encourages competitive behavior, which would be a hindrance in a team environment defined by collaboration and best results. The traditional education system continues to focus on "IQ", the measurable "I"-qualities, on grading, and thus extrinsic motivation. In contrast, the focus at the D-School is on the "We" qualities— the "WeQ"—and the intrinsic motivation that arises in creative collaboration. Clear findings from the many years of the D-School, with over 1000 graduates, show that intrinsic motivation tops extrinsic motivation and IQ grows into WeQ mode. Students consistently report the most intense learning experience of their lives at the end of the semester: "I've never learned so much in such a short time and worked so hard while having so much fun!" (Student at the D-School end-of-semester party).

The social cohesion that grows in the two-semester program is enormous. The graduates are in contact with each other long after their completion of the D-School, and some return to the D-School years later as part-time coaches. In addition, the intensive teamwork in the design thinking process releases undreamt-of creative potential in the individual and also the group, which regularly amazes both the participants themselves and their project partners. The students get to know and appreciate themselves and their team colleagues in a very intense way as they learn and work together. It is not uncommon for them to found companies together after graduating from the D-School. The start-up rate is comparatively high: 5–10 start-ups are created each year in which D-School graduates from Potsdam are involved.

The D-School team itself serves more in a role of orchestration. They design the semester program and application process, define the rough timelines with start, end, and interim presentations, put together the project portfolio and questions with the project partners, develop the method set, train the coaches, run the team spaces, and prototyping laboratories. The D-School team also ensures a relaxed and trusting atmosphere.

7 Launch into the Hybrid Learning Environment

This highly agile setting and the permanent willingness to learn—which is not only conveyed to the students but is also a hallmark of the entire team—made the D-School extremely adaptable at the beginning of the COVID-19 pandemic in March 2020. Within a few days, a remote collaboration protocol had been jointly created, which was permanently revised and supplemented in the following months. A virtual collaboration toolset was created from various software packages, and the learning and working environment, which had previously been location-bound, was virtually transferred to the digital space in a short time. A complete redesign of the program structure followed, and by the start of the summer semester in April 2020, everything was ready to set in motion remotely—with over 100 students from 20 countries.

It is also helpful to be part of the international context of the GDTA Global Design Thinking Alliance. Since 2017, 20 academic institutions in 5 continents have been sharing their design thinking experiences in this network, and reflecting, working and researching the future of the education landscape globally. The diverse experiences in dealing with the Corona crisis in different cultural areas have been compiled in an interactive online map. This map provides orientation through the jungle of available tools for communication, collaboration, facilitation, feedback, event design, etc. This collection of about 100 tools is accessible to everyone on the gdta.org website.

Now is the time to catch up on the experiences of the last few years. We want to merge our collaboration in the physical learning space of the D-School with the positive experiences of purely digital collaboration during the Corona crisis. New, hybrid learning, and working environments are just emerging that enable teamwork without the need for everyone to be physically gathered around a table. The challenge: the digitally connected team members must be able to collaborate on par with their fellow students on site. This requires not only new furniture concepts, but also new, digital communication and interaction components, which must be cleverly combined with each other. The first prototypes for a hybrid, highly flexible collaborative learning environment are already being developed with the furniture manufacturer System 180.

Flexibility, variability, and changeability were defining factors in the learning environment at the beginning of the D-School. Now in the new hybrid world, an even greater ability to change and adapt is both necessary and possible. Networking will not decrease, but continue to increase. Complexity will also increase, and we will not be able to control this development effectively and sustainably with rigid patterns of thought and action. And so we remain on the permanent search for the better, true to the motto of Audrey Tang, who concluded her presentation with the words:

Think for fun and optimize for fun – don't wait for the perfect offering

Acknowledgements My sincerest gratitude to Dr. Sharon Nemeth for her editing work.

Prof. Ulrich Weinberg Director HPI School of Design Thinking.

As early as the late 1980s, it was creative digital innovations that Ulrich Weinberg was involved with. As one of the German pioneers in the field of computer animation and virtual reality, he founded his first company in 1993 and became a professor of computer animation at the Potsdam Film Academy in 1994. Four years of tenure as vice president for technology and international relations had just passed when in 2007 the request came from HPI to establish the School of Design Thinking, which he has headed ever since. For him, the HPI D-School is a prototype for the educational landscape of the 21st century. Since 2004, he has been a visiting professor at the Communication University of China in Beijing, and the business magazine Handelsblatt counts him among the 100 innovators in Germany. At the 10th anniversary of the HPI D-School, he co-founded the GDTA Global Design Thinking Alliance, in which educational institutions from five continents now work together. He sees the greatest challenge in making the core elements of design thinking effective in traditional educational systems in order to better prepare students for the challenges of the digitally networked world. This is one of the main concerns of the WeQ Foundation, which he co-founded. Time and again, he is impressed by how quickly a design thinking team can delve deeply into a previously unknown topic and then surprise experts with new solutions. In his book "Network Thinking—What Comes After Brockhaus Thinking," he calls for a radical rethink in education and business.

Printed in Great Britain
by Amazon